Anthropology in India

Anthropology in India

Editors

H. S. Saksena
Vinay Kumar Srivastava
Nadeem Hasnain
Sukant K. Chaudhury
Sameera Maiti

SERIALS PUBLICATIONS
NEW DELHI (INDIA)

Edition: 2010

ISBN: 978-81-8387-385-7

Published by
SERIALS PUBLICATIONS
4830/24, Prahlad Street, Ansari Road
Darya Ganj, New Delhi-110002 (India)
Phone : 23245225. Fax : 91-11-23272135
E-mail: serials@sify.com

Contents

Preface vii

List of Contributors ix

PART I

1. Indian Social-Cultural Anthropology: A Brief Review 3
   Gopala Sarana
2. The Anomaly of Slow Growth of Anthropology in the South Indian Academia 28
   N. Subba Reddy
3. Some Thoughts on Anthropology in India 43
   Vinay Kumar Srivastava
4. The Status of Anthropology in Modern India 61
   Matthew Stief

PART II

5. Has Anthropology Moved out of The 'Colonial' Woods? 75
   H. S. Saksena
6. The We-They Distinction in Anthropology 86
   Julie Davis
7. Sociology and the Limits of Loyalty 98
   Ananta Kumar Giri
8. What Ails Indian Anthropology? 120
   R. Siva Prasad
9. On the Practice of Anthropology 128
   R. P. Mitra

PART III

10. The Passions and Perils of Anthropological Linguistics in India: Some Personal Reflections 147
    Kamal K. Misra
11. Museum at an Anthropology Department 177
    Kumkum Srivastava &
    Vinay Kumar Srivastava
12. Anthropology of Tourism: Insights from Nagaland 194
    Soumendra Mohan Patnaik
13. Dance Ethnography in the Anthropology of India: Prospects and Possibilities 215
    Nita Mathur
14. Career Options in Social-cultural Anthropology 234
    R. K. Kar

PART IV

15. Civilizational Approach to the Study of Indian Society: N. K. Bose And Surajit Sinha 247
    Sukant K. Chaudhury
16. Iravati Karve and the production of an Indian Anthropology 258
    Subhadra Mitra Channa
17. M. N. Srinivas at the Crossroads of Sociology and Social Anthropology: The Issue of Common Identity and the Way Forward 278
    S. Gregory
18. S. C. Dube and Indian Anthropology 304
    Yogesh Atal
19. C. von Fürer-Haimendorf: Half a Century of his Imprint on Tribal Welfare in Andhra Pradesh 328
    Urmila Pingle

PART V

20. Experiencing Anthropology in the Nicobar Archipelago 351
    Vijoy S. Sahay
21. What is not Anthropology? 389
    Binod C. Agrawal
22. The Impact of Anthropology 399
    Vinay Kumar Srivastava
23. Problematique of Unification of Social Sciences 431
    K. N. Sharma

Preface

The July-December, 2007 issue of *The Eastern Anthropologist* was devoted to the assessment of the place of anthropology in India. This issue, along with three new articles, has now been converted into a book, with the title *Anthropology in India*.

The growth of anthropology is slow and uneven in India. Taught in not more than thirty-five universities, in many of them it is not taught at the level of under-graduation, although in some states (such as Kerala), it is a school subject as well. If on one hand, anthropology departments are fewer in number, on the other hand, the impact of anthropology on other academic disciplines and the world of development is tremendous. Just because not many anthropology professionals are available, in many institutions, non-anthropologists carry out anthropological work.

The papers in this book have been grouped under five heads. The first section comprises papers dealing with the history, growth, and progress of anthropology in India. The second section takes up the problems that Indian anthropology is facing. The issues taken up here are of the colonial impact on anthropology, the distinction of the self and the other, and loyalty and sentiments for the masters of the subjects. The interaction of anthropology with the non-governmental organizations is also covered here. The third part is concerned with the special anthropologies. The fields covered here are linguistic anthropology, dance, tourism, and museum. Also included here is a paper on career options in anthropology. The fourth section is on an assessment of the contribution of some Indian anthropologists. The last section consists of papers on fieldwork experiences, the impact of anthropology, and the problem of unifying different social sciences.

List of Contributors

Ananta Kumar Giri, Madras Institute of Development Studies, Chennai.

Binod C. Agrawal, Vice Chancellor, Himgiri Nabh Vishwavidyalaya, Dehradun.

Gopala Sarana, Retired Professor of Anthropology, University of Lucknow.

H. S. Saksena, Editor, *The Eastern Anthropologist*, Ethnographic and Folk Culture Society, Lucknow.

Julie Davis, Department of Anthropology, University of California, Los Angeles, United States of America.

K. N. Sharma, Retired Professor of Sociology, I.I.T., Kanpur.

Kamal K. Misra, Department of Anthropology, University of Hyderabad.

Kumkum Srivastava, Department of History, Janki Devi Memorial College, University of Delhi.

Matthew Stief, Department of Anthropology, University of California, Santa Cruz, United States of America.

N. Subba Reddy, Centre for Economic and Social Studies, Hyderabad.

Nadeem Hasnain, Department of Anthropology, University of Lucknow.

Nita Mathur, School of Social Sciences, Indira Gandhi National Open University, New Delhi.

R. K. Kar, Department of Anthropology, University of Dibrugarh.

R. Siva Prasad, Department of Anthropology, University of Hyderabad.

R. P. Mitra, Department of Anthropology, University of Delhi.

S. Gregory, Department of Anthropology, Kannur University, Kerala.

Sameera Maiti, Department of Anthropology, University of Lucknow.

Soumendra Mohan Patnaik, Department of Anthropology, University of Delhi.

Subhadra Mitra Channa, Department of Anthropology, University of Delhi.

Sukant K. Chaudhury, Department of Sociology, University of Lucknow.

Urmila Pingle, 3-34/5, Madhuvan Enclave, Street No.4, Habshiguda, Hyderabad.

Vijoy S. Sahay, Department of Anthropology, Allahabad University.

Vinay Kumar Srivastava, Department of Anthropology, University of Delhi.

Yogesh Atal, Formerly Member, High-Powered Committee to Examine Gujars' Demands, Government of Rajasthan.

Part I

1

Indian Social-Cultural Anthropology: A Brief Review

Gopala Sarana

The first to do work of an anthropological nature were the British administrators of the mid-nineteenth century. They wanted to know about the natives and their cultures properly so that they might not violate them. Categorising the peoples of India into tribes and castes, information about their social institutions, economy, religious beliefs and practices, etc., was gathered through the official machinery. This 'other culture' study by the British administrators was in tune with the prevailing anthropological practice elsewhere also. Their work should have formed a part of the British anthropological literature but it did not materialise. The hard work done later formed the basis for founding Indian anthropology.

According to J.S. Slotkin, the background for the emergence of the science of mankind was laid in the late seventeenth and the early eighteenth centuries but the discipline could not crystallise, in the West, before the nineteenth century. My guru, Professor D.N. Majumdar, was of the opinion that in India the emergence of anthropology coincided with the founding of the Asiatic Society of Bengal in 1774. Surajit Sinha and L.P. Vidyarthi also held the same view. But the evidence to support the existence of anthropology in India or elsewhere is lacking. Occasionally essays of 'anthropologically and anti-quarian interests' were published, though not too early, in the *Journal* and the *Proceedings of the Asiatic Society*. In my view it is too far-fetched to push the beginning of anthropology in India to the 1770s and to link it with the beginning of the Asiatic Society of Bengal. It is, however, true that anthropological interest in and on India is almost as old as the interest in the subject in the West.

The government of those days was itself a source of anthropological type of work. A statistical survey of people was recommended by the Court of Directors of the East India Company in 1807 to be carried out by the government of the Presidency of Bengal. Accounts of tribes and castes indicating 'their numbers, the state of their food, clothing and habitations' were commissioned. Information was also sought about the religious aspects on the following counts: 'the number, progress and most remarkable customs of each different sect or tribe, together with payment made to the priests to know about circumstances which might bring them closer to the government or to make them disaffected'. In order to govern them properly the government desired to know about the natives and their culture.

A circular was issued in 1882 to collect more precise information about the castes and descriptions of the people of India on the basis of the census data of 1881 in addition to the information already available in the extant official documents. Herbert Risley published his four volumes on *The Tribes and Castes of Bengal* in 1891. Subsequently as the Director of Census operations, he gave us his memorable book entitled *The People of India*. At first, only British administrators turned anthropologists were conducting 'tribes and castes' studies alone. Later some Indians joined them as collaborators or assistants. Some became independent contributors also. The contemporary Western ethnographers and ethnologists were writing almost exclusively about savages or primitives. Writing about tribes and castes conjointly meant that the official ethnographer in India did not confine himself to the primitive segment only. He also dealt with a much larger part of the Indian population. L.K. Ananthakrishna Iyer's anthropological work, like that of the British administrator-anthropologists, was a compendium on tribes and castes of Kerala. His distinction lay in leading the first university department of anthropology at Calcutta.

Rai Bahadur Sarat Chandra Roy was the most outstanding self-taught anthropologist in the first quarter of the twentieth century. He was in touch with the leading anthropologists of the world like Frazer, Rivers, Marett, Dixon, etc. He called the serial publications on tribes and castes as at best 'descriptive catalogues' which were 'more general and superficial surveys that fail to furnish that exposition of kinship organisation and social system... which is needed for the purpose of scientific anthropology'. In spite of several shortcomings Roy conceded that these descriptive catalogues or ethnographic glossaries may serve as useful bases for more intensive studies of the various individual tribes and castes. Though not very profound the work of the dedicated government officials did its job of founding anthropology in India.

S.C. Roy made detailed study of several individual tribes of Chhotanagpur region and brought out his first voluminous monograph entitled *Mundas and Their Country* in 1912. He also wrote detailed monographic accounts of several other tribes. His work was essentially pre-functionalist. His monographs contained lots of information about the concerned tribe but did not acquaint the reader with how the people actually lived their lives. Roy called his procedure 'the orthodox method of the ethnographic monographs'. According to him his method consisted of concise classified presentation of the different aspects of a tribal culture. Sometimes Roy criticised the functionalist procedure and mode of interpretation. But at the fag-end of his career he declared that 'he would adopt the functionalist method if he had a chance to do his anthropology all over again'.

Several British administrators including Gordon, Hodson, Hutton, Mills, Playfair, Rivers, Stack, etc., wrote monographs on several tribes, particularly of the North-east covering their habitat, economy, and domestic life, tribal and social organisation, law, religion and folklore, etc. Roy lived in Chhotanagpur and could converse with the people directly in the language both he and his informants understood. The same cannot be said about the British administrator-anthropologists, though their monographs contained lots of information.

The anthropologists born in India conducted their studies in the same manner as was being done by the British administrator-anthropologists stationed in India. Indian anthropologists also wrote monographs on Indian tribal communities as if they were studying 'other cultures'. It will not be wrong to surmise that the anthropologists of Indian origin had an attitude of 'otherness' towards the tribal people of their own country. Between the two the British administrator-anthropologists visualized the situation more realistically and expressed their opinions more boldly than their Indian counterparts. For instance, G.S. Ghurye and others were well aware that the tribal peoples were often in close contact with caste Hindus and thus they were tremendously influenced by Hinduism. In the earlier census reports the tribals were called animists. Ghurye called them 'aborigines' or 'aborigines so-called'. It was J.H. Hutton, a Christian and a British administrator-turned into an academic anthropologist, to call a spade a spade and to designate the tribal people of India as 'backward Hindus'.

II

After the end of World War II anthropologists did not remain confined to the study of exotic and non-literate people. 'National character' and other studies of 'culture at a distance' are some examples. In India emphasis shifted from tribe to caste. A tribe was a relatively homogeneous community which maintained its identity despite outside contact. Castes were studied earlier also but now they became a primary focus of anthropological interest verging on an obsession with both Indian and foreign anthropologists working in India. A caste does not possess the autonomy of a tribe. It has to be studied only in a constellation of castes, usually though not necessarily, in the territorial limits of a village or a group of villages. Beginning in 1950s, for over fifteen years, village studies were in vogue. No co-ordinated effort was visible to cover sub-regions or regions of the country to provide a comprehensive knowledge of the way people lived in village India. However, these village studies have brought home valuable concrete data which throw light on the ordinary aspects of life of the village folk of our country. Kroeber has very insightfully remarked that these small-scale empirical (village) studies cannot tell us about 'the larger heightened elements' of the total (advanced) culture such as 'the national power, leadership, guidance, genius, resources and achievements'. It should not imply that I underrate the significance of community, in general, and those village communities, in particular. While studying caste the anthropologist found it difficult to confine himself to one village only. The study of caste was bound to spill over from one village to a group of villages, to a region and may figure in the national context as well. The anthropologist is in a dilemma because, though the above mentioned condition is true the traditional pull of the holistic approach of his discipline compels him to confine himself, in his (empirical) field investigation, to only one village taking it to be a territorially and conceptually isolable whole.

It is an accepted fact that unlike a tribe an Indian village is not an autonomous whole. It is not self-sufficient and has implications for a wider region. Yet a village can be treated as an isolable unit of study. Unlike a sociologist's or a political scientist's interest, the traditional interest of an anthropologist in a holistic perspective and face-to-face inquiry compelled him to collect his data through long-term field work. For this purpose a village is quite an appropriate unit of inquiry.

III

During the British rule in India anthropology received governmental recognition and patronage. Several governors of the Presidency of Bengal and a few governors-general of India took keen interest in promoting anthropological studies particularly through the auspices of the Asiatic Society of Bengal. A committee was constituted to encourage and direct government officers serving in Bengal to conduct ethnographic investigations. The Asiatic Society of Bengal was chosen to serve as 'a centre for reference and bureau of information' for the officers of Bengal who wanted to conduct research in the fields of history, religion, usages and folklore, not of primitive tribes alone, but of all the peoples of India.

The census operations in India began in 1881. Need was felt for more accurate information about 'the castes and the descriptions of the people of India' than was collected through statistical accounts, district manuals, gazetteers, census reports, reports of archaeological and linguistic surveys of India and through other official documents. Herbert Risley was entrusted with the task of conducting census operations in the last decade of the nineteenth century. He established an Ethnographic Survey in 1905 as a wing of the census operations. It was a landmark in the growth of anthropology in India. Census operations were given an anthropological flavour by seeking information about facets of life of different communities of India. Of course, this was done in addition to the usual head count. This trend flourished in 1931 census under the direction of J.H. Hutton. As a part of the Census Report, Hutton included thumbnail sketches of tribes, castes and other groups and communities in India. Also included in the Census Report was B.S. Guha's account of the racial elements in Indian population. Guha's description of the ethnic types was regarded as a major contribution to Indian physical anthropology. The Registrar-General of India has been assigned the task of planning and conducting the decennial census. There is a Social Studies Division as a part of the Registrar-General's office which conducts ethnographic studies among selected communities in different parts of the country. An anthropologist heads the Social Studies Division and several anthropologists on its staff undertake ethnographic and other cultural studies as a supplement to the census work.

Anthropologists work at ISRO, National Institute of Community Development, Health and Family Planning Institute, Institute of Mass Communication, Institute of Economic Growth, Demographic Research Centre, International Centre for Population Studies, Indian Agricultural Research Institute, Social Science Research Institutes, Indian Statistical Institute and several other research institutions including Tribal Training and Research Institutes. Two notable Commissioners for Scheduled Castes and Scheduled Tribes were N.K. Bose and B.D. Sharma. The former was a professional anthropologist and the latter was a civil servant with an anthropological bent of mind.

Anthropological Survey of India is the premier governmental institution for anthropological research. It was founded in 1946 with B.S. Guha as its first director. It has several regional centres including one in Andaman and Nicobar Islands. What is the situation of the Survey's regional centre at Port Blair after the Tsunami tragedy is not fully known. The head-quarter of the Survey is at Kolkata. The Survey employs several hundred professionally trained anthropologists. Its primary task is to conduct socio-cultural and biological research on different human groups and communities. It is not bound to conduct only utilitarian or practical research. The Survey is probably the biggest anthropological research organisation of its kind in the world.

IV

Museums are of vital importance for teaching and research in anthropology. There are museums in most anthropology departments in Indian universities. The most notable of them is at Gauhati University, Gujarat Vidyapeeth, and Poona University (primarily due to the efforts of Professor R.P. Srivastava). Lucknow University also deserve mention. Almost all regional centres of the Anthropological Survey of India have museums attached to them. At Kolkata there is an anthropological museum as a part of the Indian Museum. At New Delhi also the National Museum has an Anthropology Section. Manava Sangrahalaya (Museum of Man) has been established at Bhopal on the lines of Musee de L'Homme of Paris and the National Museum of Mexico City. It is managed by anthropologists.

Since the very first session of the Indian Science Congress held in 1914, there has been a section on Anthropology and Archaeology (now called the Section on Anthropological and Behavioural Sciences). Indian National Science Academy accorded a place to anthropology at its inception. Anthropology has also been recognised as an important discipline by NCERT, CSIR and ICSSR.

A subject which is not taught at the university level cannot be said to have been established. In 1918 a provision was made to teach anthropology as a subsidiary to Ancient Indian History for the undergraduate students of Calcutta University. In 1920 anthropology got recognition there as an independent discipline. At that time very few universities in the world had arrangement for teaching anthropology as an independent discipline.

Rama Prasad Chanda of brachycephalisation in east India fame was the first lecturer in-charge of the Anthropology

Department. L.K. Ananthakrishna Iyer became the regular head of the department of anthropology and continued till 1930-31 when K.P. Chattopadhyay took ever. Panchanan Mitra was a prehistoric archaeologist and H.C. Chakladhar authored a book on *Religious Life in Ancient India*. These early teachers of anthropology came from different disciplines. They carved out a broad-based subject of anthropology with biological, archaeological and socio-cultural dimensions. K.P. Chattopadhyay, T.C. Das, N.K. Bose, S.S. Sarkar and Dharani Sen enriched anthropology at Calcutta University.

The next department of anthropology was established at Madras University in 1945. For a long time B. Litt. and M. Litt. courses of anthropology were taught at Madras. The credit for converting it into a regular teaching-cum-research department, in 1970s, goes to Professor N. Subha Reddy. At Delhi University anthropology started being taught at the end of 1940's under the leadership of Professor P.C. Biswas, a product of Calcutta University.

At Lucknow University, Professor D.N. Majumdar started teaching anthropology in 1927 as a part of the course in economics. He was designated to teach tribal economy to students. He became the Head of the Department of Anthropology at Lucknow University in 1951. In a decade he raised the department to steller heights. He trained scores of students who immortalised their *guru* by their notable contributions to the subject wherever they worked. The expansion of anthropology in India has been painfully slow.

The inspiration for both academic and non-academic anthropology in India came from Great Britain. But in India anthropology is not taught in the British way. From the start anthropology has been a broad-based subject covering biological as well as socio-cultural dimensions. At least three sub-divisions of the subject—social-cultural anthropology, physical anthropology and prehistory or archaeological anthropology—are taught at the undergraduate and post-graduate levels. An entirely different situation prevails in the British universities. Due to the integrated teaching of the subject there were several contributors, in the earlier generations, who made notable research contributions to more than one branch of anthropology: D.N. Majumdar and Irawati Karve contributed to both social-cultural anthropology and physical anthropology; N.K. Bose to social-cultural anthropology and prehistory.

V

D.N. Majumdar enriched Indian anthropology in more than one way. He contributed to both physical anthropology and social-cultural anthropology. In the former he made ethnic or racial studies in Bengal, Gujarat and U.P. with P.C. Mahalanobis and C.R. Rao. He was the author of D^2 statistics which was the most sophisticated statistical tool to measure racial distance between ethnic populations in the 1950s. In social-cultural anthropology, he was in the fore-front in adopting the latest trends in both teaching and research in the subject. Besides this he also studied the tribes of Mirzapur district (in U.P.) and the 'polyandrous' Khasa of Uttarakhand. He was one of the pioneers of village studies and gave us the notions of 'rural analysis' and 'rural profiles'. Under his supervision the *Social Contours of an Industrial City* (of Kanpur) was worked out. D.N. Majumdar became distinctive among the Indian anthropologists of his time for the range, variety and depth in his researches in physical anthropology and even more so in social-cultural anthropology. He was an inspiring teacher and cared for his students who, in turn, were devoted to him and held him in high esteem. During his life time anthropology department at Lucknow University became the premier institution for teaching and research in anthropology in India. His students, who have spread throughout India and even abroad, have made Majumdar immortal by their contributions to the subject.

Verrier Elwin came to India as a missionary but got involved in anthropological work among tribal people of central India. He became a leading anthropologist of India. Unlike Majumdar, Chattopadhyay and Guha, Elwin was a 'self-selected' or amateur anthropologist. He wrote excellent monographs on the tribes of Madhya Pradesh, Orissa and Arunachal Pradesh. *Muria and Their Ghotul* is regarded as an all-time classic. For several years he was the adviser to the governor of Assam on tribal matters. He commissioned the writing of several monographs on little known tribes of the North-east. In 1940s Elwin advocated the establishment of 'national parks' to protect the tribal way of life from undesirable outside interference. This would save the tribals from exploitation by money-lenders, land-grabbers, traders, etc. Despite Elwin's good intentions and his humanitarian purpose, his suggestion of 'national park' was seen as an attempt to segregate tribal people from the people of India, treating them as 'museum objects'. This brought a bad name for anthropology.

Irawati Karve was a contemporary of Majumdar. Like him, she also made research contributions to both physical anthropology and social-cultural anthropology. In 1953 she published her book *Kinship Organization in India*. Louis Dumont and D.F. Pocock dismissed the book because they found it to be culturological rather than sociological. Such comments do not reduce the value of a work which required great effort to produce it. Karve has made quite a substantial contribution to kinship study in India. No other anthropologist has delineated an all-India pattern of kinship. Her book on kinship is a monumental contribution to Indian anthropology.

I have reservation about her method. By comparing kinship terms and corresponding behaviour she postulates a relationship of privileged familiarity between the (male) ego and his elder brother's wife for both the lower and the higher castes of Gujarat. The lower castes practice junior levirate. The higher castes do not do so now-a-days because it is repugnant to their values. She postulated that even these (higher) castes practised junior levirate in the past. When a learned *pandit* did not agree with her interpretation she presented some literary works of the Gujarat region. On examing the texts carefully the *pandit* endorsed her interpretation.

VI

The terms 'Great Tradition' and 'Little Tradition(s)' came into our vocabulary along with the anthropological study of civilisations. To Redfield, civilisation is 'expressed and recorded in the written works of its reflective, and highly creative minds'. A 'Great Tradition' of the literate few does not exist in a simpler form of living. The common people live beneath and within the high culture. The 'Little Tradition' of these people is, on the one hand, the creator of and, on the other hand, creature of the philosophy, science and fine art of the Great Tradition. In Redfield's words (1962: 302):

> in every civilization the Great Tradition is very marked: some aspects of the cultural heritage of the folk have been there developed by a self-perpetuating intellectual group into highly specialized systematized thought, often esoteric, commonly connected with religion, and in many (but not all) cases dependent upon writing for its continuance and development. The Great Tradition is one of the emergent characteristics of human society. A full understanding of China or India .... requires that we take account of the two traditions. We need to inquire in each case just what learning was special to the Great Tradition and how it developed out of the heritage of the folk. Each civilization is present in peasant village and in the more urbane scholar of the native Great Tradition—Mandarin, Brahmin or Mayan astronomer-priest. We need to learn how the one is related to the other. Does the Great Tradition continue to affect the Little Tradition: in what ways and by what means?

The Orientalist is a student of the Great Traditions and the anthropologist that of the Little Tradition and the Great Tradition.

Karve agrees with Redfield when she says that 'the great tradition is well documented in the main literary stream'. To her the difference between the 'Great Tradition' and 'Little Tradition', in particular with regard to joking relationships and junior levirate in Gujarat, had something to do with 'environmental differences' between the 'urban' and the 'rural'. Karve does not tell us what is the Great Tradition in the case at hand. Is the Great Tradition the absence of junior levirate among the higher castes of Gujarat today or its practice by them in the past, as inferred through scanning the literary sources? The higher castes are regarded as pace-setters for the other castes. Both Redfield and Karve advocate that the sacred and learned texts are the sources of Great Tradition. They do not seem to set the pattern for joking relationship and junior levirate in Gujarat because the textual prescription does not seem to agree with the prevailing practice. Tradition is a continuum in which additions, deletions or alterations go on continuously. It preserves what is of lasting value to the people. I have reservations about splitting it into Great Tradition and Little Tradition.

The above mentioned example from Gujarat makes it clear that it is very difficult to earmark the so-called 'great tradition'. The information obtained through anthropological field work must not be mixed with that obtained through the literary sources. India is a vast country with tremendous diversity. There is an underlying thread of unity but it ought not to be confused with uniformity. Hinduism allows the incorporation of local customs and practices into the main body of religion. Let us take an example. Kin marriages are prohibited in north India in all sections of the Hindu society because they are considered incestuous. On the other hand, in south India high caste as well as low caste Hindus practice uncle-niece and matrilateral cross-cousin marriages. Scanning the sacred literature of Hinduism will not help us in delineating (a single) Great Tradition regarding marriage rules in Hindu India covering the whole country.

It is sad that Karve could not finalise the enunciation of the two ideal types (north Indian and south Indian) which she was working on. Had she completed that it would have made the understanding of the unity and diversity of India and its culture much easier. Her last published work, *Yuganta,* was a seminal contribution to the anthropology of civilisation. It should open up new vistas for anthropological research in India based on the epics, the Puranas, other scriptures, folk-tales/ folk-lore and even oral tradition.

M.N. Srinivas adorned the chairs of sociology departments at M.S. University of Baroda and Delhi University, yet we shall analyse his contribution to anthropology. He raised the slogan: "social anthropology, that is, sociology". He obtained his first doctoral degree in sociology at Bombay University. Subsequently, he re-worked his material on the Coorgs for D. Phil. degree of Oxford University in Social Anthropology. This book, *Religion and Society Among the Coorgs of South India*, published by the Clarendon Press with a 'Foreword' by A.R. Radcliffe-Brown made the book an instant success.

Srinivas is famous for his notions of 'Sanskritisation', 'Westernisation' and 'Dominant Caste'. In a rigidly hierarchical society giving up beef-eating and adopting vegetarianism, discarding widow-remarriage, divorce and polluting and degrading activities are the necessary first steps toward status-enhancement. To Sanskritise or to adopt the ways of the higher-ups is the next step. Srinivas has pointed towards another trend which he calls Westernisation. While the lower castes adopt

Sanskritic practices the higher castes abandon some of them to adopt certain Western ways. Of late some politically powerful scheduled caste persons have started a tirade against, what they call *Manuwad*. They have, however, not presented an alternative in the form of Ambedkarwad or Dalitwad.

In different villages different castes may set the pattern which others in the concerned village emulate. Srinivas presented the idea of dominant caste. It may not be most numerous but is ahead of other castes in material possessions, power and authority. Srinivas worked with two of the ablest British social anthropologists of the twentieth century—Radcliffe-Brown and Evans-Pritchard. He does not, however, seem to have acquired an expertise in concept-clarification. This can be ascertained by looking at his attempt to define the concept of social structure in an essay entitled 'Social Structure' published in 1964 in the *Sociological Bulletin* (Vol. 13: 12-21).

André Béteille is the most celebrated among the students and colleagues of M.N. Srinivas. Béteille was initially trained in anthropology (with bones and stones!) at Calcutta University. But he fell in line with Srinivas's contention of 'social anthropology, that is, sociology.' He has done field work in Tamil Nadu. He has shown special interest in stratification and inequality.

Nirmal Kumar Bose was a versatile genius. He taught anthropology and geography at Calcutta University. His talent was multifaceted and multidimensional. He could talk with ease and authority on caste in Orissa and Bengal and on temple art and architecture, particularly of Orissa. His writings in Bengali and English on caste dynamics have no equals in Indian anthropology. He excavated prehistoric sites in Orissa. He was a renowned Gandhian scholar. He was the Private Secretary to Mahatma Gandhi and his interpreter during his tour of Noakhali.

As the Director of Anthropological Survey of India Bose planned and executed a survey of certain elements of culture on the lines of Kroeber's California Culture Element Survey. Though the study was a little dated it was an attempt to prepare a data-base of culture elements, particularly the material elements. Through these one could peep into the unity and diversity of India. His reports as the Commissioner for

Scheduled Castes and Scheduled Tribes had a distinctive anthropological flavour.

S.C. Dube was a self-selected anthropologist who made a valiant effort to become a broad-based anthropologist before joining the "social anthropology, that is, sociology" club. According to the need of the hour the members of this club become a sociologist or a (social) anthropologist enjoying the best of both the worlds. Hindi-speaking Dube-ji wrote a book on the Telugu-speaking village of Shemirpet in Andhra Pradesh. His book, *Indian Village* (not an Indian Village), was one of the earliest and celebrated village studies in India. It was printed under the imprimatur of the International Library of Sociology and Social Reconstruction.

An analytical and critical study of conceptual, theoretical and methodological issues in social-cultural anthropology has been the main areas of interest of Gopala Sarana. In 1959 Sarana pointed out several conceptual and terminological ambiguities and contradictions in Radcliffe-Brown's effort to distinguish social anthropology from ethnology. In 1950s his criticism, except by Murdock on kinship, was uncommon. Through detailed arguments, with evidence dug out from the writings of Radcliffe-Brown and Firth, Sarana has demonstrated that their effort to distinguish between social structure and social organisation has not borne fruit.

In 1969 Sarana rejected the idea that Malinowskian notions of function and functionalism are 'formless'. He also made an important distinction between "functioning"/functions and "having a function". This distinction has either been glossed over or has gone unnoticed by most anthropologists. A machine operates; therefore it functions. A functioning machine does some work, therefore, it performs some function. A structure is an arrangement of parts. It does not operate. Therefore, a structure cannot be said to function. If Radcliffe-Brown had kept this distinction in mind he would not be talking of the "functioning of structure".

Robert K. Merton's distinction between 'latent' function and 'manifest' function does not seem merely odd to Gopala Sarana but he finds it untenable. Merton's 'latent' function is function in the proper sense. It is deciphered by the investigating social scientist. The 'manifest' function of Merton's is really the obvious consequence of the actions of the members of a social group or a society. It should not be confused with function. The examples which Merton gave in support of the proposed distinction were utilised by Sarana to prove that the dichotomy between 'latent function' and 'manifest function' is not maintainable.

Lévi-Strauss has told us that social structure is a model built up after the reality of social relations. Sarana has presented different notions of model in science and outside science. He found that Lévi-Strauss's idea of model was not in consonance with either technical or non-technical usage. It is a common anthropological belief that social structure is rooted in material-environmental setting and cannot be divorced from social reality. An academic-conceptual model is built by the investigating scientist and not by the people themselves. Therefore, the notion of 'home-made model' is *non-sequitur*.

Methodology (of anthropology) has been of special interest to Gopala Sarana for a long time. In his book, *The Methodology of Anthropological Comparisons,* published under the imprimature of the Wenner-Gren Foundation for Anthropological Research Inc., New York, in 1975, Sarana has made a systematic analysis of comparative methods in social-cultural anthropology taking cognizance of the units, purposes (or aims), and techniques and methods of comparison. Sarana has delineated three basic comparative methods: (1) illustrative comparison; (2) complete-universe comparison; and (3) hologeistic sampled comparison.

Concept-formation-and-clarification and explanation are two very subtle and highly technical activities of a discipline. Sarana has paid special attention to this task with special reference to social-cultural anthropology. Further, elaborating the views of Kathleen Gough and joining issues with Edmund Leach, Gopala Sarana has thrown light on the possibility of a universal definition of marriage.

VII

After the end of World War II anthropologists of the West and India could not be confined to studying the exotic and the illiterate peoples. They had to go beyond tribal studies to tackle issues related to complex society.

The concept of caste is so uniquely Indian that students of Indian social system will always be interested in it. Soon after independence the study of castes and villages was conjoined for sometime but the study of caste in wider horizons and beyond the village has become quite common. Caste and politics have so much intermixed that their study cannot be ignored. Much of the empirical study of caste deals with relationship between caste status, stratification and economic and political consequences which flow from them.

Louis Dumont's *Homo Hierarchicus* is one of the most outstanding studies on the caste system in the last one hundred years. He made good use of the empirical field material including his own. Instead of concentrating on the minutest details of stratification in a particular village he rose above the level of the empirical data to postulate the ideology of caste society and contrasted that to the ideology of an egalitarian society. Unilike many social scientists—both Indian and foreign–Dumont does not condemn a caste society and refuses to consider it inferior to the so-called democratic Western egalitarian society.

Traditionally anthropologists had paid special attention to small-scale societies/communities. They adopted a holistic perspective in face-to-face inquiry to collect data through long-term field work. An Indian village may seem an appropriate unit of study because it is geographically separable from other villages. It is not a discrete cultural entity like a band or a tribe. A village in a complex civilization can be a 'unit of observation' in an anthropological study. Since a tribe is culturally autonomous it is itself the 'unit of representation' also. A village is not a 'unit of representation' because it is not culturally autonomous. According to Robert Redfield, an anthropological 'unit of representation' "for the most part has been a non-civilized group, a society and culture, easily distinguishable from the other and, without very important qualification, self-contained: maintaining its life in its own terms, endogamous, and pursuing ends and following means traditional to that group. The Andamanese studied by Radcliffe-Brown were such an entity, so were the Trobrianders of Malinowski .... Fortes has referred to such groups as 'the classical primitive isolates'" (1962 : 380).

VIII

According to Koreber, anthropologists have always desired to apperceive and conceive their subject of study both empirically and holistically. Since anthropological investigations began with small-scale or simple "authentic" societies which can be viewed as discrete wholes, how can the anthropologist studying a complex society conceive and perceive the phenomena both empirically and holistically? Through the time-honoured first-hand field work empirically he can study only a small segment of the complex Indian society. For the first time the anthropologist realizes that he is empirical in his approach but is he holistic also?

This can be done by concentrating on the study of linguistically or geographically defined communities within complex civilizations like India. In the study of a complex civilization ethnographic procedure will always remain subsidiary to dealing with the existing documents. To combine ethnographic accounts with extant documents is as difficult as to combine empiricism and holism, though it is not impossible. The Western anthropologists working in India tried to face the challenge, by postulating notions like: the 'economic frontier', 'text and context', 'great tradition' and 'little tradition', 'social organisation of tradition', etc.

Ralph Nicholas has aptly remarked that "the position of South Asian specialists in anthropology—whether British, American, Indian or Ceylonese —appears to me to be less favourable than that of specialists in several other areas." Firstly, for treating their complex society data the South Asian specialists utilise the concepts and frames of reference forged for the study of simple societies without written history. Secondly, it is the failure to divide the work, through dialogue, between those who approached India as the 'other culture' and those for whom study in India was 'self study'. The foreign anthropologists could perceive the bits and pieces of information that prove to be crucial in analysing and interpreting the data collected. Such data might escape the attention of or might seem superfluous to the native anthropologists. We should have concentrated on patron-client relationships, the position of women and their role in different spheres of life, the dynamics of the joint family system and its place in rural and urban-industrial settings and the pattern of reciprocity and redistribution in economic and non-economic transactions, etc.

The India-born anthropologists have been blamed for failing to break new grounds. In 1921 S.C. Roy lamented that very little contribution has been made by Indian anthropologists to the discipline as a whole. Three decades later N.K. Bose chided his co-professionals for leaving things for other social scientists which they could themselves do. There are no problems which Indian anthropologists have made peculiarly their own. They have followed the tracks beaten by anthropologists in the more powerful countries of the West: 'What they do, we generally try to repeat on the Indian soil'. Nearly twenty years after Bose, Surajit Sinha was in search of a possible Indian trend in social-cultural anthropology. He found that most works were oriented towards gaining approval from our peers and mentors in the West rather than concern with the goals and aspirations of the Indian peoples. Surajit Sinha found that mostly "academic patronage and linkages with Western *gurus* and *guru-bhais* continue to be a decisive factor in shaping the contour of a scholarly enterprise in anthropology in India today." Sinha has gone too far in castigating the fellow Indian anthropologists. Contrary to Sinha, Kroeber was too generous in his remark at the International Symposium on Anthropology held at New York in 1952 : India has listened both to the United States and Great Britain and wisely to herself.

From the very beginning Indian anthropology has been concerned with tribal studies. It moved from total monographic studies to study of one or more facets of tribal study, e.g. health, sanitation, education, land alienation and impact of industralisation and urbanisation. Tribals are not treated as isolates any more. Many tribal groups are now aware of the special privileges available to them under the Constitution. This, among other things, has drastically changed the situation in the tribal areas of the country. States like Arunachal Pradesh, Meghalaya, Mizoram, Nagaland are populated almost exclusively by those whom we have known as tribal peoples.

Anthropology had close links with administration during the colonial times. Since independence its area of operation and sphere of influence have alarmingly shrunk. Except for Verrier

Elwin who was the Advisor on tribal affairs to the Governor of Assam no anthropologist today occupies any such key position by virtue of being an anthropologist. The late Sarat Chandra Roy has indicated the value of anthropology in administration not merely as a technical aid. According to him, anthropology can provide a very solid foundation for good administration. His words (1921: 52-3) quoted below were written more than eight decades ago but they are very relevant even today:

> It is too late in the day to ignore the great administrative value of the knowledge of anthropology in all offices engaged in administrative work. The sympathy born of an intelligent appreciation of the customs, habits and mentality of the tribes and castes that an officer or even a business man has to deal with, is ordinarily a sure guarantee for successful work ... preference to candidates holding degrees in Anthropology in an Indian or foreign university .... will not only improve the quality of administrative work, but will afford a strong incentive for the study, and the advancement of the Science... .

In the 1940s I.C.S. trainees were given lessons in anthropology before being sent out on regular administrative assignments. Unfortunately this practice has been discontinued now. Being a student of Indian society and culture and of cultural dynamics the anthropologist is well-equipped to offer something to the young men and women who are going to run the affairs of the state. The anthropologist can bring before the mind's eye of the budding administrator the comparative cultural perspective which is sure to make him more appreciative of the other people's perspective. If these young probationers learn to take an uninvolved and detached view while scrutinising the facts before them, prior to taking decision, a lot of human misery could be avoided in this era of planned economic development wherein human factors are ignored or forgotten. Anthropology has something worthwhile to offer on these lines and in these areas.

IX

The above account does not mean that non-utilitarian study should be abandoned. The Indian anthropologists have to strike a balance between conducting research for academic purpose, for aesthetic satisfaction and the country's progress and its people's well-being. Need for planned development was realised soon after independence. For this purpose five-year plans were started in the early 1950s. Unfortunately, planning has become exclusively economic planning. Of late there has been a talk of micro-planning. With their intimate association with peoples whom they study, with their desire to learn from them rather than to teach or instruct them, anthropologists are eminently suitable to help in grass-roots/local-level planning for rounded development.

We have to understand the meaning of economic liberalisation and globalisation and their implications for the Indian people and to minimize their ill-effects. We have to shed our image of the 'doctors of the primitives or the Adivasis'. As an all-Indian institution, the Anthropological Survey of India has to play its role in delineating the contours of Indian culture through well-planned concrete studies. From time to time the Survey has carried out studies in several regions of India on topics such as the position of the weaker sections, customary laws, etc. The comprehensive mapping of different communities in India and the publication of the results in multi-volume *People of India* is an achievement in its own right. There is need to prosecute studies by pooling the institutional resources on agreed upon topics relevant to the contemporary needs of the country. However, freedom to conduct basic research through what Honigman has called 'personal approach', should not be curbed and too narrow a view of relevance will be self-defeating.

Anthropology is at the cross-roads today. The discipline as a whole is facing an identity crisis for different reasons in different places. The main reason for this is the tremendous changes in the geo-political situation around the globe. Before the World War II, there were strong European powers which had subjugated non-European peoples in Asia, Africa and the Pacific. There was also a great economic and cultural gap between the simple and non-literate peoples who were colonized and the advanced and so-called civilised peoples of the West, who had colonized them. In the traditional anthropological studies the primitives were studied by the latter with a view to comprehend the bewildering variety of human cultures. There were no local or native anthropologists to study the customs, practices and aspirations of their own peoples, except in India.

Till recently the Western anthropologist did not study a segment of his own extant culture or its past. He was known as a specialist in one non-European native culture or the other. This gave rise to the famous 'other culture' perspective so distinctive of anthropology.

The change in the world situation is both dramatic and drastic. Except for a few isolated pockets really 'simple' peoples are not available to the non-native anthropologists to investigate their work-a-day activities in the same manner as could be done fifty years or more ago. Most of the tribal groups have become parts of nation-states. Neither their ways of life nor their attitudes have remained 'simple'. Many of these peoples, particularly their political leaders, resent being treated as objects of 'study' by foreigners however noble their goals might appear to be. In some parts of the world there is a distaste for the word anthropology because of its intimate association with colonialism, particularly in Africa. It is, at least, partly borne out of ignorance and partly due to the feeling that the non-native anthropologists have shown keen interest in depicting and describing the so-called outlandish and none-too-glorious side of the life of the people investigated. This has become a real hinderance to the anthropological study of 'other cultures'—the traditional subject matter of anthropological study. The former anthropological heavens do not seem to be 'heavens' these days. The strategy of anthropological work has to be changed; 'self-study' should get precedence over 'other culture' study without abandoning the latter altogether.

When the anthropologist turns more and more homeward, the problems, the nature and focus of anthropological investigation will have to undergo change. The anthropologist will now be pitted more and more against other social scientists and humanists who have always been 'home'. He will have to make Herculean efforts to retain his identity. Indian anthropologists will not find it easy because they have mostly remained 'home'. 'Other culture' studies will also have to be pursued side by side. Anthropology has tremendous scope in India which has a multiplicity of languages and local traditions. One thing which the leading anthropologists teaching in Indian universities must come to an agreement is that they will motivate and encourage young anthropologists to undertake intensive field studies in language areas to which they do not belong.

X

In a recent comment on anthropology in India, Vinay Kumar Srivastava has pointed out how Indian Science Congress Association and Union Public Service Commission (UPSC) have given a raw deal to anthropology. Add to it the marginalisation of anthropology by Indian National Science Academy (INSA). These cases have adversely affected the growth and popularity of anthropology. He has painted a vivid picture of under-staffed university departments of anthropology with several unfilled posts making the situation worse.

He has however, made a strange statement at one place that "anthropology survives healthily outside anthropology departments". He immediately realises his mistake and accepts that "in no way does it signal the development of anthropology". He has spelled out the positive side of anthropology in the following words:

> The strength of anthropology lies in its analytical powers, in its theories, perspectives and methods. Anthropology is not a commentary on current affairs; it is not a journalistic exercise; it is not a plain description of events and phenomena. It is a theoretical examination of the facts about processes and products of human activity with an objective to know human life comparatively. Anthropology has neither preached a homogenisation of human condition nor an isolation of societies. It has drawn attention to the variegated processes that unify people as well as segregate them. Ethnicity is an outcome of these processes, so are urban enclaves, so are unions and associations. It is because of the perspectives, which anthropology offers on society, that it is regarded as a valuable and sought-after discipline. If our anthropological understanding of processes and products of human action is sound, it will automatically lead to the formulation of operational policies. Development studies look for anthropology for praxis, because praxis involves action, and action implies change. The future of anthropology will depend upon a profound realisation of its strength, which lies in the specialised knowledge it generates rather than the hopelessness of general anthropology (2004: 145).

REFERENCES

Abbi, B.L. and S. Saberwal

1969 *Urgent Research in Social Anthropology*. Simla: Indian Institute of Advanced Study.

Bailey, F.G.

1957 *Caste and the Economic Frontier*. Bombay: Oxford University Press.

Béteille, André

1974 *Studies in Agrarian Social Structure*. Delhi: Oxford University Press.

Bose, N.K.

1952 'Current research projects in Indian anthropology', *Man in India* 32: 121-33.

1967 *Culture and Society in India*. Bombay: Asia Publishing House.

Dube, S.C.

1971 *Explanation and Management of Change*. New Delhi: Tata McGraw Hill.

1974 *Contemporary India and Its Modernization*. Delhi: Vikas.

Dumont, Louis

1970 *Homo Hierarchicus*. Delhi: Vikas.

Elwin, V.

1947 *The Muria and Their Ghotul*. London: Oxford University Press.

1960 *A Philosophy for NEFA*. Shillong: NEFA Administration.

Ghurye, G.S.

1943 *The Aborigines So-called and Their Future*. Pune : Gokhale Institute of Politics and Economics.

Hutton, J.H.

1961 *Caste in India: Its Nature, Function and Origin*. Bombay: Oxford University Press.

Kroeber, A.L.

1938 "Caste". In E.R.A. Seligman (ed.), *Encyclopedia of the Social Sciences*. London: The McMillan Co.

Karve, I.

1961 *Hindu Society–An Interpretation*. Poona : Deccan College.

1969 *Yuganta–The End of an Epoch.* Poona: Deshmukh Prakashan.

1970 *Kinship Organization in India.* Poona : Deccan College.

Marriott, M. (ed.)

1955 *Village India.* Chicago: University of Chicago Press.

Neale, Walter C.

1965 'Reciprocity and redistribution in the Indian village'. In Karl Polanyl *et al.* (eds.), *Trade and Market in Early Empires.* New York: The Free Press.

Risley, H.H., E.A. Gait

1903 *Census of India,* 1910, Volume 1. Calcutta: Government of India.

Roy, S.C.

1921 'Anthropological research in India', *Man in India* 1 : 11-56.

Sarana, Gopala

1959 'A few comments on some of Radcliffe-Brown's basic concepts'. *Eastern Anthropologist* 12 : 202-09.

1967 'Model and myth in Lévi-Strauss' anthropology', *Journal of Indian Anthropological Society* 2 : 159-68.

1970 'Anthropology of Indian civilization', *Journal of the Indian Anthropological Society* 5 : 31-39.

1975 *The Methodology of Anthropological Comparisons.* New York: Wenner-Gren Foundation for Anthropological Research.

1976 'Status of social-cultural anthropology in India', *Annual Review of Anthropology,* Volume 5 : 209-25 (co-author : D.P. Sinha). Palo Alto: Annual Review Inc.

Singer, Milton

1955 The cultural pattern of Indian civilization: a preliminary report of a methodological field study. *The Far Eastern Quarterly*, Vol. 15 : 23-36.

1958 From the guest editor. *Journal of American Folklore*, Vol. 71 (281) : 191-204.

Sinha, S.C.

1971 'Is there an Indian trend in social-cultural anthropology?', *Journal of Indian Anthropological Society* 6: 1-14.

Srinivas, M.N.

1996 *Social Change in Modern India.* Bombay: Allied Publishers.

Srivastava, Vinay Kumar

2004 'Anthropology in India: A comment'. *The Eastern Anthropologist* 57: 127-52.

Vidyarthi, L.P.

1961 *The Sacred Complex in Hindu Gaya.* Bombay: Asia Publishing House.

2

The Anomaly of Slow Growth of Anthropology in the South Indian Academia

N. SUBBA REDDY

It is strange that though south India figured prominently in the writings of some of the founding fathers of anthropology, and Indian as well as foreign scholars conducted some important anthropological studies in that region during the first half of the twentieth century, the academia of the region have been rather slow and hesitant in instituting courses in the subject and train students to conduct researches on the rich cultural material available there.

As early as 1870, one of the pioneers who tried to systematize the knowledge about the evolution of social institutions, L.H. Morgan, brought out his book, *Systems of Consanguinity and Affinity of the Human Family*, as the seventh volume of the series called Smithsonian Contributions to Knowledge. That work was based on data collected from over 100 societies spread over a few continents including the then Madras Presidency of South India. In regard to some of the American Indian tribes, Morgan collected the information personally. Regarding other societies outside America, he gathered data from traders, missionaries and through the good offices of the American Consulates on the basis of questionnaires supplied by him. It is noteworthy that America established its consulate in Madras even earlier than 1870, and it was in a position to supply the information needed by Morgan, particularly on the kinship terms and usages among the Tamil, the Telugu and the Canarese. To his pleasant surprise, Morgan found that the system of classification of kin among these south Indian communities was the same as the one found among the Iroquoi, Dakota and a few other tribes of North America. Though aware of the mistaken belief of the early voyagers who, on landing in America, thought that they had arrived in India, he still could not suppress his excitement at finding such 'cultural links' between the residents of India and the American Indian tribes as to have similar systems of classifying kinsmen. His exclamatory observation runs as follows:

> When the discoverers of the new world bestowed upon the inhabitants the name of Indians, under the impression that they had reached the Indies, they little suspected that the children of the same original family, although upon a different continent, stood before them. By a singular coincidence, error was truth (1870:508).

He wanted to treat the kinship system found among the Tamil as archetypal of all societies with similar ways of classifying kinsmen. In his search for generic labels he chose to call it Turanian, which is a slight variation from the word Tamilian. In his subsequent work entitled *Ancient Society* (1877), he goes into details of how a particular type of marriage produces a particular type of kinship terminology. Pointing out that the Syndiasman type of marriage and family produces the Turanian type of kinship system, he goes on to say that while the Sineca-Iroquois group would be taken as typical of the American tribes, the Tamil people of south India would be taken as representative of other communities of Asia with similar kinship system (1870: 444). At the end of the concerned chapter, he presents the Tamil kinship terms in a series of tables (*ibid*: 56-61).

What Morgan called Turanian kinship system came to be termed as Sineca system by Lowie in his book, *Social Organization* (1950: 63) and as Iroquois-Dakota system by Murdock in his book, *Social Structure* (1960: 125). Technically speaking, it is the bifurcate-merging type of kinship system which is widely prevalent all over the world including Australia and Pacific Islands. After the evolutionist theories exhausted themselves, that system has been analyzed by the structural-functionalists to demonstrate the determining influence of the descent principle and by the alliance theorists to demonstrate the determining influence of cross-cousin marriages. It is well known that Morgan's *Ancient Society* provided the framework for most of Marxist sociology, and Engel's book, *Origins of Family, Property and State,* is largely based on the former. As such, *Ancient Society* has been translated into several languages, and Tamil kinship terms receive the attention of people in several countries of the world.

The major work of W. H. R. Rivers, published in 1906, brought to light the unique culture of the Toda of the Nilgiris, whose economy as well as religion revolved round their dairy and whose social organization encompassed a rare marriage system of non-fraternal polyandry combined with patrilocal residence. In his later work, *Kinship and Social Organization (1915),* Rivers threw light on the special feature of the Dravidian kinship system, namely the over-arching division of all the kinsfolk into parallel relatives and cross relatives.

A brief note on the pioneer Indian anthropologist, L.K. Ananta Krishna Iyer may be in order in this context. A self-made anthropologist and the first Indian to teach anthropology at the university level, Iyer was an alumnus of Madras University. Palghat where he was born and bred was then a part of Madras Presidency and was within the jurisdiction of Madras University. After serving as a science teacher in the Maharaja College at Cochin, he got the assignment of preparing reports on the castes and tribes within the province. Accomplishing a thorough job, he brought out two volumes on the subject, the first one in 1909 and the second one in 1912. On the basis of a thematic organization of that data he wrote a paper, "Marriage customs of the Cochin State" which was published in the *Journal of Asiatic Society of Bengal* in 1914. In recognition of his meritorious work, the Madras University conferred on him an honorary readership in anthropology in 1916. The visionary Vice-Chancellor of Calcutta University, Ashutosh Mukerjee, invited him in 1920 to organize the department of anthropology and train students at graduate and post-graduate levels. Thus Calcutta University was the first to establish a department of anthropology in the country. It may be mentioned that he was one of the three south Indian scholars to be invited by Mukerjee to man the top posts in the Calcutta

University, the other two being S. Radhakrishnan and C.V. Raman. While working at Calcutta University, Iyer wrote a book entitled *Lectures in Ethnography*. He also published a monograph on the Syrian Christians in 1924. The work on castes and tribes of Mysore which remained unfinished because of the untimely death of Nanjundiah was completed by Ananta Krishna Iyer while he was serving the Calcutta University (Bala Ratnam 1963: 21-22).

A few other South Indian scholars published some path-breaking papers during the first half of twentieth century. K.M. Pannikar published a paper titled "Nayar customs" in the journal of the Royal Anthropological Institute in the year 1918. In the same prestigious journal, G.S. Ghurye wrote a paper in 1923, focusing on the correlation between cross-cousin marriage and dual organization among some South Indian communities. A. Aiyappan wrote a few papers on Nayar polyandry. They were published in the British journal, *Man,* the first one in 1932, and the second one in 1934. He also wrote a paper entitled "Fraternal polyandry in Malabar" which was published in *Man in India* in 1935. Later he brought out his monograph on the Nayadis of Wyanad. His paper "Irulas and Culture Change" was published in the government museum bulletin in 1944. M.N. Srinivas completed his study of the Coorgs by 1945. The forties of the last century also saw a number of publications by Fürer-Haimendorf on the Deccan tribes like the Chenchus, Konda Reddi and Gond.

II

One would expect that the momentum of events mentioned in the preceding pages should have resulted in the starting of graduate and postgraduate courses in anthropology at the premier educational institution of South India, viz. Madras University atleast by the thirties of last century, following the example of Calcutta University. But it did not happen. When Madras University at last moved in the matter to establish a department of anthropology in 1945, it began in a modest way with a part-time diploma course. This is not to be construed as lack of earnestness. Perhaps the idea was to go step by step. For, the university cast its net very wide indeed and recruited an Austrian, U.R. Ehrenfels as reader and head of the department. There was every hope that the academic programme in anthropology would soon expand. D.N. Majumdar in his presidential address to the Anthropology and Archaeology section of Indian Science Congress in 1947, took the opportunity to refer to this signal development at Madras University and expressed his confidence about the future expansion of the discipline:

> Anthropological studies received an impetus in the recognition of anthropology as a subject for a diploma by the Madras University, and arrangements were in progress for inclusion of the subject for the degree examinations (1947: 27-8).

But the initial enthusiasm sagged very soon, and the academic programme in anthropology at Madras University stagnated for three long decades at the level of a part-time diploma course run by a single teacher. The factors responsible for it seem to be complex.

At that time (i.e. mid-forties of the last century), the curricular status of anthropology in the country was that leaving apart the Calcutta University which ran full-fledged graduate and post-graduate courses in anthropology since 1920, there were only a few other centers in the country where this subject was taught as a part of other courses. The universities of Poona, Lucknow and Delhi, did not have separate departments of anthropology at that time and did not offer post-graduate courses in the discipline as such. One or two papers in anthropology were taught along with other subjects like economics and sociology. Full-fledged departments of anthropology came to be established in those universities by about 1950. I myself studied anthropology along with other subjects in the Department of Economics and Sociology at Lucknow University. As such, I could do a bit of 'field observation' of the progress of this discipline both in the North and the South.

As the subject of anthropology was being taught only in a few centers in the country at that time, the students and teachers of this subject felt a special affinity towards one another. My teacher, Majumdar, asked me to visit the department of anthropology at Madras University and also call on A. Aiyappan who was then the Superintendent of Madras Museum whenever I visited that city. As I belonged to Nellore, and Madras was a kind of second home for people of my district, I always visited that city at least once during the summer vacations. When I called on Aiyappan during 1946-47 and expressed my desire to meet Ehrenfels, he told me that he was arranging an exhibition of the latter's paintings in the museum hall on the following day, and I could come and see the exhibition and also meet Ehrenfels. I visited the exhibition; found the paintings very impressive and told Ehrenfels that I would meet him again in the university. I did meet him the next day and it turned out to be the last time I could meet him. The next time I visited Madras University was at the beginning of my research career. By then Ehrenfels had relinquished his post and was succeeded by L.A. Krishna Iyer. I met the latter, carrying a letter of introduction from my teacher in which a request was made to give me library facility for reference work before the commencement of my fieldwork.

What I observed during my brief visits to the department of anthropology at Madras University during that phase might not yield a complete answer to the question as to why the discipline went through a long period of stagnation. But I could notice an unmistakable mismatch between the personnel recruited to run the department and the cultural milieu around them. When I went to call on Ehrenfels, I reached the university a little earlier than he did. Waiting in the verandah, I noticed a foreigner coming on a bicycle in the hot sun, wearing only knickers and not even a banian to cover his bare chest. He was none other than Ehrenfels. On the same day, I could catch a distant glimpse of the vice-chancellor, A.L. Mudaliar who was wearing a tweed coat, a tie and a turban during a blazing summer. I asked myself whether these contrasting sartorial styles could lead to a clash of cultures and consequent antipathies. Leaving the external factors aside, and looking at it ideologically, the mother-right approach of Ehrenfels could not have chimed well with the patriarchal persona of Mudaliar. Whatever it be, Ehrenfels left the university much sooner than expected.

As for his successor L.A. Krishna Iyer, it has to be noted that he was of formidable professional lineage, being the son of Ananta Krishna Iyer who had national and international assignments and exposure. One would expect that a scion of that reputed line would be a person with metropolitan life-ways. But he appeared to be one who was not willing to pull himself out of his orthodox moorings even a wee-bit either sartorially, socially or attitudinally. One factor which created an initial problem of interaction between us was that my teacher, in his letter of introduction, referred to me as his pupil and friend. Krishna Iyer paused over that line and could not conceal his difficulty in understanding how a pupil could also be a friend. Let us note that the 1950s were the times when the social and political climate in Madras and Tamilnadu was changing very fast, and politicians and administrators were looking askance at Brahmanical orthodoxy. But the lone teacher in the anthropology department chose to remain an adorable antediluvian. This underlines the anthropological truth that any project can progress only when it is in harmony with the environment.

Leaving the Madras University behind, some of the other universities in South India moved ahead to organize postgraduate courses in anthropology. The credit of being the first to offer M.A. in anthropology in the whole of South India goes to the Karnatak University at Dharwad. It happened in 1958. This was followed by the Andhra University (Visakhapatnam) which started postgraduate courses in anthropology in the year 1961. Six years later, the S.V. University at Tirupati followed suit. The Mysore University started a combined post-graduate department of sociology and anthropology in 1973, to be followed by bifurcation and the establishment of a separate department of anthropology a few years later. The prolonged stagnation of anthropology at Madras University was ended at last in 1976 by a far-seeing educationist, M. Adiseshiah, who as its vice-chancellor, expanded the department and instituted post-graduate courses in the subject. The Hyderabad Central University began with a composite department of sociology and anthropology in the year 1979 before a separate department of anthropology could be constituted in 1987.

In 1984, the Tamil University constituted Tribal Research Centre at Ooty, manned by a number of anthropologists with research experience. In 1987, the autonomous St. Xavier College at Palayamkotai in Tamilnadu, started a multi-disciplinary post-graduate course in folklore, of which anthropology was a major segment. Similarly anthropology figures in the M.A. folklore course at Madurai Kamaraj University. One paper in anthropology is being taught in the human resource development course in St. Joseph's College at Tiruchirapalli. In 1986 the Pondicherry University started a unique course in Futurology, of which anthropology was a segment. Eventually a separate department of anthropology was constituted there in 1999 with master's and doctoral programmes. Paradoxically, Kerala was the last among the states in the country to institute programmes in anthropology. It was only in the 1980s that the Calicut (Kazhikode) University instituted M.A. course in anthropology at its Tellicherry campus. Later, this campus, along with other institutions of the northern end of Kerala came under the newly constituted Kannur University.

Taking an overall view of the progress of anthropology in the South Indian academia, one cannot but express disappointment at its slow growth compared to North India. Particularly poignant are the cases of Kerala and Tamilnadu when we consider the fact that the first Indian to occupy a university chair in anthropology hailed from that region and many important studies which became landmarks in the discipline were conducted among the communities living there. The cultural material available in the region is so rich that it continues to attract scholars from far and wide to undertake field researches. To illustrate this continuing process, I may cite a few cases such as Hardgrave's study of Nadars (1969), Dumont's study of Pramalai Kallars (1986), Gough's researches on matrilineal kinship (1972), Trautmann's work on Dravidian kinship system (1981), and the current researches on the organization of Madurai Meenakshi temple by Fuller.

In the foreword to the *Introduction* volume of the *People of India*, there is a pregnant suggestion that we do not have to leave it to foreign scholars to study the Nadar of Tamilnadu or the Pattidar of Gujarat. This should not be taken to mean that foreign scholars are not welcome to study the cultures of various communities in India. Its message is that Indian institutions should produce competent researchers in anthropology so that monographs can be brought out on the country's diverse cultural phenomena to equal in quality the work of eminent foreign scholars. From that point of view, there is much lee-way to make up. In this context I cannot hide my disappointment at the lack of needed response to the objectively felt knowledge needs on the part of many South Indian universities.

In the whole of Tamilnadu, there is no other institution except the Madras University to train researchers in anthropology. The Pondichery University, which is a central institution and which has academic jurisdiction over the Andaman and Nicobar Islands should have planned for a centre of excellence in anthropology with multiple specializations. But it took thirteen years to establish a department of anthropology there, and it is run with skeletal staff and a Reader as its head. It is indeed an irony that the premier university of Kerala at Trivandrum has no department of anthropology. The irony becomes all the more galling when one recalls that one of the pioneers of Indian anthropology, Aiyappan, was once the vice-chancellor of that university. Perhaps he followed the priestly principle of monopoly over specialized knowledge which he did not want to disseminate to all and sundry. Also disheartening is the case of Osmania University, where the sociology department could claim, at one time, the association of stalwarts like Fürer-Haimendorf and S.C. Dube. Now anthropology is almost invisible in the M.A. sociology course there.

III

Towards the end, I choose to give a brief outline of a few of the unique cultural phenomena of south India which need to be studied afresh or restudied with the aid of updated conceptual and theoretical tools. It is my case that when there are things of academic and practical importance to be studied, it behvoes the universities of the region concerned to provide instruction in the concerned discipline and create facilities for research. Needless for me to stress that what I am presenting below is only a small sample of a vast and varied field.

Matrilineal societies: Well documented studies of matrilineal societies of India are but a few. In our country, matriliny is known to exist in Kerala, Lakshadweep Islands and Meghalaya. Murdock's book, *Social Structure* (1960), which draws its main data from the Human Relations Area Files, lists 40 societies as following matrilocal rule of residence in the whole world. The recent *People of India* project identifies 42 matrilocal societies in India alone. It means that a large number of matrilineal and matrilocal societies remained untraced until recently. Many of them are located in South India. To study them and prepare monographs of a good standard, requires a large band of trained researchers. A unique cultural phenomena found in Lakshadweep Islands and along the coast of Khozikode in Kerala is that the Muslim inhabitants of these places follow the matrilineal rule of descent. A study of the synthesis of two important historical and cultural streams would be of great academic importance. Of course, there are some studies on the matrilineal communities of South India, but the indication that one gets from the vast survey of the Anthropological Survey of India is that what remains to be done is much more than what could be done earlier.

The very concepts are being revised and refined. Unless the researchers keep abreast of time, their work becomes outdated before it is completed. The People of India project mentions only three categories under the rule of residence, viz. patrilocal, matrilocal, and bilocal, while Murdock mentions five categories—patrilocal, matrilocal, bilocal, partri-matrilocal and avanculocal. Additional concepts and categories have come into vogue to fit variations in institutional forms. In fact the rule of residence found among the Garo and the majority of the Khasi (in Meghalaya) where the husband moves to his wife's place of birth is not the same as the one found among the Nayar, or the Pnar section of the Khasi or Lakhshadweep islanders where both men and women live at their place of birth, and husbands only visit their wives. To bundle them together under matrilocal category is to overlook a material difference. The latterly evolved conceptual schemes used by writers like Robin Fox (1978: 99-100) with categories such as uxorilocal and natalocal (in place of matrilocal) can encompass these categories.

Conceptual refinement apart, an amplification of the functional ramifications of these distinct modes of residence would make an important contribution to ethnography. Property rights, management of economy, domestic structure, household composition, interpersonal relations, authority and command lines, internal and external interactions among the segments of the kin groups that exist in a natolocal society should be different from what exist in an uxorilocal society. Only intensive studies of matrilineal societies, some following natolocal rule of residence and some practising uxorilocal rule would throw full light on this important subject. Also deserving careful attention is the possible transition from one rule of residence to another. If there is evidence that a transition has occurred, the factors influencing the change need to be analyzed. A researcher studying the Lakshadweep Islands has reported that different modes of residence are found across the households in a single island though the norm can be clearly figured out to be natolocal. The variations in the mode of residence are said to be caused by changes in occupation and income levels of individual members or by changes in the composition of households due to demographic factors.

One caveat is due in this context. It should not be taken that matrilineal communities are confined to Kerala and Lakshadweep Islands alone in South India. There are a few matrilineal pockets in other adjoining areas too. For instance, the Mullukurumba in the Nilgiri district of Tamilnadu combine matriliny with dual organization. Such unique cultural phenomena need to be intensely researched.

Polyandrous societies: Of the three well-documented polyandrous societies in India, two are from the south (Nayars of Kerala and Todas of Tamilnadu). Once it was thought that this was a vanishing institution. But the People of India project counters any suggestion of its evanescence, because it is able to list 40 polyandrous societies. They need to be thoroughly researched. Perhaps the Toda case itself deserves an intensive re-study because of the unique combination of patriliny with non-fraternal polyandry which requires complex cultural norms to make the system work. It is possible that such complex combinations might occur in a few more societies listed by the People of India project. Variations are only to be expected in an institution like polyandry. Even where a society recognizes polyandry as its accepted norm, there may be variation in forms of marriage in individual cases. A rich family may be monogamous. A village chief may be polygynous. When such a mix becomes a recognized pattern in a society, it may be considered to be practicing polygynandry. The People of India project lists communities as practicing polygynandry, five communities as practicing non-fraternal polyandry and 28 communities as practicing fraternal polyandry. Here again, as in the case of matriliny, many more cases than hitherto known could be traced by the Anthropological Survey of India. And quite a few of them are in South India. This unique institution needs to be studied, analyzed and interpreted in relation to other features of the society like economy, demography, line of descent, age grades, hierarchical norms, etc.

Cross-cousin marriages: South India is a heaven of preferential or prescribed marriages which are not in vogue in North India. Their provenance, their frequencies and their linkages with other aspects of culture have been subjects of elaborate theses and counter-theses bearing the impress of two distinct schools of thought, one centering round descent groups and the other emphasizing alliance. The relative merits of these two lines of approach need to be tested and re-tested in reference to the norms prevailing among different groups and different regions of South India. The validity of the functionalist and structuralist interpretations of the differential preferences in respect of patrilateral cross-cousins and matrilateral cross-cousins are to be tested in the context of data from different communities and different regions of South India. The changes that are taking place in the marriage practices among the different castes and communities under the impact of modernization need to be studied with a view to assessing whether the basic principle underlying the Dravidian kinship system is itself getting transformed. Again, the consanguineal marriages prevalent in South India offer a rich field for research in human genetics which requires multi-disciplinary training in higher academia.

Rural social structure: The social structure of rural Tamilnadu is in a way distinct compared to other linguistic regions of South India. The distinguishing feature is that while the dominant castes are easily identifiable in their respective zones in other states, it is not the case in many parts of Tamilnadu, where even within a small group of neighbouring villages, power is dispersed among a few competing castes. Also the underclass in Tamilnadu (say Pallan) is more assertive compared to their counterparts in other states. This actually makes for a more dispersed loci of power than in other states.

This feature of rural Tamilnadu has been brought out by a few collaborative studies conducted by the anthropology departments of Madras and Tokyo universities among the villages of Tiruchirapally district in the 1980s. Comparative studies of other regions of Tamilnadu in particular and other states of South India in general may prove helpful in planning for rural development and local self-government.

Women's status: The status of women does vary from region to region and from one community to another. It may be related to several cultural factors like religious injunctions, rule of residence, rule of descent, property rights and preferential marriages. These variations need to be studied, as also the operation of special empowerment schemes. For instance, property rights have been amended in favour of women by legislation in some of the states in South India. But ground realities may be different from what is inscribed in the statutes. Many thrift-schemes are specially oriented towards women's participation and empowerment. Only intensive micro-studies, using anthropological methods can bring to light the underlying dynamics and help in the planning and execution of development schemes.

Folklore: The subject of oral tradition or folklore has so far occupied only a peripheral position in the anthropological studies of South India. But considering the fact that there exist what deserve to be called versions of epiclore specific to certain regions and also considering that the occasions on which they are narrated are becoming fewer or less important, in the face of changes in life-ways, there is urgent need to record them and interpret them in terms of the cultural contexts in which they figure. In Andhra Pradesh, on the occasions of traditional sacrifices offered to the village deities, bards narrate long mythic legends night after night even for a whole week in some cases. Brenda Beck recorded a similar epic lore in the Konku region of Tamilnadu which was published under the title *Three Twins*. Similar epiclores should be existing in Karnataka and Kerala too. But full texts of these oral narratives are not available. There is great need to record them and study them in relation to cognate religious practices. The journal, *South Indian Folklorist,* run by St. Xavier College, Palayamkottai, has been filling the gap to some extent. But there is a lot more to be covered.

Trans-community interactions: There are some major folk beliefs and events that cut across tribes, castes and regions which need to be studied in detail. There is a big tribal festival which takes place annually at a village called Medaram in Warangal district of Andhra Pradesh. The icons of two tribal sisters, Saralakka and Sammakka, known to be martyrs, are worshipped on that occasion. The festival draws lakhs of people, both tribal and non-tribal, from all the neighbouring districts. Last year the number of people who assembled there is said to have crossed a million. There is no full-length study of it so far. Only a short sketch of it was recently published in the journal, *South Indian Folklorist*. It needs a detailed study. Similar trans-regional centers of faith exist in different parts of South India. While there is certainly need to study and analyze the causes of conflict, there is greater need to highlight the existing amity between tribes, castes and religious communities. In the northern, interior parts of Andhra Pradesh, the images of deities of one tribe are ceremonially taken to the areas of the neighbouring tribes on specific days in a year, and the latter offer them obeisance. In many of the villages, Muslims avidly participate in Hindu festivals, and Hindus throng the Muslim shrines at some places to seek supernatural favours or to discharge their obligations in return for the benefits received. Detailed studies of such things are of national and even global importance.

Andaman and Nicobar Islands: It is high time that an advanced centre of anthropological research is established at Port Blair by the Pondicherry University (which has academic jurisdiction over the area). The variegated realities of the area, right from the tribes which are on the verge of extinction to the tribes which are yet to be contacted, with the well-adjusted Nicobarese in between, need to be studied by a band of sensitive, sagacious and dedicated researchers.

REFERENCES

Bala Ratnam
1963 *Anthropology on the March*. Madras: Madras Book Center.

Dumont, L.
1986 *A South Indian Caste: Social Organization and Religion of Pramalai Kallar*. Delhi: Oxford University Press.

Fox, Robin

1978 *Kinship and Marriage*. Penguin Books, England

Hardgrave, R.L.

1969 *Nadars*. Berkeley: University of California Press.

Lowie, R.H.

1950 *Social Organization*. London: Routledge and Kegan Paul Ltd.

Majumdar, D.N.

1947 *Progress of Anthropology in India: 1911-46*. Calcutta: Indian Science Congress and J.C.S.I.R.

Morgan, L.H.

1870 *System of Consanguinity and Affinity of the Human Family*. Washington D.C.: Smithsonian Institution.

1877 *Ancient Society*. New York: World Publishing Co. (Page numbers as per Indian Edition: Bharati Library, Calcutta).

Murdock, G.P.

1960 *Social Structure*. New York: Macmillan and Co.

Rivers, W.H.R.

1906 *The Todas*. London: Macmillan and Co.

Schneider, D.N. and K. Gough

1972 *Matrilineal Kinship*. Allahabad: A.H. Wheeler and Co.

Trautmann, T.R.

1981 *A Dravidian Kinship System*. Combridge: Cambridge University Press.

3

Some Thoughts on Anthropology in India

VINAY KUMAR SRIVASTAVA

Let me begin by expressing my deep gratitude to the Ethnographic and Folk Culture Society, Lucknow, particularly its secretary, Dr. Nadeem Hasnain, for the honour it has conferred upon me by inviting me to deliver the Dr. K.S. Mathur Memorial Lecture. I never had the opportunity of meeting Dr. Mathur during his lifetime. The sole significant memory I have of him is of March 1974 when I saw him in Professor S.C. Tiwari's room in the Department of Anthropology of the University of Delhi. On another occasion, maybe a decade later, on Professor Tiwari's advice, I prepared a set of readings on anthropology for Dr. Mathur's son who at that time was planning to appear for the Civil Services Examination.

Although I never met Dr. Mathur, I knew about him from my teachers at Delhi. As an M. A. student in sociology, I had also read his 1964 oft-referred book *Caste and Ritual in a Malwa Village*. A couple of months ago, in connection with another project, I scanned the past issues of *Man in India* and *The Eastern Anthropologist*, and read several of Dr. Mathur's writings with profit. That his 1964 book is of lasting significance may be inferred from the fact that Professor T.N. Madan, in his popular, edited volume, *Religion in India* (1992), has included excerpts from its fifth chapter.

It was a little difficult for me to choose a topic for this lecture. For the last few years, I am engaged in reading and writing about the discipline of anthropology in India, and so, I thought I would share with this august gathering some of my ideas.

II

Let me begin with an editorial statement that appeared in the inaugural issue of a journal in Delhi in 1978. The journal, called the *Spectra of Anthropological Progress* (*SAP*), started by five young enthusiasts of the Delhi Department of Anthropology, aimed to explore the possibility of bringing different anthropological specializations together. This editorial spoke of the identity crisis in anthropology: anthropology was gradually becoming 'unrecognizable', and its frontiers were merging with other disciplines. Physical anthropology was becoming more 'medicalized'; social anthropology was becoming more 'sociological' (i.e., 'merging with sociology'); and prehistory was becoming more 'archaeological and historical'. These three branches of anthropology–although, there is another one, which has remained considerably less developed in Indian universities, namely linguistic anthropology–were coexisting in a department without any interaction between them, without one getting benefited by the insights and methods of the other. An insider often felt that there were 'three departments' within one department, and one belonged to a *specialization* within anthropology rather than to the whole subject. The kind of conflict and one-upmanship that characterized qualitative and quantitative researchers was visible between physical and social anthropologists, with the former calling the latter 'story-tellers' and the latter calling the former the 'unredeemable victims of endless fragmentation.'

Certainly, the *SAP* was not the first one to draw its readers' attention to the existing scenario, because many anthropologists of those days were aware of the ceaseless–and sometimes aimless–fragmentation of anthropological interests. Many voiced their concern for the future of anthropology as an 'integrated science of man (now, human beings) in time and space', an elemental definition with which books and teachers in anthropology generally began, and still do. The *SAP* editorial briefly outlined the evolutionary growth in the subject matter of anthropology. With differentiation in anthropology, its components had become dissimilar, each one almost becoming an island in itself, and how it related to the basic concerns of anthropology remained a matter of worry. Differentiation was leading to disintegration and decomposition of anthropology, with a blurring of its foci. The need of the hour was a clarion call: to think in terms of integration.

With hindsight, I think the *SAP* editors were unconsciously impressed with Herbert Spencer's concept of evolution, the idea that integration compensates for the differentiation of parts, and they used the same for understanding the state of anthropology. Further, the concern was not to explore the possibility of a philosophy, or methodology, if any, that would unite the different specializations within anthropology, as Srivastava and Mahajan (1978) had done in an unpublished paper, in which they thought that dialectical materialism could provide a philosophical base for creating unity between biological and socio-cultural facts, thus bringing physical and socio-cultural anthropology in a relation of interdependence, where one learnt from the other. It was rather to justify one's existence in a department where the work some did was entirely different from the work of the others. It was not the coexistence of 'laboratory work' and 'fieldwork' that piqued anthropology, but the kind of work that was being done. Against this background, the catchwords of 'integration' and 'holism' (and statements like, 'anthropology is an integrated science', 'anthropology studies human beings in holistic terms', 'anthropology is a subject without frontiers and boundaries') were sought as panacea for the crises of fragmentation that the subject was facing. I think some anthropologists knew at that time that their subject was not one discipline; it was on its journey of becoming (or, had become) a 'group of disciplines', some kind of a salad where each of its components was different, but was arranged in the same bowl!

The *SAP* editors invited its readers to comment upon their editorial statement. It was heartening to note that several anthropologists (and also sociologists) cared to reply, some orally, some in writing. Without exception, the commentators agreed with the *SAP* editorial about the existence of an identity crisis in anthropology; it was not a figment of imagination, as some might have guessed. Overspecialization was taking place in different branches of anthropology, thus fragmenting the discipline in almost unrecognizable domains. However, the readers' comments covered a wide canvas: for some, the crisis was in physical anthropology and not in social anthropology; some thought the crisis was in anthropology because it had become a 'kind of rucksack' in which anything or everything could be put by simply prefixing it with 'anthropology of' (like 'anthropology of the atom bomb', 'anthropology of tubercular infection', 'anthropology of sports'); some said anthropology needed to 'modernize' its syllabi and emerge out of its image of a colonial engagement with the exotic, pre-literate, and non-civilized societies; one commentator observed that a time would come when there would be different specialists for the right and the left molar; and another commentator noted that for some in anthropology, 'culture' meant 'cell culture'!

Each specialization seemed to become an end unto itself. The question was how it related to the other branches of anthropology, on the one hand, and how it illuminated the central concerns, the goals and aims, of anthropology, if there were any. The fear was imminent that physical anthropology would become an appendage of medical science, and social anthropology would be absorbed in sociology. I heard people talk those days about the 'medicalization of physical anthropology'. Not only the research interests pursued by physical anthropologists were largely of medical value, the collaborators of physical anthropologists in their joint ventures were also medical scientists. That most of the contributors to physical anthropology journals of the world were medical scientists could be gauged by cursorily going through a recent issue of the *American Journal of Physical Anthropology* (*AJPA*). The collaborative projects might retain the term 'anthropology' in their titles (like 'anthropology of dental deformities', 'anthropology of neuro-spinal disorders'), but there was hardly any 'anthropology', as it is understood, in them. In fact, the use of anthropology in their titles was unnecessary and could be dropped without a wince. About social anthropology, it was said that the departments of sociology were providing a far intensive training in social anthropology than was the case in the departments of anthropology, where a student spent an appreciable amount of his time doing courses that he would not need for his later research and teaching. For instance, a post-graduate anthropology student in the University of Delhi reads eight and a half theory papers out of twelve in two years, and conducts half practical out of four in social anthropology in the first year of his post-graduation. His degree is in anthropology, although he specializes in Group–B (i.e., social anthropology). In comparison, a sociology post-graduate student at Delhi reads sixteen papers, in which he covers almost all the salient topics of social anthropology.

One of the observations was that the type of crisis, which bedevilled anthropology, was non-existent in other disciplines, notwithstanding the forces of differentiation in them. In other words, it cannot be concluded that differentiation necessarily led to disintegration and decomposition of discipline. Then, why was it happening to anthropology? A related question was: Would anthropology disappear with the tides of overspecialization, and its content being appropriated by other disciplines? Theoretically, one could argue in favour of anthropology being a unified and holistic discipline, and one could always think in terms of the strategies to integrate different branches of anthropology, but the micro-level reality (i.e., at the level of anthropology departments) was that the different branches of anthropology were independent disciplines. Another point of considerable merit was that it was better to speak of the integration of different specializations in physical anthropology, or integration of different branches of social anthropology, rather than the integration of physical anthropology with social anthropology. The latter was far more problematic because of the differences in which biological and social sciences were respectively conducted.

III

Twenty-five years later, let me reflect upon the identity crisis in anthropology. Since then, many changes have occurred in the practice of anthropology. The questions and queries of anthropology are different now. Anthropologists are less worried about their future and collective existence, for their subject is certainly not an endangered species. Anthropology will survive the twenty-first century and many more to follow, without being amalgamated with any discipline, either in the stream of biological or social sciences. Anthropology will survive because of its particular ways of looking at and analyzing social reality, because of its techniques, methods, and theoretical perspectives, and because it is concerned with all types of societies at all points of time. Anthropology has principally made three contributions, now not only being acknowledged but also appropriated by different disciplines, which ensure its survival: first, the perspective that the thoughts and practices of a people should be understood in terms of their cultural milieu, from an insider's perspective; second, the method of fieldwork, living with people *in situ* for a lengthy period of time; and finally, in generating a wide mass of data of comparative value about human situation from cross-cultural contexts.

Today, anthropologists are less worried about super-specializations. An irrefutable fact is that specialization is a measure of healthy growth. It does not prophesy, contrary to the analogy from paleontology, the demise of a discipline, provided the basic aims of the discipline, its methodology and distinctive approach, remain intact. For instance, the types of specialization one comes across in physical anthropology are perhaps non-existent in social and cultural anthropology, but what unifies these different specializations is a commitment that physical anthropologists have to 'Darwinian evolutionary theory in explaining and understanding the biological world' around them (Larsen 2000:2). If physical anthropology is a 'discipline', it is because its different branches share the same paradigm, the same 'philosophy', although its practitioners may disagree on the mechanisms of evolutionary change. Thus, specializations in physical anthropology are not detrimental to the discipline; rather, each one of them is a detailed (and microscopic, so to say) investigation into an aspect of biological reality. Incidentally, each issue of the *American Journal of Physical Anthropology* of 2000 carried an article by a distinguished physical anthropologist on the future of physical anthropology. A content analysis of these twelve articles (*AJPA* is published monthly) clearly points out that the paradigm of evolution and variation lies at the base of the several highly specialized studies. However, these articles do not deal with the issue of integrating physical anthropology with social-cultural anthropology; they are mainly concerned with the question of integrating the different branches of physical anthropology.

Let me now have a look at what some anthropologists regard as the 'newer issues' confronting their discipline. Earlier, anthropology and its perspectives were largely confined to its departments and organizations where anthropological work was carried out. Other disciplines generally did not evince much interest in anthropological writings, barring a couple of isolated cases; for instance, Karl Marx and Fredrick Engels spoke of 'primitive communism', and delineated the characteristics of this stage, after being inspired by Lewis Henry Morgan's *Ancient Society* (1877).

Now, the situation is different. The other social sciences have included courses on anthropological methodology and concepts in their syllabi. Although called 'qualitative methods and techniques', they are nothing but anthropological. In some such departments, their own professionals endeavor to handle these courses, while in others, they invite trained anthropologists to teach as well as guide research.

Field methods have become immensely popular in other social sciences. Legal science, for example, has termed field methodology 'non-doctrinal', which is compared to their tradition of legal research, the so-called 'doctrinal', where the cases and judgments, already available in archives and libraries, are subjected to analysis. Legal scientists are seriously considering the insights from the legal systems of pre-literate and technologically simpler societies, to which they had hitherto not paid much attention. Now, they are seriously considering the study of unwritten and customary laws, the data on which are collected through first-hand field studies. Anthropological perspectives have enriched the legal scientist's understanding of law in society. What legal anthropologists have submitted is that law is a social fact, which exists in relationship with the other social facts.

Historians of modern India often undertake spells of fieldwork. Many works on the Partition include oral evidence from those who saw that happening and suffered it. Students of history have also taken up the study of small communities, especially tribal, in which they acknowledge their debt to anthropologists. I remember my colleagues from history reading for a doctoral degree at Cambridge, undertaking studies of different aspects of the jute mill towns in West Bengal, and each one of them had carried out an empirical work with the people of these towns, following anthropological methods and techniques. Each work aimed to link the past of these towns with their respective contemporary realities. The historians' study of *dana* and *daksina* in ancient India has benefited immensely from Marcel Mauss' work on the gift; the psychologist's study of Oedipus complex has been considerably modified in light of Malinowski's Trobriand ethnography; and the students of literature increasingly use Lévi-Strauss' structuralism.

Those disciplines that at one time unequivocally argued for experimentation and quantification, psychology for example, are today correcting their partisan view by including fieldwork and qualitative methods in their researches. The students of education conduct fieldwork in micro-settings (classrooms and schools) to see the educational system in operation. One may look at examples from other disciplines, where anthropological methods and approaches are used, and the other organizations and institutions (such as medical colleges, institutes of planning and architecture, pharmaceutical industries, non-governmental organizations) where anthropology graduates are employed. I think one of the conclusions drawn from this would be that although anthropology departments have not expanded in our country, or new university departments have not come up, anthropological knowledge has definitely influenced and enriched the outside academic and developmental world, changing its perspectives by bringing in social as well as cultural factors. I shall return to this point later.

IV

As stated earlier, anthropology has championed the idea of micro-studies by 'living' with people in their natural habitats. It has profitably shown that a study of a small group (sometimes, a few dozens of people) can help us in reaching a set of common propositions about human life (Béteille 1996). In his book, Mathur (1964:3) writes:

> ...our conclusion must be based on long-term observations and investigation in a small community which an individual can handle

> by himself. Conclusions based on such studies are, in main, strictly local or at best, regional. But they do possess a certain over-all importance, since local or even regional communities are not autonomous isolated social groups but rather parts of a bigger and broader social system.

In his diary, Malinowski (1967: 119) notes: folk ideas are universal ideas. One begins with a micro-level study and attempts to formulate propositions that may be subjected to further testing and examination. For example, an urban anthropologist may begin with the intensive study of an urban neighbourhood; in anthropology of science, a scientific laboratory may be studied; in anthropology of work and leisure, fieldwork may be conducted in a government office. The focus on micro units has now considerably impressed those disciplines that traditionally began with bigger entities, such as society, nation, and civilization.

The anthropological fieldworker is a *bricoleur*, a 'jack of all trades or a kind of professional do-it-yourself person', to remember the words of Lévi-Strauss (1976). The ethnographer uses the tools of his methodological trade, deploying whatever strategies, methods or empirical materials are available with him. At the same time, he improvises newer ways of gathering information. Later, he writes about his modifications of the techniques and the ways in which he used them. That is why, the accounts of fieldwork are extremely instructive, for each fieldwork is unique and has a lot to teach the others.

In essence, the anthropological work is multi-method and multi-paradigmatic in nature. The anthropologist knows that for looking at and analyzing the social world, there are contesting paradigms, broadly termed positivist, interpretive, and critical, and each one of them has several sub-types under its head. What one chooses depends upon a variety of factors. These perspectives have also influenced researches in other disciplines, and in turn, they have influenced anthropology.

As mentioned earlier, central to the work of anthropologists is the concept of culture, which has also exercised its impact on other disciplines, although the ensemble of meanings attributed to it may differ from one discipline to another. Some still use the all-inclusive concept of culture, which embraces any manifestation of a society as well as being synonymous for 'society' itself. Some are inclined to follow the semiotic meaning of culture as enunciated by Clifford Geertz (1973): Culture implies those 'webs of significance' humankind spins for itself. Whatever may be the meaning adopted, or improvised, culture becomes an explanatory concept in these studies, accounting for differences as well as similarities between human societies. Political scientists now conduct studies of the culture of election, besides the traditional studies of voting patterns. Economists and development planners also consider the cultural aspects. Under its rubric, modern psychology has included an approach known as 'cultural psychology', the pith of which is that the researchers should 'think through cultures' in search of the psychological nature of human beings. Cultural psychology submits that individuals and traditions, psyches and cultures, psychic facts and social facts, make each other up. In addition, many examples may be drawn from biology and medicine where the concept of culture is actively used. In today's anthropology, culture is conceptualized not only as a 'way of life', one that gives people a meaning to their activities. It is also a 'way of struggle'. Armed with its instruments and symbols, people negotiate with their predicaments and face the problems of survival with fortitude.

With these examples, what I intend to show is that anthropology has considerably profited researches in other disciplines. Today, the influence of anthropology extends far beyond the narrow confines of anthropology departments and research institutes. Thus, one should not be surprised to know that agricultural scientists use anthropological techniques in learning about, and then helping in female empowerment in a village. With these examples, however, I do not wish to give the impression that the other disciplines are doing what anthropologists ought to do, but that anthropological input has broadened their intellectual horizon.

Furthermore, the anthropologist is always 'marginal' to the society he studies; it may be his own family, his own community that he selects for study, or the 'other culture' in a true sense of the term. In each of them, notwithstanding the degree of his rapport with people, he is in part an 'actor', in part an 'observer'. He is in a situation that lies between the states of 'attachment' and 'detachment'. When he becomes rather passionately involved with the local people and their culture, because of his pan-humanistic outlook, his discipline warns him of the perils of subjectivity. He is advised to control the tides of sentiment for scientific objectivity, but knows full well that his subject is a relentless struggle of involvement and detachment. This is the *raison d'etre* of 'his marginal' status. As an anthropologist, he is neither the true scientist, the forbear of objectivity, nor the native actor, the bearer of local culture.

From this status follows the creativity of the anthropologist. Here, I wish to draw your attention to Edward Said's (1999) idea that migration and marginality are the possible causes of creativity and intellectualism. Said's intellectual is an awkward outsider, someone unsettled in any one place, he is restless, transgresses boundaries, flouts norms, questions conventions and firmly held truths; he is both involved in and detached from the affairs of the world; he is able to experience the social life as an insider as well as is able to cast a skeptical look at it as an outsider. Said's model stands as metaphor for the anthropologist, who would always have the 'marginal', and thus creative, status irrespective of the location of his fieldwork. Fieldwork is an unforgettable experience–the first-hand experience of the 'other'–of an anthropologist; its essence is lost when its meaning is limited to data-collection. In this creativity lies the strength of anthropology which is one of the reasons of its impact on other disciplines and public life in general.

V

Let me now turn to the challenges before contemporary anthropology, especially in India. The context in which anthropology is now being produced is phenomenally different from what used to be in the second half of the twentieth century. At that time, the subjects of anthropology were a muted lot; they did not answer back. The anthropologist had the authority to represent them, to write anything on them, and these writings were for the consumption of scholars and the middle class public abroad. Although the people constituted the centre of the colourful text, with photographs, sketches, drawings, they had no expertise (and even, authority) to reflect upon it, to correct the understanding and vision of the anthropologist. And, the anthropologist perhaps never thought that a time would come when the people of his study would view his writings critically or reverentially, condemning him in some cases and glorifying in others. People would search for their pasts, the histories of their exploitation, in anthropological monographs. Their revivalistic movements (or movements to build their separate identity) would derive their nurturance, the details of their customary laws, from the past anthropological records. And, the anthropologist never imagined that the natives would one day rectify the errors that he had committed in his ethnography.

Now the context is different. The subjects of anthropology are now like 'middle class anthropologists'. The distinction between the 'self' and the 'other', or 'us' and 'them', is now no more than of sheer heuristic value. The cultural gap between the observer and the observed has broken down. The people now read what anthropologists write on them, including the field notes. In some cases, they demand that the first draft of the work should be shown to them so that any likely errors, or prejudiced statements, are removed. Besides this, they wish to ensure that the work includes what they want it to have, especially the 'good stories of their valour, character and life'. In addition, they also study and write about their own culture. They also engage field workers to write guidebooks on them for trekkers and visitors, as is happening in Nepal. In other words, the tradition of 'native anthropology' and 'autoethnography' is steadily rising.

The processes of globalization have brought about certain fundamental changes in people's technology, material culture, and in their ideas and rights. However, cultures are resilient objects. They have withstood the torrents of global change. There has been an increasing interpenetration between the individual life and global futures, but the people's lifestyle, their kinship and marriage, their beliefs, values and cultural models, persist almost relatively unchanged. Now people have sophisticated technological apparatuses to build and stress their identity, which implies that ethnocentrism is further reinforced. Local political bodies become powerful. People impose strict rules regarding their cultural practices and make conscious efforts to highlight their differences from others. Barriers and boundaries are emphasized far more and stringently. The contemporary world is full of contradictions: people know the world leaders but not their immediate neighbours; they know of the global happenings but not local events. They vouch for the ideology of equality in public but practice all sorts of inequality at home. Globalization does not homogenize the world.

Today's anthropology deals with this reality. It tells us that the small worlds of people are no more insulated. Modernity is happening to tribal and peasant societies all over; thus, tribal and rural poverty cannot be understood in isolation from the inequalities prevailing at the national and international levels. Today's anthropology conceptualizes the world as a conglomeration of communities which are global as well as local. Cultures are porous, but also have impregnable boundaries. Anthropological holism is an interpretive strategy of the bygone era. We today need imaginative approaches that can help us in analyzing the linkages between the local communities and other higher entities, of national and global importance.

Let me pursue an analogy. If anthropological work is some kind of a 'building', then its brick is the fieldwork. It, however, does not reduce the importance of imagination in analysis. And, there is nothing in fieldwork that requires the anthropologist to write about 'his people' abstracted from the history of modern civilizations. Fieldwork certainly does not stop us from initiating a theoretical or documentary study of a social phenomenon. However, undoubtedly, it is still celebrated, as we saw earlier, as an icon by most professionals.

Over time, in India, this commitment to go out and live with people for a lengthy period of time, around one year or so, has rather slimmed. A survey of students in anthropology departments in India will show that they go back to their communities or regions for study, where they take many cultural aspects for granted. In their fieldwork, they do not experience the stage of cultural shock, and the arduous process of rapport establishment, which is crucial for generating several insights. As they return to their own people, they are free from learning a new language of communication. Even if they venture to go to a different community, their field studies are abysmally short, sometimes not more than a fortnight, and while writing up, they heavily lean on secondary sources for a bulk of information. Although the funding agencies or universities accept these works (or theses), as the case may be, they do not see the light of publication. If the writer of these works is constrained to publish them, he has no option but to approach a lesser-known press which prints the stuff without getting it properly refereed and examined. Sometimes the writer has to bear the cost of publication.

Because our fieldwork is of inferior quality, we have not been able to produce good monographs, and have to depend upon the anthropological writings of the colonial era. Moreover, not many anthropologists in India have many fieldwork experiences to their credit. Although a fieldwork generates data for several years of writing, it does not imply that the anthropologist should not return to the community he chose initially for his doctoral study. It is noted with dismay that many anthropologists refrain from carrying out independent fieldwork or conducting a restudy of the people whom they visited decades ago. All this has implications for a sound anthropology. Ideally, one should have to one's credit a couple of field studies and good monographs emerging from them.

VI

Besides the declining standards of fieldwork, our theoretical understanding and a commitment to it has gone down the hill. The contribution of our anthropologists to pure theory was never applauding, but now many of us pursue researches for which we think that theory or theoretical insights are perfunctory. In the name of research, simple descriptive accounts are generated which are neither analytical nor comparative. There has been a rise of what are called the 'soft areas' of research (such as tribals, health, old age, population, development, ecology) where anyone from any breed of anthropology, with highly varying theoretical inputs, can find an entry. The primary job of anthropologists is to understand a phenomenon, a piece of social behaviour, as fully as possible, because of the conviction that the outline of practice, putting anthropology to use, will follow logically from a solid study. Development ethnography and the tool-kit of 'participatory rural appraisal' are not hostile to the classic ethnographic tradition. The anthropologist may become a spokesperson of a community, advocate the people's interests and participate actively for their fulfillment, formulate policies or take to task the existing prescriptions. But, these involvements of anthropologists should not be at the expense of the fundamental goal which is to understand human populations and behaviours comparatively. To reiterate, anthropology is read by representatives from other disciplines because of its explanations and a thorough understanding of human life and affairs. On the basis of this understanding what anthropologists can do is to warn the public, the planners, and the government of the consequences of changes occurring in a society. The point is that applied issues should not take precedence over their theoretical counterparts.

It is noted with concern that anthropologists are not represented in government bodies that deal with the practical issues of developing and safeguarding the interests of communities. Many decision-making bodies rarely approach anthropologists for advice. The role which Verrier Elwin and M.N. Srinivas, and some others, played in the past in these bodies was exemplary and is still remembered. The difference between these anthropologists and their present day counterparts is that the latter are 'aloof scholars'. They want to remain detached from the societies in which they live and work. They intentionally avoid making serious moral or political commitments. They hide behind their narrow interests and expertise. In the names of scientific objectivity, ethical neutrality and value freedom, which are believed to grace a scientific status to the subject, they refrain from taking sides or commenting intellectually upon the state of human suffering. Elwin and Srinivas were heard because they addressed big issues—Elwin on tribal policy and Srinivas on national integration. The anthropologist is expected to address the big issues in an integrated way, bringing out the fundamental relations between humankind, nature and society.

Anthropology is immensely useful to the understanding of the problems of the modern world provided we plan systematic studies in urban and industrial milieus, on elite societies, the rich people, and the corporate world, the areas which traditionally have not been studied by anthropologists. What inspires us tremendously is that when anthropology was singularly concerned with small and isolated societies, and was criticized for a 'tunnel vision', its moral commitments and engagements caused enough ripples in the intellectual world, with the result that it did not go unnoticed. Its paradigm might have remained in the closed cells of anthropology but not its cultural relativism, anti-ethnocentrism, and the universal respect for the so-called 'primitive people'. Now, when anthropology is dealing with human world as a whole, it has enough scope to be heard loudly, but it is incumbent upon the meaningful insights, findings of greater relevance and theoretical approaches.

Finally, let me return to the issue of specialization in anthropology with which I began. The process of differentiation cannot be stopped in any discipline or its branch. Today, we cannot take shelter under the idea of an integrated anthropology; its branches have become highly specialized and for attaining the necessary skill in any one of them, one shall have to perhaps forego those courses that really are not needed. Keeping this in mind, I think that the beginning of a specialized training in either of the main branches of anthropology (physical, social, linguistic, and archaeology) should be at the university level. However, it will depend upon the resources and specializations available in a department. Right at the entry point to the post-graduate course (i.e., what in Indian universities is known as M.A./M.Sc. previous), the student should be advised to opt for one of the specializations in which training is available in that department. However, the B.A./ B.Sc. course may have a fair distribution of courses from different specializations of anthropology. Then, we should also give a serious thought to our 'practicals' which may not only be outmoded but time consuming and a strain on one's talent and intellect.

Besides the highly specialized research in either branch (or sub-branch) of anthropology, the anthropology departments provide the unique (and ideal) place to work on culture-biology interface. Whether they are the studies of primates and their conservation, or of medical paleoanthropology, the insights can be drawn from both physical and socio-cultural anthropology, and be fruitfully combined. But the theme of 'holistic' and 'integrated' anthropology, which often becomes an emotional issue, should not pose an obstacle to the pursuance of specialized research. We should subscribe to the idea of the relative independence of our branches, which may come together for a particular research, rather than starting the 'science wars' in our departments – arguing about 'which branch is more scientific'.

An issue confronting anthropology is its subject-status, whether it is a science, to be placed in the faculty of sciences, or a subject of social study, or arts or humanities. Some anthropologists have found similarity between anthropology and literary activity, because for them the ethnographic work is like fiction writing. In India, anthropology has been classed with a variety of other disciplines, from physics and geology, to history and economics, from biological sciences to gender study and psychology. The state of anthropology is comparable to mathematics, which is neither an empirical science nor arts; it is equally logic and philosophy. In other words, mathematics can only be classified as 'mathematics', and can be read along with physics and chemistry, and also with history and sociology. In a similar vein, anthropology transcends the narrow distinctions of natural and biological sciences, social sciences, arts and humanities, or literary enterprises, and can only be properly conceptualized in the idiom of anthropology as 'anthropology'. As mathematical specialization can be best organized under the concept of faculty with many specialized departments under it, similarly the best way to organize the different specializations within anthropology, which are different subjects, is to have a faculty of anthropology comprising the departments, where each one takes care of the highly sophisticated and differentiated research and training. Specialized research is not antithetical to collaborative works on culture-biology interface.

ACKNOWLEDGEMENTS

This is the text of the Dr. K.S. Mathur Memorial Lecture delivered at the meeting of the Ethnographic and Folk Culture Society, Lucknow, on 3 March 2003. The Lecture was presided over by Dr. H.S. Saksena. I am thankful to Dr. R.P. Mitra for his comments on this paper.

REFERENCES

Béteille, André

1996 'Epilogue: Village studies in retrospect'. In André Béteille, *Caste, Class and Power, Changing Patterns of Stratification in a Tanjore Village*. Delhi: Oxford University Press (pp. 231-51).

Geertz, Clifford

1973 *The Interpretation of Cultures*. New York: Basic Books.

Larsen, Clark Spencer

2000 'A view on the science: Physical anthropology at the millennium', *American Journal of Physical Anthropology* 111 (1): 1-4.

Lévi-Strauss, Claude

1976 (1955) *Tristes Tropiques*. Translated by John and Doreen Weightman. Penguin Books.

Madan, T.N. (ed.)

1992 *Religion in India*. Delhi: Oxford University Press.

Malinowski, Bronislaw

1967 *A Diary in the Strict Sense of the Term*. London: Routledge & Kegan Paul.

Mathur, K. S.

1964 *Caste and Ritual in a Malwa Village*. Bombay: Asia Publishing House.

Morgan, Lewis Henry

1877 *Ancient Society*. New York: World Publishing.

Said, Edward W.

1999 *Out of Place, A Memoir*. Viking Books.

Srivastava, Vinay Kumar and Anil Mahajan

1978 'Towards a paradigm of integrated anthropology'. *Proceedings of the Tenth International Congress of the Anthropological and Ethnological Sciences* (Abstract: 1515).

4

The Status of Anthropology in Modern India

MATTHEW STIEF

The state of anthropology in India is worrying. Recently, in an article in *The Eastern Anthropologist*, Srivastava (2004) has examined the various areas where anthropology in India is being marginalized and "pushed to the back" of national concern and eminence. To reverse this trend and restore anthropology to its place at the forefront of Indian science it is necessary to define a progressive, unified, directed, and uniquely Indian anthropology.

To this end anthropology in India, and to a lesser extent anthropology in general, has been engaged in an extended struggle to define what in fact it is. This process of definition and estimation has been taking place externally as well as internally. The internal process of definition and direction must be intensified if it is to have a greater voice in the external process of evaluation and relegation to the backwaters of Indian science.

In this article, Srivastava (2004) examines this external process of definition and evaluation in the context of the Indian Science Congress Association as well as other indicators of the declining status of anthropology in India. Specifically, Srivastava takes issues with the regrouping, and thus external redefinition, of anthropology, along with a general redefinition and regrouping of the sciences in general, during the eighty-seventh session of the Indian Science Congress Association.

In this regrouping all the attending disciplines were administratively grouped into new and in the case of anthropology larger and more general categories. Botany was to be renamed "plant science," zoology "animal science", and physics "physical science" (Srivastava 2004:129). Anthropology, including archaeology, was to be grouped under the vague and inaccurate title of "behavioral science", along with disciplines such as psychology, education, and human biology.

The obvious reason for such a regrouping is the simple administrative convenience of having a fewer number of sections. Srivastava (2004: 130) also recalls another possible administrative concern that might have motivated such a regrouping, specifically in the case of anthropology, suggested to him by another colleague, namely that the previously independent anthropological section of the Congress was poorly attended. The colleague suggested that the poor attendance of the anthropological section was viewed as not being "respectable" and thus it was grouped with other disciplines to ensure a proper number of attendees.

In any event the motivation was clearly an external administrative one dealing with concerns far removed from the advancement of knowledge in India. It was certainly not an internally directed attempt at self-evaluation and re-direction on the part of Indian anthropologists. Nor was it an intelligent attempt to foster productive inter-disciplinary relations between related social sciences. It ignored both socio-cultural anthropology's relationship with other social sciences and humanities like sociology, political science, economies, or history as well as anthropology's internal diversity and inclusion of both biological and "behavioral" aspects.

Srivastava (2004: 130) also details several other indicators of the declining state of anthropology in India. One such indicator is found regarding the Common Admissions Test required for entrance into any programme that is a part of the Indian Institutes of Management as well as several other institutions. Srivastava notes that on the application form that needs to be submitted to take this examination the subject of graduate study needs to be selected from a large list. This list is not exhaustive however as it contains no mention of anthropology anywhere. This does seem to be an indication of the lack of emphasis by the Indian authorities on subjects like anthropology.

Srivastava (2004: 131) also points out that anthropology is not one of the subjects considered for the Commonwealth Scholarships. This is a somewhat surprising fact as most students selected for this scholarship in India find placement in universities in Great Britain and Canada where anthropology is a well-established discipline. Srivastava (2004: 132) also notes that anthropology is not one of the subjects students are required to have knowledge of for taking the Indian Forest Service Examination. The examination is focused on knowledge of physical aspects of forestry (such as biology and geology) and completely ignores the social dimensions of forests. This is despite the fact that forests in India are decidedly populated and that those people must be engaged with for any forest work to take place. This is clearly a devaluation of anthropological perspectives and contributions. What does seem to be emphasized in this case is a materialist and economically oriented model of development as modernization.

These external factors only exacerbate and make more urgent the pre-existing identity crisis of anthropology in India. This identity crisis is taking place on several fronts. Several dimensions of thought and practice in anthropology are undergoing a state of change in the present context.

Some of these dimensions are the relationship between anthropology's various sub-disciplines, and in particular between physical anthropology and socio-cultural anthropology. Also the relationship between anthropology and related disciplines such as physical anthropology and biology, chemistry, and the other physical sciences on one hand and socio-cultural anthropology and sociology, economics, history and the other social sciences on the other. In addition, there is the relationship between anthropology's colonial past and its present multinational identity.

One such dimension is the internal dynamics of anthropology. The various sub-disciplines that have historically been termed "anthropology" are changing with modern technologies and modern problems. This has created a need for internal re-evaluation of what the various sub-disciplines' relationships to one another are. More than that it creates the need to re-formulate what those relationships should be in the future, if any relationship is indeed necessary.

Historically, anthropology has been viewed as a "holistic" or "integrated" study of humanity in general. This means that anthropology has been viewed as the study of human beings in all of their aspects—biological, cultural, material, etc. While the practical necessity of specialization was present from the very beginning this generalism was strong enough to keep the various specializations categorized under a single identity.

That identity was, and in some cases still is, personified in the person of the "general anthropologist." This person is supposed to extend his area of expertise to all areas of anthropology, physical, socio-cultural, and material, so that when he studied a people he could study them in all of their aspects. This concept has in most cases, even from the very beginning of the discipline, been an abstract ideal rather than a concrete research strategy. It is generally acknowledged that the first, and one of the few, genuine practitioners of this "general" anthropology was Franz Boas (Srivastava 2004:132).

It can be seen clearly that this ideal will lead an anthropologist to limit his research on a people to a more shallow "general" level of analysis that would be possible with a more specialized approach. Nor did the combination of expertise in both physical and socio-cultural anthropology in a single person imply that the two modes were integrated into a combined approach. Rather the general anthropologist would do a little of this and a little of that to try to paint a "general" portrait of a community.

This limitation has meant that greater and greater levels of specialization have characterized the evolution of anthropology. This process has reached its climax in the ever more numerous sub-disciplines such as medical anthropology, forensic anthropology, linguistic anthropology, etc., that characterize American anthropology in particular. The "general" anthropologists is thus dead in most parts of the world.

However, he lives on in India and the reasons for his perseverance in the Indian academic climate add to the list of challenges anthropology in India faces today. Many anthropologists in India still cling to this notion of holism and "integration" in the form of general anthropology. It is significant that most Indian anthropologists who subscribe to this view are by training physical anthropologists (Srivastava 2004: 134). This exodus of physical anthropologists to the realm of general anthropology suggests that something might be lacking in the academic environment that physical anthropologists are forced to endure in India. The most obvious reason for this dissatisfaction is the laboratory conditions that physical anthropologists have available in India. Setting up a laboratory is a very expensive process and most departments in India are able to do it only in a very limited way, if at all. Beyond this, maintaining a laboratory with the most modern devices and setting up new laboratories to accommodate new techniques and areas of interests is extremely expensive.

Unfortunately in India these funds are simply not available to most anthropology departments. Funds to set up cutting edge laboratories inevitably go to medical research centres and other types of biological scientists. The result of this is that many departments with physical anthropology programmes are relegated to studying such topics as anthropometry and dermatoglyphics. Such departments can only teach students about other dimensions of human biology in the abstract without providing them with any concrete laboratory training. Thus, physical anthropologists in India tend to turn to areas of interest that do not require intensive laboratory work such as "surveys of health and illness, demographic variables, old age, ecological adaptation, adoption of family planning measures" (Srivastava 2004:134). Such areas are of course valid fields of study and highly relevant to Indian society. They are however highly complex issues that involve both physical and socio-cultural elements interacting in a dynamic way. The problem lies in that by approaching them as a general anthropologist the proper training is not there in either physical or socio-cultural anthropology. The result is an inadequate *imitation* of socio-cultural anthropology by physical anthropology without effectively drawing on the strengths of each.

The only way to approach such problems effectively is with a team of well-trained physical and socio-cultural anthropologists working together in an integrated manner. That integration can only come through a conscientious look at the *boundaries* that distinguish the two sub-disciplines. Only by trying to understand, and thus acknowledge, what separates the two sub-disciplines can one hope to forge a plan whereby specialists trained in their own discipline can work together effectively. That understanding and working together is the only effective way of creating a true integration of the study of the various aspects of humanity into a single powerful analysis. By actively attacking the very concept of anthropological specialization general anthropologists cripple this effort.

The lack of resources available to physical anthropologists is not the only reason for the continued existence of the general anthropologist in India however. The insistence on an unthinking conglomeration of the various sub-disciplines is encoded in the very structure of many departments and the Civil Service Examination on anthropology.

In anthropology programmes in India that have both socio-cultural and physical anthropology programmes represented in their departments students are required to study both physical and socio-cultural anthropology simultaneously. The only opportunity for specialization occurs in the second year of post-graduate education. For the entire period of B.A./B.Sc. education there is no opportunity for a student to specialize in one aspect or the other. This trend continues throughout the entire first year of M.A./M.Sc education as well. This is in contrast to anthropology programs in America, for instance, where students are required to take only one introductory course in each of the main sub-disciplines of physical anthropology, cultural anthropology, and archaeology before concentrating on the specialization of their choice.

In addition, the Civil Services Examination for anthropology now requires a detailed knowledge of all branches of anthropology (Srivastava 2004:137). Rather than being able to opt to take an examination designed for physical anthropologists or socio-cultural anthropologists respectively all students are required to cover both topics and more besides. The examination demands expertise in topics as diverse as human evolution, socio-cultural anthropology, medical anthropology, and the anthropology of international relations. The general anthropologist framers of such an examination are waging war on the very concept of specialization within anthropology.

This identity crisis, the struggle between general and specialized anthropology, within the discipline is mirrored in the identity crisis of anthropology's relationship to other disciplines in the social sciences like sociology, economics, political science, and history. The same issue of boundaries emerges in this context—how boundaries are to be drawn, whether they are to be a help or an impediment, what their uses might be, what their dangers might be.

Specifically, in the Indian context, anthropology's relationship with sociology becomes ambiguous and in need of clarification. Historically anthropology and sociology have been distinguished in terms of subject matter. While on one level it seems obvious that their subject of study, humanity, is in fact identical, it must be remembered that both anthropology and sociology emerged in the context of colonialism. In that context the world was divided in two, and remains divided if somewhat more subtly, between the modern "self" and the primitive "other." Anthropology and sociology evolved somewhat separately from one another as the study of the "other" and the "self" respectively. Initially all academics interested in the topic of studying humanity hailed from the modern, and western, "self" category. While this remained the case, the distinction between the study of the "self" and the "other" remained relatively unproblematic from their point of view. However, as time progressed and academic ideas, and even whole institutions, were imported into the newly colonized "other", the "other" inevitably was drawn into the debate. With the entrance of this no longer entirely "other" into the discourse, on a somewhat more level played field, the previously unproblematic distinctions between "us" and "them" were seriously undermined.

Unfortunately, social science in the west has been somewhat insulated from this profound change in the nature of the relationship between the social scientist and the subject of study. Anthropology responded by scouring the world for ever more primitive, ever more "other", peoples untainted by colonialism. Sociology simply continued to focus inward on the societies in which it was born.

Social scientists in India could not afford to ignore it however. The realization of a shift in the relationship between subject and scientist was integral to their identity as social scientists. For them that new relationship was complex and highly problematic. Initially, Indian anthropologists attempted to deal with this ambiguity by continuing in the tradition of foreign anthropologists and studying the most remote parts of India possible. Thus they were able to set up a distinction between their urban "self" and the rural "other". There is some tension with this approach and the mutual identity as Indian between the Indian anthropologist and his rural subject; both would have fallen under the category of "other" to the western anthropologist.

The Indian sociologist maintained his identity as a sociologist by focusing his attention on the study of the urban in India. The western sociologist, in studying his own society, traditionally also studied the urban within his society. There is thus an identity imposed between the exotic, the "other", and the rural; all subjects thought to be within the realm of anthropology rather than sociology. As the disciplines progressed however, both anthropologists and sociologists began to look outside of their traditional fields of study. This process was taking place both inside and outside of India. Sociologists and anthropologists began to study both the urban and the rural. Accompanying this shift was a new interest in research topics that are associated with the urban and the rural. Sociologists, while studying the rural began to turn their attention to traditionally anthropological subjects such as kinship and ritual. Anthropologists began to turn their attention from isolated tribal communities to the more integrated communities being analyzed in terms of caste. While this shift initially was limited to village studies in an attempt to preserve some semblance of the "other", it quickly and rationally progressed to studies of caste in urban areas and of inequality and power in general, subjects traditionally limited to sociology.

On the level of the greater community of social scientists the position of Indian sociologists in particular was seen as being vague and ambiguous. To the sociologists working in the western world sociology was not simply the study of urban communities but the study of modern, industrial, and above all *western* communities, both urban, and increasingly, rural. According to this line of thinking, any study of Asian or African societies is inherently anthropological in nature. Béteille (1993:301) reports that, particularly in American universities, sociologists trained in India and studying Indian society are invariably presented as anthropologists in the west regardless of their long and rigorous academic training.

One conclusion that could be drawn from all of this ambiguity is that there is no fundamental distinction between subjects like sociology and anthropology. Or rather that such distinctions are historical constructions based on the legacy of colonialism and thus represent a hindrance to a powerful analysis of human society rather than a valid distribution of labor.

A practical result of such a conclusion would be to combine anthropology and sociology departments into a single unit, and this has in fact been done on several occasions both in India and in England. Béteille (1993: 293) recalls the course of one such department in England at Manchester in his personal experience. He notes that a joint department of anthropology and sociology was set up in 1949 by Max Gluckman. By the time of Béteille's second visit in 1965 a second chair of the department had been set up for sociology, though nominally the department still remained a unit. Only a few years later the department split apart completely. On subsequent visits, Béteille was told that it was a rare instance that the sociologists and anthropologists that had previously been a part of a single administrative unit would interact at all.

Forcing anthropology and sociology departments, or other academic bodies, together can be thought of as a kind of mutual attempt at imitation. Identifying the two disciplines with one another to the extent that a single administrative system is adequate, or even necessary, is to necessitate an internal, and mutual, re-evaluation of the two historically distinct disciplines. But, to force the issue by placing the two disciplines within a single department limits that evaluation to a relatively shallow level by assuming and enforcing through practical reality that the two are in fact identical. Thus the analysis will necessarily result in the conclusion that anthropology and sociology are fundamentally the same and need to be placed together; the result of the analysis will in fact be predetermined. This will have the effect of the two disciplines trying to reform themselves in the image of the other without having a clear idea of what they, or the other, really are. The result of this lack of clarity is a chaotic and ultimately incoherent process. Because of this chaos and lack of clarity whatever insights might have been gained through cross-disciplinary approaches are also suppressed.

Thus, the analytical benefits that might balance the chaos and difficulty of such a premature merger and provide a motivation for the continuation of the project are nullified. The result of this is that such attempted mergers have tended to fall apart quickly into distinct administratively and geographically separated entities.

In order for true integration to be possible there must be clear analytical benefits that outweigh the practical difficulties and the academic politics of blind mergers such as the ones discussed above. This applies equally to attempted mergers between socio-cultural anthropology and other social sciences like sociology into joint departments and the long standing historical union between socio-cultural and physical anthropology. In the former case, it is totally without benefit to simply and blindly force the two disciplines into proximity with one another based on nothing other than the ideological notion of their ultimate unity. In the latter case, the pre-existing union will remain little more than a myth created for the sake of academic identity rather than a truly integrated, functioning, and holistic analysis of human beings in all their aspects.

The only way to create true integration is to identify and analyze the precise boundary areas that distinguish these disciplines from one another, only by having knowledge of these frontiers can it become possible to navigate them intelligently and effectively. To do this it is necessary to identify issues that require more than one discipline to understand them effectively. Some examples of these kinds of issues in the case of the junction between anthropology and sociology would be inequality, poverty, class, caste, and power. An example of an issue needing an intelligent cooperation between socio-cultural anthropology and physical anthropology would be the study of endemic and ethnically specific diseases.

It is a profound mistake to attempt to create such integration by trying to destroy such boundaries rather than attempting to understand them. To really understand what unites disciplines like anthropology and sociology and socio-cultural anthropology and physical anthropology one must first direct one's attention to what these disciplines actually are. One must examine the history of the disciplines, assess the present state of the disciplines, and establish a direction for the future, mutual and integrated, growth of the disciplines.

It is essential for that growth that boundary areas between anthropology and other disciplines and within anthropology be developed and concentrated on. It is through such boundaries, one could call them frontiers, that new seminal work is created. Though these areas have been relegated to the margins in the past it is their very marginality that makes them important and deserving of time, attention, and resources. The problems that anthropology faces in India at the margins of the western dominated anthropological institution may thus ultimately be a source of great strength. For by virtue of their position being so inherently problematic and ambiguous they are uniquely placed to push the boundaries of modern anthropology and create truly new and exciting work.

REFERENCES

Béteille, André

1993 'Sociology and anthropology, their relationship in one person's career', *Contributions to Indian Sociology* 27 (2): 291-304.

Srivastava, V.K.

2004 'Anthropology in India: A comment', *The Eastern Anthropologist* 57 (2): 127-152.

Part II

Part II

5

Has Anthropology Moved out of The 'Colonial' Woods?

H. S. Saksena

The colonial roots of anthropology, as an emergent social science in the nineteenth/twentieth century, has been a matter of extensive comments and debate whenever the present status and state of the subject comes up. In this context the discussants have been raising the ethical/value angle as well as the methodological issues of scientific objectivity and neutrality in anthropological researches, and also the perils involved in doing/practicing applied anthropology and furthering tasks set about by developmental anthropology, and on to the direction that 'social engineering' can take.

Salmone (2006) makes an excellent review of the role of some prominent American foundations/funds in financing research by both the British and American anthropologists in Africa and Asia during the pre and post World War II period which significantly helped the colonial rule and later the Cold War, as well as the Vietnam agenda of the U.S.A. He, *inter alia*, discusses the role of stalwarts like Malinowski, Fortes and others, and how Malinowski's applied anthropology was criticized by Herskovits. Salmone (2006:290) concludes that:

> But the effort to reconstitute the discipline using this 'common denominator', experience as a ritual image for the profession's straits was unsuccessful. There has been a steady retreat from the tougher

> ethical standards that emerged from the bloody battles at AAA (American Anthropological Association) meetings in the sixties and early seventies. The stronger ethical codes have been watered down and ignored as the recent scandal over Chagnon's research (Napoleon Chagnon was supposed to have meddled into Yanomani—an Amazon tribe—affairs) has demonstrated.
>
> It is time now for the AAA to find the courage to make this fact, once again, clear. It is important to state, once again, that secret research under the guise of fieldwork is just wrong. It is not those who seek to bring the truth into clear and sharp focus who are wrong. It is not those who hate the darkness who endanger anthropologists. Rather it is those who seek to excuse those who have violated the code of a self correcting science and the dictum that no harm shall come to those we study because of our work who are wrong and endanger anthropologists and the humanistic goals of the profession.

But, it is becoming apparent that the commitments of a section of American anthropologists to a 'committed anthropology' are far deeper. The annexed 'The Big Story, Armed to Help' from the *New York Times* (*Indian Express*, 8 October 2007) throws ample light on an experimental Pentagon programme called the 'Human Terrain Project'.

A debate in *Anthropology Today* carries this particular story still further back in time. David H. Price who has written extensively on the 'tortured past' of anthropology (2007a and b: 17-22) reveals *in extenso*, how anthropology and anthropologists have been featuring in the agenda of the CIA, US Army and the US government. He mentions *Kubark*, a 1963 instruction manual of the U.S. Army to guide the interrogations and torture procedures that emerged in the 1960s and continue in the present era in the infamous Abu Ghraib and other such detention camps established by it for persons who have been detained for years together from Afghanistan and Iraq. It is well known that these camps have been declared as zones where the Human Rights protocol or other legal remedies to help the detainees were inoperative as per a Presidential fiat.

The interrogations also spanned the use of some drugs and various kinds of torture (or coercive interrogation) where an earlier sponsored research by two anthropologists–Alan Howard of California and Robert Scott of Cornell–relating to 'the analysis of stress in the human organization' had been used, and many other such sponsored covert researches. But this research was aimed at understanding the role of stress in disease. Price remarks that even though covert funding programmes by CIA (research on stress for example through Human Ecology Fund) had widely influenced American researches in anthropology, psychology and behavioural sciences during 1950s to 1970s, the American anthropologists have been surprisingly reluctant to learn any lesson and prevent its repetition. He has called it a system that 'in effect buys a part of the specialist in order to enlist his aid in pursuing the intelligence implications of his research'. He also mentions Margaret Mead's association with the agenda. On the whole, however, Price concludes that most of this kind of work was done unwittingly by the scientists. Connecting this 'past' (Cold War years) to the present, Price is apprehensive that 'given the present day War on terror' the intelligence agencies are once again seeking help from the academics. Hence there is some urgency to critically examine the past interactions so as to be mindful of the outcome. He finds that more anthropologists are working today openly for military and intelligence agencies than in the past. Moreover, some scholars programmes are now advertising and funding students covertly placed in the universities in pursuance of this agenda. Gonzalez of the San Jose State University, U.S.A., through his 'comment' (2007b: 23) discusses how exactly Raphael Patai's 'outdated ethnography', *The Arab Mind*(1973), has featured as an 'essential reading' for the U.S. Army's Special Warfare School and beyond that provided basics regarding the 'other's' (Iraqi) mind for the manual (*Kubark*).

Earlier Gonzalez (2007a: 14-19) had critically examined the different aspects of use of social sciences in the situations of counterinsurgency–as situations in Iraq and Afghanistan and earlier in Vietnam are called. He examines the contents of an insurgency manual released by the US Army in Dec. 2006 (*Counterinsurgency*–FM 3-24).

> It is the first US Army manual dedicated exclusively to counterinsurgency in more than 20 years. At least one anthropologist played a role in preparing the 282 page document: Montgomery McFate, a cultural anthropologist from the US co-authored a chapter entitled 'Intelligence in counterinsurgency' with a military intelligence specialist. In addition, the Pentagon adapted the work of Australian infantry officer David Kilcullen for an appendix entitled 'A guide for action'. Though the media has reported that Kilcullen is

> an anthropologist, he in fact holds a Ph.D. from the School of Politics of the University of New South Wales..... (Gonzalez 2007a: 14).

Gonzalez notes that Kilcullen had conducted stretches of fieldwork in West Java and East Tumor during 1994-2000 and used multi-disciplinary fieldwork techniques including anthropological techniques and analysis.

Gonzalez remarks that the involvement of anthropologists in such tasks —the use of 'cultural knowledge' to wage a war on terror—has become increasingly evident since 2001 and comments:

> The 2006 American Anthropological Association (AAA) meetings included a special panel featuring four anthropologists working with military and intelligence agencies—an event which in someways heralded the revival of militarized anthropology.

The contents of Chapter 3 are the manual–essentially a primer on cultural relativism and social structure—and the appendix which is a collection of counterinsurgency guidelines for manipulating local social relationships in order to pry insurgents away from bases of support. Gonzalez finds that the manual 'generally reads like a manual for *indirect colonial rule*', without using the 'taboo words' like empire and imperial but at the same time using historical examples from British, French and Japanese colonial counterinsurgency campaigns in Malaya, Vietnam, China and Algeria. The manual charters a path to 'a culturally informed occupation with native power-brokers co-opted by coalition forces'. The result will be a lighter colonial touch with less 'collateral damage' and a lower price tag.

Here, we may raise the question: Is not this what neo-colonialism is all about? To quote Gonzalez again:

> Is it anthropology at all? That McFate, Kilcullen and others have committed social science to goals established by the Pentagon–goals that under the Bush administration include missions resembling colonial style police operations in the Middle East and Central Asia–is indicative of a rapidly evolving approach to counterinsurgency".

To top this there is a reported broad shift within the Pentagon with 'warrior-intellectuals' having social science Ph.Ds and headed by General David Petraeus, a Ph.D. from Princeton in international relations The Human Terain System has been set up by Pentagon in the last seven years with pilot teams in Iraq and Afghanistan as an organizational response to the situations there. Thus counterinsurgency operations are clearly the latest phase in the 'weaponisation of anthropology'.

Summing up the arguments for oppositional forces to such an use of anthropology, Gonzalez (2007a: 19) tersely says:

> The crass use of 'anthropology' and 'cultural knowledge' in the military deserves fuller and deeper analysis. A preliminary approach might include exploration of the degree to which anthropologists who write military field manuals (as opposed to academic texts) have adhered to the contemporary professional standards. Should not anthropologists be responsible for conducting work that reflects current anthropological theoretical and ethical concerns? Answering this question affirmatively would surely preclude consulting work for counterinsurgency projects.
>
> The potential consequences of anthropologists engaging in counterinsurgency work would be wide-ranging with multiple impact on military personnel as well as those living under occupation. But when such work is performed clandestinely this undermines and endangers the work of anthropologists more generally, not to mention their families and informants, potentially putting them at risk. It is plausible that "once Thai peasants or Somali clansmen learn that some anthropologists are secretly working for the US government, they begin to suspect all other anthropologists. Anthropologists have a professional obligation to one another not to conduct slash and burn field work" (Gusterson 2003: 25). Those serving the short term interest of military and intelligence agencies and contractors end up harming the entire discipline in the long run, particularly in an era of rapid global communication...... If the discipline moves towards open cooperation with counterinsurgency efforts today, what is to keep it from moving towards more covert cooperation tomorrow–or eventually, towards a mercenary anthropology in which cultural knowledge itself is used as a weapon.

And interestingly, a footnote in Gonzalez's 'comment' brings forth the changing perspective to a 'participant' (anthropologist presumably):

> For example, one has only to follow Marcus Griffin's blog to see where things are heading: 'there probably is no Other anymore. The Other is Us.... This is the underlying reason why I am trying so hard to immerse myself in Army culture.....' and 'I am about a month away from deploying to Baghdad as part of the US Army's new Human Terrain System and have almost gone completely native..... I cut my hair in a high and tight style and look like a drill sergeant... I shot very well with the M9 and M4 last week at the range.... Shooting well is important if you are a soldier regardless of whether or not your job requires you to carry a weapon' (2007b: 23).

How the community of anthropologists in America is by and large reacting to this situation has also to be discussed here. The annual meeting of the AAA in November 2006 adopted two resolutions: one condemning torture and the use of anthropological knowledge as the element of torture and the other condemning US occupation of Iraq. The resolutions thus articulate a set of values and ethical concerns shared by many anthropologists (2007a: 19). The AAA had in its meeting of 2005 set up an Ad-Hoc Commission on the Engagement of Anthropology with the US Security and Intelligent Committee precisely to address the ethical challenges for anthropological work. The Commission was expected to deliver its report in the 2007 meeting (Butler and Flores 2007: 27).

Anthropology Today, June 2007, also carries a response from Montgomery McFate of the US Institute of Peace and the anthropologist whose contribution to the manual has been so forcefully criticized by Gonzalez. McFate argues that if Gonzalez was so concerned with 'building bridges between peoples' as he had written elsewhere then why he was taking a position of intellectual isolationism towards the military. McFate regards this moment as a real opportunity for positive influence of anthropology which should not be lost as 'nobody owns anthropology'. He further argues that:

(i) Anthropology has many intellectual trajectories which by no means form a unified theoretical or ethical whole;

(ii) The plea that knowledge (anthropological in this case) has been 'misappropriated suggests epistemological censorship'–the very nature of knowledge is to escape its bonds; and

(iii) Gonzalez's assertions mean that the national security community should not use anthropology for any purpose that Gonzalez personally deems unethical.

McFate, an the contrary, believes and finds from his experience that anthropological knowledge applied to military problems has the power to save lives, socio-cultural knowledge reduces violence, creates stability, promotes better governance and improves military decision making. He defends his role pointing out that after a long divorce the discipline (anthropology) has a chance to become directly relevant to national security and urges other anthropologists to enter the national security arena.

Kilcullen, the other 'co-accused' in this case, has also presented his views (2007: 20) under the title 'ethics, politics and non-state warfare'. He points out that field evidence suggests that the more anthropological knowledge is available to counterinsurgents the more human are their operations. According to him:

> the evidence suggests that anthropological knowledge (properly applied by people who understand both the discipline and the security environment) does contribute to the greatest good of the greatest number, and its use in counterinsurgency is therefore ethical, in my view (*ibid*).

And this exactly portrays the new strategy called 'armed social work' (*Indian Express*, 8 October 2007). How effective is this 'armed social work' is certified by Colonel Woods as 'Call it what you want, it works'. And a senior officer of the US Army argued before the U.S. House Armed Services Committee that:

> during the present 'cultural phase' of the war intimate knowledge of the enemy's motivation, intent, will.... cultural environment has proven to be far more important for success than.... smart bombs, unmanned aircraft.... (Gonzalez 2007a: 17).

This leads to the imperative questions: works for whom? Or in whose interest? As well as the structural functional consequences of this military anthropology or armed social work which can easily be designated as counterinsurgency or occupationary anthropology? The likely consequences, if long-drawn epistemologically, interestingly remind me of the end-results of a long field stay of a team of anthropologists in *The Three Sirens*, an isolated small islandic society projected in a very readable work of fiction by Irving Wallace (1964). The protagonist professor of anthropology and the team-leader here is said to be modeled on Margaret Mead. The face-off portrayed through anthropological field techniques leaves both the field workers and the social field devastated and changed irretrievably.

In our country also there have been accusations of CIA funding institutions and of American anthropologists covertly trying to hone means to subvert or manipulate our nascent democratic processes. My guru, Professor D.N. Majumdar, can be credited with being instrumental in getting the largest Ford Foundation grant of its times for social research. It was a collaborative research project between Cornell and Lucknow universities based in the Department of Anthropology, Lucknow University, for three years beginning in 1953-54. However, Majumdar was probably acutely aware of its implications and tried to closely monitor the kind of work the American team members were doing in the rural areas of western and eastern U.P. I remember his visit to Rankhandi village in Saharanpur district, the field centre for a large inter-disciplinary research team in western U.P. of which I was also a member in 1954-55. While discussing the research foci of the senior most American researcher, he became suspicious of the intent of certain questions in a questionnaire used by him for exploring the factors influencing rural communication and decision making processes. Subsequently, this and other issues led to his withdrawing from the project, which was wound up. Majumdar's own studies which were a part of it were taken over for financing by the Research Programmes Committee of the Planning Commission. N. Subba Reddy had in 1955 written a series of articles in a Lucknow daily about the case. I am also reminded of an interesting description of an Indian anthropologist Professor M. E. Opler (Cornell University's Co-Director of the Project) had engaged for the Rankhandi team. In the course of our conversation at Dehradun in mid-1954 he described the anthropologist as an 'excellent technician', and that made me think, whether anthropology when it was applied, facilitated manipulations of human behaviour in some particular ways.

It seems that anthropology is once again in a phase where the inter-play of world powers aided by the forces of globalization would keep it linked to a variety of emerging situations which have been labelled as neo-colonization, state-clientele, war on terror, counterinsurgency and so on. In many of these conflicts the issues that arise move around ethnic claims, cultural and/or political autonomy, recognized human rights, moral boundaries of a nation- state, with of course a spectrum of political and international relations underpinnings. George M. Foster, while receiving the Thomas Jefferson Award for International Anthropology had in his inspiring speech identified four primary conditions (among others) essential to peace and international understanding. He went on to discuss how anthropologists had continued to contribute in each of these areas. The identified primary conditions were: (i) meeting the basic needs of individuals; (ii) respect for human rights; (iii) enjoyment of national security by citizens of all countries; and (iv) promoting confidence in the good intentions and goodwill of the citizens in other countries. And then he elaborated how IUAES was planning to enrich the role of anthropologists in this endeavour (Foster 1986: 139-145). The dawn of the twenty-first century, however, seems to have initiated a different kind of anthropological approach for conflictual situations. Therefore, this appears to be the time when anthropologists from different countries—and India has a large community of them—react to such situations and formulate their approach on the bases of what anthropology's basic tenents and strength are. Needless to add that in India also some low-intensity conflicts have been going on, often with international shades.

REFERENCES

Butler, Udi Mandel and Carlos Y. Flores

2007 'Conference–Critical intersections/dangerous issues', *Anthropology Today*, 23 (3): 26-27.

Foster, George M.

1986 'The role of anthropology in the enhancement of peace and international understanding', *The Eastern Anthropologist*, 39 (2): 139-45.

Gonzales, Roberto J.

2007a 'Towards mercenary anthroplogy? The new US army counterinsurgency manual FM-24 and the military-anthropology complex', *Anthropology Today* 23 (3): 14-19

2007b 'Comment–Patai and Abu Ghraib', *Anthropology Today* 23 (5): 23.

Kilcullen, David

2007 'Comment: Ethics, politics and non-state warfare', *Anthropology Today* 23 (3): 20

McFate, Montgomery

2007 'Comment: Building bridges or burning heretics', *Anthropology Today*, 23 (5): 21.

Patai, R.

1973 *The Arab Mind*. New York: Scribner

Price, David H

2007a 'Buying a piece of anthropology-Part 1: Human ecology and unwitting anthropological research for the CIA', *Anthropology Today* 23(3): 8-13.

2007b 'Buying a piece of anthropology–Part Two: The CIA and our tortured past', *Anthropology Today* 23 (5): 17-22.

Salmone, Frank A

2007 In the name of science: The Cold War and the direction of scientific pursuits, *The Eastern Anthropologist* 59 (3-4): 275-294.

The New York Times

2007 'The Big Story: Armed to help', Lucknow: *Indian Express*, October 8.

Wallace, Irving

1964 *The Three Sirens*. London: Cassell and Co. Ltd.

Annexure

LUCKNOW | MONDAY | OCTOBER 8 | 2007

ARMED TO HELP

US commanders say their combat operations have come down in parts of Afghanistan and Iraq after the induction of anthropologists. But critics say this is political misuse of the social sciences. DAVID ROHDE balances the debate

SHABAK VALLEY, AFGHANISTAN

IN this isolated Taliban stronghold in eastern Afghanistan, American paratroopers are fielding what they consider a crucial new weapon in counterinsurgency operations here: a soft-spoken anthropologist named Tracy.

Tracy, who asked that her surname not be used for security reasons, is a member of the first Human Terrain Team, an experimental Pentagon programme that assigns anthropologists and social scientists to American combat units in Afghanistan and Iraq. Her team's ability to understand subtle points of tribal relations has won the praise of officers who say they see concrete results.

Col Martin Schweitzer, commander of the 82nd Airborne Division unit working with anthropologists here, said that the unit's combat operations had been reduced by 60 per cent since the scientists arrived in February, and that the soldiers were now able to focus more on improving security and health care for the population.

In September, US Defence Secretary Robert M. Gates authorised a $40 million expansion of the programme, which will assign teams of anthropologists and social scientists to each of the 26 American combat brigades in Iraq and Afghanistan. Since early September, five new teams have been deployed in the Baghdad area, bringing the total to six.

Yet criticism is emerging in academia. Citing the past misuse of social sciences in counter-insurgency campaigns, including in Vietnam and Latin America, some denounce the programme as "mercenary anthropology" that exploits social science for political gain. Opponents fear that, whatever their intention, the scholars who work with the military could inadvertently cause all anthropologists to be viewed as intelligence gatherers for the American military.

Hugh Gusterson, an anthropology professor at George Mason University, and 10 other anthropologists are circulating an online pledge calling for anthropologists to boycott the teams. In Afghanistan, the anthropologists arrived along with 6,000 troops, which doubled the American military's strength in the area it patrols, the country's east.

A smaller version of the Bush administration's troop increase in Iraq, the buildup in Afghanistan has allowed American units to carry out the counter-insurgency strategy here, where American forces face less resistance and are better able to take risks.

Since Gen David H. Petraeus, now the overall American commander in Iraq, oversaw the drafting of the army's new counter-insurgency manual last year, the strategy has become the new mantra of the military.

In interviews, American officers lavishly praised the anthropology programme, saying that the scientists' advice has proved to be "brilliant," helping them see the situation from an Afghan perspective and allowing them to cut back on combat operations.

Afghans and Western civilian officials, too, praised the anthropologists and the new American military approach but were cautious about predicting long-term success.

Officers shrugged off questions about whether the military was comfortable with what David Kilcullen, an Australian anthropologist and an architect of the new strategy, calls "armed social work." "Who else is going to do it?" asked Lt Col David Woods, commander of the Fourth Squadron, 73rd Cavalry. "You have to evolve. Otherwise you're useless."

The anthropology team here also played a major role in what the military called Operation Khyber. That was a 15-day drive late this summer in which 500 Afghan and 500 American soldiers tried to clear an estimated 200 to 250 Taliban insurgents out of much of Paktia Province, secure southeastern Afghanistan's most important road and halt a string of suicide attacks on American troops.

In one of the first districts the team entered, Tracy identified an unusually high concentration of widows in one village, Colonel Woods said. Their lack of income created financial pressure on their sons to provide for their families, she determined, a burden that could drive the young men to join well-paid insurgents. Citing Tracy's advice, American officers developed a job training programme for the widows.

In another district, the anthropologist interpreted the beheading of a local tribal elder as more than a random act of intimidation: the Taliban's goal, she said, was to divide and weaken the Zadran, one of southeastern Afghanistan's most powerful tribes. If Afghan and American officials could unite the Zadran, she said, the tribe could block the Taliban from operating in the area. "Call it what you want, it works," said Colonel Woods. "It works in helping you define the problems, not just the symptoms." The process that led to the creation of the teams began in late 2003, when American officers in Iraq complained that they had little to no information about the local population. Pentagon officials contacted Montgomery McFate, a Yale-educated cultural anthropologist working for the Navy who advocated using social science to improve military operations and strategy.

The New York Times

6

The We-They Distinction in Anthropology

JULIE DAVIS

In this paper, I shall examine the varying aspects of anthropology, mainly the history of anthropology, national anthropology, and Indian anthropology to illustrate the we-they distinction. The we-they distinction refers to the dynamics of 'us versus them' in anthropology. In the history of anthropology it was colonialism vs. the indigenous people, in national anthropologies it is Western countries vs. developing nations, and in Indian anthropology it is Western anthropology vs. native anthropology. The we-they distinction has reconstituted itself from colonialism into the international anthropological core in which it has manifested itself into the central and periphery debate between Western and developing nations.

History of anthropology

Anthropology emerged out of colonialism that forced the natives of many countries to succumb to imperialist governments. Some of the first anthropologists were government officials that implemented the colonial administration's 'tactics' to make the natives serve their imperial needs. Srivastava (1990) elaborates on the role of early anthropology and the intentions of the officials who later on became the first anthropologists. He writes:

> Administrators, political agents and military officers, who had qualified the civil service examination, were sent to the non-Western

> world the colonial rulers of Britain, France, Portugal, Spain and Holland wanted to bring under their hegemonistic control, with the explicit purpose to rule, siphon off the resources for building industrial empire at home, and to extend the control to interior, often inaccessible, areas (1990: 304).

This passage highlights the first purpose of anthropology as being aimed towards the needs of the foreign government. At that time, the task of the early anthropologist was to implement the control over resources, local polity, and to assert imperialist culture over the natives. It is in these tasks that anthropology emerged as the *'bastard child of colonialism'*. Anthropology studied humans in space, time, economically, religiously, socially, physically, etc., to pursue the ends of colonization by exploiting the natives.

The beginning of anthropology did not end here, though missionaries came to teach and religiously convert the natives. Adventure seekers arrived in search of 'exotic' lands and recorded their experiences in their travel accounts. Armchair anthropologists sprang up behind their desks publishing articles in secluded academic circles. At this time, anthropology began to take shape, but it was not yet institutionalized.

With the colonial start of anthropology, the discipline grew, but many biases remained. Westerners produced monographs about primitives, pre-literate, and non-western societies. Western anthropologists became the arbitrators of the we-they distinction and obsession with the exotic other increased. Srivastava (1999: 549) comments on the findings in social anthropological fieldwork in the early twentieth century:

> The we-they distinction, or the distinction of the self and the other, was the pith of the anthropological work... That the 'they' was qualitatively different from the 'we' constituted the discourses. Anthropologists wrote what they thought was right, proper, and just, on and about the primitives, who were mute, who did not answer back... the monographs thus produced were for the literate, white, western public.

This quotation explains how Western anthropologists sought to learn about non-Western cultures, but in doing so, the anthropologists interpreted their foreign surroundings through a hegemonic view. Anthropologists asserted their culture as being on top as the "we" in the we-they equation. Those who were not part of the "we" were known as "they", and "they" were to be viewed as primitive.

With the processes of colonialism and the we-they contrast, the formula for "modernizing" simple societies began. Srivastava (1990: 305) explains the hardships natives were forced to endure as a result of modernization, when he states:

> It involved uprooting of the communities from their cultural moorings and traditional habitats. People who squatted on the resources needed for bringing about industrial revolution at home, were ousted. It was in this phase that anthropology emerged.

In this quotation, anthropology emerges out of the colonial need for resources that resulted in the exploitation of natives. During the modernizing period, anthropologists wrote about exotic practices performed by the group under study. The Western curiosity of the exotic other filled monographs and the discipline became orientalist in nature.

After the modernizing period, anthropology grew and many Western anthropologists who conducted their fieldwork in Africa, India, and the Pacific Islands were able to publish their findings back home. Gradually, this process led to the canonization of Western anthropology that was conducted on non-Western or so-called "primitive" societies at the time. The anthropological literature that was being produced exacerbated the we-they distinction in which Western scholars took the central position in the discipline. In this next passage, Freedman (1978) explains some of the processes that not only aggravated the we-they distinction, but also gave rise to the canonization of Western anthropology:

> When anthropology was about primitive societies, the primitives were the subject matter and Western civilized men were the students. The fact that anthropologists and their 'objects' were mutually exotic and, in the normal course of events, often separated by great physical distances, was a strength to the discipline. It could promote one kind of objectivity: the observer was totally from outside and unencumbered by the presuppositions of those under study. (One might add that the ethnographer did not then have to face the possibility that the people he described would read what he wrote about them.)

The quotation analyzes the hierarchy in the anthropological discourse that emerged with foreign fieldworkers' fascination with the exotic. Western anthropologists explained the native's practices in their own terms with inferred ideology that did not represent the native's rationality or motives. The concern with exotic anomalies and primitiveness allowed the foreign anthropologists to romanticize the culture, exaggerate differences, and manipulate cultural contexts. The Western fieldworker's search for the causes of diversity ignored the group's affinity and unity, which could have been discovered through existing habitats and historical experiences (Srivastava 1990: 310). However not all Western anthropology of this time was ethnocentric, but Western dominance did emerge as a result of primitives being their "object" of study. Freedman (1978) also notes that the foreign anthropologist and the natives were mutually exotic to one another and this created objectivity in the field. The objectivity resulted from the foreign anthropologists not being part of the society or tribe under study, which in turn released the fieldworker from the norms and biases within that particular group.

After World War II, the fate of anthropology changed from the 'practice of' to the 'practice in' as a result of the liberation from colonial rule. The 'practice of' and the 'practice in' are two terms identified by Srivastava (1990) that refer to the types of anthropology conducted before and after the Second World War. The 'practice of' is identified as colonial anthropology that aimed to bring the colonies under Western imperialist control. The main feature of colonial anthropology was that the discipline did not work to protect the people, and sought to understand the natives for the purpose of exploiting them. In contrast to the 'practice of' anthropology, the 'practice in' anthropology is concerned for the welfare of the people. The idea of the 'practice in' anthropology is functional in which it combines the people's perspectives, integration between physical and social anthropology, and development programs (Srivastava 1990: 302) The 'practice in' anthropology has brought about a change in the we-they distinction in which anthropologists, from previously colonized countries, were rebuffing the ethnographies from the 'practice of' period. The shift in the discipline towards the 'pr^ctice in' anthropology gradually assimilated the natives as part of the 'we'. After the natives became educated in English, they started to re-examine the

Western anthropologists' writing on their culture (Srivastava 1999:549). It was in the reviewing of the anthropological writings of the colonial and modernizing period that the discipline came to take on a more humanistic viewpoint.

National anthropologies

The change in the discipline towards 'practice in' anthropology ushered in a new wave of anthropologists from developing nations, although Western anthropology has remained at the centre. Even though anthropology has taken on a humanistic role, few developing nations have been able to create a department to serve their own national needs. Perhaps many Third World countries have the biggest need for social, physical, developmental, archeological, and linguistic anthropology to emerge as their activists in the changing world. It comes as a sad fact that the countries that require the help and insights of the anthropologists the most do not even have their own institutions to support them. Sarana and Sinha (1976) comment on the lack of anthropological institutions in South Asia when they write:

> To the best of our knowledge, anthropology has not been accorded independent academic recognition in Afghanistan, Pakistan, Nepal and Bangladesh, although there are some anthropologists working in basically non-anthropological institutions.

This quotation sheds light on the fact that a discipline for the peoples' needs cannot gain enough clout in many developing countries to support itself nationally and internationally.

The inability of many developing countries to support a functioning anthropological institution has allowed western countries to occupy the centre of the discipline and push the work of scholars of developing nations to the periphery. The dynamics between the centre and the periphery of anthropology had reinvented the we-they distinction. The new form of the we-they distinction represents the inequality that still persists in the discipline. The struggles of developing nations make it difficult to advance the discipline at the same rate as Western countries, and as a result, the work of many Third World scholars is not being recognized. Gerholm and Hannerz (1982) reflect on the lost voices of academics in the developing world when they quote J.P.S. Uberoi. They write:

> There is no "world community of science" unless that phrase be another name for the national and international science of rich nations... It subordinates the national science of the poor to the national and international science of the rich. It confirms our dependence and helplessness and will not end them. The reasons for these effects are simple and fundamental: the national and international systems inherently are synonymous for the rich but opposite for the poor.

This statement highlights the frustrations that academics in developing nations confront in the international scholarly circles. There are many factors that anthropologists of the developing countries struggle against and the Western countries do not give a second thought. For example, it is almost a prerequisite that anthropologists write their ethnographies in English, which is usually their second language, to gain international recognition. And yet, the steps that lead up to the publication of their work is highly strenuous. Third World anthropologists have to fight for the funding of their fieldwork, tracking down research material in libraries with limited resources, and use out of date technology. For these reasons, it is not difficult to understand why the we-they distinction still remains with Western anthropology at the centre, and developing nations' anthropology at the periphery.

With Western anthropology at the centre and the anthropology of developing countries at the periphery, this has resulted in diverging practices in the two spheres. One of the core features contributing to the divide in the recognition of anthropological work is the sociology of knowledge. The sociology of knowledge refers not to one's own education and actual knowledge, but rather the methods one comes to learn about how to acquire knowledge, thinking habits, problem solving, and incorporating theories. The sociology of knowledge relates to how students of different peripheries and nations critically think and reason. It may be said that one's own process of analyzing is a cultural construct. It may also be a cultural construct as to which mental habits are understood more by the centre and the periphery. In addition, outside factors, and one's access to resource also contribute to the sociology of knowledge. In this next statement, Gerholm and Hannerz (1982: 15-6) discuss how a student's environment affects the topics he or she may choose to study. They write:

> Big-city universities, neighbors of slums as well as of public bureaucracies, may choose their anthropology differently from those which seem to be close to no social problem other than the conflict between town and gown.

This quotation highlights an inner truth that the type of interests students may pursue often depends upon the world around them. It should also be noted that certain subjects might be valued more by one sphere than the other. It is unfortunate that the prospect for a middle class student in a developing country to receive publication for their work is very slim. However, in many Western universities there are numerous student journals that give the opportunity of publishing to the average student. The sociology of knowledge and the availability of resources are contributing factors to central and periphery spheres, which reinforce the we-they distinction.

While the sociology of knowledge and environment are deciding factors between Western and developing nations' anthropology, on the other side, many nations' anthropologies have their own theoretical core. Some countries' core is shaped by the national situation. For example, South African anthropology adopted the politics of apartheid to their national core. In addition, many scholars claim that post-statehood Zionism has shaped Israeli anthropology. However, in contrast to South Africa's and Israel's national anthropologies, some states do not develop their own theoretical core despite their high levels of nationalism. Quebec is a Canadian state with extreme levels of nationalism, and yet there is not an established nationalist anthropology at its core. From these examples, one can see that South African and Israeli anthropology is at the periphery of the international academic sphere. It can be deduced that both South African and Israel have anthropological cores shaped from the collective experiences of their countries. The national factors that shaped South Africa's and Israel's core anthropologies do not permeate far into the international centre though. Perhaps, Quebec has not created a national core because the state has not faced the violent conflict and turmoil that South Africa and Israel have experienced.

Indian anthropology

Indian anthropology also has its own national discipline, but Indian scholars still rely on the international cannon and colonial monographs to aid their research. In this next quote, Sundar *et al.* (2000) describe the merging of Western and Indian anthropology when they write:

> While it is true that sociology and anthropology in India have been significantly shaped by theories and scholars of the West, local influences—theoretical, institutional, and national—have also played a major role in shaping the disciplines.

This quotation renders thought to the process of how Indian scholars relate Western theories (especially in social anthropology) to India. With the combination of Western theories and the cultural-social composition on the Indian sub-continent, the problem arises in the relationship between what Indian students study in American textbooks, and what they experience when they step outside the classroom (Béteille, n.d.). Thus, there is a need for Indian scholars to get away from Western theories, but that does not go to say that Western models cannot be applicable or valuable.

Many fundamental topics that are covered in Indian anthropology, such as caste, kinship, religion, panchayati raj system, and tribal development, are Indian specific and relate to India's vast social matrix. While it can frequently be difficult to relate Western theorists to India, Béteille (1971) demonstrates how Weber's definition of class is different from caste. The distinction between the social functions of two terms is derived from a comparison in the marketplace where one's class can determine the changes in the distribution of property. Béteille (1971:7) explains:

> While market forces seem to have played a relatively unimportant part in the traditional system of Sripuram, they cannot by any means be ignored today. The existence of such forces, which bring about changes in the distribution of property, makes it necessary to study the class system as a thing in itself, governed by properties which are in part independent of caste.

The passage is an example of an Indian scholar relating Western theories to Indian society. In this passage, one can determine that an anthropologist or sociologist conducting fieldwork should not consider caste to mean one and the same as class.

Class in India has separate functioning properties that are independent from caste. One striking feature between the two is that class can be moveable, while one is born into one's caste. Indian social anthropology reflects both spheres of influence while maintaining the Indian scholar's perspective as to what extent Western theories pertain to India.

In moving away from the discussion of Western theories combined with Indian anthropology to some of the central problems in Indian physical and social anthropology, one is reminded of overspecialization and the lack of Indian anthropologists conducting fieldwork abroad. The overspecialization in physical anthropology has resulted from researchers joining forces with biomedical institutions. The factors that have attracted physical anthropologists to other disciplines are lack of up-to-date technology which has made the physical anthropology less laboratory oriented. In addition to physical anthropologists being drawn to other hard sciences, in striking contrast the unavailability of up to date technology has also led physical anthropologists in the opposite direction and closer to social anthropology. The movement of physical anthropology back towards social anthropology is demonstrated in bio-behavioural sector in which emphasis has been relegated to anthropological demography, medical anthropology and ecological anthropology. Social anthropologists originally developed all of the named bio-behavioral sectors (Srivastava 2000:37). Thus, it can be said that physical anthropology is splitting in two directions: one side is straying away towards harder sciences, while the other end is becoming more integrated with social anthropology. Most Indian anthropologists prefer the incorporation of both physical and social branches.

The second commonly cited issue in Indian anthropology is that most Indian anthropologists only conduct fieldwork within India, which usually centers on the town or state they grew up in. The positives and negatives of native anthropologists doing fieldwork in their home are debatable. Native anthropology tries to properly represent their own culture through an internal understanding of their society and cultural framework. Sarana and Sinha (1976: 209) examine the positive contributions of native anthropologists when they explain:

> ... [Indian anthropologists] should throw light on those aspects of Indian culture that we are more competent to deal with than any foreigner because we have learned the goals, values, and ideals of our culture through enculturation. This means that we have to undertake the study of those aspects of our culture that are of vital importance.

This quotation reflects the advantages of the native anthropologist in which the fieldworker does not have to learn a new language, culture, and gain acceptance in the group under study. Native anthropology is also attractive by which it enables an indigenous scholar to rebuke previous writings that might have been conducted on their culture during colonization. Furthermore, a native anthropologist can work on the development of their home in local, district and national policy making processes.

However, in contrast to the internal advantages of native anthropologists, many of these scholars come from privileged backgrounds that can become detracting factors in their work. In many developing nations, the class or caste origin is equivalent with their academic background (Gerholm and Hannerz 1982: 25). While a Brahmin fieldworker may find him or herself an insider in their native home, however, they are a person holding a hierarchical status and might, knowingly or unknowingly, conduct their analysis from a top-down perspective. Also, the Brahmin anthropologist may find his interactions with people during his or her fieldwork to be governed by certain social institutions. For example, in his book, *The Remembered Village,* Srinivas (1976) at times cited his interaction with the Mysore villagers as being constructed by purity and impurity social actions that were appropriate to his caste. The position of a Brahmin fieldworker can be both beneficial and a variant in one's study. The Brahmin fieldworker can participate and interact easier with the group under study because the people understand his position in society. Although, while the Brahmin's interaction with the group under study may come naturally, the fieldworker could take the structure of social institutions for granted and overlook relevant characteristics of the study. On the other hand, a foreign anthropologists will be an obvious outsider to the group under study, and people will find it difficult to interact with the fieldworker in the beginning. However, the role of the foreign anthropologists can also be beneficial as a result of the fieldworker concentrating on subtleties in the relations between people, or major cultural characteristics that might be considered as "given" to the native anthropologist.

I attempted in this paper to examine the history of anthropology, national anthropologies, and Indian anthropology. The colonial beginnings of anthropology engendered the we-they distinction and reinforced a hegemonic view that was later on exacerbated in the international discipline. The international discipline has further institutionalized the we-they distinction in which Western anthropology is at the centre while in previously colonized and developing nations anthropologies are at the periphery of the discipline. The Westernization of anthropological core is difficult for developing nations to permeate as a result of differences between Western and developing nations' sociology of knowledge. Finally, Indian anthropology is a strong example of a national anthropology with its own theoretical core that does, however, use Western theories to aid their research, although, Indian anthropology is yet another instance of the we-they distinction that emerges in the field with regards to relating Western theories to India, and native anthropologists vs. foreign anthropologists.

REFERENCES

Béteille, André

1971 *Caste, Class and Power: Changing Patterns of Stratification in a Tanjore Village.* Berkeley, Los Angeles: University of California Press.

Béteille, André

n.d. The teaching of sociology in India. Manuscript.

Freedman, M.

1978 'Social and cultural anthropology', *Main Trends of Research in the Social and Human Science* 1(II), 3-176.

Gerholm, Tomas and Ulf Hannerz

1982 'Introduction: The shaping of national anthropologies', *Ethnos* 47(1): 5-35.

Sarana, Gopala and Dharni P. Sinha

1976 'Status of social-cultural anthropology in India', *Annual Review of Anthropology* 5: 209-25.

Srinivas, M.N.

1976 *The Remembered Village*. Delhi: Oxford University Press.

Srivastava, V.K.

1990 "'Practice of' and 'practice in' anthropology", *The Eastern Anthropologist* 43 (4): 301-23.

1999 'The future of anthropology', *Economic and Political Weekly* XXXIV (9): 545-52.

2000 'Teaching anthropology', *Seminar* 405: 33-40.

Sundar, Nandini, Satish Deshpande and Patricia Uberoi

2000 'Indian anthropology and sociology', *Economic and Political Weekly* XXXV (24): 1998-2002.

7

Sociology and the Limits of Loyalty

ANANTA KUMAR GIRI

> Intellectual life is first of all conflict and disagreement, teaching may give the opposite impression when initiates relate to novices what we claim to know; but the forefront where ideas are created has always been a discussion among oppositions. This heartland of disagreement is difficult to avoid; to deny it is to exemplify it. This is not say that no agreement ever happens.
>
> Randall Collins (1998:1)

> Sociology confers on you an autonomy, especially when you don't use it as a weapon against others, or as an instrument of defence, but rather as a weapon against yourself, an instrument of vigilance.
>
> Bourdieu (1990:27)

> To follow in the most demanding and authentic way, it implies 'anacol,' the not following [..] in order to follow in a consistent way, to be true to what you follow, you have to interrupt the following.
>
> Jacques Derrida (2003:7)

Debates and discussions in an intellectual field help us to come to terms with our existing condition and work towards its needed transformation. Debates and discussions have been very much part of traditions of sociological reflections in India. In the 1950s there was a debate about the "book view" and "field view" of studying Indian society in which the works of M.N. Srinivas and Louis Dumont were discussed (cf. Das 1995). A recent debate has arisen on the need for Indian social sciences to overcome their entrenched parochial fixations and be simultaneously interested in fieldwork at home and the world. The present writer had initiated such a dialogue as a response to an earlier essay on the subject by Ramachandra Guha (Giri 2003; Guha 2003). On the issue of our parochial fixation I had written:

> Many of us from India now go to all parts of the world as students and teachers but how many of us are interested in carrying out study of other cultures and societies? [..] In India we accuse other scholars, especially from the west of ethnocentrism but what needs critical self-reflection here is an entrenched parochial fixation in Indian scholarship (Giri 2003: 3605).

I had also written:

> The same problem of parochial fixation which is camouflaged as loyalty to roots is compounded when we come to social science research in rest of India. [..] How many people from universities in Orissa work on Bengal what to speak of working in far off areas such as Kashmir and Meghalaya? Is it that difficult to send our students to do fieldwork in other parts of the country far from the place where our home is? The problem here is not at all one of resource but a lack of vision and total insensitivity to our responsibility of understanding the other and the world. We have an indispensable responsibility to understand our self and therefore all of us have a responsibility to work on local issues and problems but does not this also call for an integrally linked engagement with the other and the world both empirically and theoretically? (*ibid*).

A. M. Shah (2003) and Yasmeen Arif (2004) had made valuable rejoinders to this argument. On the issue of parochial fixation of Indian sociologists not doing enough fieldwork outside India, Shah argues that this has not been the case, i.e. sociologists from India, particularly the Delhi School of Economics, have always been engaged with societies and cultures other than one's own.[2] In this context what Arif writes in her article, "Passages out of India," deserves our careful consideration:

> Notwithstanding A.M. Shah's statements on this, particularly in the way they interlocute M.N. Srinivas' thematic concern with the study of 'other' societies, I will still have to say that out of the 97 PhDs awarded by the Department since its inception in 1959, not more than a couple are based on direct field work in locations outside India. A very few others, in ratio, would have been on and about locations within India which are removed from the students' personal universe (Arif 2004: 301).

What André Béteille, himself a student of Srinivas and presently a doyen of world sociology, writes also helps us to put in perspective our parochial fixations and predicament:

> Sociologists in India have been much more confined in their interests, and in the early decades of independence their work ran the risk of being absorbed into Indian studies. *It is true that India offers enormous scope for comparative studies within its own boundaries but the development of the subject has undoubtedly suffered from the absence of sound empirical work by Indian sociologists on societies other than their own.* New entrants into the profession feel discouraged when they find that western sociologists write freely about all societies whereas the leaders of the profession in their own country have very little to say about societies outside India (Béteille 2002: 4; emphases added).

Béteille also tells us how very few Indian scholars work on societies and cultures other than their own:

> [..] Indian research scholars [..] rarely choose to do fieldwork in a region other than the one to which they belong; this enables them to dispense with the trouble of learning a new language, and it allows them to take other shortcuts that in the end detract from the quality of their fieldwork (Béteille 1996: 234).

On this issue of parochial fixation of Indian scholars, Shah writes:

> Giri makes a grand statement, 'The problem here is not at all one of resources but a lack of vision and total insensitivity to our responsibility of understanding the other and the world' (Shah 2003: 4491).

Shah considers this statement grand but by characterizing this adjectivally does it help us to address the issues and challenges at hand? The key question here is what is our approach to criticism, self as well as social? Such an adjectival mode of quick judgment and apriori fixation is akin to what Bourdieu talks about the violence of classification:

> The logic of the classificatory label [in this context labels such as "grand" and "careless"] is very exactly that of racism, which stigmatizes its victims by imprisoning them in a negative essence (Bourdieu 1990: 28).

The key question once again is: can we and should we be critical of ourselves and the traditions with which we work?

Shah concludes his article with a suggestion that one's own backyard is as good as "Trobriand Islands." Shah quotes Srinivas:

> As an overprotected Brahmin..boy growing up on college road, I experienced my first culture shocks not more than fifty yards from the back wall of our house... The entire culture of Bhandikeri (the area behind our house where lived a colony of shepherds, immigrants from their village, located a few miles from Mysore) was visibly and olfactorily different from that of college road. Bhandikeri was my Trobriand Islands, my Nuerland, my Navaho country and what have you (Shah 2003: 4492).

But in the very next pages Srinivas also writes:

> There are also important differences among 'the others.' A Sholiga tribesman in the elephant-infested jungles of the Biligiri mountains, about 60 miles from my house, would be very different from my neighbor while a Naga or a Mizo in the North-Eastern Hill areas would be even further removed. There are then varying degrees of the 'other,' and in the extreme case 'the other' can be totally different culturally from the self (Srinivas 1992: 142).

Therefore how to read Srinivas's statement—"Bhandikeri was my Trobriand Islands, my Nuerland, my Navaho country and what have you"? Should we read it literally? As Shah himself acknowledges, despite Srinivas himself having done fieldwork only in his native Karnataka, Srinivas's commitment was to a broad-based comparative sociology and anthropology. As Srinivas urges us to realize in his co-authored article with M.N. Panini, 'The Development of Sociology and Social Anthropology in India':

> Paradoxical as it may seem the very need to understand Indian society requires from Indian sociologists a commitment to a comparative approach in which the problems, processes and institutions of their society are systematically compared with those of neighboring countries in the first instance, and later with other developing countries [..] There are also areas and problems which should be studied on a global basis, for instance, backwardness and poverty, ethnicity, urbanization, generation gap and student unrest (Srinivas and Panini 1992: 181-182).

But in what way did Srinivas realize this project of a global comparative sociology and anthropology from India? In this regard, Shah writes:

> Aware of the constraints of circumstances in India, Srinivas followed two main strategies to put his vision into practice. First, he devised for BA and MA students of sociology syllabi that were comparative. He introduced a number of books on Africa, America, Australia, Europe and parts of Asia other than India along with India in the

> syllabi both at Baroda and Delhi. [..] If such student went on to do research in his own society, his knowledge and understanding of other societies would help him to understand his own society better (Shah 2003: 4491).

But the whole question is whether the project of a global comparative sociology and anthropology be realized only by having courses on other cultures or does it also call for fieldwork in other cultures and societies?[3] Is there any contradiction between an aspiration for a global comparative sociology and anthropology and the literal belief, not necessarily of Srinivas himself as Srinivas had a much more subtler sense of self and other, that one's backyard is one's Trobriand Islands? It is Srinivas himself who also tells us:

> The phrase 'studying one's own society' needs some clarification: very few are ill-advised enough to take up their natal village or town or quarter for study (Srinivas 1989b: 177-178).

A great contribution of Srinivas to post-independent Indian intellectual landscape is his emphasis on fieldwork (Béteille 1996). Srinivas, Béteille and many of the founders of the Department of Sociology of University of Delhi plead for fieldwork as an integral part of sociological and anthropological engagement. In the words of Béteille:

> Sociology and social anthropology are empirical disciplines which will languish in the absence of a deep respect for facts and close attention to their observation and description; in other words, a disciplined as against a self-indulgent attitude towards facts (Béteille 1996: 247).

But what is our preparation for nurturing respectful observation of and relationship with facts? In many of our centers of sociological learning, there is not much training worth the name either in statistical method or fieldwork?[4] In Department of Sociology at Delhi School of Economics and at the Center for the Study of Social Systems, Jawaharlal Nehru University— two of our premier centers of sociological teaching and research— now students begin their empirical research and ethnographic fieldwork only when they reach the doctoral level. Students here even in their post-MA M. Phil. research do not do fieldwork. With such a "solid preparation in and for fieldwork" then it should not be a surprise that tradition of empirical research is weak in India (Béteille 1996). But the reason for this weakness is not the invasion of the barbarians or the proponents of cultural studies and deconstruction as some scholars (Guha 2003) might suggest but our own lack of training in and commitment to fieldwork and nurturance of habits of empirical research.

For Béteille, sociology and anthropology are empirical disciplines but this begs the question of the meaning of the empirical? Is empirical reality only what we observe and is it so unproblematically amenable to observation in the way we know it in traditions of empiricism and anthropological traditions of participant observation? Does not the domain of the empirical consist of multiple layers of reality, as Roy Bhaskar (2002), the philosopher of critical realism, would challenge us, and in understanding this stratified reality in which the empirical and supra-empirical interpenetrate to what extent empiricism is adequate? In putting forward the view of sociology and anthropology as empirical disciplines are we uncritically following empiricism as an epistemology as well as ontology? Moreover for being empirical does a person or a discipline have to be empiricist? A collapse of the empirical and empiricist epistemology and ontology impoverishes the nature of sociological engagement as sociologists proceed with a naïve sense of reality without letting themselves being challenged by both the empirical and supra-empirical dimensions of reality. This self-confident sociological empiricism is also based upon little foundational reflections on the nature of our assumptions, assumptions of reality thus based upon a divorce between philosophy and sociology, rather than a mutually enriching and transforming dialogue between the two.

We are grateful to Srinivas and Béteille for emphasizing fieldwork in Indian intellectual engagement. But is it a question of either theoretical engagement or fieldwork? In case of Srinivas himself, as Srinivas writes in his autobiographical reflections, 'Itineraries of an Indian Social Anthropologist,' while proceeding to do fieldwork among the Coorgs in South India Srinivas himself wanted to write on theories of society taking some Indian traditions of thought as his point of departure. But he could not proceed on this because of threat of lack of fellowship for such a work from his mentor G.S. Ghurye:

> While the field study of Coorgs in their forested mountains had its appeal for me, I was troubled by the fact that I was becoming a chronicler of customs and not the theoretician of society which I wanted to be [..] I thought I should take up a 'theoretical subject' for my PhD. I went to the late Professor M. Hiriyana in Mysore whose understanding of Indian philosophy was profound and asked him whether a person who did not have a knowledge of Sanskrit could make a study of how the relation between individual and society was formulated in Indian thought. Hiriyana said I could undertake such a study. But the project was nipped in the bud by Ghurye who told me that no fellowship would be forthcoming if I chose a theme which did not involve fieldwork. Ghurye took a dim view of my hankering after 'theory.'
>
> I was bitter with Ghurye at that time but in retrospect I cannot help being thankful to him for being firm about fellowship being available for fieldwork only (Srinivas 1989a: 190-191).

But what happened to this desire for theory in Srinivas in his subsequent years? If there is a disdain for theoretical engagement in Indian sociology and anthropology could it be linked to such foundational experiences?[5] Indian sociology and anthropology began with a dualism between book-view and field-view but as Srinivas himself tells us there was a part in him which wanted to be a theoretician of society. And as Béteille writes nearly sixty years after this foundational experience of Srinivas in his own autobiographical epilogue:

> Perhaps it was a mistake to have presented the book-view and field-view as if they stood in complete mutual opposition. A comprehensive scheme for the understanding of Indian society and culture must find a place for the book-view as well as the field-view [..] (Béteille 1996: 247).

II

Arif (2004) raises a number of important questions on the issue of parochial fixation of Indian social scientists. For her, the issue here is not only one's desire to work on other cultures and the availability of mentors but also crucially of funding. Arif argues that the issue here is not only of desire to work in other cultures and societies and availability of interested mentors. The crucial issue lies in availability of funding for such work and also the issue of institutional insularity. From her own experience of carrying out fieldwork in Beirut, she shows us how in India there are virtually no institutions which support field work in other cultures and societies. Thus Arif quite rightly writes:

> Apart from combating possible intellectual insularity towards a research agenda that falls outside the 'local,' a sustainable interest in 'other cultures' in India has to be nurtured through various interconnected institutional and practical measures (Arif 2004: 302).

Thus for overcoming our parochial fixation we need transformation of our ethos, existing institutions such as universities, University Grants Commission and Indian Council of Social Science Research, as well as creation of new institutions.

Arif welcomes the plea for more nuanced theoretical engagement on the part of Indian social scientists but wonders whether in this context dialogue with Indian traditions is a must: "If my specific research agenda is best informed by theoretical reflections that have not emerged from the category of the indigenous, should that be a predicament about my 'responsibility' as a student of social science in India?" She suggests the difficulty of taking part in such a dialogue as we do not have adequate preparation in languages such as Sanskrit, Persian and Pali for this. But this itself calls for appropriate pedagogical transformations. Her question also raises important issues about the nature of theories that we deal within social sciences as well as to the nature of dialogue itself. The theoretical frames that we deal with reflect specific socio-cultural presuppositions, for example the social theory we deal with being primarily Euro-American reflects particular socio-cultural presuppositions. As India is not just an empty slate for application of sociological theory originating from elsewhere there is a need to engage ourselves with a dialogue on the presuppositions of theories that we are dealing with. The emergent theoretical reflection is not an extension of the indigenous but emerges from open-ended and mutually interrogating dialogue between reflections on self, culture and society in a specific locale such as India, Europe and Japan and more universalizing theoretical models. But this dialogue is a dialogue of exploration, not of apriori assertion about the timeless virtue of "Indic wisdom." For example, if one is engaged in a dialogue between contemporary critical theory and insights of texts such as *Bhagavad Gita* and *Upanishads* then one does not treat the latter as storehouses of wisdom. The objective is not to make a war between 'native view' and the established "metropolitan hegemony" but a "better understanding of human society," as Arif so inspiringly aspires for and through this to transform sociology into varieties of planetary conversations.

Arif also raises important questions about the nature of relationship between self and other in extending one's anthropological engagement to other societies. For Arif, an important question is whether in doing fieldwork in other countries as Indian anthropologists we are also constituting these 'places' as 'field sites for empirical research' within a "gaze." But doing fieldwork in other countries is not destined to be done in an "otherizing gaze" and despite our inherent finitude in any self-other relationship, an effort to understand other culture and society can be carried out in a spirit of mutual learning and transformation—transformation of our initial starting points. This calls for, as Arif herself writes, "new epistemologies of understanding":

> The impasse has to be dislodged, in terms of both empiricism and theory, preferably in the same breath, to create new epistemologies of understanding rather than create innumerable contrasts of interpretation (Arif 2004: 303).

Arif also challenges us:

> .. a critical reflection on some new modalities of interaction between parochial selves and hegemonic others, on the outside and inside must be worth the effort (*ibid*).

This indeed is a key challenge but addressing this is not only an epistemological task, it also calls for work on ontology, exploring what may be called an "ontological epistemology of participation" (Giri 2005b). In the spirit of the very important question that Arif has raised it may be helpful to explore this pathway further.

To begin with, the very categories of "parochial self" and "hegemonic self" can be further opened up both epistemologically and ontologically. Self is not only parochial, self has also a connected and relational dimension which is an aspect of its transcendental dimension. Similarly the other is not just hegemonic, the other also has a potential and desire to love and understand despite all problems of violence and history.[6] Therefore a new modality of interaction between self and other calls for multi-dimensional realizations in case of both self and other, i.e. there is a universal dimension in the so-called parochial self and a non-hegemonic dimension in the hegemonic other. But cultivation of this new modality of interaction is not possible only epistemologically or sociologically, it also involves work on self and ontology.

An important task here is to realize the foundational limitations of modernist social science in raising some of these issues. Modern social research is part of the epistemic privileging of modernity to the neglect of ontological nurturance and the new epistemology of understanding that we need has to transcend this modernistic primacy of epistemology (cf. Connolly 1995; Giri 2004). Such a foundational interrogation and seeking of transcendence helps us realize that social research is not just an epistemic activity; it also calls for cultivation of appropriate virtues transcending the conventional boundaries between epistemology and ontology. John Greco writes:

> Just as virtue theories in ethics try to understand the normative properties of actions in terms of the normative properties of moral agents, virtue theories in epistemology try to understand the normative properties of beliefs in terms of the normative properties of cognitive agents (Greco 2001: 136).

Virtue epistemology makes activities of research "person-based rather than belief-based" (*ibid*). While in epistemology there is a move towards "virtue epistemology" in ontology there are moves towards "weak ontology"[7] as pioneered by Vattimo (1999), "practical ontology" and "critical ontology" as striven by Dallmayr (1987, 1991), ontology of self-expansion as suggested by Roy Bhaskar (2002) and "ontological anthropology" as striven by Clammer *et al.* (2004), which interestingly embodies a "relational epistemology" (Clammer *et al.* 2004: 17). Vattimo's weak ontology embodies vulnerability, self-emptying (*kenosis*), love and non-violence; similar is also Dallmayr's strivings of a practical ontology which touches the height and depth of a practical spirituality. We can bring together "virtue epistemology," "weak ontology," "practical ontology," "ontological anthropology" and ontology of self-expansion and nurture the ground for an ontological epistemology of participation.

Ontological epistemology of participation as it embodies transformative border crossing between epistemology and ontology can build upon creative experiments in both philosophy and transformative practice, for example those of Gandhi and Heidegger. Taking inspiration from Heidegger the engagement of research here becomes a time and space of laying open oneself and realization of co-being (cf. Dallmayr 1993). The time of research becomes both a time of communication and silence[8]—a time of "lived time"— and the space of research becomes a space of dwelling, in fact a "poetics of dwelling" (cf. Ingold 2004), rather than building. But ontological epistemology of participation also goes beyond the notion of fixed ontology and preoccupation with mastery in early Heidegger; in fact it strives to supplement Heidegger with Gandhi and thus transforming any association of ontology with a Nazi politics of annihilation. While Gandhian experiments had an ontological dimension, Gandhi was also continuously interested in learning. A way out of the modernist privileging of epistemology and neglect of ontology is not to valorize ontology at the expense of the epistemic practices of learning and inquiry. Here we can supplement Heidegger with Gandhi, not only in politics but also in epistemology, thus rescuing us from complicity with any politics of mastery in the name of the resoluteness of *Dasein* and making *Dasein* and self an involved and emergent participant in learning (cf. Bourdieu 1991; Dallmayr 2001; Srinivasan 1998).[9] One arresting aspect of Gandhi's life and work is his insatiable passion for learning and experiments with truth. At the ripe age of eighty when he was traveling from village to village and trying to calm the fire of communal violence in riot-torn Noakhali, he was devoting an hour everyday to learning the alphabets of the language of the locality, Bengali. It is this passion for learning and self-cultivation which can make us humble and rescue us from the danger of using our knowledge, including the knowledge generated out of our research, as an aid to our will to power—an instrument of authority, including ethnographic authority; it can help us realize that what we need is not so much "self-mastery" as an "ethics of sevanthood," and a "pathos of shakenness" (cf. Giri 2002; Shanks 2001). Here ontology emerges as much from contestation, conversation and learning as it is an initial participant in self and science.

In ontological epistemology of participation, there is attentiveness to and interpenetration of both the subjective and the objective and the whole challenge is to arrive at an objective in spite of our irreducible subjectivity. This calls for a new conception of both the subjective and the objective. Subjective also refers to the dimension of transcendental or non-dual self in the actor / subject / scientist and this would be a companion of an aspired for objectivity. As Eric Fromm tells us:

> Objectivity does not mean detachment, *it means respect*; that is, the ability not to distort and to falsify things, persons and oneself (Fromm 1950: 105).

Furthermore,

> To be objective is possible only if we respect the things we observe; that is, if we are capable of seeing them in their uniqueness and interconnectedness (*ibid*: 104).[10]

Ontological epistemology of participation differs from participant observation as it is conventionally understood. Bourdieu (2003: 282) asks of participant observation: "How can one be both subject and object, the one who acts and the one who, as it were, watching himself acting? As an alternative Bourdieu proposes *participant objectivation*: "By participant objectivation I mean the objectivation of the subject of objectivation, of the analyzing subject—in short the researcher herself?" (*ibid*). But how can one watch oneself acting and be both subject and object? Does it not involve work on oneself or cultivation of some kind of witnessing self what is called *sakhi pursusha* in Indian spiritual traditions or impartial spectator by Adam Smith (cf. Sen 2002; Smith 1976)? Can this be only epistemic and doesn't it also involve some ontological work on oneself? Bourdieu speaks about "epistemic reflexivity" (cf. Bourdieu and Wacquant 1992: 38). His application of statistical analysis to self-understanding is helpful but does it also not involve ontological nurturance?

In this context, historian and philosopher F.R. Ankersmit's (2002) most recent discussion of the methodology of historical representation helps us understand the work of ontological epistemology of participation in a new way. Ankersmit tells us that historical representation of a period may present a "coherent whole of developments on domains that are incommensurable with each other" such as the "cognitive, ethical, aesthetic, religious or technical preoccupations of a period" (Ankersmit 2002: 234). For Ankersmit such a connected picture and free movement "from one domain to another" is possible because of historical representation. He goes on to write:

> If we ask ourselves how representation may enable us to do this, the answer is that *the unique contribution of representation [..] is that it involves the knowing subject [..] The self is activated by representation in a way that would mean the end of objective knowledge*. And from the point of view recommended by representation, suddenly a common ground can be discerned for domains that seemed hitherto completely unrelated and incommensurable (*ibid*; emphases added).

Here Ankersmit presents the example of epistemology and politics in seventeenth century France. For Ankersmit,

> at first sight seventeenth-century rationalist philosophy and absolutism will have nothing in common for us. But then the historian may suggest the point of view of the transcendental ego [or it may emerge from any self-initiated historical engagement, not just from historian as a professional expert], of a self that withdraws from the world but in order to get a firmer hold of it (*ibid*).
>
> And this point of view makes us aware of what the Cartesian self, doubting all knowledge in order to gain access to absolute certain knowledge, has in common with Louis XIV withdrawing from the bustle of Paris to Versailles in order to confirm his absolutist mastery of France (*ibid*).

Thus the perspective of transcendental ego born of historical inquiry and representation, an engagement in which all of us seeking souls can participate, not only professional historians, helps us understand the connection between epistemology and politics in seventeenth century France. For Ankersmit, one may not totally identify with such a perspective which emerges from our work of historical representation but nonetheless it shapes our personality and what we are. From the perspective of the calling of an ontological epistemology of participation, what Ankersmit writes deserves our careful considerations:

> *Nevertheless, becoming acquainted with the possibility of many such points of view will add each time, a new, though tiny stone, to the mosaic of our personality. And in the end this cannot fail to have its effect on the kind of person that we are* (*ibid*: 235; emphases added).

III

Ontological epistemology of participation as it crosses the boundaries of self-certain epistemology and fixed ontology seeks to bring both virtue epistemology and virtue ethics together (cf. MacIntyre 1999). What are some of the virtues in an ontological epistemology of participation? To begin with, it is gratitude. Life begins and is nourished further by gratitude, so does science and scholarship. Shah wonders whether I have forgotten my MA studies at the Delhi School of Economics. No. I am ever grateful to my teachers at the School as well as to our earlier pioneers such as Srinivas but this gratitude itself urges us to ask questions, explore further. This is different from loyalty. The calling of creative social research, for that matter science or philosophy, can not proceed by loyalty but by gratitude. However, sociological reasoning itself may have its limitation in understanding the limits of loyalty. Sociology not only in India but also in its Euro-American home suffers from an intractable problem of loyalty. The primary loyalty of sociology has been to modernity[11] but is it not committing both epistemic and ontological violence in its modernist epistemology of understanding where not only subjects of sociology but also sociologists themselves live a variety of forms of life simultaneously—traditional, non-modern, modern as well as postmodern? In this context sociology's loyalty to modernity needs to be transcended by a mode of gratitude which while making us grateful to modernity does not make us its prisoners. It is an important challenge of a sociology of Indian sociology to understand to what extent its practitioners suffer from an *apriori* post-traditional and modernistic telos or are they open simultaneously to tradition, modern and post-modern as co-constitutive dimensions of reality that we are seeking to understand.

Sociology also has been a loyal subject of nation-state but in this loyalty, it has forgotten its duty to both critical aspirations of people in such contested spaces as Kashmir as well as post-national and cosmopolitan formations which challenges the easy equations between society and nation-state (cf. Mathur 2005; Oommen 2004; Beck 2002). It is encouraging that there is some acknowledgment of the limits of nation-state in sociological engagement. Ulrich Beck (2002) in this context argues that understanding many of the sociological themes such as inequality challenge us to go beyond the nation-state but the present-day conventional sociology reflects the biases of a methodological nationalism. Beck challenges sociology to overcome its loyalty to methodological nationalism and embrace a new one of methodological cosmopolitanism. Even though Beck's cosmopolitan sociology is primarily Euro-American[12] and has very little planetary conversations as to the very conceptions of self, culture, society, sociology and social theory it is an important move in going beyond the complicity of sociology in the project of the nation-state. Similarly in Indian sociology there is a move now to go beyond the confinement of the Indian nation-state and to look at our engagement from a broader South Asian and comparative global vantage point.[13]

Sociology has also been loyal to varieties of ideologies. In each of these axes—modernity, nation-state justification, and ideology—our challenge is to understand the limits of loyalty and the significance of gratitude. Shah's rejoinder challenges us also to understand the problem of loyalty to our pioneers. Sociology like any tradition of learning is enriched by the ongoing creative work of pioneers who are alive even in their physical absence but this calls for a relationship of gratitude, which in turn is nurtured by systematic learning and training about their works and methods,[14] and continued critical and creative explorations rather than only ritual ancestor worship.

ACKNOWLEDGEMENTS

I am grateful to Abhijit Dasgupta of Department of Sociology, Delhi School of Economics, for his comments on the draft of this paper. This was then subsequently presented as part of my presentation, "Understanding South Asia and the World: Sociology and the Limits of Loyalty," at the national seminar on "Towards a Sociology of South Asia," Jan 26-27, 2006, Center for the Study of Social Systems, Jawaharlal Nehru University, New Delhi. I am grateful to M.N. Panini and Amit Kumar Sharma for their kind invitation and to the participants especially Dipankar Gupta, M.N. Panini, Nilika Mehrotra and V. Sujatha for critical posers. None of my interlocutors however are responsible for the views presented here.

NOTES

1. We are grateful to Shah (2003) for telling us that R. Jayaraman, one of the early students of Srinivas, had completed his doctoral work on Sri

Lanka, and Anand Chakravarty who had done fieldwork in another society other than the one in which he was born was not originally from Bengal but from Andhra Pradesh. Though it would have been helpful instead of advising us to look at the annual reports of the Department of Sociology, University of Delhi, Shah had helped us with some detailed facts and figures including the nature of the project about the Pakistan Area Study Program and the North Eastern Hill Areas Program in which the department took part.

2. Because of many constraints fifty years ago, Srinivas might have had to take recourse to course work on other cultures as an important companion to comparative orientation of Indian scholars but do we do justice to the outstanding legacy of Srinvas by repeating the same strategy now? Is there not an indispensable need to combine coursework on other cultures with fieldwork in some of these?

3. In this context, Sujata Patel tell us that "..to this day Delhi University's Department of Sociology does not teach quantitative methodologies" (Patel 2002: 277). Patel furthermore writes: "Unlike the sociologists from Lucknow, Srinivas did not place his sociology in context with a debate and discussion with Marx and Weber or other thinkers. He was also against the survey method being popularized by American sociology, and disapproved of its teaching in Indian universities because, in his opinion, it diluted the qualitative understanding of the structure..." (*ibid*).

4. Exploring this is not a matter of "Oedipal struggle" about which Patricia Uberoi (2000) writes in her reflections on sociologists reflecting on their own profession in India.

5. Here Said's (1978) reflections on the self-other relationship in *Orientalism* can be supplemented by a new hermeneutics and spirituality of this as suggested in pathways of *Beyond Orientalism* charted by Fred Dallmayr (1996).

6. In the words of Vattimo: "..We derive an ethics of non-violence from weak ontology, yet we are led to weak thought, from its origin in Heidegger's concern with the metaphysics of objectivity, by the Christian legacy of the rejection of violence at work within us" (Vattimo 1999 : 44).

7. Consider here what Niklas Luhman, the sociologist of communication, writes: " [We need] to make a digression at this point and consider whether the participation of consciousness is not perhaps best conceived as a silence" (Luhman 2001: 16).

8. It must be noted however that in his later seeking Heidegger himself made a shift from his earlier preoccupation with resoluteness. As Dallmayr helps us understand in an original reinterpretation of the Heideggerian pathway: "..Heidegger's middle and later writings came to see the pitfalls and streamlining effects of linear power- seeking and to adumbrate a realm beyond power and impotence, domination and submission under the rubric of a 'power-free' (*machtlos*) dispensation that allows being (s) 'to be' (Dallmayr 2001: 190).

9. This is similar to Bhaskar's (2002) perspective of dialectical universality and Hardt and Negri's (2004) perspective of multitude simultaneously paying attention to uniqueness and commonality.

10. For Anthony Giddens (1994), sociology is essentially characterized by "a post-traditional telos" and for Béteille (2002: 6)), "sociology is a modern and not a postmodern.. discipline."

11. Another limitation here is that Beck's methodological cosmopolitanism seems to be primarily epistemic and does not involve work on ontological nurturance and transformation as suggested in the pathway of ontological epistemology of participation (cf. Giri 2004; Giri 2005b).

12. In a seminar on this theme convened by M.N. Panini at Jawaharlal Nehru University recently (January 27-28, 2006) several participants challenged Indian sociology to go beyond the nation-state perspective and adopt a broader civilizational and regional perspective. In his concept note, Panini writes: "The need for such a seminar arises from the fact that social scientists working in the region tend to be confined to their own niches and do not look out across national boundaries to make comparisons and evolve perspectives that may generate new insights in the understanding of South Asian cultures and communities" (Panini 2006: 1). In this seminar J.P.S. Uberoi and T.K. Oommen, among others, led this move to go beyond the limitations of Indian and South Asian sociology by adopting a civilizational and frontier perspective. But in his keynote address André Béteille quite rightly challenged us to go beyond programmatic statements and be engaged in serious comparative studies across the borders. He also challenged us to acknowledge that just as there are limits in reifying the nation-state there are also limits in reifying the region. For example, for him, sociologists in Pakistan would find enriching not only sociological work from other South Asian countries but also from Iran.

13. Béteille (1997: 98) challenges us to understand the problem of amnesia in Indian sociology: "In India, each generation of sociologists seems eager to start its work on a clean slate with little or no attention to the work done before." Cultivating a relationship of gratitude to our pioneers' challenges to overcome this amnesia and be engaged in creative memory works. But this itself is nurtured by systematic training in history of sociological, anthropological, and social thought in India and South Asia in Indian universities which, in most cases is only conspicuous by its absence. Our amnesia of our pioneers may be related to this lack of training in traditions of social thinking in India. In this context, the proposed work of gratitude and memory work has significant pedagogical implications: in schools of sociology and anthropology in India there is a need for teaching the work of our pioneers as well as many other related thinkers. Apart from this, there is also a need for a critical discussion of our contemporary fellow sociologists and anthropologists. Post-independent India has produced some seminal sociologists and anthropologists of world significance but except pioneering figures of an earlier generation such as G.S. Ghurye and M.N. Srinivas it seems there

is not even a single M.Phil. work critically discussing works of scholars such as J.P.S. Uberoi, André Béteille, T.K. Oommen and Veena Das what to speak of full length doctoral work on their works. This is also a part of our amnesia but here again much of this may be related to the character of our pedagogy and training.

REFERENCES

Ankersmit, F. R.

2002 *Political Representation*. Stanford: Stanford University Press.

Arif, Yasmeen

2004 'Passages out of India', *Economic and Political Weekly*, January 17:301-303.

Beck, Ulrich

2002 'The cosmopolitan society and its enemies', *Theory, Culture and Society* 19 (1-2): 17-44.

Béteille, André

1996 Epilogue: Village studies in retrospect. In *Caste, Class and Power*. 2nd Edition. New Delhi: Oxford.

1997 'Newness in Sociological Inquiry', *Sociological Bulletin* 46 (1): 97-110.

2002 *Sociology: Essays on Approach and Method*. Delhi: Oxford University Press.

Bhaskar, Roy

2002 *Reflections on Meta-Reality: Transcendence, Everyday Life and Emancipation*. New Delhi: Sage.

Bourdieu, Pierre

1990 *In Other Words: Essays Towards a Reflexive Sociology*. Cambridge: Polity Press.

1991 *The Political Ontology of Martin Heidegger*. Cambridge: Polity Press.

2003 'Participant objectivation', *Journal of Royal Anthropological Institute* (N.S) 9: 281-294.

Bourdieu, Pierre and Loic J. D. Wacquant

1992 *An Invitation to Reflexive Sociology*. Cambridge: Polity Press.

Clammer, John, Sylvie Piorie and Eric Schwimmer

2004 'Introduction: The relevance of ontologies in anthropology: Reflections on a new anthropological field'. In John Clammer *et al.* (eds.), *Figured Worlds: Ontological Obstacles in Intercultural Relations*: 3-22. Toronto: Toronto University Press.

Collins, Randall

1998 *The Sociology of Philosophies: A Global Theory of Intellectual Change*. Cambridge, MA: Harvard University Press.

Connolly, William E.

1995 *The Ethos of Pluralization*. Minneapolis: University of Minnesota Press.

Das, Veena

1995 *Critical Events: Anthropological Perspectives on Contemporary India*. Delhi: Oxford University Press.

Dallmayr, Fred.

1987 *Critical Encounters: Between Philosophy and Politics*. Notre Dame: University of Notre Dame Press.

1991 *Between Freiburg and Frankfurt: Toward a Critical Ontology*. Cambridge: Polity Press.

1993 *The Other Heidegger*. Ithaca, NY: Cornell U. Press.

1996 *Beyond Orientalism*. Albany: SUNY Press.

2001 'Resisting totalizing uniformity: Martin Heidegger on the *Macht* and *Machenschaft*'. In *Achieving Our World: Toward a Global and Plural Democracy*. Lanham, MD: Rowman & Littlefield.

Derrida, Jacques

2003 'Following theory'. In Michael Payne and John Schad (eds.), *Life After Theory*. London: Continuum.

Fromm, Eric

1950 *Man for Himself*. London: Routledge and Kegan Paul.

Giddens, Anthony

1994 'Living in a Post-Traditional Society'. In Ulrich Beck, Anthony Giddens and Scot Lash (eds.), *Reflexive Modernization: Politics, Tradition and Aesthetics in Modern Social Order*. Cambridge: Polity Press.

Giri, Ananta Kumar

2002 *Conversations and Transformations: Towards a New Ethics of Self and Society*. Lanham, MD: Lexington Books.

2003 'Social science research: Call of home and the world'. *Economic and Political Weekly*. August 23, 3605-08.

2004 'Self-Development, Inclusion of the Other and Planetary Realizations'. In Ananta Kumar Giri *et al.* (eds), *The Religion of Development/Development of Religion*. Delft, Netherlands: Euborn.

2005a *Reflections and Mobilizations: Dialogues with Movements and Voluntary Organizations*. New Delhi: Sage.

2005b 'Creative Social Research: Rethinking Theories and Methods and the Calling of an Ontological Epistemology of Participation'. Madras Institute of Development Studies: Working Paper.

Giri, Ananta Kumar (ed.)

2004 *Creative Social Research: Rethinking Theories and Methods*. Lanham, MD: Lexington Books and Sage, New Delhi.

Greco, John

2001 'Virtues and Rules in Epistemology'. In Abrol Fairweather and Linda Zagzebski (eds.), *Epistemology: Essays on Epistemic Virtue and Responsibility*: 117-141. Oxford: Oxford University Press.

Guha, Ramachandra

2003 'The ones who stayed behind', *Economic and Political Weekly*. March 22.

Hardt, Michael and Antonio Negri

2004 *Multitude: War and Democracy in the Age of Empire*. London: Penguin.

Ingold, Tim

2004 'A circumpolar night's dream'. In Clammer *et al.* 2004: 25-57.

Luhman, Niklas

2001 "Notes on the Project 'Poetry and Social Theory' ", *Theory, Culture & Society* 18 (1): 15-27.

MacIntyre, Alasdair

1999 *Dependent Rational Animals*. London: Duckworth.

Mathur, Shubh

2005 'Torture, empire and nation', *Economic and Political Weekly*, March 5-11: 993-995.

Oommen, T. K.

2004 *Nation, Civil Society and Social Movements: Essays in Political Sociology*. Delhi: Sage Publications.

Patel, Sujata

2002 'The profession and its association: Five decades of the Indian Sociological Society', *International Sociology* 17 (2): 269-284.

Pillai, P. V.

1985 '*Hind Swaraj* in the light of Heidegger's critique of modernity'. In Nageswar Prasad (ed.), *Hind Swaraj: A Fresh Look*. New Delhi: Gandhi Peace Foundation.

Said, Edward

1978 *Orientalism*. New York: Random House.

Sen, Amartya

2002 'Justice across borders'. In *Global Justice and Transnational Politics: Essays on the Moral and Political Challenges of Globalization*. Cambridge, MA: The MIT Press (pp. 37-51).

Shanks, Andrew

2001 *What is Truth? Towards Theological Poetics*. London: Routledge.

Smith, Adam

1976 *A Theory of Moral Sentiments*. Oxford: Oxford University Press.

Shah, A. M.

2003 'The matter of facts', *Economic and Political Weekly*, October 18, 4491-92.

Srinivas, M. N.

1989a 'Itineraries of an Indian social anthropologist'. In *Cohesive Role of Sanskritization and Other Essays*. New Delhi: Oxford University Press.

1989b 'The insider versus outsider in the study of cultures'. In *Cohesive Role of Sanskritization and Other Essays*. New Delhi: Oxford University Press.

1992 *On Living in a Revolution and Other Essays*. Delhi: Oxford.

Srinivas, M. N. and M. N. Panini

1992 'The development of sociology and social anthropology in India'. In Srinivas (1992: 151-188).

Srinivasan, Amrit

1998 'The subject of fieldwork: Malinowski and Gandhi', In Meenakshi Thapan (ed.), *Anthropological Journeys: Reflections on Fieldwork*. Hyderabad: Orient Longman.

Uberoi, J.P.S.

2002 *The European Modernity: Truth, Science and Method*. Delhi: Oxford University Press.

Uberoi, Patricia

2000 ' "Déjà vu?" Seminar'. Retrieved from *http://www.india-seminar.com/2000* on Nov. 11, 2004.

Vattimo, Giani

1999 *Belief*. Cambridge: Polity Press.

8

What Ails Indian Anthropology?

R. Siva Prasad

Anthropology, like the other disciplines, has its peaks and troughs. Unlike the others, its peaks are more undulating and this may be attributable to its growing divergence or gulf between its subdivisions (read physical/biological, social/cultural, archaeological/pre-historical and linguistic anthropologies). We have a tendency to identify our glory with either some eminent personalities or always try to bask in the glory of the past and hide behind the reality. This attitude of ours does not take us anywhere. Instead, we slide down in the estimation of our peers elsewhere. Therefore, it is essential for us to take a critical look at the troughs that the discipline is undergoing and take corrective steps well in time; otherwise, we will be in pits.

II

One might take comfort in looking at the spectrum of anthropologists who were, and are, employed in divergent disciplines or public spaces at both national and international levels (Sarana and Sinha 1976). This gives us some pyrrhic satisfaction but will not lead us anywhere to strengthen the course of development of the discipline. Scholars point out the growth of anthropology was slow as compared to sociology (Sarana and Sinha 1976: 212). Why was it so? We need to find the answers for this lagging behind. One of the prominent reasons being, unlike anthropology, the sociologists have only one all-India professional body or association. We have not one but a handful of them. There is a need for a single unifying all-India professional forum or body for the anthropologists[2] with a number of research committees (RCs) dealing with its subdivisions as well as interdisciplinary concerns. People should be free to join the RCs and can organise their own regional or national conferences, and each can report to the all-India body. We need to start somewhere like this to rejuvenate and rekindle the spirit of anthropology.

When we talk of anthropology, we are always reminded that 'holism' is its hallmark. We are, however, not clear about how the holism operates within or between or across its subdivisions. Many a times, it is not even properly understood. Even if it was stated in terms of its linkages, it is always at a very superficial level or only in a general sense it is discussed. In fact, there are only a handful of scholars who have really tried to work it out in the past. However, such attempts are only countable and they were largely in the early stages of the founding of anthropology departments in India.

Every anthropology student is taught about what is anthropology–it is a science of man (read human); it studies about man and his works; or it deals with all that is related to human beings. Then they are told about anthropology and its several branches and also its relationships with other sciences (natural as well as social sciences and humanities). Every anthropology student in India studies the basics of physical/biological, social/cultural and archaeological/prehistoric anthropology, and afterwards a student gets into specialising in any of its subdivisions. The problem actually arises here and afterwards when the linkages are given a complete go by. Instead, some kind of one-upmanship takes place at this stage and each tries to vie against the other as rival disciplines, though they actually are not.

It is true that any growing discipline, like a family, tends to branch off and establish its independence from the other members of its family. It is also natural that each branch evolves its own course of events and direction (Srivastava 2000). Integration across its subdivisions can only be of a limited value and cannot sustain only on sentiments. The acrimony between its subdivisions is due to suspicion and lack of mutual respect towards each other. Each tries to score points over the other. In fact, we do not need enemies from outside. Subdivision feuds, like factional feuds, are its nemesis.

III

We have different approaches to look at anthropology and there are wide agreements and disagreements about them. When we talk about British anthropology, biological or archaeological anthropology are never taught along with social anthropology. In most of Europe, it was social anthropology which was taught as anthropology. In this context, we find the influence of British anthropology, especially that of A. R. Radcliffe-Brown and E. E. Evans-Pritchard on Indian sociology through M. N. Srinivas much more. Srinivas used to state that Indian culture does not permit the division of social anthropology and sociology (this he reiterated more emphatically in his key note address to the XI International Sociological Congress held in Delhi way back in 1986; see also Kolenda 2001). He believed that Indian sociology is more of social anthropology than sociology in the American sense. As the last student of Srinivas, I used to have discussions on this and he used to explain why Indian sociology and social anthropology are not very different. On the contrary the Indian anthropology is shaped more on the lines of American anthropology, which encourages an integrated anthropology consisting of physical or biological, socio-cultural, archaeologica and linguistic anthropology.

When we attempt to understand the state of anthropolog in India we need to look at it at five levels: 1) the theoretical o conceptual; 2) of integration, or lack of it, across its differen branches (emotive level); 3) the methodological; 4) of competenc (level of meeting the challenges of reality); and 5) of leadership A stock-taking on these levels, which are interdependent, wi really enable us to understand the situation that we are in toda and throw us opportunities to take corrective steps to espous the cause of anthropology as a discipline to surge ahead.

At the theoretical or conceptual level, we have a handful (native anthropologists who have made some noteworth contributions. By and large, we still continue to analyse ou society and culture from a western theoretical vantage poin

The point is not to argue against the western theoretical perspectives but to look more inwardly. Why we were unable to develop our own theoretical or conceptual perspectives is really the one that we need to ponder over. Is it something to do with our curriculum or training? Or, is it something that we were not motivated to focus on? Is it that we doubt our capabilities of evolving our own perspectives to reflect on our society and culture? Where does the problem lie?

In India, physical or biological, socio-cultural and archaeological anthropology are prominent in their presence in the curricula of anthropology departments. Only a handful of departments teach linguistic anthropology in the country. Integration is really problematic even in those departments with all the branches operating. Some branches get more priority over the others in recruitment as well as in their operation. Physical or biological anthropologists claim that they can handle socio-cultural anthropology papers (Srivastava 1999, 2000), while the socio-cultural anthropologists will not be able to do justice in teaching physical or biological anthropology as it is science.

The problem is one of attitude. The physical anthropologists think that they are scientists and are superior to social anthropology, which they do not regard as a science. I witnessed this tendency in a number of contexts. As a matter of fact, archaeological anthropology is relegated by both physical and social anthropologists to a lower position, sometimes to the point of no relevance. When recruiting teaching faculty, preference is given to physical or social anthropology, in that order, and only when there are 'adequate' representations, archaeological anthropology gets a chance, otherwise it will be taught by any one. In case of physical anthropology, the physical anthropologists would want that only specialists should teach the subject, and they claim the scholarship to teach social or archaeological anthropology. So the contrary should also be true in a logical sense, as social as well as archaeological anthropologies[2] also require some proficiency and also they can teach the other papers as well. It is this attitude of some that comes in the way of real integration of the subdivisions[3]. How can we talk of integration under such prevailing mental frameworks? An emotional talk of integration does not cut ice any longer. How do we overcome this to achieve a harmonious relationship?

We need to be more practical and have to work out the areas of integration which can be taught as such by persons from the subdivision areas together. In other words, we need to democratise our teaching and development of the discipline. This can be a beginning for the development of a more integrated discipline of anthropology with its core concerns more focussed, while the rest branch out and also develop linkages with the other sister disciplines. So there is really a need for an honest soul searching amongst us the anthropologist to whatever ilk that we belong to. Srivastava places some propositions before us in his writings on 'The Future of Anthropology' (1999) and 'Teaching anthropology' (2000), which merit some serious consideration.

This invariably leads us to the question of methodology and depth of enquiry in our quest of anthropological knowledge of our society and culture. Compared to all the other disciplines, anthropological method is more holistic, intensive, participative, and anthropocentric. For a socio-cultural anthropologist, intensive ethnographic fieldwork is the patented trademark. How much of it is in vogue today is a question mark. We hardly find any intensive fieldwork undertaken by students (Srivastava 1999, 2000) as well as most of the faculty today, who indulge in writing theses, articles, and books prolifically without undertaking any intensive fieldwork. To our horror, many publish articles[4] with a week's, or less than that, fieldwork. With this kind of academic contributions how can we take anthropology forward? Some Indian journals do not even edit the articles, leave aside peer reviewing.

Let us face it. The quality of works is an important concern and so long as we do not give credence to it we cannot arrive in the competitive international horizons.[5] The quality of some of the journals and the articles or books coming out from the Indian anthropologists of calibre are really far and few. Most of the publications are publications only on paper and are hardly referred to. If reviewed very strictly, they will get screened out at the entry level itself. Publishing today has become an industry. Editing volumes or plagiarised publications have become the order of the day. I am not against those who are making sincere attempts to bring out edited volumes with some focus and also not against those brining out anthologies of conferences. Under these conditions, where there are hardly any people concerned about the quality and depth of information, how can we expect anthropology to lead the other disciplines in methodological rigour? In fact, the others have taken to anthropological method while the anthropologists have completely forgotten about their own methods. In turn, now anthropologists make use of the short-cut methodologies and claim that they have in-depth information about the culture or society that they have studied. We need to introspect whether the same rigour of intensive fieldwork is also missing among the other subdivisions of anthropology.

This leads us to the fourth level, the level of meeting the challenges of reality or the level of competence. It is a truism that the level of competence is dependent on the depth and thoroughness of knowledge that we possess about the issues at hand, which implies that we need to have a holistic perspective of the problem and look at it from the point of view of the natives for discovering better understanding of the issues that are being investigated. The tendency to adopt some models evolved by someone else in a different socio-cultural milieu does not require any level of competence. This does not add anything to the anthropology of knowledge. The level of competence gets reflected only when we deal with the problems that are at hand more reflectively and conceptually. The level of competence is not dependent only on whether one is well versed with quantitative and qualitative methodologies but on the level of understanding and evolving critical theoretical or conceptual points of view. The tendency among some Indian scholars is to find whether one has used any theoretical perspective, be it structural-functionalism, structuralism, Marxism, cognitive anthropology, postmodernism, or whatever you have, to qualify a work to be worth looking at. They forget the fact that there can be many other perspectives that one can have or may adopt a concoction of diverse perspectives or may have something new tried by the scholar that can merit for competency. We have evolved long ago from the apes and we do not need to copy anymore the others but use our minds to evolve better. Let us be different from Xerox machines.

Why Indian anthropology is in such a mess? The answer invariably will lead us to the question of leadership or lack of it. In other words, there is a crisis of enlightened leadership that can rise above partisan and narrow considerations. Let us not forget that mediocrity breeds mediocrity. Let us take the bull by its horns.

IV

There are no shortcuts for a healthy development of anthropology. There is a need for serious introspection and we need to identify the problems and their solutions collectively. There is an urgent need today for capacity building at the level of the departments, updating curricula, reinforcing the fieldwork tradition and evolving collective responsibility. Anthropology is a science of democratic learning and sharing, and it is a humanising science. Therefore, there is no place for autocratic leaders at any level of its operation. Together we sail and divided we sink. No one, I am sure, is interested in sinking and, therefore, let hundred flowers bloom than have *Strobilanthes kunthiana* (*kurinji*, in Tamil), which blooms once in twelve years or a monocarpic plant which blooms once in its lifetime.

NOTES

1. The recent forming of the Indian National Confederation and Academy of Anthropologists (INCAA) is a welcome trend and there is a need to sustain the spirit and we should not any longer get embroiled in the quagmire of narrow politics, be they sub-divisional, regional or of any other kind. We need to learn from our past mistakes but not repeat them.
2. As a matter of fact, we all know, even the social anthropologists as well as archaeological anthropologists, like the physical anthropologists, are trained in the foundations of physical anthropology along with social and archaeological anthropology, but it is assumed that they cannot handle introductory papers of physical anthropology. In course of teaching one can acquire proficiency in any branch of anthropology and there are a handful of examples that one can look for.
3. Srivastava (2000) argues for a federal structure of teaching and governance. There is a need to respect every sub-discipline as an equal partner than regarding some as more than equal.
4. We were always told, 'publish or perish'. In this context, it is better to perish than publishing perishable stuff, which does not help the growth of the discipline.

5. This is true not only in the arena of our publications but also in the realm of recruitments. Some of our selection committees have their own biases, prejudices and are not above board. The committees are usually constituted with people from all the major subdivisions of anthropology. When recruitments are made a social anthropologist becomes qualified to judge a physical or archaeological anthropology candidate, and similarly a physical or archaeological anthropologist with the other subdivisions. Why this logic is not extended to teaching is not fathomable.

REFERENCES

Kolenda, Pauline

2001 'Mysore Narasimhachar Srinivas, Biographical Memoirs'. *Proceedings of the American Philosophical Society* 145 (3): 374-376.

Sarana, Gopala and Dharni P. Sinha

1976 'Status of social-cultural anthropology in India', *Annual Review of Anthropology* 5: 209-225.

Srivastava, Vinay Kumar

1999 The future of anthropology. *Economic and Political Weekly*, February 27.

2000 *Teaching anthropology. www.india-seminar.com/2000/495495%20vinay%20kumar%20srivastava.htm*

9

On the Practice of Anthropology

R. P. Mitra

Applied or application aspect in the practice of human sciences like anthropology needs to be problematised as these subjects are concerned with human beings. It is easier to distinguish applied from pure research in natural sciences (like physics and chemistry) as these subject do not directly deal with human beings. Knowledge in these subjects can be about unraveling the mysteries of nature as in pure research or it could be application of this knowledge for human welfare and usage in the case of applied research. The situation is different in anthropology, which is directly concerned with human beings and understanding of human behaviour that arises in a socio-cultural context. Human well being and primacy of human interest are the very ends of the discipline, and knowledge must contribute to better understanding of human beings. In other words human welfare and well being are built in the very practice of anthropology. The gap between generation of knowledge to satisfy one's intellectual proclivities and the practical use of that knowledge is not very wide. Therefore, the natural sciences division of research into pure and applied categories needs to be reexamined in the case of practice of anthropology. van Willigen (1993:7) has identified twelve different roles of applied anthropologists, viz., as policy researcher, evaluator, impact assessor, need assessor, planner, research analyst, advocacy, trainer, cultural broker, administrator, change agent and therapist. The information, product and action involved in applied anthropology derive from basic anthropology only. The difference lies in the milieu in which anthropology is practiced and the ends its serves. On this basis we can distinguish between anthropology of and anthropology for in the practice of anthropology.

With the emergence of knowledge economy based on production and management of knowledge as a prime mover of economic growth, the anthropological knowledge and skills have come to acquire an added significance. Anthropology has found admirers from across the board. One keeps hearing of anthropologists being hired by different organizations. Sapient, a software developing and electronics firm, has more than two dozen anthropologists on its staff. Anthropologists are also employed in such renowned companies such as Intel, Kodak, Whirlpool, AT&T, General Motors and Hallmark (Boss 2001). The same is the case in India also. Large numbers of students, after completing their degree in anthropology, are working as policy analysts, social researchers, media professionals, managers, administrator and business consultants. What do they do there? Do they find what they learn as part of their training in anthropology useful? This paper deals with some of these issues. It examines what anthropology has to offer in the contemporary globalizing world. For this, I conducted interviews with those who have studied the subject and are now employed out, to know their views about the relevance of anthropology in what they are doing? Data were also drawn from interviews with academicians who are frequently part of multidisciplinary project and policy making teams.

There is definitely a greater awareness now of anthropology and the role anthropologists can play in handling social issues. When we were students in closing decades of the last century the oft-repeated statement from scholars of other disciplines was 'anthropology is a subject that has not got its due recognition'. The present trends indicate that all this is fast changing and there is a greater realization of the discipline's worth in new areas of applications. If anthropology was the study of exotica in the last century, this century is seeing a greater involvement of anthropology in handling frontline issues ranging from urban problems like development, poverty, disaster management, business and industry (see MacClancy 2002). This paper is an attempt to examine the relevance of socio-cultural anthropology in handling issues which till recently were considered as being beyond the traditional confines of the discipline.

A common thing that worries all generations of anthropology students is job opportunities in the discipline. Which jobs are available for anthropologists outside academics? If we look at the employment section of the newspapers or the regular employment news, the weekly published by the publication department of the Government of India, jobs with essential qualification as anthropology are hardly advertised. This gives an impression that jobs in anthropology are either few or are not advertised in a way jobs in other fields are advertised. My guess is that the latter statement is closer to reality than the former. This is borne out by the fact that there are not many anthropology students in any department I know of, who are not gainfully employed. Some join teaching after finishing their study. However, most by choice or compulsion take up jobs outside academics, where their work may or may not involve the direct use of anthropology. In some fields, like development and health, they are employed as anthropologists. Others may be working in fields like marketing where they may not be primarily employed as anthropologists, i.e. for their specialized knowledge of the discipline. Most of them are quite successful and doing fairly well in these organizations. I was told during my interactions with them that although they are in fields which are very different from anthropology, they do not face any difficulty in switching over to new areas. One reason for the success of anthropologists is undoubtedly their individual skills, but along with this the students feel that the training in anthropology also contributed to a great degree towards their success. That means the subject of anthropology teaches them not only specific skills but also equips them with certain functional and transferable skills. Irrespective of the nature of their jobs (whether closer to traditional fields of anthropology or far removed) they agree that studying anthropology has made a difference to what they contribute at their work places. Thus the anthropological knowledge is not restricted in application to the field of anthropology only.

Anyone studying anthropology acquires a perspective which is relevant in fields as diverse as administration, call center, marketing, banking, hotel and financial institutions. Srivastava (1999: 545) has noted how the bureaucrats who have studied anthropology as one of the subjects in the civil services examination became comparative, analytical, field oriented and contextual, and how they understood human predicaments better after learning the discipline.

Contribution of Anthropology

What is this anthropological perspective and how does it provide them an edge over their colleagues from other disciplines? I posed this question to a number of anthropologists working in non-academic settings. Sandeep Chachara, a post graduate in anthropology, working in the U.S. Aid India, feels that the most important contribution of doing anthropology has been the ability to see politics in apparently non-political situations. It is anthropology that has taught him to go beyond what is visible. Bijoy Mohanty, another anthropologist working in the same organization, felt that the most important lesson from anthropology is not to jump to conclusions based on impressions. Mohanty, who has done fieldwork in Sri Lanka, Afghanistan and Sudan among other such difficult places, said he never felt stranger or out of place in any new situation. Exposure to a wide array of cultures and situations has prepared him better to handle this. Both of them agreed that working in adverse conditions comes much more easily to an anthropologist than to others.

Avanish Kumar, who teaches policy research, feels that the primacy of interest of the people and emphasis on understanding them in their own terms are important things anthropology has taught him. Meerambika Mahapatra, a doctorate in anthropology, working with the Indian Council of Medical Research, feels that training in methodology especially the skill of combining qualitative and quantitative methods is a unique feature of anthropology. She feels the anthropological approach provides an edge over others in project formulation. The subject has taught her among other things the ability to ask the right kind of questions to solve any problem. Alka Sabharwal, who works as a consultant in the development sector, feels that training in anthropology has enabled her to understand the development issues through the perspective of community. She feels people from other disciplines never take this seriously. If it is done it only represents the opinion of the educated and powerful few. Anthropologists only have that sensitivity to give equal significance to the voices of the 'muted' lots (like women and those who are marginalized).

One interesting fact which I came across while interviewing these people is that a number of them told me that they consistently draw upon the knowledge of social anthropology without being consciously aware of it. They found it difficult to sight specific instances how they have applied the knowledge of anthropology? This is because the perspective which anthropology provides is not a separate, clearly bounded and an identifiable unit. All of them (I interviewed) have done anthropology varying from 5 to 10 years[1]. The long association with anthropology has a great impact on them. It has left an indelible mark and their total vision has become anthropological. As a result anthropology is so ingrained in them that they have no alternate way of looking other than of anthropology. Whatever they do and any activity they perform whether it may be in the household, personal life or work place, it is anthropological. The discipline deeply touches the learner and a true student of the subject cannot be non-anthropological or un-anthropological whatever be the circumstances. The situation can be compared to a scientist. A scientist may not do science all the time. All his activities may not be guided by rationality, logical consistency and objectivity his discipline demands of him. He may be scientist while working in the laboratory but in personal life he may subscribe to irrational behaviour like magic or witchcraft. However, an anthropologist can not segregate himself from the subject even when he is not doing anthropology. As a result, it becomes difficult for them to isolate specific instances of how anthropology is useful for their work. One of them, who studied anthropology till post-graduation compared anthropology to a magic wand. Just as a magic wand transforms an individual similarly doing the subject transforms an individual's perspective of how he thinks and acts in this world. Pink (2006: 11) identifies some of the distinctive features of anthropology, which I have listed below.

1. Recognition of culture as one of the important determinant of human actions.
2. Significance of empirical understanding through fieldwork. What Nolan (2003:119) referred to as 'understanding inductively from the ground up rather than by imposing theories before hand'.
3. Emphasis on the processes rather than on the outcome. According to Ray (2006:677) what distinguishes anthropologists from economist is that while the research in economy emphasize more the outcomes or findings which help in precise predictions, the anthropological findings on the other hand emphasizes predictions based on process. The anthropologists focus on relationships, values, and power dynamics involved in any situation for prediction.
4. Cross-cultural skills and being trained in looking at things holistically, relatively with empathy.
5. Specialization in doing an ethnographic form of research.
6. Uncovering the implicit meaning: Understanding both implicit and explicit meaning of things. Recognition of the significant role of the implicit factors behind what is explicit.
7. Atomistic and holistic understanding: A systematic way of approaching an issue by breaking it down into its constituent units, i.e. simplification of complex things and the opposite of it, i.e. looking at things in an integrated manner. This combination of atomizing a phenomenon, then integrating to understand holistically is a unique feature of the discipline.
8. Ability to observe patterns in actions and behavior (which apparently look arbitrary) in social situations.
9. Flexibility towards handling new ideas, complexities and the ability to work in a multi-disciplinary team.
10. Rigour of work and the capability of working in difficult situations like conflict zones and disaster affected areas.

It is not that these skills have suddenly assumed significance and are in demand outside the discipline. In fact, applied anthropology has a long history and is an established sub-discipline in its own right within anthropology (see Chambers 1987; Bennette 1993; van Willigen 1993). In its initial years, anthropology was part of training imparted to the new entrants of British colonial service to understand the native culture better (Forde 1953). There were criticisms of anthropologists for assisting colonial administrators in facilitating colonialism or neo-colonialism, an allegation that was based more on sensationalism than facts. It is now well established that although some of the studies were funded by the colonial administrators yet these works rather than assisting in controlling and governing the people promoted a more humane and sympathetic understanding of the people. In independent India, anthropology right from the beginning, found favours with the government and anthropologists were active partners in social and economic development programs especially in tribal and rural areas. Well known anthropologists like Verrier Elwin, D. N. Majumdar, L. P. Vidyarthi and S.C. Dube acted as advisors to government and actively combined pure/basic with applied research.

What has changed in the present scenario is that anthropologists are employed not only in the traditional fields of applied anthropology (like health, education and development) but also in sectors like marketing and business. Anthropological perspective has found newer applications in the changing globalizing knowledge based economy. Information and knowledge are replacing capital and energy as the primary wealth-creating assets, just as the latter two replaced land and labour 200 years ago (see Doz and Williamson 2001). Technological advancement has rendered distances obsolete leading to a phenomenon called globalization, thus resulting transformation in economic organization, social regulation, political governance and ethical regimes, which are redefining the core dynamics of social, cultural, and economic life (Collier and Ong 2002: 12). Broadly there are three types of change that are simultaneously acting upon social and cultural life.

(a) Global forces, represented through the flow of goods, information and technology, are giving rise to global culture, a force that tends to bring about homogenization.

(b) Response and resistance of the local to the global forces through strengthening of local cultures and identities.

(c) A new synthesis brought about by globalization of the local and localization of the global.

For any organization to succeed in contemporary situation, these three forces simultaneously need to be taken into account. Let us take a case study to understand how the anthropologist can contribute in the present competitive business scenario.

The case study relates to an advertisement campaign being planned for a paint company which wanted to launch a floor polish. The company approached a marketing firm where the anthropologist was employed in the consumer research division. The firm provided detailed information about the product. The company claimed that the product was different from all available floor polishes because it had a special compound, which the company referred to as SKS which provides additional shine and does not wither easily. The company claimed that it spreads evenly on the floor and is a stable compound; as a result it does not melt or freeze with a change in temperature. The compound has a high reflective index, as a result it shines when light falls on it. The company wanted to create an advertisement highlighting the above mentioned features of the product. The advertising agency started with a consumer research to determine what should be the form and the content of the advertisement. The anthropologist who was one of the members of the team suggested that they should actually visit construction site to see how people take decision to buy a floor polish. When the fieldwork was carried out it was found there were three set of players involved in decision making regarding buying of a floor polish. The first is the polishing contractor, second is his paid workers who actually do the polish, and the third is the house owner himself. The shopkeepers do not play an important role in decision making as the consumers often demand for a floor polish with a particular brand name. The three groups have different motivations to buy a polish. The contractor and the workers are usually interested in a product that shines with minimum of effort. The house owner is primarily interested in a polish that not only shines but the shine lasts long. Further it was found that house owner buy the floor polish mainly on the advice of their construction worker, who are present on the site. The contractor who employs them only talks of floor polish and very seldom patronizes any particular brand. It is the workers who do the actually polishing and are present when the owner is going to buy the polish; they advice the house owners regarding a product. Often they insist upon a particular brand to be purchased so as to get the desired result. So the feed back was given to the copywriters and the creators that for the advertisement to be successful:

- It should target both the house owners as well as the workers who do the actual polishing.

- The advertisement should not only emphasise the long lasting nature of the shine, it must also mention something about the ease of using the product to appeal to the workers and the contractors.
- Most of the workers being from Hindi speaking rural belt of U.P., M.P. or Rajasthan, the advertisement should use folk music and the simple local language prevalent in these areas. The images or sound used in the advertisement should be a mix of urban places and rural set up so that it satisfies the imagery of both the house owners as well as the workers.
- Majority of the workers being illiterate, the advertisement should emphasize on the visuals display rather than on the text or technicalities of the product.
- As the workers mostly have access to radio as a form of mass media, the advertising campaign should focus on radio advertisement of the product.
- Further, it was felt that merely advertising would not push the product as workers already had their tested brand which they would like to follow. Therefore, some kind of incentives needed to be provided to the workers to switch their brand loyalty. It was suggested to the client that they must put two five rupees coin inside the container of the polish. This will be for the worker who generally opens the tin of polish and mixes it. This money can be adjusted in the retailer profit as the retailers do not play an important role in pushing the product. Therefore a marginal decrease in the retailers' margin will not affect the sale.

Where did the anthropologist made a difference in the above mentioned case study? He made a difference by adding a new perspective to look at the things by shifting the focus from decision making (outcome) to the process involved in it, thereby helping in the understanding of these process and the reasons for buying a particular product. He added a new dimension in the campaign by changing the focus from the product to its users. The company and the other people in the advertisement agency wanted to emphasize the specialty of the product; the anthropologist shifted the focus to the user of the product.

This innovative alternative way of understating the world is of great significance in the present business scenario, which itself is becoming extremely complex due to increased competition in the market. Due to globalization, products originating at different places are competing with each other at the same market. In such a situation only those products can succeed which meet the expectation of the consumers and satisfy their needs. Consumer thinking is also undergoing a rapid transformation. Newer ethics and values (like environmentalism) inform consumer choices (Pant and Alberti 1997:7). In other words, the consumer today is better aware and discerning. As a result, new business thinking demands a deep concern with the culture of the consumers (ibid.7). The same product can have multiplicity of functions. For example, it was seen that many people in slums were using the glow of the cell phone screen as a torch light. As a result it led to installing of torch lights on the lower end cell phones. Such demands and information cannot be collected through mere surveys and interviews because often, like culture, such demands are non-sentential. Question answer type of research based on interview and survey cannot articulate these demands. They require direct observation of the product use *in situ*. Someone has to visit the actual site of the product use to understand the needs of the consumers. The site could be a hotel lobby, a hospital room or a work place. Who else can do this better than an anthropologist? Pant and Alberti (1997:11) have identified the following areas of anthropological application in the business world.

1. Study of marketing and consumer behaviour.
2. Identification of non-economic factors which affect consumers' decision to buy a product. This includes the role of kinship, family and peer group, symbolic meaning and prestige value attributed to a product. Different meanings and significance attributed to products in different groups based on criteria like age grade, gender, occupation, region and ethnicity.
3. Intercultural communication and developing advertising material.
4. Work place ethnographies and study of organization culture.
5. Providing inputs about new social trends and business opportunities by identification of the emerging cultural scenarios and moral regimes, in providing inputs for strategic thinking.
6. In strengthening the community organization relationship by encouraging corporate groups to fulfill their social responsibility, integrating organizations with the community and thereby generating the goodwill for the organization in the community.
7. Evaluation of socio-economic impact of a new project and to identify resistance and address the grievances of local population about a project.

How can an anthropologist do it while others cannot? The answer lies in the way in which an anthropologist is trained.

He is trained to recognize the importance of culture and cultural processes in determining human actions (see Chambers 1987: 315). An anthropologist is methodologically 'culturalist'; culture is the central unit in anthropological analysis as against the methodological 'individualistic' orientation in other social sciences, e.g. economy (Rao 2001: 14). This difference of emphasis has a major role in determining how human behavior is understood. For example, economists take a more positivistic view of human behavioral preferences and constraints emanating from a rational individual. Individual operates with self-interest, strategizes to maximize benefits and minimize costs and make rational choices in this world. Anthropologist, on the other hand, takes a more nuanced view. Human behaviour is not always rational, self centered or strategic; there are other determinants which are context specific. They are determined by the culture of a place. Search for culture orients an anthropological inquiry in a different way compared to specialists from other disciplines. This is because culture unlike an individual is not tangible. It is not visible, therefore it requires a different level of methodological empiricism to understand and explain cultural processes. Anthropology over time has developed an intellectual body of knowledge in dealing with this abstract concept. According to Chambers (1987: 316), there are three strategies used by applied anthropologists to study events with respect to time, viz. social accounting, social evaluation and social forecasting, dealing with present, past and future dimension of any events respectively. Social accounting deals with the estimate of the social needs and desires of the people at a particular place and time. It provides a baseline data for further decision making. Two approaches were identified under this, viz. strategy need assessment and resource assessment (*ibid*: 317). In evaluation research, anthropologists are concerned with impact assessment of various policy interventions in the fields like health, education or nutrition program that has already been implemented in a community. In evaluation, the focus is on the past activity; on the other hand anthropologists also are also adept in social forecasting. Here they are primarily concerned with making projections based on information collected from the field. Thus anthropologists have the skill not only to study the present and the past; they are also capable of assessing the future

An anthropologist is trained to commence a study without a questionnaire. The first task is to know the people before trying to learn what they know (MacClancy 2002:5). It is important for an anthropologist to gain the trust and the confidence of the people so that the actual behavior can be noted in their natural surroundings. Anthropologist begins with a premise that people would like to represent themselves publicly in a particular way which may not correspond to their actual behaviour. There are no preconceived notions in the mind of an anthropologist. If he is working in a familiar place the study begins with estranging the familiar, i.e. making the familiar strange (*ibid:* 9). The methodology is inductive and the understanding begins with people, although being grounded does not mean that the larger picture is lost sight of. He is trained to understand the micro in macro context and at the same time tease out the influences of macro in shaping the micro. Another factor which anthropologists are always prepared for is serendipity or chance finding. An anthropologist knows that there are many things which are discovered by chance; therefore he is prepared for the unexpected things. It can be said that in many ways the success of an anthropological inquiry is measured in finding out the unexpected.

The distinct approach of anthropology is to situate a problem or an event in a social setting, which is an organized space where social interaction takes place. Every social setting has certain objectives and activities are directed toward fulfilling those objectives. There are positions available in a social setting. Individuals can become players or participants of a social setting by occupying these positions. Players in a social setting bring with them their own expectations, objectives and goals. Broadly there are two sets of objectives around which activities are arranged. First there are those which are institutionalized objectives of a place and then there are those which the social actors bring in with them. It is not necessary that these two may coincide. Actors may themselves have different motivations for actions. They may interpret and give meaning to things differently. For example the term 'customer' may have different association for different employees in a shop. In a case study of sportswear shop, Gobo (2008: 169) showed that the concept of customer has three different meanings for employees of the store. 'When the managers use the term customer, they have more of an abstract notion associated with them; the term is often used as rhetoric to establish their authority over the junior staff. The head of the departments, when they use the term customer, they are referring to more concrete individuals, which help them to win competition over the other departments. As head of the department with the largest sale at the end of day receives a bonus, for him more the number of customer the better it is. On the other hand, those for those who manned the counters customers are not always a welcome entity. Only a few in numbers are a welcome sight after that, they start looking at a customer as an essential nuisance one who distract him for essential activities like arranging the stocks and tidying up the counter'. The anthropological expertise lies in determining such meanings which actors give to their actions. The anthropologists do so by unearthing the social conventions that define a social space. Conventions, which according to Gobo (2008: 162), are expressed in banal rituals and ceremonies of everyday routines. And through listening to talks and looking at contexts, anthropologists make explicit the tacit knowledge through which people operate.

This raises an important question that if knowledge is power then will not unearthing of such knowledge lead to complete control of the people; further, if such knowledge were to fall into the hands of unscrupulous people, it may prove detrimental to the interest of the people. Anthropologists gain their knowledge by winning peoples' trust and confidence and therefore an anthropologist has to be doubly careful in ensuring that no harmful effect comes to the community or the respondents. It poses a challenge when we are talking of use of *anthropology for* certain purpose. Because in this case the anthropologists also have to keep in mind the interest of the employer or the client who engages an anthropologist. But such a situation should be seen as an opportunity in settings like business which are driven by pure economic rationality. The client or the employer could be acquainted with peoples' point of view and how incorporating the interest of the consumers can best serve the business interest of the clients themselves.

Whenever an anthropologist may find himself in a situation of conflicting loyalties, divided between the agency where employed and the interest of the people, it is the latter that has to have the priority. It is easier said than done. But it is the tact and skill of a good anthropologist to create that space to refigure a product, program or a project to take care of the interest of the people. We live in a society where interview, observation, and conversation play a dominant role in the creation of social reality (Gobo 2008: 318). From doctor's clinic to recruiting people for jobs in radios and television, interviews are the predominant form of social construction. Similarly observation as an activity is being utilized more for understanding others. As the demand for knowledge and innovation become the new driving force in the economic sphere, anthropology finds itself in a unique position. Anthropology in its quest for understanding the other has evolved into a discipline known for its 'fertility in generating new ideas' (Benthall 2002:11). According to Benthall (*ibid:* 14), anthropology has enabled society to look at its own back thereby unmasking the hidden and marginalized and helped the society to question its own prejudices and biases. Many disciplines like cultural studies, dalit studies, human rights and women studies have been greatly influenced by the theories and methods which primarily originated in anthropology. There is a great demand for ethnographers in business, marketing and all other fields which rely on interaction with other human beings. It is important that in chasing these remunerative opportunities the basic strength of anthropology as an inventor of new ides should not be lost. There is a need to draw on a fine balance between anthropology as a service discipline contributing to the others and anthropology as an independent quest with its own body of objectives in a quest for newer perspectives.

NOTE

1. I am thankful to V. K. Srivastava for developing this argument.

REFERENCES

Bennett J. W.

1996 Applied and Action Anthropology: Ideological and Conceptual Aspects. *Current Anthropology*, Vol. 37, No. 1, pp. S23-S53.

Benthall J. (Ed.)
2002 *The Best of Anthropology Today*. London and New York: Rutledge.

Boss, S. J.
2001 *Jobs for anthropologists*. In the Christian Science Monitor I February at *http://www.brianhoey.com/*

Chambers, E.
1987 Applied anthropology in the post Vietnam era: Anticipation and Ironies. *Annual Review of Anthropology* 16: 309: 37.

Doz Y. and P. J. Williamson
2001 *From Global to Metanational: How Companies Win in the Knowledge Economy*. New York: Harvard Business School Press.

Forde, D.
1953 Applied Anthropology in Government: British Africa," in A.L. Kroeber (ed.), 1953. *Anthropology Today*, Chicago. The University of Chicago Press.

Gobo, G.
2008 *Doing Ethnography*. London and New York. Sage Publication.

Isha R.
2006 *Outcomes and Process in Economics and Anthropology*. In *Economic Development and Cultural Change*. Chicago. The University of Chicago Press at: *http://econpapers.repec.org/article/*

MacClancy J. (Ed.).
2002 *Exotica No More Anthropology on the Front lines.* Chicago. The University of Chicago Press.

Nolan, R.
2003 *Anthropology in Practice: Building a Carrier Outside the Academy*. London: Lynne Rienner Publication.

Ong A. and S. J. Collier (Eds.)
2004 *Global Assemblages: Technology, Politics and Ethics as Anthropological Problems*. UK: Blackwell Publishing.

Pant D. R. and F. Alberti
1997 Anthropology and Business. In Economia e Impressa vol. 11 Line paper no 42, at *http://www.biblio.liuc.it/liucpap/*

Pink, S. (Ed.).

2006 Application of Anthropology. In S. Pink S. (ed.) *Application of Anthropology: Professional Anthropology in the Twenty-First Century* Pink S (Ed.). New York: Berghahn Books.

Rao V. and M. Walton (Eds.)

2004 *Culture and Public Action*. New Delhi: Permanent Black.

Srivastava V. K.

1999 The Future of Anthropology. *Economic and Political Weekly*, February 27, 545-52.

van Willigen, J.

2002 *Applied Anthropology: An Introduction.* West Port and London: Bergin and Garvey.

Part III

10

The Passions and Perils of Anthropological Linguistics in India: Some Personal Reflections

Kamal K. Misra

If we want to understand the role of languages in people's lives, we must go beyond the study of their grammar and venture into the world of social action, where words are embedded in and constitutive of specific cultural activities such as telling a story, asking for a favour, greeting, showing respect, praying, giving directions, reading, insulting, praising, arguing in court, making a toast, or explaining a political agenda.

Duranti (2001)

The background

Let me begin with a note of clarification that I am not writing about the current deplorable status of a scholarly domain like 'Anthropological Linguistics' with any euphoria, but with a deep sense of anguish, as I am simply captivated since my student days by sheer versatility of this subject and its immense significance in the study of culture. Personal passion and fascination notwithstanding, I find today that anthropological linguistics is relegated to a state of oblivion and I would not be surprised if the next generation of anthropologists in India would not know what anthropological linguistics should be like. Let me suggest here that my assertion is certainly not speculative, rather based on some hard facts. In his most objective analysis of the *U.G.C. Status Report on Anthropology* of 1982, Srivastava (2000) notes that:

> A closer reading of this document [U.G.C. Status Report] suggests that besides the three well-known branches (viz. physical, archaeological, and social/cultural), it also considered linguistic anthropology as an important component of anthropology. With dismay, it noted that linguistic anthropology was taught in 'only one or two universities' (p. 12) ... As a large number of universities did not teach linguistic anthropology, one could easily infer that none of the anthropology departments were in fact truly integrated.

This hard reality is not unfamiliar to colleagues in anthropology in India; what hits hard is that there is only apathy, if someone really strives to continue teaching anthropological linguistics. Contrarily, there are myriad pleas and excuses not to make a strong case in favour of teaching and researching upon the subject, realizing fully well that its willful abandoning amounts to questioning the very foundation of anthropology, which is universally construed to be integrative and holistic. Suffice to mention here is that for no valid reason worth its name, anthropological linguistics is buried alive in India, although theories and methods in anthropology have relied heavily on linguistics, and anthropologists time and again look at theories and methods of linguistics for inspiration (cf. Lévi-Strauss 1963). It seems, therefore, pertinent to have a glance at the status of anthropological linguistics from the inception of anthropology in the West as well as in India, its contribution to the study of culture, and probable reasons for its demise in India while it is still considered an integral part of anthropology in rest of the world. Since there is no status or trend report available, as far as I know, on the origin, development and peril of anthropological linguistics in India, I would urge the readers to consider the contents of this paper purely as my personal reflections as a teacher of anthropology for the last three decades.

The debate on terminology

Before I proceed further, it is appropriate to resolve the terminological wrangles that have fraught anthropological linguistics from the middle of the 1960s. Although the study of native languages had a significant presence in anthropology by the beginning of the twentieth century, which was evidenced from the title of Franz Boas' *magnum opus*, *Handbook of American Indian Languages* (1911), the status of language study in anthropology was still ambiguous. This was despite the fact that linguistics in anthropology was considered as a means to other anthropological ends, practical or theoretical, or both. By the middle of the last century, anthropological linguistics had many synonyms, such as "Linguistic Anthropology", "Ethno-linguistics", "Linguistics in Anthropology", "Sociolinguistics", etc. With the inauguration of the journal of *Anthropological Linguistics* in 1959, the debate began with the title of the journal itself. It was said that

> ... there was no such field. There is linguistics, there is linguistics in anthropology, and there is linguistic anthropology, but if we wish our terms to have unambiguous and pertinent reference, there is no anthropological linguistics (Teeter 1964: 878).

Teeter further asserted that

> Four probable interpretations for the proposed name come to mind, the first redundant, the second tendentious, the third unduly restrictive, and the fourth illogical (loc.cit).

He was of the opinion that anthropological linguistics implied "... *all* of linguistics as studied by the anthropologist", and therefore, in all fairness, was "Linguistics in Anthropology" or "Linguistic Anthropology", and not "Anthropological Linguistics", which for him was a distinctive *part* of Linguistics, and "... is both a chameleon and a chimera" (*ibid:* 879). Hymes reacted to Teeter's reservations with a focus on the paradigmatic structure of the problem and viability of anthropological linguistics in a limited sense (1966: 143-153). However, both of them agreed that linguistic anthropology was a preferable term than anthropological linguistics, given its scope and applicability.

The debate did not end there. It rather resurfaced when some believed that anthropological linguistics was strongly rooted in linguistics, while others asserted that

> Linguistics is an *cffshoot* of Anthropological Linguistics. It emerged as a separate discipline so as to meet challenges of studying the language in its total structure, bringing out its phonological,

> morphological, syntactic and semantic significance, the purpose being to progressively develop oral cultures as written cultures (Bayer 2005; emphasis added).

For example, Foley (2000) claimed that

> ... anthropological linguistics views language through the prism of the core anthropological concept, culture, and, as such, seeks to uncover the meaning behind the use, misuse, or non-use of language, its different forms, registers and styles.

Contrarily, linguistic anthropology was often construed by many others as a sub-field of anthropology influenced by folk and performance studies, literacy and education, cognitive science, interactional sociology, social cognition, and child language acquisition. It studies language as a cultural resource and speaking as a cultural practice, thereby recognizing speakers as social agents who make their world.

My intention here is not to get entangled in futile terminological debates. I would rather consider anthropological linguistics as an integral branch of anthropology that helps to understand culture with the language and speech, no matter who is engaged in it—an anthropologist or a linguist. What is important for me is the praxis or application of the subject in cultural analysis (and by implication in anthropology), rather than whether or not it is a branch of linguistics or anthropology. I tend to agree with Duranti (1997) who considers:

> ... language as a set of practices, which play an essential role in mediating the ideational and material aspects of human existence, and, hence, in bringing about particular ways of being-in-the-world...; a powerful tool in everyday practice, and not a mirror of social realities established elsewhere.

I also agree with him that central to linguistic anthropology is *performance*, *indexicality* and *participation*.

This 'spurious' dichotomy between the terms used can easily be understood when we look at the early contributors to anthropological linguistics. In fact, a linguist like Sapir, whose early training was primarily in Germanic, was deeply induced by Boasian anthropology and had contributed so much to language and culture that the distinction between linguistics and anthropology was literally blurred in his teaching and research. This blurring is also revealed from the titles of some of the textbooks published in the recent past that fundamentally deal with the interface between language and culture. While many authors have named their textbooks on the subject as *Linguistic Anthropology* (Duranti 1976 and 2004; Hickerson 1980), others have named them as *Anthropological Linguistics* (Foley 2000; Greenberg 1968; Misra 2000), thus relegating the war on terminology to the background.

It is well-known to the anthropological fraternity in India that both British and American Anthropology had a direct influence on the trajectory of development of the discipline in this country. But in some areas this impact was discreet, as in the case of anthropological linguistics. While studies on tribes, castes, peasants, cities and civilizations were modeled after the pioneering works of American and British anthropologists, the prominent casualty was anthropological linguistics. It is a bizarre reality that while anthropological linguistics is one of the four major branches of anthropology in the U.S.A. and an essential component of cultural anthropology, it has not impacted much on the course of development of anthropology in India. The situation is not much different in case of the departments of linguistics, where the thrust was on the structure of language, and either no attention was paid to anthropological linguistics or it was equated with the study of tribal languages and dialects. Before I proceed to examine the status of anthropological linguistics in India, it is pertinent to have a glance over its development in the U.S.A. and Britain that had profound impact on Indian anthropology in its formative period (Vidyarthi and Rai 1976).

Language in Boasian anthropology and after

It is not my intention in this section to attempt an elaborate review of the history of anthropological linguistics in the U.S.A. and Britain, which has been done earlier by many (cf. Ardener 1971; Duranti 1997, 2001 and 2004; Foley 1997; Beeman 1997). I would rather present a sketchy picture to show how anthropological linguistics occupied the centrestage in anthropology, how its significance was underscored in cultural studies by the founders of anthropology, and how the trend of research in the subject became vigorous over the years drawing theories and methods from linguistics, psychology, sociology, cognitive science, etc., whereas nothing of the sort happened either in Indian anthropology or linguistics.

Although Franz Boas formally introduced linguistics into anthropology in the U.S.A. as a part of the "four field approach", intellectual interest in Native American languages goes back to the early periods of its colonization. The founder of the Rhode Island, Roger Williams, seems to have compiled a small dictionary of Narragansett (Beeman 1997) much before the formal introduction of linguistics in Boasian anthropology. In the nineteenth century, the Smithsonian Institution and the Bureau of American Ethnology (BAE) supported a large number of studies on grammar, dictionaries and compilation of folklore of the Native Indians as a commitment of the U.S. government for its tribal people, which apparently evoked tremendous intellectual interest in linguistic study and research.

Boas' study of Inuit culture and language in the Arctic had as much lasting impact on his passion for linguistic research as for his anti-evolutionary theoretical proposition of 'historical particularism'. His introduction to *Handbook of American Indian Languages* (1911) was against the contemporary popular notion that there was necessary correlation between language, culture and race. He maintained that each culture followed an independent path of development as it adapted to a given physical and social environment. And this holds good for language as well. Eventually, Boas suggested the doctrine of 'linguistic relativism', which meant that "... no human language can be seen as superior to any other in terms of its ability to meet human needs" (*ibid.*). His emphasis was to counter the stereotype that Indian languages were 'primitive' ones when compared with non-tribal languages. As Hass aptly summarized:

> ... Boas's most important theoretical contribution to the study of linguistics was his promulgation of the concept of linguistic relativism, that is, that each language had to be studied in and for itself. It was not to be forced into a mold that was more appropriate to some other language. Side by side with this was his insistence on seeing the language as a whole (Haas 1978).

It was also Boas' conviction that human cognition could be studied by analyzing linguistic information elicited from the native speakers. This exercise helped in model building on the functioning of language, about which the native speaker was usually unaware. Boas (1911) maintained that

> we must insist that a command of the language is an indispensable means of obtaining accurate and thorough knowledge, because much information can be gained by listening to conversations of the natives and by taking part in their daily life, which, to the observer who has no command of the language, will remain entirely inaccessible.

Boas' emphasis on the study of language in anthropology was carried forward by Edward Sapir to new heights. Sapir, in all fairness, had a wide-ranging interest in anthropological linguistics that included language and gender, historical linguistics, psycholinguistics and the study of Native American languages. And yet, he did not drift from Boas' basic position of linguistic relativism. His ideas largely matched with that of the German linguist, Wilhelm von Humboldt, who held that each language was conceptually *sui generis*. While endorsing this view, Sapir (1964) held that

> Language is not merely a more or less systematic inventory of the various items of experience which seem relevant to the individual, as is so often naïvely assumed, but is also a self-contained, creative symbolic organization, which not only refers to experience largely acquired without its help but actually defines experience for us by reason of its formal completeness and because of our unconscious projection of its implicit expectations into the field of experience.

Perhaps his most outstanding contribution was his conceptualization that language served as a filter through which the world was constructed for purposes of communication, which was carried forward by his student Benjamin Lee Whorf, and was later popularized as "Sapir-Whorf Hypothesis" by Harry Hoijer. From his study among the Hopi Indians, Whorf contended that "Grammatical Structures were seen not just as tools for describing the world, they were seen as templates for thought itself" (Beeman 1997). His comparison of the conceptualization of time in Hopi and Standard Average European (SAE) languages and wrong inferences drawn from the English words such as "*empty* gasoline drums" and "spun *limestone*" became popular examples among the students of anthropological linguistics and reinforced his contention on the relationship between language and thought (Misra 2000).

Sapir's idea of linguistic relativity was further corroborated by Whorf in his own characteristic fashion and was articulated in the distinction between the overt and covert grammatical categories of various languages (Carroll 1956). For example, while in Spanish, gender is an overt category, in English it is largely a covert category and made explicit in specific circumstances. Duranti (2001) is of the view that this distinction is a precursor to Chomsky's much acclaimed distinction between 'surface' and 'deep' structures of language.

The foundation laid by Sapir and Whorf that language as the symbolic guide to culture and thought was loosely adopted by the proponents of cognitive anthropology or ethno-science in the late 1950s and early 1960s. The study of colour categories by Conklin, diseases and their classification by Frake, componential analysis of kinship by Goodenough, ethno-biological classifications of Berlin, etc. emphasized without any ambiguity that people's logic of categorization of cultural phenomena is the key to the understanding of cognitive processes underlying their cultural behaviour. I have elsewhere called it as the use of linguistic epistemology in cultural analysis (Misra 2000).

With the publication of Chomsky's revolutionary work, *Syntactic Structures*, in 1957, the focus of linguistic studies shifted from descriptive study of phonology and morphology to the study of syntax as the principal formal structure of language. The Transformational-Generative (T/G) Grammar provided the basic paradigm for the formal linguists, whose primary focus was the exploration of language structures. The practice of fieldwork was almost abandoned by the formal linguists, who considered linguistics as a mental phenomenon, an innate human capacity, and thus a branch of cognitive science under the most influential direction of Chomsky (Beeman 1997). Contrarily, around this time anthropological linguistics turned its attention to the study of language use in social and cultural context. At this juncture, anthropological linguistics diversified into the study of primate language abilities, sign languages, non-verbal communication, behavioural origin of human speech, and so on, in the writings of Charles Hockett, Philip Lieberman, among others.

When Chomsky was looking at language ability from a mentalistic perspective and as a human universal capacity, it was Dell Hymes, who turned his attention essentially to the diversity with regard to how language was used in social life. "Instead of ignoring differences for the sake of creating a homogeneity that can be more easily accessed through a scientific method, Hymes assumed that an anthropological programme for the study of language must start from the assumption of heterogeneity" (Duranti 1997). "Ethnography of Speaking" was thus born as "a theory of speech ... a system of cultural behaviour; a system not necessarily exotic, but necessarily concerned with the organization of diversity" (Hymes 1971). Hymes' diversity proposition was lent tremendous support in the writings of Labov, who demonstrated that even within the monolingual communities, linguistic variation is an inescapable feature which is due to social stratification (Labov 1966). Gumperz's (1968) notions of 'repertoire' and 'speech community' further corroborated Hymes' diversity *mantra* by pointing out how the speakers routinely switch their speech within a range of linguistic varieties that include language, dialect, style, and register.

Anthropological linguistics in the U.S.A. in the last two decades and a half has diversified enormously with an emphasis on interdisciplinarity to study highly complex linguistic behaviours in many different contexts. The contextuality of language production has gone beyond the conventional units of analysis of word or sentence to include speech community, speech events, speech acts as well as the notions of registry and variety (Duranti 2001). It has moved far beyond the earlier framework to taking up questions like discourses; linguistic nationalism; language policies and politics; ethnopoetics; linguistic construction of social categories such as race, class, gender, personhood and status; space in language and cognition; music and language; different genres of language such as ritual languages, metaphors and verbal art including oration, narration and theatrical performance; induced language and linguistic engineering; etc.

Language study in British anthropology

During its formative years, anthropological linguistics in Britain was not given as much importance as it was given in the U.S.A. Hension (1971), while analyzing the history of linguistic research in early British anthropology from 1850 to 1920, notes that

> In contrast to the American or the French approach, very few British anthropologists considered that language required study in its own right within the bounds of their discipline. With the exception of Müller, who from his half-century of teaching in Oxford falls here into the British context, they merely used it as *supplementary evidence* to support and extend theories developed within anthropology. Language was indeed such a peripheral interest that very few ideas evolved any further at the end of the period... (italics added).

Nevertheless British anthropology had taken on itself the study of racial and linguistic distribution all over the world and was keen on establishing relationship between race and language. At this juncture, British anthropology was influenced by the comparative linguists, who proposed that there existed a positive correlation between language and race, until E.B.Tylor (1881) pointed out that the equation between language and race was false, as evidences were rife that people of one race spoke many different languages and same language was spoken by different racial groups.

The significance of language study in British anthropology gained momentum with the assertion of Malinowski on the complimentarity between ethnography and linguistics. In fact, Malinowski asserted, "Linguistics without ethnography would fare as badly as ethnography would without the light thrown on it by language." True to his conviction, Malinowski had written a long essay on language, and particularly, translation of magical formulae, in his *Coral Gardens and their Magic*.

> Magic formulas cannot really be translated, he maintains. They have no comprehensible semantic content. They do, however, accomplish cultural work within Trobriand society. They are therefore functionally situated. In order to 'translate' such material, the ethnographer must provide a complete explanatory contextualization for the material. Otherwise it can make no sense (Beeman 1997).

This brand of functional theory of language had drawn the attention of very few committed scholars in Britain like J.R. Firth and Edwin Ardener. Edwin Ardener's edited title, *Social Anthropology and Language*, although published way back in 1971, is still considered as an excellent source book for the beginners of anthropological linguistics in British universities.

Although the study of language was never at the centrestage of British social anthropology, the contributions of Parkin (1984), Grillo (1989), Bloch (1975, 1998), Finnegan (2002) to anthropological linguistics cannot be wished away.

Dell Hyme's articulations of the relationship between linguistics and ethnography had an influential impact on British anthropologists in the 1970s and early 1980s, resulting in academic collaboration between North American and British scholars (e.g. Gumperz and Roberts, Heath and Street, Hymes and Bernstein, and Heller and Martin-Jones). This was the time when the United Kingdom Linguistic Ethnography Forum (LEF) was formally launched with the prime assumption that language and the social world are mutually shaping, and that close analysis of situated language use can provide both fundamental and distinctive insights into the mechanisms and dynamics of social and cultural production in everyday activity. Therefore, even now American empiricism provides an important model for British work, and the ongoing production of rich and sophisticated conceptual frameworks in North American linguistic anthropology continues to be an invaluable analytic resource (cf. Duranti 2001). During the 1990s the United Kingdom witnessed further consolidation of language studies with various brand names without, of course, much of it being a part of the departments of social anthropology. Under the overarching British Association of Applied Linguistics (BAAL) the movement took off with the contributions from many different intellectual genres such as New Literacy Studies, Interactional Sociolinguistics, Critical Discourse Analysis, Interpretive Applied Linguistics, and so on.

Indian anthropology and the study of Language

The pre-Independence scenario

Although Saraswati (1993) has forcefully claimed that our Smritis and Dharma Shastras, dating back to the pre-Christian era, were perhaps the most ancient texts in anthropology ever produced on earth, academic anthropology was undoubtedly the product of European expansion over the world during the last three or four centuries (Srinivas 2002). When the British administration had firmly rooted itself in India by the middle of the eighteenth century, there was a felt need to understand the cultures and customs of the native subjects for better administration by the colonial government. As a result of this, in 1769 A.D., Henry Verelst, the then Governor of Bengal and Bihar stressed the need to study customs of leading families by the revenue supervisors (*ibid.*). To further illustrate this tendentious move, Mahapatra (2006) writes that "As early as 1807, the Court of Directors of The East India Company made a formal decision to acquire anthropological information on India, as 'such knowledge would be of great use in the future administration of the country' (Roy 1921)". Francis Buchanan was appointed by the Governor-General in Council to undertake an ethnographic survey to enquire into the conditions of the inhabitants of Bengal and their religion (Buchanan 1820). In pursuit of this policy of The East India Company, the British government of India sponsored many anthropological/ ethnographic regional studies. E.T. Dalton (1872), H.H. Risley (1891), Edgar Thurston (1909), R.V. Russell and others undertook regional studies in eastern and northeastern India, Bengal Presidency, Madras Presidency (which covered the major part of South India), [and] Central Provinces of India. These were preceded by Abbe Dubois' *Hindu Manners, Customs and Ceremonies* and Walter Hamilton's multi-volume gazetteers, *A Geographical, Statistical and Historical Description of Hindostan and Adjacent Countries* (Srinivas 2002). This was the foundational phase of the development of anthropology in India, roughly spanning from the 1770s until the early twentieth century. While Majumdar (1950) names this as the 'formulatory' phase of Indian anthropology, Vidyarthi and Rai (1976) prefer to call it 'formative', and in Srinivas' (2002) terms, it was the time when the foundation of Indian anthropology was laid. As said earlier, the primary focus of this phase was to study and understand cultures and customs of the Indian population. These studies made occasional reference to the languages and dialects of the people they studied, without probing into the intricacies of the relationship between language and culture.

When the first department of anthropology was established in 1920 at Calcutta University, the research agenda of the department confirmed more or less to the colonial tradition of writing ethnography on caste and tribes of India. This trend is clearly visible in L.K. Anantha Krishna Iyer's ethnography on Mysore and Cochin Castes and Tribes, and on the Syrian Christians of Kerala. Around the same time, S.C. Roy was writing exhaustive monographs on the tribes of India, such as the Munda (1912), the Oraon (1915), the Birhor (1925), *Oraon Religion and Customs* (1928), Hill Bhuiyas (1935) and the Kharia (1937), not much different from the British-oriented descriptive tradition. It was but natural that in the early twentieth century, W.H.R. Rivers' monograph on the Toda (1906), Seligman and Seligman's on the Veddas of Sri Lanka (1911), Radcliffe-Brown's on the Andaman Islanders (1922), Hutton's ethnographic notes (1931) were considered as profound exemplars for the Indian anthropologists to orient their anthropology to describe the cultures of Indian tribes and castes.

> Anthropologists like P.N. Mishra, ... K.P. Chhatopadhyay, T.C.Das, D.N. Majumdar in the east and north India, and G.S. Ghurye, Irawati Karve, L.K. Anantha Krishna Iyer and A. Aiyappan in the western and southern India provided the initial stimulus to organize scientific anthropological researches by conducting field expeditions, writing books and articles and by training researchers for anthropological researches on tribal and rural cultures (Vidyarthi and Rai 1976).

Since two founding fathers of Indian anthropology—K.P. Chattopadhyay and G.S. Ghurye—were students of W. H. R. Rivers, the ethnographic tradition was perpetuated in its early years.

It will not be fair to conclude hastily that Indian anthropologists during this time were only following the imperial strategy of collecting the bulk of ethnographic materials on Indian castes and communities for use in the administration, they were also sensitive to what was happening around them. For example, S.C. Roy wrote in 1912 that

> with the opening up of the country by roads and railways under the British rule and the gradual deforestation of the country and even the increasing restrictions on the use of forest, these forest tribes (the Birhor and the Korwa) are slowly but surely dying out partly from famine and partly from loss of interest in life (quoted in Mahapatra 2006).

Similarly, T.C. Das' publication of *Bengal Famine* of 1943 was a radical critique of the Denial Policy of the colonial government that was discussed in the British Parliament and forced the imperial government to appoint a fact-finding committee to initiate corrective measures (*ibid.*).

Reverting back to our main concern of the study of language in Indian anthropology, it is not hard to find the lack of spark in this direction amidst extensive ethnography of castes and tribes, despite the fact that the foundation of modern linguistics was laid in India in 1786. Of course, India had the rare distinction of nurturing high intellectual linguistic tradition even in the pre-Christian era. The Sanskrit grammar of Panini, dating back to the fifth century B.C., consisting of nearly 4000 aphorisms divided into eight chapters, was a fully formulated system of Sanskrit grammar, Panini himself standing at the end of a long line of precursors of which 64 are named but whose works have entirely perished (Misra 2000).

On 2 February 1786, to be precise, modern linguistics was born on Indian soil, when the British judge and an ardent student of Asian languages, Sir William Jones, in his address to the Asiatic Society of Bengal at Calcutta said,

> The Sanskrit language whatever be its antiquity, is of a wonderful structure; more perfect than the Greek, more copious than the Latin, and more exquisitely refined then either, yet bearing to both of them a stronger affinity, both in the roots of verbs and in the forms of grammar, than could possibly have been produced by accident; so strong, indeed, that no philosopher could examine them all three, without believing them to have sprung from some common source, which, perhaps, no longer exists.

Jones outlined the family tree model of linguistic relationships, which could be termed as historical linguistics or comparative philology, focusing on the Indo-European language family. Within a generation comparative philology established itself as a discipline. Scholars such as Jacob Grimm, Franz Bopp, August Schleicher, etc., reconstructed the Proto-Indo-European lexicon. Eventually, other language families, such as Sino-Tibetan and Hamito-Semitic also began to be studied from this perspective. Franz Boas was perhaps inspired by this trend and in addition to his ethnographic research used comparative method to the study of Native American languages.

The observations of Sir William Jones on the significance of Sanskrit language notwithstanding, the British East India

Company purported to promote English in India with the argument that it was a country rife with internal dissensions and devoid of any semblance of homogeneity in its culture, language or polity. In 1835, a young British officer in India, Thomas Babington Macaulay (later Lord Macaulay) strongly advocated to teach English (instead of local Indian languages) and European science and technology in public schools that were supported by the government. He said,

> We have to educate a people who cannot at present be educated by means of their mother-tongue. We must teach them some foreign language.

Lord Macaulay further argued,

> The question now before us is simply whether, when it is in our power to teach this language, we shall teach languages in which, by universal confession, there are no books on any subject which deserve to be compared to our own. ... All the declamations in the world about the love and reverence of the natives for their sacred dialects will never, in the mind of any impartial person, outweigh the undisputed fact that we cannot fine [sic. find], in all our vast expire, a single student who will let us teach him those dialects unless we will pay him....Why then is it necessary to pay people to learn Sanscrit and Arabic? Evidently because it is universally felt that the Sanscrit and Arabic are languages, the knowledge of which does not compensate for the trouble of acquiring them. On all such subjects the state of the market is the decisive test (Hay and Quereshi 1958: 46-48; quoted in Rangila, Thirumalai and Mallikarjun 2001).

Despite Macaulay's passion towards English language and English education in public schools in India, in conjunction with ethnographic survey, the Linguistic Survey of India was started in 1896 with Grierson as its in-charge. The mandate of the Survey was to codify the native languages/dialects spoken in India that resulted in a multi-volume series on Indian languages. The Census of India also contributed to recording the local languages/dialects as a part of its decennial exercises from the nineteenth century. Although language census was not included in the 1870 Census of India, subsequent Censuses began collecting information on language, using different terms like 'mother-tongue', 'parent-tongue', 'language ordinarily used', 'language ordinarily spoken in the household', etc. Padmanabha (1978), the former Registrar-General of Census of India, however, contends that

> ... this lack of uniformity in concepts did not vitiate the data on language as is evidenced from the language returns in the successive censuses which show fair consistency.

Although it was strictly not anthropological linguistics *per se*, research on many local Indian languages, including tribal languages, in the late nineteenth century India continued both by the scholar-administrators and missionaries. There was a movement of a sort to compile and edit tribal language dictionaries to meet the needs of the contemporary and future researchers and linguists. Besides Grierson's multi-volume *Linguistic Survey of India* (1906), P.O. Bodding's *Santali Dictionary* (1929-36), Rev. E.W. Clark's *Ao Naga Dictionary* (1911), Alexander Campbell's *Santali-English Dictionary* (1899-1902), R. H. S. Hutchnison's Lushai language vocabulary (1897), A. Nottrott's grammar of the Kol language (1903), E.G. Phillip's outlines of Garo language (1904), A. Mcdonald and M.G. Momin's Garo-English dictionary (1910), G.B. Mainwaring's Lepcha dictionary (1898), Edward H. Man's dictionary of the central Nicobarese language (1889), Nissor Singh's Khasi-English dictionary (1906), etc., are indicative of the early interest in studying tribal languages in India. But it failed to provoke enough interest among the teachers and young scholars in the teaching departments of anthropology to pursue language studies. Some of the early students of Calcutta University department of anthropology recall that linguistic anthropology was never a part of their syllabus. This is notwithstanding the fact that most of the early monographs mentioned in passing in their introductory chapters the language family to which the tribe/community studied belonged to without further elaborating on it.

The post-Independence scenario

Indian anthropology in the post-Independence period responded vigorously both to the theoretical trends in American and British anthropology as well as to the developmental concerns within the country. Kathleen Gough's Tanjore village study, F.G. Bailey's land, caste and mobility study, Scarlett Epstein's Mysore village study, David Mandelbaum's Indian society, Louis Dumont's study on caste, A.C. Mayer's analysis of kin, caste and village, etc., heavily influenced many Indian anthropologists like Surajit Sinha, Satish Saberwal, R. S. Khare, L. P. Vidyarthi, T. N. Madan, André Béteille, among others. The elder generation of anthropologists, such as G. S. Ghurye, D. N. Majumdar, M. N. Srinivas, Irawati Karve, N. K. Bose, K. P. Chattopadhyay, T. C. Das, A. Aiyappan, continued to contribute to the diversification of Indian anthropology and provide it with a stable foundation to grow further. But admittedly, anthropological linguistics was relegated to oblivion, as there was little attempt to understand culture and social organization with the idiom of language and linguistic behaviour. This vacuum during, what Vidyarthi and Rai (1976) call the analytical period beginning with 1950, and what Srinivas and Panini (1973) name as the period of diversification, foreclosed the prospect of anthropological linguistics to grow in India. This is very clearly evidenced from the following reviews on the development of anthropology in India.

In 1962, Madan and Sarana edited a volume titled, *Indian Anthropology: Essays in Memory of D.N.Majumdar*, which contained 19 well-written essays by the students and associates of Majumdar, which portrayed contemporary research in the anthropology of India. Many renowned scholars, including Bailey, von Fürer-Haimendorf, Chattopadhyay, Karve, Ramakrishna Mukherjee, Dube, Mayer, etc., contributed to the volume. Out of the 19 essays, four were on prehistoric archaeology, seven on biological anthropology, eight on social and cultural anthropology, and none on anthropological linguistics. It was indicative of the lack of interest in the subject among the leading anthropologists of contemporary period.

From a review of the status of social-cultural anthropology in India by Sarana and Sinha (1976) in *Annual Review of Anthropology*, it is quite evident that anthropological linguistics had not drawn much of attention of the contemporary anthropologists. They write,

> Before detailing the background of contemporary anthropology in India, we should like to say a few words about the discipline in general. We have been invited to write on social-cultural anthropology, the study of man. But it is appropriate to state at the outset that social-cultural anthropology in India is a subdivision of anthropology in the sense that the term is understood in the English-speaking countries. The other two major subdivisions of anthropology are physical (biological) anthropology and prehistory or

> archaeological anthropology. In recent years, some institutions of higher learning and research have begun to teach linguistic anthropology as well (Sarana and Sinha 1976).

While Sarana was at Karnataka University, Dharwad, he had started teaching anthropological linguistics, and since then it has been a part of their curriculum. At Utkal University, Bhubaneswar, I was taught anthropological linguistics as a part of my specialization in social anthropology in the second year of the Master's programme. I am told that the subject is still being taught at Utkal University, but evidently without a strong research programme.

Sarana and Sinha have argued that anthropology in Indian universities is taught as an integrated discipline unlike in British universities. They hold the opinion that

> Curiously, although the first inspiration for both academic and nonacademic anthropology in India came from Great Britain, Indian anthropological teaching has not followed the British pattern. At present, full-fledged departments of anthropology, covering all branches of the discipline, are conspicuous by their absence in British universities. Most of the famous British universities have departments of social anthropology, not anthropology. But in India, beginning with Calcutta University, practically all the universities teach anthropology as an integrated discipline although there has been more emphasis on the development of social-cultural anthropology (*ibid.*).

The integrative anthropology that Sarana and Sinha talk about is evidently devoid of anthropological linguistics, barring a few, as indicated above. As Srivastava (2000) notes, except Punjabi University, Patiala, there is no other university in India that has a department of anthropological linguistics and there are only a handful of anthropology departments where anthropological linguistics is taught. At least in Britain linguistic ethnography is still alive, although in a low key, outside the departments of anthropology, whereas in India, anthropological linguistics is neither within nor outside the anthropology departments. The situation is getting further worsened day by day. I remember, I was teaching anthropological linguistics at the department of anthropology of the University of Hyderabad since 1989 as a 'core' course in alternate semesters until 1996, when it was relegated to an 'elective' status. In all our wisdom, the very idea of considering anthropological linguistics not as a core course in anthropology was the beginning of the end of the subject. It gained popularity, nevertheless, as an elective course, not only in the school of social sciences, but also in the school of humanities with the regular presence of students from the department of English language and literature with our own students. But there were fewer opportunities now to offer the course with the department prioritizing teaching the core courses rather than the electives.

Danda (1995) while reviewing the development of anthropology in India suggests that

> The integrated discipline of Anthropology consisted of three major sub-streams like Prehistoric Archaeology or Palaeo-anthropology, Physical Anthropology, and Social/Cultural Anthropology each having a number of sub-sub-streams specifying areas of their respective research operations.

Danda also prefers not to mention about anthropological linguistics, which was already a non-entity within the integrated framework of Indian anthropology. In his scheme, probably, it is a 'sub-sub-stream' in the domain of social/cultural anthropology. In a similar vein, in reviews by Sahay and Singh (1998), Hasnain (1991) and others on the development of anthropology in India, anthropological linguistics has not found any place.

With the demise of anthropological linguistics among the anthropologists in India, research institutions like Anthropological Survey of India (AnSI), Central Institute of Indian Languages (CIIL), Census of India, and the Tribal Research Institutes, which have trained linguists on their rolls, have been studying languages in general, and tribal languages in particular, no matter how feeble the attempt might seem. The language and grammar of the Nicobarese, Chenchu, Juang, Kharia, Lodha, Mal-Pahariya, Ghatoli-Pahariya, Thadou, Onge, Gade Lohari, Andamanese, Bhotia, etc., have been studied by the AnSI and published subsequently. Simultaneously, CIIL has consistently engaged itself in the study of the languages of tribal and indigenous people of India. Linguists from CIIL have conducted several field studies to collect data on tribal languages all over the country. Several grammars and bilingual dictionaries have been published and several others are either under preparation or in print. Its website lists 105 tribal languages that its researchers have studied. It also has studied 12 endangered languages in India that include the Andamanese, Bondo, Didayi, Jarawa, Kota, Kurukh, Onge, Sentinelese, Shompen, Singpho, Sulung and Toda. A bibliographical survey of resources in tribal languages was also published by two librarian colleagues, Ramaiah and Kanakachary (1990), enlisting the Austro-Asiatic, Dravidian, Indo-Aryan and Tibeto-Burman families of tribal languages in India for the benefit of the researchers. Shukla's (1985) socio-linguistic study of Bastar is an important contribution to tribal languages, where the author laments in his preface,

> It is a real pity that many Western linguists do not have India in their linguistic map, for they either forget or ignore completely India's contribution to grammar, phonology, and philology... Indian society will have much more to contribute in this regard, and we in India would welcome any sociolinguists interested in our activities and having a strong desire to cooperate with scholars in other parts of the world.

There is, however, no reason to lament on the lack of interest of the Western scholars, but certainly of our own scholars, who are very well trained to undertake such projects.

Among the Indian linguists, Anvita Abbi's (1997) edited volume, *Languages of Tribal and Indigenous Peoples of India: the Ethnic Space*, comprising 26 essays, sets out systematic descriptions of India's tribal and indigenous languages that not only constitute as many as five distinct language groupings: Andamanese, Austro-Asiatic, Dravidian, Indo-Aryan, and Tibeto-Burman, but also cover the vast geographical space: from the Himalayan ranges to the Bay of Bengal. Exploring the structures of these languages of India, the authors focus specially on language change, language demography, sociology of language, languages in contact, and social status of the indigenous speech communities in India. Many linguists and a few psycho-linguists have evidenced keen interest in the study of language policy vis-à-vis tribal languages in education (cf. Misra 2005), which are published in the journal, *Language in India* from time to time. In more recent times, attention of the concerned linguists is diverted towards the endangered languages with the formation of Foundation for Endangered Languages. At the end of the day one painfully finds that the versatility and spread of anthropological linguistics as a tool to understanding how language is used in concrete and culturally significant social encounters, its contribution to the study of human bio-cultural evolution and the development of writing, etc. are replaced by what we might loosely call applied anthropological linguistics and its bearing on language acquisition and education. There are, however, some very commendable exceptions such as Saraswati's (1982) ritual language, Krishna Nandan Prasad's (1990) bilingualism among the Ho, Goswami's (1981) speech distribution, Behera's (1998) linguistic adjustment, Ray and Tat's (2003) ritual language of the Bauls of Birbhum, Pande's (1983) analysis of kinship terms, and Roy Burman's (2004) study on non-verbal communication among the tribal people of India.

Although there is no recorded evidence to support my views on the demise of anthropological linguistics in India, I consider three factors most important from my own experience. The foremost among them is the pattern of composition of anthropology departments in British universities. Since not many established British anthropologists are engaged in language research with the result that linguistic ethnography is left to the linguists and others. In the Indian university system, being profoundly influenced by the British university system, it is but obvious that anthropological linguistics was not given its due in Indian higher education. Further, the influence of American anthropology on Indian scholars was mostly in the areas of village, caste and civilization studies, and many significant contributions like the study of speech variation by John Gumperz (1961) could not engage the attention of Indian anthropologists. Even the contributions of American scholars like Murray Emeneau, a former student of Sapir, on Dravidian linguistics, have a more profound influence on Indian linguists than anthropologists. In the process, Indian anthropologists could not seize the opportunity of being benefited from the experience and expertise of the American scholars.

The second important factor that I consider leading to the demise of the subject is the lack of incorporation of anthropological linguistics into the integrated anthropology curriculum during the formative years of anthropology departments in the country. As a result, many scholars either did not have or had a vague idea about the significance of anthropological linguistics in cultural studies. There was no strong research tradition in these departments of producing quality Ph.D. works on language as was in other areas of anthropology. Some of these scholars, who are now occupying the position of decision-makers at different levels, do not appreciate the idea that anthropological linguistics has enormous significance in the study of culture. Therefore, it is erroneously assumed that integrated anthropology in India has a tri-partite division rather than a four-fold one. The sub-discipline prejudice is so strong in Indian anthropology that division and re-integration of the departments have become a common feature of the history of anthropology departments in India, and the scholars opine that when three sub-disciplines have become unmanageable, why to encourage a fourth one. Srivastava (1999, 2000) in his review notes that many departments are single sub-discipline departments, and where all three are present by historical accident, one is always dominant, leading to bitterness and heart-burning.

The third factor, to my mind, is an insidious impression among many anthropologists regarding the efficacy of anthropological linguistics. It is not uncommon that anthropologists in India have started leaning heavily towards many populist themes these days that attract better funding and to ensure better employability in the 'development' sector. I do not say that these are irrelevant, but I do not remember coming across a good Ph.D. thesis on kinship or language as on reproductive and child health or ethno-medicine or assessment of NGO activities or self-help groups. This trend is a reflection of our changing pedagogy. It should be realized that we live in a multi-cultural and multi-linguistic country and we have an urgent task before us of understanding particular social-cultural phenomena and the uniqueness of human thought through the prism of language that the people use. This has also enormous potential in policy making in the fields of education, law, insurance, etc. (cf. Misra 2000, 2005).

Epilogue

Anthropologists are well aware that languages embody the history and traditions of people and researches reveal that from rural Australia to Siberia to the U.S.A. to South Asia languages are dying. It is said while there are about 7000 languages spoken around the world today, one of them dies out every two weeks (*The Hindu*, 2007). There is no disagreement to the conviction of K. David Harrison that

> when we lose a language, we lose centuries of human thinking about time, seasons, sea creatures, reindeer, edible flowers, mathematics, landscapes, myths, music, the unknown and the everyday (*ibid.*).

The study of speech communities, communicative competence, verbal arts, greetings, language acquisition, linkage between habitual thought and language, gender and language, contact languages, code-switching, multilingualism, sign languages, gesture and literary practices, language and identity, language and religion, language and social inequalities, language ideology, and many other domains lead to our understanding that language is undoubtedly one of the very powerful tools in understanding the intricacies of culture and social activities. But the question remains who can better study these domains than an anthropologist with his rich exposure to the culture under question. Once Sapir had aptly remarked,

> ... the attempt to master a primitive culture without the help of the language of its society will seem as amateurish as the labours of a historian, who cannot handle the original documents of the civilizations which he is describing.

Many might think that anthropological linguistics caters merely to the needs of social and cultural anthropology. But the interface between physical anthropology and language is equally strong as it is between culture and language. Researches in physical anthropology have already demonstrated how physiological adaptation during the process of hominization has eventually made humans capable of speaking (cf. Misra 2000). Besides, there are suggestions that genetics may have a bearing on speech production and speech variation (Luchsinger 1940; Tarnoczy 1947; Darlington 1947; etc. in *ibid.*). Even prehistoric archaeology is a definite facilitator of the study of historical linguistics or comparative philology to a considerable extent. The archaeological finds may be used to study the processes of divergence and convergence of languages. On the other hand, language provides authentic evidence for the reconstruction of cultural history of civilizations and the processes of diffusion and integration. I think, techniques like glottochronology and lexicostatistics can reveal the approximate age at which two or more languages and cultures separated from a common stock (*ibid.*).

Therefore, anthropological linguistics, I believe, can truly integrate otherwise disparate branches of anthropology, thus transforming it into a holistic science of the humans. It can also integrate linguistics with sociology, psychology, cognitive science and other cognate disciplines, as it is trans-disciplinary in nature. What seems urgent to me is to sensitize the anthropology fraternity, particularly the younger generation, about the efficacy of the subject. It has already taken root in the West, and hence, Duranti notes that

> In contrast to earlier generations of students who started from a fascination with linguistic forms and languages... or from their use in concrete and culturally significant social encounters..., students today typically ask questions such as 'What can the study of language contribute to the understanding of this particular social/ cultural phenomenon (e.g. identity formation, globalisation, nationalism)? The formulation of this type of question conceives of language no longer as the primary object of inquiry but as an instrument for gaining access to complex social processes... for many young scholars today linguistic anthropology is a tool for studying what is *already* being studied by scholars in other fields (2003).

I have little doubt in my mind that if anthropological linguistics could be revived from its state of peril and practiced in right earnest would definitely contribute to the processes of reintegration of anthropology as a holistic discipline and forge an unwavering link between all those disciplines that are committed to the study of human societies and cultures.

REFERENCES

Abbi, Anvita (ed.)

1996 — *Languages of Tribal and Indigenous Peoples of India: The Ethnic Space*. Delhi: Motilal Banarasidass Publishers Pvt. Ltd.

Ardener, Edwin (ed.)

1971 — *Social Anthropology and Language*. London: Tavistock.

Bayer, Jennifer Marie

2005 'Missing links–From research to development', *Language in India* 5, May.

Beeman, William O.

1997 'Linguistics and Anthropology'. In Thomas Barfield (ed.), *Blackwell's Dictionary of Anthropology*. London: Blackwell.

Behera, D. K.

1998 'Linguistic adjustment of Telugu speaking immigrants in Western Orissa', *Man in India* 78 (1&2): 27-43.

Bloch, Maurice

1975 *Political Language and Oratory in Traditional Society*. London: Academic Press.

Bloch, Maurice

1998 *How We Think They Think*. Colorado: Westview Press.

Boas, Franz

1911 *Handbook of American Indian Languages*. Bureau of American Ethnology, 40, Part I.

Bodding, Paul Oleff

1929-36 *A Santhali Dictionary*. Oslo: Kommisjon Hos Jacob Dybwad.

Campbell, Alexander

1899-1902 *A Santhali-English and English-Santhali Dictionary*. Pokhuria: The Santhal Mission Press in three parts, Part-I, 1899, Part-II 1900 and Part-III 1902.

Carroll, J.B. (ed.)

1956 *Language, Thought and Reality: Selected Writings of Benjamin Lee Whorf*. Cambridge, MA: MIT Press.

Clark, Rev. E. W.

1911 *Ao Naga Dictionary*. Calcutta: Baptist Mission Press.

Danda, A. K.

1995 *Foundations of Anthropology: India*. New Delhi: Inter-India Publications.

Duranti, Alessandro

1997 *Linguistic Anthropology*. Cambridge: Cambridge University Press.

Duranti, Alessandro (ed.)

2001 *Linguistic Anthropology: A Reader*. Malden, MA: Blackwell Publishers.

Duranti, Alessandro

2003 'Language as culture in U.S. anthropology', *Current Anthropology* 44 (3): 323-335.

Duranti, Alessandro (ed.)

2004 *A Companion to Linguistic Anthropology*. Malden, MA: Blackwell Publishers.

Finnegan, R.

2002 *Communicating: The Multiple Modes of Human Interconnection*. London: Routledge.

Foley, W.A.

2000 *Anthropological Linguistics: An Introduction*. Cambridge: Cambridge University Press.

Greenberg, Joseph, H.

1968 *Anthropological Linguistics: An Introduction*. New York: Random House.

Grillo, R. (ed.)

1989 *Social Anthropology and the Politics of Language*. London: Routledge.

Goswami, B. B.

1981 'A preliminary note on speech distribution of Lakher', *Man in India* 61(3): 289-292.

Gumperz, J. J.

1968 'The Speech Community'. *International Encyclopaedia of the Social Sciences*: 381-386, New York: Macmillan.

Haas, M. R.

1978 'Boas, Sapir and Bloomfield: Their contribution to American Indian linguistics'. In Mary R. Hass, Selected and Introduced by Anwar S. Dil, *Language, Culture, and History: Essays* (pp. 194-206). Stanford, CA: Stanford University Press.

Hasnain, Nadeem

1991 *Readings in Indian Anthropology*. New Delhi: Harnam Publications.

Henson, Hilary

1971 'Early British anthropologists and language'. In E. Ardener (ed.), *Social Anthropology and Language*: 3-33. London: Tavistock.

Hickerson, N. P.

1980 *Linguistic Anthropology*. New York: Holt, Rinehart and Winston.

(The) Hindu

2007 'Global hotspots of endangered languages'. Thursday, September 20:26.

Hutchinson, Robert Henry Snyed

1897 *Vocabulary of the Lushai Language*. Calcutta, Bengal Secretariat Press.

Hutton, J. H.

1931 *Census of India*, Vol.I. Simla: Government of India Press.

Hymes, Dell

1966 'On "Anthropological Linguistics" and congeners', *American Anthropologist* 68 (1): 143-153.

1971 'Sociolinguistics and the ethnography of speaking'. In E. Ardener (ed.), *Social Anthropology and Language*: 47-93. London: Tavistock.

Labov, W.

1966 *The Social Stratification of English in New York City*. Arlington: Centre for Applied Linguistics.

Lévi-Strauss, C.

1963 *Structural Anthropology*. New York: Basic Books.

Lieberman, Philip

1984 *The Biology and Evolution of Language*. Cambridge: Harvard University Press.

Madan, T.N. and Gopala Sarana (eds.)

1962 *Indian Anthropology: Essays in Memory of D.N.Majumdar*. Bombay: Asia Publishing House.

Mahapatra, L. K.

2006 'Anthropology in policy and practice in India'. In Carole E. Hill and Marietta L. Baba (eds.), *The Globalization of Anthropology*. Berkeley: National Association for Practice of Anthropology, University of California Press.

Mainwaring, George Byres

1898 *Dictionary of the Lepcha Language*. Berlin, Unger Print.

Majumdar, D. N.

1950 *The Affairs of a Tribe: A Study in Tribal Dynamics*. Lucknow: Universal Publishers Ltd.

Man, Edward Horace

1889 *Dictionary of the Central Nicobarese Language*. London, W.H. Allen.

Manoharan, S.

1980 'Language of the present Great Andamanese', *Journal of the Indian Anthropological Society* 15 (1): 43-55.

Misra, Kamal K.

2000 *Text Book of Anthropological Linguistics*. New Delhi: Concept.

2005 'Future of Tribal Languages and Scripts in India'. Paper presented at the National Conference on Tribal Situation in Contemporary India, Department of Anthropology, University of Delhi, 28-30 March.

Padmanabha, P.

1978 'Indian Census and anthropological investigations'. Paper prepared for the X International Congress of Anthropological and Ethnological Sciences, New Delhi.

Pande, S. V.

1983 *A Socio-Linguistic Analysis of Kinship Terms in a Polyandrous Society*.

Parkin, D.

1984 'Political language', *Annual Review of Anthropology*: 345-84.

Prasad, K. N.

1990 Incidence of Bilingualism among the Ho Tribe of Chotanagpur. *Man in India*, 70(2), 155-168.

Ray, Manas and Suparna Tat

2003 'A study on the nature and structure of ritual language of the Bauls of Birbhum, West Bengal', *Man and Life* 29 (3&4): 117-138.

Rivers, W. H. R.

1906 *The Todas*. London: Macmillan & Co.

Radcliffe-Brown, A. R.

1922 *The Andaman Islanders: A Study in Social Anthropology*. Cambridge University Press and Glenco, Ill: The Free Press.

Ramaiah, L. S. and M. Kanakachary

1990 *Tribal Linguistics in India: A Bibliographical Survey of International Resources*. Madras: T.R.Publications Private Ltd.

Rangilla, R. S., M. S. Thirumalai and B. Mallikarjun

2001 'Bringing Order to Linguistic Diversity: Language Planning in the British Raj', *Language in India* 1 (6), October.

Roy, S. C.

1912 *Mundas and their Country*. Calcutta: City Book Society.

1915 *The Oraons of Chotanagpur*. Ranchi: Bar Library.

1925 *The Birhor, A Little Known Jungle Tribe of Chotanagpur*. Ranchi: Man in India Office.

1928 *Oraon Religion and Customs*. Ranchi: Man in India Office.

1935 *The Hill Bhuiyas of Orissa*. Ranchi: Man in India Office.

1937 *The Kharia*. Volumes I and II (with R.C.Roy), Ranchi: Man in India Office.

Roy Burman, B. K.

2004 'Non-verbal communication among the tribal peoples of India', In P.K. Misra (ed.), *Studies in Indian Anthropology*. New Delhi: Rawat Publications.

Sahay, V. S. and P. K. Singh

1998 *Indian Anthropology*. Allahabad: K. K. Publications.

Sapir, E.

1964 'Conceptual categories in primitive languages'. In Dell Hymes (ed.), *Language in Culture and Society*. New York: Harper & Row.

Sarana, Gopala and D. P. Sinha

1976 'Status of social-cultural anthropology in India', *Annual Review of Anthropology* 5: 209-225.

Saraswati, B. N.

1982 'Ritual language: A transanthropological perspective', *Man in India* 62 (1): 103-107.

1993 *Sacred Science of Man*. Calcutta: Institute of Social Research and Applied Anthropology.

Seligman, C. G. and B. G. Seligman

1911 *The Veddas of Ceylon*. Cambridge: University Press.

Shukla, H. L.

1985 *Socio-Cultural Approach to Tribal Languages*. New Delhi: B. R. Publishing Corporation.

Singh, Nissor

1906 *Khasi English Dictionary*. Shillong: Eastern Bengal and Assam Secretariat Press.

Srinivas, M. N.

2002 *Collected Essays*. New Delhi: Oxford University Press.

Srivastava, V. K.

1999 'The Future of Anthropology', *Economic and Political Weekly* 34 (9): 545-52.

2000 'Teaching Anthropology', *Seminar* 495, November.

Teeter, Karl V.

1964 ' "Anthropological Linguistics" and Linguistic Anthropology', *American Anthropologist*, 66: 878-879.

Tylor, E. B.

1881 *Anthropology: An Introduction to the Study of Man and Civilization*. London: Routledge.

Vidyarthi, L. P. and B. K. Rai

1976 *The Tribal Culture of India*. New Delhi: Concept Publishing Co.

Whitehead, G.

1925 *Dictionary of the Car-Nicobarese Language*. Rangoon.

11

Museum at an Anthropology Department

Kumkum Srivastava &
Vinay Kumar Srivastava

This paper deals with the place of museum in an anthropology department. It illustrates this with an example of the museum in the Department of Anthropology, Delhi University, focusing principally on the part that deals with material culture.

The Department of Anthropology at Delhi University was founded in 1947. Professor P.C. Biswas (1947-1968) was the first person appointed to teach anthropology and also head the department. He had his early training in anthropology at Calcutta, and then, read for a doctorate at Berlin. His doctoral dissertation was an ethnological study of the Santhals. He was regarded as one of the few 'general anthropologists', who contributed impressively to both physical and social anthropology and supervised doctoral dissertations in both fields. The university also made two other appointments at that time–Mrs. Freda Mukherjee (1947-1951) and Mrs. Hilda Raj (1947-1953).

The first batch of students for a Master's in anthropology was admitted in 1948. Some of them later became well-known anthropologists of the country—Indera P. Singh, J.D. Mehra, and S.C. Tewari. The department was housed initially in a couple of rooms in the earlier biology block of the Faculty of

Science, before being shifted to the first floor of the Faculty of Arts building.

In its formative years, the teaching of anthropology did not have the notion of twin specializations—in physical/biological anthropology and social/cultural anthropology—as it now has. Teaching was imparted to students in all branches of anthropology, barring linguistic anthropology. In their respective doctoral dissertations, it was left to students to explore one or the other aspect of human society and population. If the special area investigated was predominantly biological, the dissertation was classified as in physical anthropology. Similarly, if the student focused on the socio-cultural life of people, the dissertation was deemed to be in social anthropology. However, each doctoral dissertation submitted at that time had chapters on both biological and socio-cultural aspects of the people under study. In mid-1950s, the department introduced the system of twin specializations–specialization in physical anthropology was called 'Group-A', whereas in social anthropology 'Group-B'. A similar kind of specialization in archaeological anthropology was not introduced in the department. However, when the syllabi were revised in 1984, two papers in archaeology were introduced among the common options for the students of physical or social anthropology.

From the beginning, an important area of anthropology has been the study of material culture. A typology of culture respectfully upheld in the 1960s was of material and non-material culture, although no one subscribed to the supremacy of one over the other, as was the case in anthropology before the Second World War. A study of material culture guided one to the principles of technology, on the one hand, and social organization, on the other. Ethnographers collected tools and implements for analysis in the course of their field studies, and later transferred them to museums, where they became exhibits, with a short write-up on their characteristics and cultural contexts.

The Delhi Department of Anthropology had a theory and a practical paper on technology and material culture in its Master's course. When a bachelor's programme was introduced in anthropology in 1962, the course on technology and material culture was moved to the B.Sc. (Hons.) curriculum, and removed from Master's syllabi. As a post-graduate course in a subject was (and is) continuous with that of the undergraduate course, the department felt that the student who had done a Master's in anthropology would obviously had studied material culture in his graduation. That a significant number of students in Master's in anthropology came from other disciplines, and had not studied material culture was never a moot point. Till 1984, there was a theory paper and a practical course on material culture in the second year of B.Sc. (Hons.), but with the revised syllabi (in 1984), the theory paper was dropped and the practical course on material culture was brought forward to the final year. This was taught in relation with a theory paper on cultural ecology. The course on material culture introduced the students to the department museum.

II

To teach material culture, as well as to introduce students to cultural diversity, each anthropology department needs to have a museum. In fact, one of the essential requirements for starting an anthropology department is a museum, howsoever small it may be. The museum located in an anthropology department differs from other museums in following respects.

First, it is generally not intended for public. It is essentially meant for teaching and research. Although, it will be wrong to say that it is not open to public, it makes no efforts to inspire public visitations. However, in case people want to visit it, it definitely welcomes them. Sometimes, school children visit the Delhi anthropology museum after seeking permission from its head. On Flowers' Day, which Delhi University observes on the last Friday of February every year, when a large number of the families of university employees visit the sports ground where the show is held, many visit the anthropology museum. A visitor to the department spends some time in the museum. When a paper titled 'Social Formations and Cultural Patterns' was introduced in the B.A. (Hons.) syllabus of history, college students made an annual visit to the museum for purpose of study. The point to be emphasized here is that the anthropology department museums are not strictly 'public places' and, at the same time, are not strictly 'private'. Lying in between the continuum of the 'private' and the 'public', they sometimes become 'exclusively private', when an examination is being held, and become 'public', when a dignitary visits the department.

Second, no museum can represent all cultures; a group of museums may claim to do that. There exist specialized museums, and within that category, they must be able to represent all strata of the population. Anthropology department museums are largely concerned with a documentation of the material culture of the so-called 'small-scale societies'. This does not imply that they turn a blind eye to the changes that are surfacing in these societies. Museums have to keep pace with the all-round changes that occur in societies, particularly those societies the study of which is central to anthropology.

Anthropology museums rally around certain kind of societies because anthropology is still understood as a subject dealing predominantly with the scientific and interpretive understanding of 'simple' (tribal and peasant) societies, notwithstanding the fact that in theory, anthropology defines itself as the study of all human beings in time and space. Because of anthropology's inalienable association with tribes and peasants, its museums are truly subaltern, for they provide a respectable place to cultures that had been ignored in other subjects overwhelmingly concerned with complex and modern societies. Therefore, anthropology museums represent the people at margins and peripheries, and hence have much to teach. They also help correct the ethnocentric vision.

Furthermore, as anthropology is an integrated study of biological and socio-cultural facts, its museums have both biological and cultural exhibits. Let us have a look at the Delhi anthropology museum (or, perhaps, which we can call now the 'museum system'). It is divided into two parts–the main hall (which during Lord Mountbatten's time was used for dance parties) is the residence of material cultural exhibits, while the rectangular room next to it is generally called 'physical anthropology museum'. It is perhaps, we are told, the only museum of physical anthropology in anthropology departments of India that has the stuffed representations of the three great apes (gorilla, chimpanzee, and orang-utan), besides other stuffed primates (like the slender lemur, tarsier, etc). It also has a good collection of primate crania and bones, in addition to several plaster casts of fossil men. Some fetuses have also been stored here in formaldehyde solutions. The physical anthropology museum is also used as a classroom and 'laboratory', where students draw both material cultural and physical anthropological specimens. Archeological material (mainly in the form of stone tools) is dispersed in both these museums wherever space is available. The real, fragile and exotic artifacts are kept in glass-cases, while the thousand others have been piled up in open shelves in both the museums. Compared to them, all material cultural exhibits are in glass-cases, accessioned and locked.

This brings us to the issue of governance of the museum system. Interestingly, the list of the exhibits in physical anthropology museum is kept by the department store in-charge, while that of the material cultural exhibits is with the museum. Archaeological specimens are unrecorded, and except those in glass-cases, the rest are not in any one's particular governance, in the sense that physical anthropological and material cultural exhibits are the responsibility of the store and museum respectively. Each year, the students of B.Sc. (Hons.) second year visit an archaeological site and collect artifacts. They then prepare a short report evaluated at the time of annual examinations. These collections eventually find their way to the department museum. For some months, they may remain in the rooms of archaeology teachers, who also have their personal collections, which they use for instructional purposes in their classes and give to their students to draw and learn.

Artifacts given to students for the purpose of identification and description invariably come from the personal collection of the teachers. This however does not apply to either the material cultural or the physical anthropological exhibits. The teachers in both these courses are completely dependent upon the museum exhibits for teaching aids. They may have their private collections, but for the course, they select specimens from the museum. Whilst archaeological collections are mounting each year, with each field visit of the second year contributing a plethora of specimens, the other two 'museums' of material culture and physical anthropology have almost 'frozen' with no new exhibits being added to them. For instance, the last material cultural exhibit was acquired in the museum on 29 May 1986, when a native Hopi Indian artist from Lowie

Museum of Anthropology, University of California, Berkeley, gifted a doll, locally called *hoo-lee*, to the museum.

The history of the department museum spans from December 1948, when the first collection of specimens came from Red Fort authorities, to May 1986, when the last exhibit was accessioned. We were told that in the last nineteen years, some gifts to the museum have definitely come but are yet to be accessioned and displayed. The museum has acquired exhibits in the manner detailed below (see Table 1):

(1) Individuals

(a) Gift: Artifacts and objects collected, purchased, or received (as gift) during one's field study or visit have been *gifted* to the museum.

(b) Purchases: Artifacts and objects *purchased* during one's field study have been given to the museum, for which the individual was reimbursed from the grant for the museum.

(2) Institutional Gift. A set of artifacts and objects has come as a *gift* from an institution, such as the Red Fort authorities, or the Anthropological Survey of India.

(3) Fieldwork Collections. The department has acquired, either through *payment* or as *gift*, several collections during the yearly field studies that its students of B.Sc. (Hons.) final year and M.Sc. final have carried out in different parts of India.

(4) Departmental Purchases. The department has *purchased* several items from emporia and curio shops, from the funds that were available to it. Most of these purchases were made during the month of March when the funds had to be exhausted lest they lapsed.

Presently, the museum has a total of 1,157 objects, of which 712 (61.54 per cent) have come from individuals; 205 (17.72 per cent) are gifts from institutions (viz. the Red Fort authorities have gifted 62, the Anthropological Survey of India, 59, and the Registrar General's Office, 84); 80 (6.92 per cent) are fieldwork collections; and 138 (11.92 per cent) are departmental purchases. The source of 22 (1.90 per cent) objects is not listed in the department records. Of the 712 objects, 473 (66.43 per cent) are gifts, whereas 239 (33.57 per cent) were purchased by individuals for the museum.

III

When senior members of the department were questioned about the factors that led to the expansion of the museum, and any significant memory associated with it, they unfailingly spoke of the late Prime Minister, Jawaharlal Nehru. That he was a great lover of tribes and a friend of Verrier Elwin is known to almost all anthropologists. In his birth centenary year (1989), a number of articles were published on his understanding of tribal India, and the contemporary relevance of his Foreword to the second edition of Elwin's *A Philosophy for NEFA*. But what many are unaware of is his commitment to the development of anthropology museums. His visit to the anthropology museum in the mid-1950s is still fresh in the minds of the senior and retired members of the department. They remembered Nehru asking questions about the significance of material cultural objects in tribal life. He himself knew quite a lot about their lives. For him, a visit to the museum was an academic pursuit; it was a curious sojourn, and a discovery of his own self. In the words of J.D. Mehra, his visit to the anthropology museum was far 'above the mundane and the routine'.

Envisioning the potentiality of the Department of Anthropology to develop into a major research centre, Nehru advised his office to send his personal collection of tribal objects to its museum. The first set of sixty-five items, consisting of objects from tribal Orissa, Madhya Pradesh, Assam, Naga Hills, and Mysore, arrived on 5 September 1955. Exactly a month later were added forty items, mainly from Assam, NEFA, and Naga Hills. They consisted of a wooden and a silver quiver, which the Assam Hills Tribal Union had presented to him. It also had the Naga *dao* with which Nehru inaugurated the Aijal-Lungleh road at Bawngkawn on 3 April 1953. Welcome addresses of different leaders at Nehru's visits to tribal areas were also sent to the department museum. For a long time, they were exhibited in a separate showcase in the museum. However, when the limitation of space was being felt with the multiplication of objects, they were kept in a steel almirah. Ninety-three items from Bastar (then in Madhya Pradesh) came from Nehru on 19 October 1956, followed by forty items from NEFA, Punjab, Naga Hills, and Rajsthan on 23 October 1958. The last gift from him in the form of a letter from Abraham Lincoln arrived on 10 February 1962. It was displayed in a glass-case, but was unfortunately lost when the department was shifted in 1966 from the Faculty of Arts building to its present location. In total, Nehru's contribution to the department museum consists of 239 objects, which is 50.53 per cent of all the items (473) that came to the museum as gift.

Nehru's daughter, Indira Gandhi, closely followed her father's example, though she could never visit the department museum. On 25 January 1964, when Nehru was alive, she sent three items of the Murias of Bastar, which included a fan and a shawl, to the department museum. From then on till 24 February 1984, Mrs. Gandhi sent a total of 79 objects to the museum (i.e., 16.71 per cent of the items that were received as gift). In other words, both Nehru and his daughter have contributed 67.23 per cent of the objects that came as gift to the museum. And, of the total items in the museum, the total contribution of the two Prime Ministers is 27.49 per cent. That is the reason why the department is eternally indebted to the Nehru family for its contributions to the museum, and the senior, retired faculty members of the department remember Nehru's visit with nostalgia. In fact, the museum acquired 51.24 per cent of its collection in the decade 1950-9, courtesy Nehru. The fame of the anthropology museum spread far and wide. Many visitors came to see its collection, prominent among them were R. Gates, B.S. Guha, and Prince Charles, who particularly came to the campus of Delhi University in 1980 to have a look at the places associated with Lord Mountbatten.

IV

Among the well-known scholars who gifted objects to the department museum were Surojit Sinha, Sakuntala Paranjape, J.D. Mavalwala, M.N. Srinivas, T.N. Pandit, and P.D. Khera (see Table 2). One of the teachers of the department, Abhimanyu Sharma, who died prematurely in September 1978, was a great collector of material cultural objects. Among other ethnographic locations, he had also done his fieldwork with the Kachins of Burma. During his lifetime, he gave some exhibits to the museum, but after his death, on the request of his family members, the department appointed a committee to look into his collection, decide about the approximate cost of each object, and recommend it to the museum. On 4 March 1982, the department bought his personal collection of sixty items from

Kachin and Garhwal areas for a sum of Rs. 2,606. After Nehru and Mrs. Gandhi, it was the biggest collection coming from an individual to the museum.

From the yearly grant that came to the museum, it was able to acquire certain specimens. The most expensive item it has so far bought is a bronze framed Nataraja lamp, purchased on 26 March 1965 from Madras Handicraft Emporium, New Delhi, for Rs. 275:63. The model of a dugout canoe of the Andamanese that it has was bought from Calcutta in 1951 for Rs. 75. Presently, the department receives a yearly grant of Rs. 5,000 for the museum, which is spent mainly on its maintenance.

As said earlier, the glorious period of the museum, when it expanded under the patronage of Nehru, was the decade 1950-9. In the following decade (1960-9), the museum acquired 18.92 per cent of its objects, and was also shifted to its present location in the central hall of the department (see Tables 3 and 4). In addition, a museum curator looked after it. Kamlesh Guha, a student from Calcutta anthropology department, was the first curator of the museum. He later earned his doctorate under the supervision of M.N. Basu and P.K. Bhowmick on the analysis of museum objects in Calcutta and Delhi anthropology museums. In the articles he published in reputed journals (including one in *Ethnos*), he showed that in addition to the field, the museum could also be a site of study.

V

The decline of the institution of museum in the department began after Guha's retirement. In 1991, the university abolished the post of the museum curator, which was in lecturer's pay time-scale. Instead, it was converted into the post of a 'technical assistant', in 'C-grade', however the qualifications for this post remained the same as they were for the post of museum curator. Second, since a course on material culture is not taught at the Master's level, the post-graduate students have minimal contact with the museum. However, in M.Sc. (Previous), since they study courses on archaeology and primates, they at least have a chance to see the museum. If they happen to study physical anthropology in the final year of their M.Sc., they study palaeoanthropology, because of which they retain their relations with the museum. Some M.Sc. (Final) social anthropology students do work on material culture for their dissertations, and M.Phil. students can also write their theses on material culture. No student has however researched on museum exhibits or the museum itself.

Till the time, there was a theory paper on material culture in B.Sc. (Hons.), the museum was taken quite seriously. One would see students moving around the museum with copies of Lips' *Origin of Things*, Royal Anthropological Institute's publication *Notes and Queries on Anthropology*, and M.N. Basu's slim book on material culture, and carefully looking at the exhibits. Now, as stated earlier, there is only one practical course on material culture in B.Sc. (Hons.) final year, where the students learn to draw and write about forty specimens representing different cultural contexts (such as foraging, horticulture, pastoralism, agriculture, etc). The description of the specimens, we are told, is not original but borrowed word-by-word from the practical files of students who have passed out, a tradition that is difficult to break.

For the last nineteen years, we said earlier, the museum has not accessioned any article, although some gifts have definitely come in. Grant received from the university for the museum is spent mostly on its maintenance, rather than on acquiring new objects. The financial assistance to the museum needs to be increased for it genuinely requires more glass-cases and spotlights. When Prince Charles was scheduled to visit the museum, the university spent a lot of money on 'beautifying' the museum, but since then, not much has been done.

VI

Notwithstanding the kind of anthropology departments that have come up in India, some virtually without any museum, no one will ever dispute the significance of museum in anthropology or that anthropology could be taught without it. The truth is that the museum remains at the core cf teaching and research in anthropology. It is well known that anthropology museums in many universities fund ethnographic researches. They also publish journals and research periodicals. Many famous ethnographers and anthropologists have been associated with museums. And, several path-breaking ideas in the history of anthropology had their origin in the study of museum exhibits.

One of the criticisms of anthropology museums that has come from within the subject is that our museums are 'static', 'frozen', and 'timeless'. They do not represent the changes that have come in the discipline of anthropology with the passage of time. Anthropology has reacted sharply and satisfactorily to the challenges posed to its subject matter by the forces of globalization and the theoretical perspectives of post-modernity. However, the criticism of anthropology museums, as mentioned above, does not hold true because a large number of well-funded anthropology museums of the world have evocatively represented the glimpses of the post-modern world. At the same time, they have not lost sight of the multicultural, plural, and diverse world in which we live, and which will continue to retain its diversity albeit the vast technological and social organizational changes. That is why a totemic pole is as much dear to the anthropology museum as are the pictures and technology of the hair styles of punks!

The case of the Delhi anthropology museum shows that one of the pivotal factors responsible for its de-centering is the decline in studies of material culture. However, in the last decade, especially due to the work of certain archaeologists who branched out into culture studies and anthropologists who focused on the study of consumption patterns, the study of material culture is regaining its past glory. In years to come, the anthropology museum will not just be a teaching adjunct. It will emerge as an active place of research, a place to think, as behind every material object are the intricate principles of social organization. The emergence of disciplines like museum anthropology and research interests like 'anthropology *in* museum' and 'anthropology *of* museum' in recent years amply testify to this.

Table 1
Mode of Acquisition of Objects

S.No.	Mode of Acquisition	Number	Percentage
1.	Individuals	473	61.54
	i. Gift	239	
	ii. Purchases	712	
	Total		
2.	Institutional Gift	205	17.72
3.	Fieldwork Collections	80	6.92
4.	Departmental Purchases	138	11.92
5.	Not listed in records	22	1.90

Table 2
List of the items which certain individuals either purchased for the museum or gifted to it. Those bearing the asterisk (*) mark were purchased for the museum.

S. No.	Date	Name	Number of Items	Ethnographic Context
1.	3 July 1949	Surojit Sinha	20	Ho, Singhbhum District.
2.	16 December 1949	B.B. Verma	14	Oraon, Chotanagpur.
3.	14 January 1950	Sakuntala Paranjpaye	1	Australian Aborigines (boomerang)
4.	20 March 1950	R.N. Kawatra	16	Bhil, Udaipur and Dungarpur.*
5.	27 December 1950	S.C. Tewari	8	Raji, Village Askote, Almora.*
6.	1 April 1952	B.B. Verma	21	Ho and Oraon, Chotanagpur.*
7.	15 April 1952	J.D. Mehra	21	Assam*
8.	9 October 1953	S.K. Kaul	1	Gonds, Madhya Pradesh (leaf umbrella).
9.	25 November 1953	N. Kumar	1	Abor, NEFA (hat).
10.	20 December 1953	Mrs. Hilda Raj	1	Emu, Australia (egg shell).
11.	1 January 1954	J.D. Mavalwala	24	Uttar Pradesh (clay toys).
12.	10 February 1954	Mrs. Gill	3	Tibet

table1 contd.

S. No.	Date	Name	Number of Items	Ethnographic Context
13.	15 February 1954	H.L. Seth	1	Ceylon (Sri Lanka) (model of a cart).
14.	15 June 1954	Indera P. Singh	8	Manali, Kullu Valley.
15.	13 July 1954	P.C. Biswas	5	Kashmir.*
16.	16 October 1954	S.K. Kalra	15	Khasi and Jaintia Hills.*
17.	16 October 1954	Indera P. Singh	6	Simla Hills.*
18.	17 November 1954	Abhimanyu Sharma	2	Burma
19.	5 September 1955	Jawaharlal Nehru	65	Orissa, Madhya Pradesh, Assam, Nagaland, Mysore.
20.	5 October 1955	Jawaharlal Nehru	40	Assam, NEFA, Nagaland.
21.	21 October 1955	Abhimanyu Sharma	6	Dacca, East Pakistan (now Bangladesh).*
22.	19 October 1956	Jawaharlal Nehru	93	Bastar.
23.	15 August 1957	T.N. Pandit	11	Kashmir
24.	14 October 1957	S.K. Kalra	3	NEFA.
25.	16 October 1957	Ms. Toris	5	Assam.
26.	9 December 1957	T. Rao	18	Andhra Pradesh.
27.	4 July 1958	S.K. Kalra	3	NEFA.
28.	10 August 1958	S.K. Kaul	1	Lahaul Valley (footwear).
29.	23 October 1958	Jawaharlal Nehru	40	NEFA, Nagaland, Punjab.
30.	12 January 1959	Flt. Lt. S. Gautam (I.A.F.)	1	Ziro, Subansiri Division, NEFA (basket of the Daflas).
31.	11 August 1960	Divyadarshi Kapoor	1	Kinnaur, Himachal Pradesh (a pair of snowshoes).*

table1 contd.

S. No.	Date	Name	Number of Items	Ethnographic Context
32.	9 October 1960	M.N. Srinivas	1	Mysore (bamboo clapper of the Kheddas).
33.	19 December 1960	Swami Jitpuri	4	Bhils, Rajasthan.
34.	10 February 1962	Jawaharlal Nehru	1	Abraham Lincoln's letter
35.	9 March 1962	Shamsher Singh	6	Bhils, Rajasthan.
36.	10 March 1962	Swami Jitpuri	1	Pangi Valley (one pair of Pangi chappals).
37.	4 April 1963	S.B. Mani	1	Tanjore District (harp).
38.	7 December 1963	Kamlesh Guha	2	West Bengal
39.	25 January 1964	Indira Gandhi	2	Muria, Bastar (bison-horn head-dress).
40.	27 July 1964	Biswajeet Sen	2	NEFA
41.	31 July 1964	R.P. Naula	2	Gaddi, Himachal Pradesh (woolen rope).
42.	21 October 1964	G.S. Parashar	2	Rajasthan.*
43.	4 November 1964	B.S. Barar	3	Pangi Valley.
44.	9 December 1964	Biswajeet Sen	2	Brokpas, Ladakh.
45.	20 February 1967	K.N. Vasu	1	Kerala (scythe).
46.	1 January 1968	B.R. Ghosh	18	Khasi and Jaintia Hills.*
47.	12 January 1968	S.C. Tewari	33	Ranchi and Tibet.*
48.	29 March 1968	S.C. Tewari	5	Tibet (prayer wheel, strike-a-light with pouch).*
49.	1 April 1968	Indira Gandhi	6	Assam.
50.	17 October 1968	D.K. Bhattacharya	3	Korku, Amroha District.
51.	15 March 1969	Sibani Dattagupta	1	West Bengal*
52.	30 October 1969	Harish Baveja	3	Palampur, Kangra.*

table1 contd.

S. No.	Date	Name	Number of Items	Ethnographic Context
53.	16 December 1969	D. Anand	5 pictures	Gujars, Himachal Pradesh.*
54.	30 July 1970	N.C. Sharma	10	NEFA*
55.	5 November 1974	Indera P. Singh & Sarvesh Kumar	5	Lahaul-Spiti
56.	17 December 1974	P.C. Joshi	2	Kumaon (iron pick).
57.	7 July 1975	Indira Gandhi	9	Africa (drum, cap, wooden tribal statue).
58.	20 October 1976	V.C. Channa	1	Kashmir (gown).
59.	5 April 1977	Indira Gandhi	15	Nagaland
60.	18 May 1979	S.C. Tewari	1	Raji, Pithorgarh.
61.	19February 1981	Indira Gandhi	18	? (bow and arrow, waist-basket, toe rings).
62.	4 March 1982	Abhimanyu Sharma (posthumous)	60	Kachin area and Garhwal.*
63.	24 February 1984	Indira Gandhi	26	Africa
64.	16 July 1985	P.D. Khera	2	Muria, Bastar.
65.	31January 1986	I.S. Marwah	3	Jotsoma Village, Nagaland.*
66.	29 May 1986	Hartman H. Lomawaima	1	Hopi (doll).

Table 3
The yearly acquisition of exhibits in the museum

S.No.	Year	Exhibits acquired	Per cent
1.	1948	62	5.36
2.	1949	39	3.38
3.	1950	25	2.16
4.	1951	32	2.76
5.	1952	67	5.80
6.	1953	62	5.36
7.	1954	64	5.53
8.	1955	116	10.02
9.	1956	106	9.17
10.	1957	47	4.06
11.	1958	46	3.97
12.	1959	28	2.42
13.	1960	6	0.51
14.	1961	-	-
15.	1962	8	0.70
16.	1963	19	1.64
17.	1964	28	2.42
18.	1965	42	3.63
19.	1966	14	1.21
20.	1967	4	0.34
21.	1968	78	6.74
22.	1969	20	1.73
23.	1970	94	8.13
24.	1971	-	-
25.	1972	-	-
26.	1973	-	-
27.	1974	7	0.60
28.	1975	9	0.78
29.	1976	1	0.08
30.	1977	15	1.30
31.	1978	-	-
32.	1979	1	0.08
33.	1980	-	-
34.	1981	18	1.56
35.	1982	67	5.80
36.	1983	-	-
37.	1984	26	2.25
38.	1985	2	0.17
39.	1986	4	0.34

Table 4
Years of acquisition of museum exhibits

S. No.	Years	Percentage of exhibits acquired
1.	1948-9	8.74
2.	1950-9	51.24
3.	1960-9	18.92
4.	1970-9	10.97
5.	1980-6	10.12

12

Anthropology of Tourism: Insights from Nagaland

Soumendra Mohan Patnaik

The study of tourism is still an emergent specialty concerned with the study of touristic motivations, roles, relationships and institutions and their impact on tourists and the societies which receive them (Cohen 1984). From being viewed as commercialized hospitality, democratized travel, modern leisure activity, modern variety of traditional pilgrimage to seeing it as an expression of basic cultural themes, an acculturative process to a type of ethnic relations and even as a form of neo-colonialism, touristic studies have it all under their purview. Anthropologists view tourism as an interaction between cultures and subcultures. Seen in this way, it becomes a process involving the generation of tourists, their travel and subsequent encounter with people in a host society. Such an encounter implies interaction between tourists, their agents and hosts, which affects the people and cultures involved (Nash 1981).

Understanding tourism: Anthropological insights

Weaver (2000: 2) defines tourism as:

> the sum of the phenomena and relationships arising from the interaction among tourists, business suppliers, host governments, host communities, origin governments, universities, community colleges and non-governmental organizations, in the process of

> attracting, transporting, hosting and managing these tourists and other visitors.

Tourism is defined as the activities undertaken by "tourists". The World Tourist Organisation defines "tourists" as temporary visitors staying at least twenty four hours in the country visited and the purpose of whose journey can be classified under one of the following heads: (a) leisure—recreation, holiday, health, study, religion and sport; and (b) business (family mission, meeting) (IUOTO 1963:14). Tourism as an organized industry is a post-World War II phenomenon. It was after the war that it came to dominate all social classes in industrialized western societies, a result of the rising standards of living and shortening of the work year. For many small communities and even nations with limited natural resources or few industries, tourism forms the mainstay of their economy.

Today, it is considered to be one of the most profitable industries with very low investment. Policy makers have for long realized its potential as a revenue generator and in many places tourism is simply too attractive an option for governments to ignore. In spite of being a topic of research for almost three decades, tourism retains its stimulating freshness as a subject area for anthropological research.

Tourism is widespread among all human cultures at all levels. While tourism is more easily identifiable in agricultural and industrial societies, even 'simpler' societies provide sufficient evidence of touristic behaviour. It is this and the resultant intermixing of people and cultures that makes the field a continuously evolving challenge albeit a fascinating one. There is a plethora of conceptual approaches to the study of tourism in India.

This study concentrates on four principal issues—the tourist, relations between tourists and locals, the structure and functioning of the touristic system and importantly, the consequences of tourism. Motivations behind travel range from intrinsic ones, like self-actualization and fulfillment of long-term psychological needs to religious fulfillment, exploration, research and even drifting. The encounter between tourists and their hosts rests on the people's interactions, perceptions and attitudes. Such encounters are transitory, non-repetitive and asymmetrical and the participants are oriented towards achieving immediate gratification rather than maintaining long-term relationships. This aspect can lead to problems for both the hosts as well as the guests. Since no one is concerned with long-term consequences, the relationship between hosts and guests is open to deceit, exploitation and mistrust. The pressure of tourism may transform the customary hospitality into a hybrid tourist system hitherto non-existent. Economic motivations and professionalisation set in and rule the relationship between the hosts and guests. Modern tourism is an ecological, economic and political system that is complete and global. The tourist industry hinges on an army of transitional actors—hotels, travel agents, companies, tour operators, and even government organisations and cultural centres. The structure of the tourist industry at the global level has important repercussions for the national and local levels in the host countries.

The impact of tourism is by far the most intensely researched area in the anthropology of tourism. Most studies distinguish between socioeconomic and socio-cultural impacts of tourism. The socioeconomic impacts cover issues like income generation, employment generation, prices, distribution of benefits, ownership and control, development and government revenue, etc. While the positive effects of tourism cover the aspects given above, the tourism industry often involves the penetration of outsiders. This frequently leads to a loss of local control over the industry. Where large scale professionalization occurs due to interference by outsiders it yields minimal benefits for the locals. It is here that the introduction of small scale, locally owned, lower standard "craft"/ cultural tourism is needed. The gross earnings may be less in such a form of tourism but the benefits are locally retained and the disruptive effects are minimized.

The socio-cultural impacts of tourism are numerous ranging from community involvement in wider frameworks, the nature of interpersonal relations, the basis of social organization, the rhythm of social life to migration, division of labour, stratification, distribution of power, deviance and customs and art. Tourism integrates the local economy with national and often international systems. As dependence on external factors increases, diffuse solidarities and individualisation, change in local interpersonal relations and even conflict situations arise. In simple and traditional societies, tourism leads to an expansion of the economic domain roping in those activities within the system that were previously unaffected by economic criteria. Certain customs and arts become commoditized and inter-personal relations lag behind economic considerations. Furthermore, tourism being a seasonal activity disrupts the rhythm of social life, interfering with traditional patterns of life especially in agriculture based economies. The generation of employment due to tourism may disrupt migration of locals but it also attracts outsiders to the area resulting in increased pressure on resources and competition.

A ubiquitously noted impact of tourism is on the division of labour among the sexes. Women and other sections of the population that traditionally did not form a part of the labour force get drawn in and become a part of the institutional setup (hotels, art shops, other services). This changes the equations of the division of labour within the household and may even lead to conflict and deviance in the family structure. By placing greater emphasis on the economic domain, tourism results in a change in the criteria for stratification in a particular society. This becomes especially significant in the case of tribal and simple societies as this has wider ramifications on social strata and institutions like marriage. A revaluation of local resources due to the new use they are put to may change fortunes of a community or individuals. What was previously defunct may suddenly become valuable or vice versa. This may lead to an increase in social disparities and unequal distribution of benefits that usually accompany it.

Among the less studied consequences of tourism are its effects on the political system and interests. Tourism may give rise to new political interests, leading to pluralization of local power structures. Customs and art are often commoditized for touristic purposes. While this may lead to their eventual preservation, what is also possible and has been recorded is the emergence of tailor-made, "phony" folk culture and art to cater to tourist tastes. Global forces are opening up the hitherto remote and inaccessible sites for tourist purposes like northeast parts of India. Earlier visits to these areas required special permission due to sensitive political situation. It is interesting to note that not only international organizations but central and state governments are more than keen to showcase these untouched beautiful 'exotic' lands for tourist purposes. In the virtual absence of industrial activity tourism is being promised as an attractive earning option for local populations. Being inhabited largely by tribal populations with their 'exotic' long abandoned customs like 'head hunting' and unique dress styles, a state like Nagaland opens up interesting options.

In this paper[1] the focus is on how the state government is trying to showcase the cultural heritage of Nagaland. What according to them is the tourist potential of the state with special reference to local aspirations, logistics and other considerations? How tourism impacts the local cultures? And, what is the nature of people's involvement in tourism highlighting (a) community participation and management; (b) gender differences; and (c) marginal groups The paper also highlights the emerging critical issues in a changing scenario.

Tourism is seen to play a significant part in balanced sustainable development and generates benefits for the poor. The World Tourism Organisation believes that the power of tourism can be more effectively harnessed to address the problems of poverty more directly. One of the cornerstones of sustainable tourism is the well being of poor communities and their environment. Because of its various attractions, Nagaland is being seen to be in a unique position to differentiate itself from its competitors by highlighting its rich and unique natural and cultural assets through the promotion of tourism.

The Government of Nagaland notified its Tourism Policy on January 23, 2001 with a view to ensure sustained growth of tourism. The policy recognizes the main constraints of tourism development in the state and highlights the objectives of the programme for future development. The prime objective of the policy is to provide for planned development of tourism based on promotion of domestic and international tourism. It will *inter alia* involve the identification of potential areas of tourism, strengthening of infrastructure, integrated development of tourism facility and marketing of tourism products. Promoting the conservation and enhancement of natural resources, particularly the flora and fauna, forests and other unique features of the state through regulated development and promotion of rural, ethnic, cultural, ecological and adventure tourism are the other objectives of the Tourism Policy.

Nagaland tourism vision statement

A Nagaland Tourism Vision was also formulated in 2001, through extensive interaction with various segments of the people of the state, both at the Government and the public level. It calls for developing tourism to reflect and reinforce the uniqueness of Nagaland's rich history, and its natural and cultural resources, to develop tourism so that there are 'no serious negative socio-cultural impacts' on the society of Nagaland, emphasizes the local participation and equitable socio-economic benefits. It also focuses on the importance of environmental regeneration, effective marketing and integration of the State's tourism resources with other states in the northeast. Through tourism development the state government is seeking to harness resources for the overall development of the state by creating infrastructure suitable for tourism that in long term would serve the people.

My field visits to different parts of Nagaland were meant to identify the trends in community participation of locals, government officials and the civil society organizations. Interestingly we found that there was an initial enthusiasm towards tourism development as the state has been able to develop in some measure interest in these activities by emphasizing the economic gains and employment potential of the tourism industry. Community participation and democratic functioning so inbuilt in Naga society is conducive to such trends. At different levels, meetings were called, in which the representatives of different sections of society participated and discussed the issues.

Naga history

The Naga had their own political system of chieftainship. In 1215 A.D. Naga area (Patkoi) was invaded for the first time by an outsider—Ahom Sukhapa. He had to use tremendous force to subdue Nagas, who rebelled several times. However, Ahom successors were friendly with the Nagas resulting in a significant expansion of the Ahom kingdom. The relations between the Ahom kings and the Naga people were maintained through a confederation, which was periodically held in the capital of Ahom Kings. The Nagas (Angami and Rengma) came under Kachari rule in the thirteenth century. The Angami had little contact with the Kachari state, while Rengma maintained socio-economic relations with it by supplying iron implements in exchange for salt.

The British entered the Naga Hills for the first time in 1832 but had a hostile relationship with the Naga. In 1836, when political conditions were stable, the American Baptist Mission entered the Naga Hills. In their first contact in the Konyak territory, the missionaries carried out a combination of educational, economic and religious activities. From the beginning of the Naga mission, the conflict between Naga culture and Christianity was evident. G.W. Clark, a renowned missionary, made strenuous efforts to bring an end to head-hunting and blood feuds that characterized the Naga culture.

The Ao Naga area has a long history of Christianity. A mission centre was opened at Impur in 1894 where churches of not only Ao but also those of Sumis, Lothas, Changs, Phoms and Sangtams were built. Impur gradually grew into an educational centre. The Kohima centre covered Angami, Rengma, part of Sumi, Zeliang and Kuki tribal areas. In postcolonial India, the course of development followed the same pattern to a great extent. This period saw the crystallization of Naga identity and these people shared a turbulent relationship with the Indian state on the question of autonomy and governance.

The cultural matrix of Nagaland

The Naga tribe is divided into different sub-tribes, each having its own dialect, distinct dress pattern, jewellery, headgears, beads, tattoos and festivals. However, all believe in a common history and share a sense of belongingness. In spite of the fact that more than 95 per cent of the population professes Christianity, the Nagas have retained their traditional festivals associated with different phases of their day-to-day life. Slash and burn cultivation forms the primary occupation, further supplemented by hunting, fishing, trapping, animal husbandry, weaving and basket making. With the advent of Christianity, head-hunting practices and dormitory institutions (*morung*) have been abandoned. The statutory village council consists of clan elders. It continues to be influential, despite the introduction of statutory village and area councils. Customary laws are followed in settling disputes in all these councils.

At present, Nagaland is divided into sixteen districts and each district largely houses members of individual tribe. Angami Nagas are one of the dominant Naga communities of Nagaland. Presently they are concentrated in Kohima district. The Ao are found in Mokokchung district. The Chakhesang inhibit cold and hilly terrain of the Phek district. Mon district is inhabited by the Konyak. The Phom exclusively inhabit the Longleng district which was previously a subdivision of the Tuensang district. The Yimchunger are also concentrated in Tuensang district.

Tourism in Nagaland is relatively a new development due to long drawn insurgency movements. Christainity, education and opening up of the state to global influences has however created new waves of aspiration and ambition. The development process in Nagaland has been pretty uneven. A clear stratification in terms of early beneficiaries of fruits of development is evident as the northern districts remain underdeveloped whereas the southern districts like Kohima and Mokakchung clearly show signs of modernization. In Nagaland's march on the path of development, the northern districts of Mon and undivided Tuensang (including the new districts of Longleng and Kiphere) have never been the stakeholders and remain neglected. Bureaucracy and state politics is largely occupied by the Ao and Angami whereas in the insurgency movement the Sumi and the Naga from underdeveloped districts are predominantly present.

Local responses

Local residents, district level officers, NGO workers and members of the youth clubs and student unions in the Northern part of Nagaland feel that the fruits of development and modernisation are not reaching this part of the state. Some of the NGO activists even used the phrases like "step-motherly treatment" to describe the ways in which state administration responds to local needs and demands. Maintaining anonymity, some district officers even admitted that their transfers to either Mon or Tuensang are punishment postings. The people of Mon and Tuensang nurture a sense of alienation in relation to the residents of Kohima and Mokokchung. In fact, the Aos of Mokokchung were the first converts, who took the advantage of western education and occupied important positions in the state bureaucracy. On the other hand, the Konyaks, Khimaniungans and Yimchungers and other tribes of these districts got converted to Christianity only in last fifty years leading to a differential access to western education and government jobs. This area has a lot of tourism potential as much of its traditional cultutre is still intact. The area was never under the British rule; it was an unadministered area. It was only after Indian independence in 1947 that these areas became a part of the Indian Republic.

In the meeting with the stakeholders at Tuensang it was pointed out that there is no 'tourist officer' at the district headquarters. Tourism department has not been able to make its presence felt in the district. The local youth do not seem to know much about tourism. It was felt that they need role models or examples citing the success stories of tourism not from far off places in India or abroad, but from their immediate neighbourhood.

There was a stark contrast between the composition of stakeholders who attended the district level workshops at Mon and Tuensang. While a large number of youth and students, some of whom were tourist guides, both men and women attended the workshop at Mon, the workshop at Tuensang was attended mainly by government officers. No women stakeholder attended the workshop at Tuensang. It seemed that the state was going slow on capacity building. Awareness programmes require differential inputs in these two districts.

It was also found from the tourist guides of Mon that the tour operators at Kolkata, Guwahati and Kohima generally discourage the foreign tourists to visit Mon and Tuensang in the absence of any local contacts. The youth of Mon town feel that there should be effective linkages, both institutional and electronic, between foreign tourists and local tourist guides.

The interested officials and stakeholders felt though that in spite of bad roads, the districts of Mon and Tuensang have a lot of potential to attract Special Interest Tourists (SIT) who intend to explore adventures in cultural tourism. In these areas, the impact of Christianity being relatively new, the traditional Konyak Naga culture is still evident in various forms. The institution of Ang and associated practice of polygyny, the Ang's house, his personal granary and separate apartments for different wives, his court where he meets his counsellor are showcased as places of attraction for tourists from abroad. The traditional slate houses of Khiamniungans and the ancient remains of head hunting practices are supposed to constitute a source of unending fascination for the tourists.

The district of Zunheboto is also relatively backward in comparison to the neighbouring districts of Wokha and Mokokchung. Though it has potential for cultural and eco-tourism, it never had adequate exposure to tourism. The district officials, members of CCF (Concerned Citizen Forum) and NGO personnel feel that the district has been neglected as far as tourism activity is concerned. There is no tourist officer in the district. The tourist officer of Kohima used to attend the district development board meeting. One of the reasons for inadequate tourism exposure of the district is the prevalence of insurgency. As mentioned earlier, the NSCN K-group is active here. The local tour operators and tourist guides from other districts admit that they have avoided Zunheboto in the past only for security reasons. However, after the commencement of peace talks things have changed.

The Sumi have a lot of tolerance and are warm-hearted people; they are forgiving and hospitable. Professing these qualities makes the area very conducive for visitors and the promotion of tourism, but the experts emphasise a lot of capacity building. The inhabitants of the area voice their preference for a local person as the tourist officer, for he/she would then be able to understand the different cultures prevalent in the area and propagate a separate cultural council for each, forwarding the formation and registration of cultural troupes with the tourism department. A success of such a situation can be seen at Mokokchung where cultural groups perform their items on invitation whenever VIPs come over. Items are called "legs" and Sumi stepping is different from other Naga dances. The dance is performed with atleast 20-30 people adorned with traditional cultural items like headgears and bangles, and an individual can earn up to Rs. 50 a day through his/her performance. It was further pointed out that the area is largely mountainous, covered with thick forests which nest a number of the rare species of birds. This could serve the purpose of adventure and eco-tourism.

Wokha comes in between Kohima and Mokokchung. Due to its locational advantage, it can be developed as a tourist site. The traditional method of preparing jaggery by the Lotha could be one of the attractions for rural tourism.

Mokokchung (in contrast to these districts) is more exposed to tourism. The number of Ao youth in tourism industry is already significant. The people recognize the need to preserve their traditional culture and a number of training centres have been opened to promote the making of local traditional artefacts.

Youth resources

Tourism has led to a high level of motivation and aspiration among the youth. Most of the tourist guides and local tour operators are young men and women from different parts of Nagaland. However, the process of capacity building among local tourist guides has been confined to a few tribes—Angami. Chakhesang, Ao and Konyak. The youth from Rengma, Pochury, Khiamniungan and Yimchunger needs to be linked with tourism activities of the state. Tourism has generated self-employment among youths in the absence of institutions which would require differentially trained human resources. People are not only open but also enthusiastic to the idea of providing paying guest facilities to foreign and domestic tourists.

The Konyak youths are forthcoming. Both men and women joined the training programme/workshop organised at the district level. The Konyak are availing the tourism opportunities in whatever form they come to them. Some of them are working with tour operators at Kohima and Dimapur. Two of them have moved to Delhi to join a travel agency. However, the number of youths working in tourism industry are very few in comparison to their Ao or Angami counterparts. Konyak youths are also doing various government jobs. Honesty, truthfulness, hard work, sincerity and dedication are the qualities that were traditionally valued by Konyak culture even before the advent of Christianity.

Interestingly, the Ao of Mopungchuket village in the district of Mokokchung have realized that the art of basketry and weaving requires specialised skills which are available only with the elders and aged. The younger generation completely lacks such skills. Due to the initiative of Mopungchuket Community Tourism Society and other associations concerned with tourism, the youngsters are attending learning sessions on basketry, weaving and other forms of folk art under the supervision of village elders. But the educated youth is generally shy of learning these skills which leads to thin attendance. Unless such initiatives are accompanied with adequate incentive packages it would be difficult to sustain the interest of the youth.

Local expectations

The Konyak areas in the district of Mon receive a lot of foreign tourists. The question arises: what are the expectations of local people from these tourists? The Ang of Shangnyu village was of the opinion that whenever the foreign tourists come, they only take few photographs, ask them to show some traditional baskets, jewellery, shawls and simply go away. The accompanying tourist guides do not make any attempt to answer their queries; He/she is only bothered about what the tourists want to know and not in what the local people want to know from the tourists. The Konyak of Shangnyu village find such an interaction meaningless from their point of view. Any attempt to promote rural tourism in such areas should ensure mechanisms and strategies by which the local people can relate themselves meaningfully to such interactive sessions.

The Konyak also find a difference in the behavior of tourists from India and abroad. While the foreign tourists are prompt buyers of traditional handicrafts, the Indian tourists take a long time to decide. Even if they decide to buy, they offer a very low price. Indian tourists are welcome to Konyak land but given an option they would like to have more foreign tourists. And they would enjoy the company of foreign tourists more, if they can find some meaning in such meetings. It was very clear in our interactions that they clearly weigh their options in choosing to be hosts.

The Konyak of Shangnyu village prioritized their needs. They expected the following things from the government: (i) construction of road; (ii) maintenance of Ang's court; (iii) adequate water supply; (iv) provision of government jobs for village youth; and (iv) maintenance of the village museum. In tourism development the state government has to clearly take note of the local issues.

Cultural diversity

The scenario at Tuensang is different. Inhabited by six different ethnic groups (Chang, Phom, Sangtam Khiamniungan, Yimchunger and Sumi), the district has the unique potential of exposing the tourists to six different cultural styles of life. By adopting six villages as model villages for respective tribes, tourists from different parts of India and abroad can have glimpses of their traditional houses, handicrafts, dresses and ornaments, styles of wearing and textile designs—all in a considerably compact location. Khiamniungans are known for their exotic traditional houses with stone roofs. At present only two houses of Noklak are having stone roofs.

Besides, some of the local NGOs are also working in the field of alternative medicine and flori-culture. This area is also known for different varieties of orchids. The Eastern Farmer's Association (EFA) of Tuensang town is working in the field of herbal medicine. It is documenting the medicinal value of rare species along with the associated local knowledge. It has already prepared a catalogue of such plants and their curative value. Apart from the large variety of medicinal plants, this area is also known for different varieties of paddy. Traditionally this area had fifty-one varieties of paddy grown in shifting cultivation.

Border trade

The districts of Mon, Tuensang and Kiphere have strategic location on the international border between India and Myanmar. Opening of International Trade Centres (ITC) at Pangsha of Noklak sub-division of Tuensang district and at Longwa village of Mon district would not only facilitate border trade but also unleash new kind of market forces. On the insistence of the local villagers, the ADC, Noklak, was planning to organise a weekly market beginning from the second week of December 2003. Villagers from Burma need salt, spice and eatables from their Indian counterparts. In exchange they bring wild animal meat, horn, baskets, beads (of necklaces) which the Khiamniungans use. The very idea of trading across the international border by local communities is seen to be a factor in tourist attraction.

Impact of tourism

Inflow of tourists into an area, where the host communities have not understood the intricacies of social interaction between tourists and themselves can lead to unforeseen consequences. After the relaxation of Restricted Area Permit (RAP) by the Government of India in April 2000, the inflow of foreign tourists to Nagaland increased almost six times in the last two years. The flow of domestic visitors has also increased substantially in the last few years. Some NGOs (especially Christian aided) are critical of the implications of tourism, while others perceive it as a mixed bag.

Some of the educated Konyak felt that though all sections of Naga are 'vulnerable' to tourism induced change, it is more so in their case. In the past, the Konyak were influenced by the Ao's version of Christianity. It was only at a later stage (after receiving education) that they have understood the real meaning of the Bible. It was different from the ways the Ao have made them understand. So the Konyak nature of "getting influenced easily" has to be kept in mind while promoting tourism in this area. Tourism development efforts have to be coupled with components of conservation/preservation of Konyak culture.

When the foreign tourists visit these tribal villages, they look for antique pieces of jewellery, spears, baskets, wooden sculptures and other traditional items possessed by the families of tribal aristocracy. Demand for such exquisite pieces of art has tempted the local villagers to sell them at prices considered very high in local standards. The international tourist does not mind paying little more as he/she is sure of the authenticity and antiquity of the artefact.

In the last two-three years, this has become almost a trend in the villages of Mon, Shangnyu, Chui, Longwa of Konyak area. Most of the authentic and antique pieces have been lost in the process of unmindful selling. Realizing the grave threat it poses to the rich cultural heritage, the officers of the tourist department in collaboration with the local tourist guides, undertook a campaign making people aware of the invaluable worth of such pieces of art. Since the present generation cannot reproduce such art forms they should preserve them for posterity. They conducted meetings with the villagers to make them realize the importance of these cultural items, but without much success.

Mistaking us for tourists, one of the Konyak women brought an old piece of basket to be sold at Rs 1000. This basket was being used in her household and when she saw us she was tempted to sell 'something' for ready cash. And the item she could immediately decide on was this basket. The accompanying tourist officers and guides were visibly upset about this. They explained to the lady the consequences of her action, and also reminded her that they have already done so in the past. The local people might take time to realize the seriousness of such a trend, but any attempt to promote rural or cultural tourism among the ignorant villagers would definitely have its own fall outs.

Drug trafficking

Heroine and other forms of narcotics change hands when the tourists are in Nagaland. Most of the international visitors, especially the tourists from west Asia (Pathans) come to Noklak sub-division of Tuensang for drugs. It is, therefore, very important to know the kind of people or local links through whom the tourists come.

The local people have now gained a greater level of movement and exposure and often travel to Kohima for the purpose of both education and employment; this leaves them vulnerable to vices like drug addiction and commercial sex which are becoming more and more rampant in urban areas. The youth begin with alcohol, then move to taking cough syrups (like phensedryl) before moving on to more serious drug abuse. Alcoholism though acceptable in men is greatly tabooed among women, reducing their chances of marriage. Thus, of these young addicts the family might still protect and cater to young men while the women fail to find acceptance in their own families thus pushing them more towards social insecurity and vulnerability leading to commercial sex. Some NGOs are openly warning the residents of pernicious effects of tourism.

Commercial sex work

Tourism has led to cultural exposure especially to the evils of modernity. Commercial sex work was unheard of in traditional Nagaland. But with rising contact with outsiders, it is coming up. Until very recently flesh trade was carried out mainly by women from Bangladesh. It was confined only to Dimapur and Kohima. But these days, commercial sex work is spreading rapidly to different towns. It is feared that it might have entered into every big town in Nagaland. In Dimapur, it is openly practicised in selected pockets. Some of the local informants in Tuensang feel that the possibility of commercial sex work coming from Myanmar cannot be ruled out. Cities like Kohima are already seeing a number of Naga girls in sex trade; the most obvious causes that have been quoted are that of alcoholism, drug addiction and broken families. The urban social parties, fashion shows, peer pressure, etc., are pulling more and more youth towards these vices. Further a test sample of 250 from among the sexually high-risk women showed an HIV prevalence of 15-20 per cent in the population. Thus the opening up of the Naga culture to the outside world is leading up to a number of social as well as health hazards. The church is also shying away from its responsibility. The local girls fall into the traps of sex trade due to the dire need for cash, which they require for drug. The link between drug addiction and commercial sex work cannot be ruled out. This situation is alarming.

Benefiting few

It was also observed in Mopungchuket that only a few rich, educated and forthcoming families participate in various activities of community tourism. Others generally stay away or are not in a position to take part in tourism activities. Paying guest accommodation is provided to tourists by few host families. Closer examination of the decision making process at the community level regarding identification of host families might reveal interesting details. However, during our stay at Mopungchuket Senso Mungdang rest house, one of the village council members *(gaon burha)* received us at the *morung,* the traditonal youth dormitory, entertained us with local songs (groups songs), and received some cash from our team members. On the same night we had dinner with our host's family enjoying the traditional Ao delicacies. At the time of payment for the dinner, to our surprise, we found that the hostess happened to be the wife of the same person whom we had paid in the *morung*. Distribution of benefits was seen to be uneven in the community. Some of the village youths staying at Kohima own Tata Sumos and rent them out as taxis to the tourists coming to Nagaland. In many cases tourism-fueled development has often led to increased wealth stratification in host communities. Thus the possibility of benefits of tourism not reaching larger sections of the society is a matter of concern.

Insurgents are not coming in the way of tourists as in most places we found a parallel tax extraction economy. They in fact have little problem with the foreign tourists in whom they find a good source of income whereas they are very suspicious of the Indian tourists. Insurgents were quite ambivalent towards these changes.

Emerging gender concerns

The Nagas, having a tradition in warfare and militancy, treat their women in a way specific to their culture. In the traditional Naga culture women were treated with dignity and respect. Naga women enjoyed more rights in traditional marriages. For example, among the Chang the husband had to make a promise to the wife's family clearly declaring the patch of forest he would give as compensation in case he betrayed her. Such promises were always made in the presence of the mediator who negotiated the marriage, and other influential persons of the village. Adoption of Christianity required change in customary marriage practices, and as a result, Chang women were deprived of their traditional rights.

In traditional Naga society, however, women had little role in decision making, both in domestic and politico-jural domains. Women were almost invisible in the field of governance. Among the Naga, being patriarchal and patrilineal, women virtually got no inheritance. The division of labour between men and women centred around traditional gender roles. While men were busy in hunting, including 'head hunting', women engaged in agricultural work, cooking, taking care of children and looking after the household chores. Women were considered the backbone of traditional economy.

Weaving is a woman's job. Weaving a shawl requires one to two months depending on the amount of time she is able to give amidst other household responsibilities. The family granary, located little away from the house to avoid fire, is under the direct supervision of women. Men do not interfere in women's job. However, it is the woman's responsibility to ensure that family members get food in time and the granary does not run out of stock. Nowadays women are able to generate some income by selling these shawls in the nearby market. But, among the more traditional set ups, though the woman is responsible for making the artefact, it is usually the man who sells it and gets the financial benefit; thus, in spite of the fact that the woman is an earning member, she lacks social power. The implications of tourism are also gendered. They have opened up work opportunities for young women. Besides, the traditional gender roles necessitate that the Naga woman acts as a good hostess to tourists.

Naga women are the repository of local knowledge. One of the Chang women of Tuensang said that during her forefather's time the area had fifty-one varieties of indigenous paddy. But only twenty-three varieties survive today. On asking her how did she know such exact details, she came up with an astounding answer. Each variety of paddy was associated with a specific song which the women sing while husking it. There were fifty-one songs associated with the husking of paddy which some of the older women remembered, but today they could only hear twenty-three songs in their area. The state needs to realize that the success of sustainable tourism development plan depends on the ability to identify, preserve and document the rich oral tradition and local knowledge of the Naga.

The Naga men treat their women with great care and respect. Eve- teasing is unheard of. The women feel safe even while roaming alone. This is definitely a positive indicator for domestic and international visitors. Foreign tourists, especially women, can safely move around without any security risk.

Revivalism and identity assertion

The issues of tradition and modernity loom large in contemporary Naga community life. Christianity has undermined the traditional glamour of Naga rituals, folk songs, dormitory life and other aspects of their rich cultural heritage. With a growing realization that it is the 'ethnic' or 'traditional' which sells in the tourism market, there have been attempts on the part of local people to revive age old traditions. The state government has taken several steps in this direction but the achievements are far from the expectations. The church is clearly sceptical of these activities.

One of the steps the Departments of Tourism and Arts and Culture have taken is to build a community museum for the preservation of cultural items. The village of Shangnyu has one such museum with an entry fee of Rs. 500 for a group. The key lies with the Ang. Traditionally the Ang's court used to house different types of cultural items such as large wooden cots made out of a single piece, exquisite bamboo baskets, spears, *dao, mithun* and elephant heads, human skulls and other artefacts which were regarded as prized possessions. Most of them were given to the Ang as gifts by chiefs of other villages. The weapons and some other items belonged to the entire village.

When the government is building community museums most of the items of Ang's court are shifted to a new building which is not in tune with the local architecture. In fact, by putting the cultural items in a museum, which is built next to Ang's house, we are removing them out of context to an extent that the meaning gets diluted, if not lost. On our visit to the villages of Shangnyu and Chui, we found out that the traditional Ang houses have shrunk considerably. The tourist guide/interpreter would often say that the house extended further with huge campus when he visited it last year.

In the Chui village, a sprawling Church building has been recently constructed just in front of the Ang's houuse. In past, the villagers buried the human skulls on persuasion of the Church. But now they feel that had those skulls been there, the village would have attracted more tourists. Exploring the possibility of preserving these artefacts in the Ang's court itself is a better option so that they are not dissociated from the context. Preservation of culture in real life spaces would not only convey more meaning to the tourists but also make tourism in Nagaland more lively and exciting.

The processes of cultural revival are being facilitated by various tribe specific *culture clubs*. They are making every effort to identify the so called 'culture experts' who know the folk songs, traditional styles of singing and dancing, which distinguished one tribe from another. They organize and celebrate traditional festivals in their respective areas from time to time. Some felt that there was a need to infuse a sense of dignity in the traditional cultural items. The youth are collaborating in documenting the traditional Naga culture through literature, music and films, thereby asserting their identity. The contemporary Naga youth are not only taking pride in their culture but also making sincere efforts to reinterpret the tradition, so that the posterity searches for the cultural power not from without but from within. This is definitely a welcome trend for ethnic or cultural tourism.

NOTE

1. This paper has emerged out of my work with the World Tourism Organization, UNDP, and the Government of Nagaland, for which I assessed the potential impact of tourism. Intensive anthropological fieldwork was conducted in different parts of Nagaland intermittently from November 2003 to March 2004. Thanks are due to these organizations and Nilika Mehrotra for support.

REFERENCES

Ao, M. Alemchiba

1970 *A Brief Historical Account of Nagaland.* Kohima: Naga Institute of Culture.

Bhattacharya, P. K.

1975 'The position of Naga women,' *Highlander : Biannual Research Bulletin,* 3(1).

Cohen, Erik

1984 'The sociology of tourism: Approaches, issues and findings,' *Annual Review of Sociology,* 10: 373-92.

International Union of Official Travel Organisations Document

1963 *The United Nations' Conference on International Travel and Tourism.* Geneva.

Lim, Francis Khek Gee

2007 'Hotels as sites of power: Tourism, status and politics in Nepal Himalayas', *Journal of the Royal Anthropological Institute* (*NS*), 13(2): 721-738.

Mehrotra, Nilika

1992 'Angami Naga women: Some reflections on their status," In S. M. Channa (ed.), *Nagaland: A Contemporary Ethnography*. Delhi: Cosmo Publishers.

Nash, D.

1981 'Tourism as an anthropological subject,' *Current Anthropology*, 22 (5): 461-481.

Roy Burman, B. K.

1973 'Perspective on Nagaland,' *Highlander : Biannual Research Bulletin,* 1 (2).

Weaver, David

2000 *Tourism Management*. Brisbane: John Wiley and Sons.

13

Dance Ethnography in the Anthropology of India: Prospects and Possibilities

NITA MATHUR

The discursive spaces in which the intellectual currents in the discipline of anthropology in general and the practice of social anthropology in India in particular are located entrench determinate hierarchal positions of power. Writings on society and culture in India that gained currency in the colonial period (and laid the foundation for the ones that followed) were those that made use of western concepts and analytical models eschewing local concepts and ways of understanding with greater heuristic potential. Many of them employed conceptual categories that were eurocentric and imputed meaning to social reality that tightened the grip of colonialists. The debate started by Louis Dumont and David Pocock on the need to develop sociology of India that filled the columns of the journal, *Contributions to Indian Sociology,* between 1957 to 1960 received inputs from the best sociologists and anthropologists well up to the 1980s and continues to be discussed even in the present day, though in different fora. More specifically, Saberwal (1983:1) raises a fundamental question:

> How does an intellectual tradition, arising out of a civilization with particular kinds of intellectual and social habits and resources become domesticated in another civilization whose intellectual habits and recourses have been very different?

The growing awareness about the inadequacies in the broad-based anthropological theories calls for reformulating anthropological practice and re-defining the subject of anthropology in the Indian context (see Ghurye 1943; Srinivas 1955; Mukherji 1958; Gough 1968; Singh 1986). Concomitant with the processes of indigenization of concepts and ideas for the practice of sociology and social anthropology in India is that of identifying dimensions of social and cultural reality that have a distinct salience in the culture. Last few decades have seen burgeoning of interest in the issues of ethnic identity, impact of globalization on local culture, consumer society, popular culture, and related aspects within the framework of postmodernist discourse. The paradigm of postmodernism lays broad-based theories and metanarratives to rest in favour of polyvocality, multiple realties, and cultural autonomy. In fact:

> Though post-modern ethnography privileges discourse, it does not locate itself exclusively within the problematics of a single tradition of the discourse, and seeks, to avoid grounding in the theoretical and commonsense categories of the hegemonic western tradition (Tyler 1986: 129).

Meaningful ethnography in contemporary times legitimates understanding of cultural realities in non-Western contexts from the vantage point of local perceptual, conceptual, and metaphysical aspects. The process is inevitably accompanied with widening of the scope of the discipline in order to accord cardinality to dimensions other than those that have long constituted the core area of concern. Against this backdrop, aspects of culture that had hitherto remained ignored or found only limited space in ethnographies lend themselves for intensive exploration. There is consequent shift in focus from the conception of culture as a set of shared beliefs and values that may or may not be expressed (see Almond and Verba 1963; Parsons and Shils 1951) to culture as a "set of public ally shared codes or repertories, building blocks that structure people's ability to think and to share ideas" (Eliasoph and Lichterman 2003: 735).

Taking off at this juncture, the present essay seeks to explore how the "public ally shared codes or representations" in a classical dance form are imbued with meaning(s) and message(s) in real life situations. The domain of break dancing, bar dancing and other forms of popular dance referred to by Hanna (1992) as 'social dance', however, lies beyond the scope. More specifically, the focus is on the construction and transmission of knowledge characteristic of Tamil Brahmin culture through the use of narratives and gestures in Bharatanatyam which is one of the classical dance forms of India. The understanding is that dance constitutes a vital component of culture in a general sense and of the Tamil Brahmins culture in a particular sense. The main agenda is to decipher the operative processes in culture. The dance has been used as a gateway for entry into the culture of Tamil Brahmins with the purpose of demonstrating how knowledge which is distinctive of the culture is construed in the dance; and how hand gestures used in dance are employed to convey information in non-dance situations too. The social significance and meanings of gestures and narratives in dance is deciphered. The purpose is to identify the fine nuances that integrate dance with mundane lives of people, here Tamil Brahmins. In doing so what emerges is a dance ethnography in which dance is situated in the matrix of social relationships. The essay begins with the concept of dance ethnography in anthropological literature, then presents a case study of dance ethnography and concludes with reflections on the prospects and possibilities of dance ethnography in anthropology of India. The concept of dance ethnography is used here to privilege the strategy of treating performance as an agency of culture. This marks a shift from 'dance as representation' to 'dance as participation' in anthropological writings.

Dance ethnography

At the outset, distinction, though a subtle one, may be made between dance in ethnography and dance ethnography. A large number of ethnographies, particularly those produced in colonial times were, in effect, based on cultural appropriation of difference (Martin 1992). The scope of dance in such ethnographies was confined to description as cultural exotica, as queer performance, or at best as part of 'irrational' religious behaviour often as an appendage without much significance. The focus was on the components of movement, style, and performance. In later ethnographies, however, dance was assigned a more prominent place in being treated as an inseparable part of culture. Most of the ethnographies and other anthropological writings on culture and lifestyles of people incorporate the element of dance in the context of religious experience, trance and ecstasy, leisure, entertainment and informal means of interaction, and competition and welfare (Sachs 1937; Durkheim 1915; Bailey 1957; Marshall 1962; Rappaport 1979). There are also those that treat dance as a means for release of pent-up emotions and drives. One of the earliest references to the cathartic value of dance is that of Herbert Spencer (1862), who explains the efficacy of dance (as also music and laughter) as an outlet of emotions in the form of nervous energy that becomes intensified when their expression in the course of daily life is plugged. Later writings such as those of Evans-Pritchard (1937) on Azande beer dance as a channel for expression of sexual desires; of Margaret Mead (1928) on children's dance in Samoa as providing release from repression and subordination by adults in different situations; and of Gluckman (1965) on Swazi first-fruit ceremony enfolding opportunity for release of anxiety and tension accruing from prolonged period of shortage and economic insecurity strengthen the proposition. Another category of writings on dance draws on its role in the maintenance of social order. Radcliffe-Brown's interpretation of dance among the Andaman Islanders (1964) is based on the homeostatic model in which dance was interpreted as an expression of collective emotion which centripetally pulls an individual who had gone astray into the social order. Social anthropologists and sociologists have also tended to explore dance in the framework of social stratification (more so in societies that have identifiable dances of the upper and lower classes) as an index of rural-urban contrasts especially by way of shedding light on the differences in performance of a single dance form in rural and urbanized locales. This is concurrent with the constant flux between the rural and urban styles of presentation (Lange 1977).

What comes out clearly is the fact that while dance has been recognized as an integral component of culture, the reference to dance is only scattered, dispersed, and in clearly delimited contexts in the writings of social anthropologists and sociologists. Equally important is to note the excessive emphasis on stage dance as shared experience, often at the cost of explaining movements in terms of social codes and the symbolic significance of dance in totality. Here, perspectives of those who perform the dance and of those for whom the dance is performed acquire greater significance. It is only in the last decade or two that dance studies have been able to carve a niche in anthropological and sociological writings. This is accompanied with the rise of dance ethnographies born out of a distinct methodology of research. According to Sklar (1991), dance ethnography derives from the following propositions: (i) dance is a kind of cultural knowledge hence it is more than a set of stylized and codified movements performed as end unto themselves rather they embody cultural history, beliefs, values, and feelings of a people; (ii) local contextual information about social values, symbolic codes, beliefs all constitute the framework within which dance is purposed and within which it may be understood appropriately; and (iii) understanding the social significance and meaning of the movements in dance is crucial.

In the context of concert dance, Martin (1992: 103) writes:

> The dancers constitute themselves in anticipation of performance. This anticipation bears the anxiety of uncertainty, of something that can be completed only through its communication. The performance is the execution of an idea by dancers whose work proceeds in expectation of an audience that is itself only constituted through performance.

In corollary, dance in society may provide an understanding of the way of life of a people and all that is critical to in-depth understanding of a culture. The idea of dance as cultural understanding may be used to develop complete ethnographies because,

> The aim of anthropological works is not simply to understand dance in its cultural context, but rather to understand society through analyzing movement systems (Kaeppler 1992: 151).

This offers greater potential for dance writings in India because of the fact that dance is enmeshed with the lifestyles of people as their warp and woof rather than being ephemeral in character—created by a performer for the limited period for which the performance lasts. The scope of dance ethnography in the anthropology of India is considerably widened in that the way of life as cultural reality and dance as aesthetic manifestation of creative energies coalesce. Dance may, therefore, be understood as part of the total design of life and thought since complete lifestyles revolve around it at the physical level (as movement enfolding cultural construction of identity in the matrix of symbolic configuration, experience and expression of emotions and rituals) and at the philosophical level (as enfolding the vision of life and cosmic order).

The dance of Bharatanatyam among Tamil Brahmins: A case study

The dance of Bharatanatyam proliferated in the temples in Tamil Nadu as part of service rendered to the male deities by a distinct category of women devotees known as *devadasi*s. The term *devadasi* literally means servant (*dasi*) of the god (*deva*). Young girls were initiated into the devadasi way of life, which consisted of learning the skill of serving the male deity in the temple. One of the ways of doing it was appeasing him through dance. They underwent a long period (often spanning several years) of rigorous training that was intercepted with rituals marking different stages of proficiency. An important marker was the ritual of *gajjai puja* (or worship of ankle bells) which signified the adeptness of the devadasi in performing astutely to the rhythm set by the drummer and other musicians. It was only after the *gajjai puj*a that the devadasi could wear the ankle bells in the course of her training. When the teacher was satisfied with the performance of the devadasi, he would organize an *aragaetrum* - her first performance before the devotees in the temple. This was an important occasion in her life because following it, she was wedded to the god himself through a set of elaborate rituals. She stayed in the precincts of the temples serving him as a wife and continued to do so throughout her lifetime. In line with the practice of the husband performing the last rites of his wife, the funeral pyre of a devadasi was lit with fire brought from the temple. In the Hindu thought, a married woman remains auspicious so long as her husband is alive. The devadasis were often referred to as *nityasumangali* (or the ever auspicious) because they were never widowed hence their auspiciousness as married women was never annihilated. People invited the devadasi on important occasions, e.g. life cycle rituals with a belief that her presence would bestow auspiciousness to the event.

Apart from performing in the temples as part of *nityaseva* (daily service) devadasis would dance in front of the deity's chariot in processions. Since Tamil Brahmin men managed the affairs of the temples and performed rituals consisting primarily of incantations, chanting, and singing of hymns that also formed the code of symbols and language of the dance, their interaction with the devadasis and the association with their dance was intense. Another reason why Tamil Brahmin men associated themselves with the dance was that it was treated as a form of worship and serving the god which was one of their prime duties ordained in the religious texts. Later, when the anti-nautch movement (prohibiting the initiation of young girls into the devadasi way of life) was launched and the dance could not be performed in temples, Tamil Brahmins protected and perpetuated it zealously in many ways. The elders encouraged the young girls in their families to undergo the training in dance. Several men learnt to perform themselves, some of them would even wear women's dresses and make performances in public. Over the years, the dance earlier popular as *dasi attam* (dance of women servants), came to be known as Bharatanatyam and got entwined with the culture and lifestyle of Tamil Brahmins. Since dance is regarded as a form of rendering worship, menstruating girls (who are believed to be polluted for a period of four days) do not attend dance classes. Gaston (1991: 166) cites the following words of a Brahmin dancer:

> Because you are already committed, you must perform, but there was an idea of pollution so I kept some distance from the cymbals and musicians. You will pollute them if you touch them. We would not drop flowers in front of the image or bow down in front of the icon on the stage.

In their own homes menstruating girls are treated as 'untouchables' and made to remain confined to a limited space. The men keep away even from their shadow for the fear of getting polluted.

The earliest exposure of a Tamil Brahmin to the dance is when a pregnant woman watches live performances (on stage or now on the television too) with a conviction that the child in her body would develop deep and abiding interest in the art. Children, particularly girls, enthusiastically accompany their parents and grandparents to dance recitals. A fairly large number of them seek admission in dance schools. Enrolment in a dance school is accompanied with a series of rituals and prayers evoking the blessings of the gods and the dance teacher. Most of them enthusiastically practice at home all that they learn in the dance school, so perfection is not far to fetch. With the passage of time, initial hesitation, inhibition and shyness give way to confidence. Children form friendships with co-learners and develop bonds of trust and affection with teachers. Those who learn from the same teacher share a common identity and exhibit solidarity. This overshadows quarrels, strife, and competition as each one strives to receive greater attention and appreciation of the teacher. The dance teacher (*nattuvanar*) is not a distant figure. Children address men teachers as *tattha* and women teachers as *akkal,* which are also kinship terms for father's father and father's sister respectively. In the kinship system, *tattha* and *akkal* combine authority and affection in a way that children joyfully follow their direction. The dance teachers often know the children's anxieties and apprehensions as also their problems relating to regular studies as also familial affairs. Many children confide in the dance teachers and tell their little secrets and all that they are unable to say to the elders in the family.

Children may be seen humming the song of the dance softly or trying to hold a glass of water or comb the hair in different styles so as to choose the one they find most graceful and adopt it in their daily lives. The dance provides alternative ways of performing mundane activities. More interestingly,

> Parents encourage the children to learn dance because, in their own words, it etches erect posture and makes common, daily activities controlled, polished and graceful. A child who has learnt dance even for a short period of time is distinguished by the style of, say turning the head, pointing out to somebody, or to dance, their walk and everything they do will appear feminine (Mathur 2002 : 127).

The people perform mundane activities such as rocking a child in the cradle, grinding rice in pestle and mortar in a way that follows a rhythm, which make them less tiresome.

In another context, Radcliffe-Brown (1964) explains the significance of rhythm exercises in that they place a constraint on the individual both from within (since the impulse to yield themselves to the constraining rhythm comes from their own organism) as also from without (since it is the sight of friends dancing and the sound of singing and marking time that occasions it). The body and mind are compelled to submit to the constraint which produces pleasure of a distinct nature. A large number of Tamil Brahmins say that they attribute their sensitivity to the exposure to dance and music, which encourages them to appreciate the elements of rhythm and regularity in their lives. At another level, they are able to connect the rhythm in personal lives with the universal rhythms exhibited in the form of, among others, the waxing and waning of moon, cycle of seasons, rise and fall of waves in the ocean and other natural phenomena. They explain that in this sense, cultural rhythms are only a part of universal rhythms and one who is able to understand the interrelationship between the two, acquires emotional and spiritual maturity and success and failure in mundane life fail to toss him/her.

A large part of the dance consists of stylized presentation of stories that are drawn from the sacred texts. A dancer, therefore, enacts specific events from the lives of the gods. The impact on her as also on those who watch her do it is so tremendous that they tend to re-count and re-live the performance event in course of the day. People, particularly women say that their response to a situation, their ways of behaving and interacting with others on a day-to-day basis is often derived from portrayals and presentations of similar situations in the dance. In everyday, non-dance situations their actions are largely influenced by what they see or perform in dance. One example is that of a young mother whose child began to cry incessantly in the night. With no help at hand, and with no success to quieten her, she remembered one dance performance in which the dancer enacting the role of Yashoda (the foster mother of Krishna, the dark hued god, who put the child in a cradle, then took him in the arms and sang a lullaby. Inspired by Yashoda's success, she followed the sequence. The fact that she derived inspiration from a dance situation is far more important then the physical efforts by which the child was put to sleep. The meaning and message in dance are extremely important for those who understand them.

The dance consists of fifty-two gestures (*mudras*) of the hands through which the stories are enacted. Each gesture carries a defined set of meanings. The folds and extensions of fingers forming the gestures depict animals (e.g. *sarpa-siras mudra* in which the palm is hollowed by bending the fingers and thumb depicts the head of a snake). Apart from the snake head, the *mudra* also denotes the ears; religious symbol (e.g. *trishula mudra* in which the first three fingers are extended while the thumb and little finger touch each other). The *mudra* denotes, among others, Lord Shiva's trident. It also denotes the number three, and a wood-apple leaf. Cultural ingenuity lies not simply in drawing morphological similarity between the form(s) a *mudra* depicts, but in conveying abstract ideas, emotions, relationships and processes on the one hand and in the multiplicity of depictions that each one is used to make. The gestures are polysemous, the same gesture can take on different meanings in different contexts. One example is that of the *sikhara mudra* in which the fingers are rolled inwards to form a fist while the thumb is stretched out. It is used to denote a bow, bell, pillar, tooth, as also silence, the acts of untying the girdle, embracing, pounding (food grains) and physical strength. The dancer uses the same *mudra* for a combination of depictions in the course of a performance. Her choice depends on the theme and idea being depicted and the appropriateness of the combination with the movement of the body, the facial expressions, and the basic rhythm to which the song is set. In actual practice, therefore, a *mudra* may be seen to be embedded in the complete performative matrix. One is struck by the use of these *mudras* in daily life. Men and women, for example, ring the bell as part of the every day worship at home in the *sikhara mudra*. It is common to see the use of this *mudra* in regular conversations. Often, it is not easy to say whether dance is drawn from daily life or daily life is greatly influenced by dance.

The dance provides an effective means for channelising the basic drives and emotions that have hitherto remained crammed up in the mind. The basic instincts energize psychic processes and operate compulsively in the unconscious realm of the mind while at the conscious level they remain under the control of the ego (Jung 1954; Preston 1990). The pressure of yielding to cultural norms, restrain on talking and laughing aloud and similar other compulsions restrict the inner psychic processes among children. It has been mentioned that in the process of growing up, several children accumulate emotions as unresolved repression and tension (Mathur 1997). In the dance, children are able to perform feats such as flying over oceans, killing demons effortlessly, and carrying mountains in the hands that are not possible in real life. This provide a means of compensating for their failures and inabilities in lived lives. The fantasy (or make-believe element) in dance and creative movements is known to reach out to the inner recesses of the mind that effectively mobilize the blocked psychic context. Dance gathers further relevance in the case of girl children who are subjected to more intense and severe conditions of stress than boys and are required to discharge the major responsibility of maintaining and handing down of traditions.

Cultural ideologies of gender differences are reproduced in dance largely through the narratives to which the performance is set. Several of them establish the role of women in families as mothers, sisters, daughters, and daughters-in-law. There are also narratives that bespeak of women as yearning for a glimpse of their beloved. Such themes reinforce ideas of women's subservience to men. The men, in turn, derive notions of self-supremacy. Feminists argue that men have laid down patterns of interaction for women. It was the men who wrote the religious texts that continue to sanctify and regulate relations between genders. Again, they taught the dance to devadasis, wrote the songs and played the instruments to which women would dance. Both, literally and metaphorically, women seem to dance to the clichéd tune of men. The men have presented the image of women as dependent and subordinate to them. Women have, in turn, idealized it. An eight year old boy expressed his opinion about women in following words:

> Girls are dirty. I don't like young girls. They are weak, they cry. Once some girls in school teased me. I gave them one blow. They started crying and did not come near me again. Girls cannot fight an intruder, I can. I can be a better cook than them. Girls cannot cook well because they do not consult cookery books. I don't depend

> on girls. I can wash my own clothes in the machine. Girls cannot recite Shakespeare (he laughs). I will never marry. I don't want a sister.

The mother accepted his ideas and made no intervention. This is not to say that no Tamil Brahmin woman has a voice of her own. The younger generation does appreciate feminist ideology with emphasis on gender equality and empowerment of women but the cultural system does take a long time to manifest the change in values and ideals.

Prospects and possibilities

Commonplace understanding of dance in a culture is limited to the conception that there are dancers at one end and audience at the other, and that the relationship between them is mediated by the dance. Surely, dance in a culture more so in India has wider spread in that it is entwined with the life philosophy itself. The Indian view of civilization revolves around the concept of *sabhyata*. The term *sabhyata* is derived from *sabha* which means, 'shining together' and 'assembly of men in harmony.' The concept of *sabhyata* is not so much about refinement as about perceiving the rhythm of existence integrating creativity, experience, expression and collective identity in different processes of life. This encourages tolerance towards others and ready acceptance, not repulsion of new ideas. The image of civilization is explained through the metaphor used extensively by Kabir and other seers—that of weaving of fabric of civilization which is likened to a woven fabric designed by gods. Seers and laypersons continue the process of weaving and only add on to it through their own efforts. They weave forward and weave backward maintaining the pattern. The purpose is to enlarge the fabric (i.e., expand the civilization) without loss of the pattern (i.e., the design of life). All that a person does in daily life, the corpus of thoughts that are generated in the mind and the impressions that are formed need to be in consonance with the basic design. This lays out the configuration for developing lifestyles and leading lives.

Sabhyata subsumes apparent contradictions and divergences within its fold treating them not as oppositions but complements to the larger pattern of life. Auspiciousness and inauspiciousness, fertility and sterility, all define cultural reality. The seemingly opposing characters are connected, if nothing else, by the principles of convertibility and transformation. Inauspicious becomes auspicious and the sterile becomes fertile through rituals, incantations and sacrifices. The potential of godliness coexists with that of being evil and demon-like. The ultimate objective of human existence is to develop one's godliness and minimize the demonic character. At the aesthetic level, this notion gets translated into the classical or the canonized tradition and the folk or the performed tradition. The interplay between them is evident in the *genres* of dance, music, and theatre. A civilized person is regarded as one who is endowed with the sensitivity to recognize the harmony in sentient beings, insentient things, phenomena of nature, and the processes of life is a manifestation of play (*lila*) of the gods. Both gods and devotees are known to dance. The image of Krishna dancing on the hood of the thousand-headed serpent instills fearlessness and reinstates the god's commitment to deliver devotees from evil. Somewhat akin to the dance of Krishna is that of goddess Kali on the burning grounds (which represents the preparing of the human heart for devotion and piety by consigning illusions and worldly attachments to flames) and Nataraja–the Lord of Dance (conveying messages of devotion, liberation and renunciation from worldly life). The dance of the gods affirms the cosmic order (*rta*) which signifies regularity, uprightness and justice in the cosmic processes. Dance becomes a means for acquiring as also manifesting spiritual fulfillment. Several devotees and seers as Meerabai, Sri Ramakrishna, Swami Vivekananda, and Chaitanya Mahaprabhu are known to have danced with spontaneity in sheer ecstasy.

In order that devotion to the gods is fruitful, the aspirant has to strive to avoid all thoughts that are not associated with the gods and go about the mundane activities with an attitude of surrender to them. As aids to establishing an intimate and personal relationship with the deity, a devotee engages in hearing the praises of the deities, praising the deities, chanting their names, remembering the deities all the time, and serving the deities by worship and by doing 'good deeds' in their name (Walker 1983). This entails exercising restraint on negative emotions such as anger, disgust, and jealousy that cross the mind. Dance contains the potential to control the mind (which is believed to be inherently volatile) since it is a way of, as all forms of Indian art, about which Vatsyayan (1998) affirms, *sadhana* (referring to the means of achieving a state of total release or liberation from the so-much-ness of life), *yoga* (referring to the means of attaining adeptness or efficiency in whatever endeavour one undertakes), and *yajna* (referring to the means of making dedicated offering of the best that one has to the gods). Furthermore, the dance articulates the abstract principles of life (philosophy and world-view) by which people to whom the dance belongs live. In the classical dance forms that commonly portray lives of the gods, the dancer acquires the identity of the character she performs, though for a brief while. The merit of her dance lies in the ability to engross the audience to an extent that each one transcends the personal, individual identity and experience the presence of the deity amidst themselves.

The folk dances are characterized by active participation of the audience in the sense that often there is no neat dichotomy between the dancers and the audience, for many among the audience have been dancers earlier or may join the group in future. The thrust is not so much on the perfection of performance as on the participation and involvement of the community. In the Indian context, several dance forms convey a vision of life which lays emphasis on harmony and integration of human life with nature and environment. Dance, particularly among the indigenous people and villagers (i.e. those who live in the lap of nature) has a bearing on the means of subsistence at two levels. The first consists of performance as part of ritual or celebration of different stages in the processes of subsistence. Among the rice cultivators, for example, there are dances at the time of sowing, transplanting, and harvesting. At the second level, the nature of dance is determined by the means of subsistence itself. Vatsyayan (1976) explains this more clearly by stating that often the *jhum* cultivators hold the seeds in one hand and scatter them with the other. The result is crossing-over movement of the arms, so typical of some of the dances of the north-east region. Similarly, the paddy growers have to bend low and move in receding order for transplantation of the seedlings which finds manifestation in the dances of rice growing communities. The wheat cultivators, in contrast, harvest the grain by bending forward but holding themselves higher than the paddy growers. The dances of those who hold implements with long handles are invariably erect with inconspicuous bend of the torso. In earlier times, the daily routine of people comprised spinning and weaving, drawing water from the well, cleaning of utensils, looking after the domestic animals and other activities, most of which have permeated the fabric of their dances. The movement of the spinning wheel and gurgling of water finds place in the Gidda dance (an exclusively women's dance of Punjab), the weaving of cloth on looms finds place in the dance of Lai Haraoba (the dance of the Meiteis of Manipur); the journey to the well and process of drawing of water find place in the dances of Lambadis and Paniharis (of Rajasthan). In fact, the act of balancing of pots for drawing water has been transformed into a competent skill in the Bhawai dancers of Rajasthan. This is also true of the martial dances in several parts of the country in which the twin acts of attack and defence are performed without the immediacy of the actual event.

Anthropological studies on dance in India are few, fewer are dance ethnographies. This is despite the fact that dance ethnography in India affords considerable potential for the following reasons: (i) the multiplicity and richness of dance forms; (ii) co-existence of the folk and classical dance traditions with continual flux; and (iii) integration of dance tradition with traditions of other forms of art on the one hand and with mundane life on the other as a complex whole. Attention may be fruitfully directed toward "how images of dance and its production affirm and challenge basic social arrangements and doctrines about them" (Hanna 1988: 250). Indian dances have greatly inspired American choreographers. Apart from the articulation of sacred knowledge, an important dimension of anthropological study of dance in India is that of patterns of interaction between teacher and disciple, and among teachers and disciples, gender images, and social and cultural change. In the present day, several teachers are experimenting with the dance. Thus there are now mergers and combinations of movements from different dance forms.

The intervention of technology has made tremendous difference not only to the imagery and rendering of the dance but also to the performer-audience relationship. In the context of dance studies in India, the intense relationship between the performers and audience characterized by a sense of participation of the audience in the dance and the dedication of the performance by the dancer to the audience. Evidently, images viewed at one's convenience through the electronic media create a virtual distance between the two and an entirely different impact on the viewers. It also provides the convenience of repeated takes and re-takes (which is not possible in a live-performance) to dancers for making flawless presentations. The performer-audience relationship undergoes transformation as does the role of dance in culture which is itself set in a globalizing framework. In contemporary society governed largely by consumer culture and globalising trends, both classical and folk dance forms traverse beyond local spheres and in the process re-invent themselves, often several times. Though cultural organizations do define the parameters of the performative *genre*, producers of tourist programmes package them for non-traditional audiences within the place of their origin and spread as also outside it, even across national borders (Zarrilli 2000).

In a general sense, Turner (1967) explains that in a performance the principal meanings, values, and goals of a culture that govern and explain a people's behaviour may be seen 'in action'. A meaningful performance, therefore, is one in which archetypal roles and cultural identity is re-played. The relation between art and collective life pervades the construction of social reality and its experience. According to Geertz (1983), works of arts materialize a way of experiencing. They bring a particular cast of mind into the world of objects where others can look at it. The patterned symbols in art through which an idea or a set of ideas are conveyed are largely shared by members of a cultural group. Among other forms of art, dance elucidates this most appropriately because of its dynamic nature referring to its creation, existence, and evanescence each time in a performance and the powerful impact it generates on the minds of the dancers and those who see the dance within the limited period of time in a dance event. It, therefore, affords immense potential for innovation, re-configuration and versatility because of which it continues to be relevant to the culture over several decades.

REFERENCES

Almond, G. and S. Verba

1963 *The Civic Culture*. Princeton, N.J.: Princeton University Press.

Bailey, F, G.

1957 *Caste and the Economic Frontier*. Manchester: Manchester University Press.

Durkheim, E.

1915 *The Elementary Forms of the Religious life*. London: George Allen and Unwin.

Eliasoph and Lichterman

2003 Culture in Interaction. *American Journal of Sociology* 108, 4.735-794.

Evans-Pritchard, E.E.

1937 *Witchcraft, Oracles and Magic among the Azande*. London: Oxford University Press.

Gaston, Anne-Marie

1991 'Dance and the Hindu woman: Bharatanatyam re-ritualized'. In Julia Leslie (ed.), *Roles and Rituals for Hindu Women*. London: Printer Publishers.

Geertz, C.

1983 *Local Knowledge: Further Essays in Interpretive Anthropology*. New York: Basic Books.

Ghurye, G. S.

1943 *The Aborigines so-called and their Future*. Poona: Gokhale Institute of Politics and Economics.

Gluckman, M.

1965 *Custom and Conflict in Africa*. New York: Free Press.

Gough, K.

1968 'New proposals for anthropologists', *Current Anthropology* 9 (5): 403-407.

Hanna, J. L.

1988 *Dance, Sex and Gender: Signs of Identity, Dominance, Defiance and Desire*. Chicago: University of Chicago Press.

1992 'Moving messages: Identity and desire in popular music and social dance'. In James Lull (ed.), *Popular Music and Communication*. Newbury Park: Sage Publications.

Jung, C. G.

1954 *The Development of Personality*. London: Routledge.

Kaeppler, A.

1992 'Theoretical and methodological considerations for anthropological studies of dance and human movement', *Ethnographica* 8: 151-157.

Lange, R.

1977 'Some notes on the anthropology of dance'. In J. Blacking (ed.), *The Anthropology of the Body* (ASA Monographs). London: Academic Press.

Marshall, L.

1962 '!Kung Bushman religious beliefs', *Africa* 32:221-252.

Martin, R.

1992 'Dance ethnography and the limits of representation', *Social Text* 33: 103-123.

Mathur, Nita

1997 'Dance and the child', *The Eastern Anthropologist* 50: 247-257.

2002 *Cultural Rhythms in Emotions, Narratives and Dance*. New Delhi: Munshiram Manoharlal.

Mead, M.

1928 *Coming of Age in Samoa*. New York: William Morrow.

Mukherji, D.P.

1958 *Diversities*. Delhi: People's Publishing House.

Parsons, T. and E. A. Shils.

1951 *Toward a General Theory of Action*. Cambridge,Mass.: Harvard University Press.

Preston, E.

1990 'Mind and matter in myth'. In Barnbay and D'Aeierno (ed.), *C.G. Jung and the Humanity: Towards a Hermeneutics of Culture*. Princeton: Princeton University Press.

Rappaport, Roy A.

1979 *Ecology, Meaning and Religion*. Richmond, Calif: North Atlantic Books.

Radcliffe-Brown, A.R.

1964 *The Andaman Islanders*. New York: The Free Press.

Saberwal, S.

1983 'For a sociology of India: On multiple codes', *Contributions to Indian Sociology* 16(2): 289-294.

Sachs, C.

1937 *World History of the Dance*. New York: WW. Norton and Co.

Singh, Y.

1986 *Indian Sociology*. New Delhi: Vistaar publications.

Sklar, D.

1991 'On dance ethnography', *Dance Research Journal* 23, 6-10.

Spencer, Herbert

1862 *First Principles*. London: Williams and Norgate.

Srinivas, M. N.

1955 *India's Villages*. Bombay: Asia Publishing House.

Turner V.

1967 *The Forest of Symbols*. Ithaca, NY: Cornell University Press.

Tyler, S.A.

1986 'Post-modern ethnography: From document of the occult to occult document'. In Clifford and Marcus (ed.), *Writing Culture: The Poetics and Politics of Ethnography*. Delhi: Oxford University Press.

Vatsyayan, K.

1976 *Traditions of Indian Folk Dance*. New Delhi: Indian Book Company.

1998 'Philosophy of Indian dance', In S. J. Cohen (ed.), *International Encyclopedia of Dance*, Volume 3. New York. Oxford University Press.

Walker, B.

1983 *Hindu World*. New Delhi: Munshiram Manoharlal.

Zarrilli, P. B.

2000 *Kathakali Dance- Drama: Where Gods and Demons Come to Play*. London and New York: Routledge.

Career Options in Social-cultural Anthropology

R. K. Kar

At the very outset, I deem it prudent to recapitulate what exactly we mean by the two terms, career and anthropology.

Career, according to the *Oxford Dictionary* refers to: (i) Course or progress through life or history, (ii) way of making a livelihood and advancing oneself, and (iii) personal advancement and success in life. *Chambers Twentieth Century Dictionary* also refers to "advancement in profession or occupation" as its meaning. When we talk of career, we definitely mean something more than the least ones of salary and some security. It should, as a matter of fact, offer so much more.

With regard to anthropology, I feel, I should emphasize that like any other lively discipline, it is constantly in a process of redefinition, and probably as such calls for an operational definition. The discipline initially came into being as a scientific study of the primitive cultures. But, incidentally, its traditional subject matter is gradually evaporating before its eyes. The accelerating demise of the traditional tribal societies is one of the reasons why anthropologists are increasingly turning from the investigation of small-scale exotic societies to the small-scale process of social interaction in large or complex societies. At present, it practically studies all types of human cultures and communities as well as their problems. As a matter of fact, an anthropologist always tries to understand and evaluate the emerging social issues of varied types at micro and macro levels; and from that angle it is a discipline with a commendable elastic horizon. Over a period of around one hundred and fifty years of its life, anthropology has been able to distinguish itself reasonably well both in terms of systematic attainment of knowledge as well as in its application to the service of mankind.

In this backdrop of the subject, and also in the backdrop of a very fast changing scenario of Indian society in particular; and global society in general, we need to examine the relevance of the discipline before we initiate a discussion on career options in anthropology.

II

I have observed elsewhere (Kar, 2001) that standing on the cusp of a new millennium, face-to-face with formidable challenges and equipped with equally powerful technologies, while attempting a self-appraisal, it cannot be denied that during the last century we have been able to solve a variety of difficult problems in the realms of engineering, medicine and technology. However, when it comes to solving human social issues, we do not seem to be much better than we were some two or three thousand years ago. The world is still a place of massive sufferings. Starvation, malnutrition and undernutrition, and premature deaths, etc., are a commonplace fate for millions of people. Yes, it is a fact that we have obtained a kind of mastery over the physical world; and to some extent, over the complexities of biological reality. But, at the same time, we do not seem to have that kind of wisdom which might enable us to make the greatest use of our lives. We very often get bogged down in racial, ethnic, religious, linguistic, regional and political conflicts. It is thus something of a paradox that we are more capable of dealing with the mysteries of the universe than we are with the complexities of ourselves and our social systems.

This paradoxical reality, I believe, makes it apparent that the anthropological understanding of our society itself as a problematic feature of human existence will continue to have a genuine relevance, until it is demonstrated that the advances in science and technology have brought about improvement in social relations among people.

Today, as we look for a new way of educating men and women who can both understand and cope with our intricate, just emerging universe with its tremendous contradictions, discrepancies, potentialities and dangers, it is being increasingly recognized that before a man can become an engineer, an administrator or a statesman, a production manager, a marketing executive, or even a poet, he must be made somehow into an educated man; that is a whole man, to whom nothing in the world is alien, to whom no path of possible exploration is blocked or closed; and I am confident, anthropology is the best suited discipline to meet this need. Anthropology, as we all know, is a discipline of the whole, the whole of man's history, the whole of man's being. Concern with ethical and other value issues is a part of anthropological tradition (e.g., the concept of cultural relativism). Combating ethnocentrism or regionalism has been named frequently as one of the main objects of teaching anthropology. Cultural relativism is sometimes treated as the whole substance or essence of the anthropological point of view. This orientation can however be acquired and internalized only by someone who is himself or herself, in true sense of the term, wholly involved and immersed in the discipline and its points of view.

It may relevantly be noted here that anthropology can be pursued both as a professional career as well as liberal education. Margaret Mead (1967) opines that anthropology is peculiarly fitted to fill a tremendous need in liberal education. It tries to conjoin, rather than fragment, the knowledge of man. It can be taught so as to give understanding of the farthest past of man and yet with close relation to the life today. The essence of a liberal education, according to her is to share the full identity, made possible by one's civilization. Anthropology's inclusive and integrating approach offers a broad avenue for such learning. The fundamental values of anthropology, she believes, are eternal and are essential for wisdom, and perhaps for a meaningful survival. A student of anthropology should hold them, not as distant ideals, but as the very essence of the work he or she does.

The relevance of the discipline is thus apparent to the effect that anthropology not only provides its students with a background for a new philosophical approach, but it also gives them a meaningful and satisfactory way of putting together the bits and pieces of knowledge about man and his achievements which they have acquired from other courses and sources.

III

With a foundation of anthropology, a student's career options are really very wide open. We need to remember that traditionally education in anthropology is accompanied by extensive field training that contributes towards orienting a mindset with high degree of objectivity and cross-cultural appreciation. A formal training in the discipline equips one with analytical ability; intellectual curiosity; critical thinking skills; knowledge of research methodology; ability to manage, evaluate and interpret large volumes of data. It equips one with social adeptness; tenacity of accurate record-keeping and attention to details; capacity to conceptualise; advanced oral and written communication skills; and willingness to network and share ideas with others.

In light of the culturally diverse global workforce and markets, as a matter of fact, there is a growing demand for personnel with the background of anthropology who possess a keen understanding of human behaviour; and can offer an anthropological perspective when conceptualizing and projecting future socio-economic trends and issues. Barring teaching and research, in Tribal Welfare Institutions/Organisations, Anthropological Survey of India, Community Development Projects of various types, in non-governmental organisations (NGOs), different world organizations (e.g. UNESCO, UNICEF, WHO, World Bank and ILO etc.), museums, archives, tourism related establishments and many other allied organizations, quite a good number of job opportunities can be found.

The Anthropological Survey of India (ASI) that was established in December 1945, has now grown into the world's biggest anthropological organization with the largest number of professional anthropologists and scholars of allied disciplines working in it.

With regard to the NGOs vis-à-vis career option in anthropology, it may be noted that the sixth five-year plan (1980-85) stated that the country is dotted with numerous examples of highly successful voluntary organizations. It however, admitted that considering the vast pool of motivated individuals available in the country, what has fructified so far by way of organizational effort is not even a fraction of the potential. Role of voluntary organizations in the development process got a further fillip in the seventh plan (1985-90) where it was declared that serious efforts would be made to involve voluntary organizations in various development programmes to supplement the government efforts. The sustained trends of encouragement towards the voluntary sector continued in the approach paper to the tenth plan also. There, it has been emphasized that voluntary sectors deserve encouragement because they help ameliorate some performance related problems of central and state plans (2001: 6-7).

It remains a fact that the NGOs, because of their closeness to people and with their relatively less rule-bound, non-bureaucratic, non-formal and flexible structures and operations, have been doing a commendable job in the last several decades. They are now working in all conceivable sectors for welfare and development of all sections of Indian society. It is a bit difficult to get an accurate figure of the number of NGOs in action at present in India. As per the record of the Government of India (2001), there are around 14,000 NGOs that have received grants from various government departments/ ministries. But, the actual number would be more as many NGOs are functioning without government grants. As reported by Saikia (2003: 56), there are at least 421 NGOs that are functioning in the state of Assam only.

A good number of studies (Gomes 1989; Khan and Thomas 1989; Sachchidananda and Prasad 1994; Vijaya 1994; Saikia 2003) reveal that the NGOs accord higher priorities to the activities for social development and are mostly engaged in the field of education, health, relief and rehabilitation, and slum development, etc. Activities for economic development come next in their priorities. They also act as partners of the government in the implementation of programmes for rural development. They also sometimes take the mantle of working as advocates, critics and pressure groups on behalf of the community. A good number of the NGOs are working exclusively for the development of tribals.

While focusing on the problems faced by these organizations, the studies by and large put emphasis on the facts that the dearth of qualified and committed workers and poor rapport with the people are the woes of most of them. Probably to overcome these problems and woes, at least to a great extent, the NGOs of late are showing increased preference to recruit more and more anthropologists on their staff. A good number of our students are working in different voluntary organizations and to the best of my knowledge, they are enjoying the jobs and doing well in their assignment.

Placement opportunities for anthropology graduates in different world organisations are also increasing. The World Bank, for example, has planned to hire fewer economists and more anthropologists. Anthropologists, the Bank feels, will best be able to understand the financial needs of business in other countries. It is assumed that anthropologists will make the projects of the World Bank more relevant and cost-effective.

Table 1 presents an illustrative sampling of career options in the discipline.

IV

While dwelling some more on the issue in global perspective it seems that the most impressive increase in anthropology's scope and options is observed in the U.S.A. It is really encouraging to note that the interest as well as respect and demand for the subject are steadily growing there since around last two decades. The number of anthropology students continue to rise in the universities there. According to an assessment made by the American Anthropological Association, during the decade 1987-97, the number of anthropology majors nationwide increased by 109 per cent. At Northern Kentucky University, it was the maximum (close to 300 per cent). The number of Master's degree awarded went up to 60 per cent, and the number of Ph.D. degree by 35 per cent. The 1999 edition of *Newsweek's Career and Graduate School Guide* lists anthropology as "one of the hot careers of the future". The November, 2001 issue of *Cincinnati Magazine* makes a similar claim for anthropology careers and observes: "employers have been snatching up anthropologists as if they were nuggets at the Gold Rush". According to the magazine, among the companies that hire anthropologists are

Table 1
An illustrative sampling of career options in anthropology

Sl. No. 1	Role/Position 2	Possible Setup/ Employer 3	Remarks, if any 4
1.	Anthropologist	Anthropological Survey of India	There are positions below and above.
2.	Archivist	Archives of different types	There may be different positions.
3.	Bank Development officer	Commercial Banks. World Bank	
4.	Community Development Officer	Relevant Government Departments/Projects	
5.	Community Health Educator	Directorate of Health, N.G.O., W.H.O.	
6.	Child Development Project Officer (CDPO)	UNICEF Sponsored Project	
7.	Development Officer/ Field Officer	L.I.C.I. and allied organizations	
8.	District Research Officer	Tribal Research institutes	There are positions below and above.
9.	Education Officer	Central Board of Workers' Education, Directorate of Education/Adult Education, N.C.E.R.T., UNESCO	
10.	Labour Welfare Officer	Relevant Government Department, Industries, ILO	
11.	Linguist	Institutes of languages, Relevant Government Departments	There are positions below and above.
12.	Marketing Researcher	Marketing Research Organisations, Mass Media Organisations, Commercial Banks, World Bank.	

table contd.

Sl. No. 1	Role/Position 2	Possible Setup/ Employer 3	Remarks, if any 4
13.	Medical Anthropologist	Directorate of Health, ICMR, UNICEF, WHO	
14.	Museum Keeper	Museums of different types and levels	There are positions below and above.
15.	News Correspondent	Mass Media Organisation	
16.	Rural Development Officer	Relevant Government Department/Project	
17.	Social Scientist	Indian Council of Social Science Research, Council for Social Development	There are positions below and above.
18.	Social Worker	NGOs	
19.	Teacher/ Researcher	Teaching/ Research Institutes	
20.	Urban Planner	Relevant Government Departments	

AT and T, General Motors, Hallmark, Intel, Kodak, Sapient and Whirlpool.

Earlier, the job advertisements rarely stated that a particular company or agency was specifically hiring an anthropologist. They would only list the kind of skills that incidentally the anthropologists are better equipped with. But, of late, more and more job advertisements do specifically state that the individual to be hired should be an anthropologist or an archaeologist. Not only the contract archaeology companies advertise for archaeologist, but so do some government agencies like the National Park Service. Some social organizations also sometimes engage anthropologists to evaluate their effectiveness in the community. Hallmark Greetings Cards recently advertised to hire an anthropologist who could conduct an ethnographic survey of when and how the Americans use greeting cards.

The February 18, 1999 edition of *USA Today* ran in its "Money" section a cover story titled, "Hot Asset in Corporate: Anthropology Degrees". The concluding observation was:

> as companies go multinational and crave leaders for a diverse workforce, a new hot degree is emerging for the aspiring executives: anthropology.

Among the companies with anthropology degrees of the executives, the article listed Citicorp, Hallmark, Hanseatic Group, Hauser Design, Hoffman-La Roche, Koss, Motorola, National Semiconductor, Nynex, Sun Microsystems and Xerox. Motorola even trains its employees to do "anthropological analysis", as it believes "important social research can't be gained by gazing at computer screen." The August 16, 2002 issue of *USA Today* ran a letter to the editor praising liberal arts subjects like anthropology. Wrote accountant Christina Hardin:

> Many of the country's top professional employers recognize the value of a liberal arts education. They hire liberal arts graduates because they demonstrate a combination of academic preparation, intellectual versatility and strong leadership skills that make them indispensable in the work force.

While exploring career options in anthropology, it is however, important that one should be sure of his or her particular interests, skills, values and personality preferences. Because the only way to be successful in any pursuit is to love what one is pursuing.

Before I put the curtain down on this rambling exercise, I would like to suggest the budding anthropologist to ask himself what he really enjoys. If he thinks what he would enjoy doing in life is anthropology, only then he should proceed with a career exploration in the subject. Kindly permit me to conclude this with one of my very favourite quotes that I generally do not miss to tell my students:

> Anthropology is more than a career. It is a way of life. In everything I do, I'm an anthropologist (Sharlottee Neely).

REFERENCES

Gomes, L.

1989 'Role of voluntary and other organizations in development', *Yojna* 33 : 28-31.

Government of India

2001 *The Report of the Steering Committee on Voluntary Sector for Tenth Five-Year Plan (2002-'07).* New Delhi: Planning Commission.

Kar, R. K.

2001 'Anthropo-historical appraisal of a migrant population in Assam, North-east India'. *Presidential address, Anthropology and Archaeology Section, 88th session of Indian Science Congress.*

Khan, M.Z. and M.E. Thomas

1989 'Role of voluntary agencies in rural development', *Social Change* 19 (1): 3-12.

Mead, Margaret

1967 'Anthropology and education for the future'. In D.G. Mandelbaum, *et al.* (eds.), *The Teaching of Anthropology.* Los Angeles: University of California Press.

Sachchidananda and A. Prasad

1994 *Tribal Development and Voluntary Action: A Case Study of the Badlao Foundation.* New Delhi: Inter India Publication.

Saikia, Dip Kumar

2003 *Role of Voluntary Organizations in Child Welfare in Kamrup District of Assam.* Unpublished Ph.D. thesis, Gauhati University, Guwahati.

Vijaya, P.L.

1994 'School and drop-outs or barefoot veterinarians: Lesson from a non-formal education project', *Vikalpa* 19 (1): 33-34.

Part IV

15

Civilizational Approach to the Study of Indian Society: N. K. Bose And Surajit Sinha

SUKANT K. CHAUDHURY

The scriptural tradition of Indian society is very strong and well built since ages. Therefore, it is a well-known fact that Indian civilization is one of the oldest and ancient civilizations of the world. Both Nirmal Kumar Bose and Surajit Sinha analyzed the civilizational perspective in the context of tribes in India. They spoke about a holistic perspective where all groups and communities are an integral part of Indian society. Bose said that Indian civilization was built over a sub-structure of caste. Throughout India, caste system has almost the same pattern with some local variations. At the cultural level, these communities were left free to practice their own faiths and rituals and these faiths combined together to give rise to Hinduism.

Bose tried to compare the Indian civilization with that of the European. He said that civilization of Europe was built up in an atmosphere torn by wars, which were sometimes caused by large migration. Europe succeeded in building up a unity, at the altar of which cultural pluralism had to be sacrificed. The two civilizations thus made their own contributions to the totality of human civilization. Indeed, they have tended to be complementary to one another (Bose 1972a). On the aspect of tribe, he said that they are an essential part of civilization, and since times immemorial, they were in regular contact with the Hindu civilization. On the other hand, Sinha said Indian civilization has adopted complex strategies in observing tribal enclaves and frontiers into the body politic of the caste-peasant level of the civilization. However, he said that the tribes, nevertheless, continued to maintain their distinctive identity (Sinha 1980).

Both Bose and Sinha did not concentrate on working in any single field of enquiry or area. In fact, Sinha was a student of Bose; both hailed from West Bengal, hence both had much influence of Eastern Indian culture. Profession-wise they followed almost similar assignments. Bose was the editor of *Man in India* from 1958 to 1972, and after his death in 1972, Sinha became its editor till 1986. Bose was the director of the Anthropological Survey of India from 1959 to 1964, and Sinha became its director from 1969 to 1975. Besides, Bose started his academic career as an assistant lecturer in pre-historic archaeology in Calcutta University in 1937. Later on, he became a reader in human geography and continued in the same capacity till 1959. Later, he served as the Commissioner for Scheduled Castes and Scheduled Tribes from 1967 to 1970.

Bose worked on a variety of topics in general and understanding tribes and their transformation in India in particular. The tribes he studied include Juangs of Pal Lahara (Orissa) and Mundas of Chotanagpur. During his stint as Commissioner for Scheduled Castes and Scheduled Tribes, he produced informative and analytical reports and their extracts have been published in his book titled *Anthropology and Some Indian Problems* (1972b). Bose, probably, was one of the original thinkers and indigenous anthropologists, who questioned the western approaches to the understanding of Indian society. He was one of the finest field-workers. He had been a wanderer, cutting across different communities and regions in India. He has been truly termed as a field-scientist by Béteille (1975). Though, he did not concentrate on a specific community, yet he focused on various aspects of Indian civilization. It has later come to be known as the civilizational approach to understand Indian society. His articles entitled, "The Hindu Method of Tribal Absorption" (1941), "Some Aspects of Indian Civilization" (1971) and "An Anthropological View of Indian Civilization" (1972a) provide the base for the civilizational approach. In a nutshell, the approach is concerned with how the tribal communities in India interact with other societies, particularly caste based communities. Further, he rejected the idea of complete isolation of tribals from the wider society.

Delivering the sixth N. K. Bose Memorial Lecture in 2006, Mahapatra (2006) observed that Bose had been a nationalist to the core and had interrupted his studies several times to participate in the movement initiated by Mahatma Gandhi. He was very close to Gandhi and for sometime, served as his personal secretary. He wrote many books on Gandhi including *Selections from Gandhi* (1934), *Studies in Gandhism* (1940), *My Days with Gandhi* (1952), and *Mahatma Gandhi and One World* (1966). He worked on Indian culture and said that both the cultural content and acculturation were vital processes in establishing a democratic way of life in India. On this aspect his books include: *Cultural Anthropology* (1929), *Culture and Society in India* (1967).

In 1949, he wrote *Hindu Samajer Garen* in Bengali which was later translated into English with a longish introduction by Béteille (1975), entitled *The Structure of Hindu Society*. It provided a bird's eye-view of Indian society and culture, including the problem of its integration. Béteille said that Bose emphasized a proper understanding of Hindu civilization, which required a different approach than the one applied to understand the tribal community of North America, Melanesia or Australia. It was in this sense that Bose saw kinship between his work and that of the American anthropologist, A. L. Kroeber (Béteille 1975: 1-2).

Remarking upon Indian civilization, Bose(1971) said that the

> multiplicity of fractional views of truth was a dominant element in Hindu religious thought and it is of significance that it spread from one corner of India to ancther eventually even pervaded some forms of non Brahmincal thought in the country in later times. .....this also brought about uniformity in Indian civilization as much as the productive organization of caste and of property relationship had done in other spheres of life.

Further he said:

> when we view the whole of Indian civilization there is a greater diversity in the material aspect of life and multiplicity of caste, religion faith and sect. In India each guild was encouraged to follow its own dharm which was guided by the advice of colleges of the Brahmin which were either located in centers of learning or of pilgrimages (*ibid*).

Béteille said that Bose spoke of two models of Indian civilization—(a) Brahminical; and (b) tribal.

The Brahmanical model may also be called the caste-model, which is based upon ranking and hierarchy. Probably, it is a superior model, not because of its political system or ideology, but because of its superior technology. Such a technology produces enough to support and sustain a large population. As we know, everything is ranked in Hindu society, from food to clothing, to occupation and also bride-giving and bride-taking. But, it is not an undemocratic structure. It is democratic in the sense that all other communities are allowed to exist with their own practices. The tribes became caste, adapted to their rituals which Bose called the Hindu method of tribal absorption. He described it in the following manner—one person, two persons. one family, two families came into contact with their Hindu neighbours and in course of time became attached to the Hindu economic system, and then were absorbed partially within the social fold also. The tension between one section of the people and another was not intense because the gap between rich and poor was not much. Besides, while the tribals are attracted by the gods and goddesses of Hindus, the Hindus also quite often, adopted the gods and goddesses of tribes. Undoubtedly, the mode of absorption of Hindu rituals and other cultural traits by the tribals was slow.

Going back to the Brahmanical model, Bose said that it was a super-structure. He further said:

> There was a superstructure guiding the religion and cultural life of the community as a whole. Each small component called a *jati* was left free to pursue its own rights and ceremonies, so long as it did not militate against the moral codes of Brahmincal society.

Bose mostly took Indian civilization synonymous with Hindu civilization. Further, he said that through ages Hinduism has tried to promote ideas and spiritual exercise, designed to promote the growth of every individual soul in this direction.

Individuals and communities have been encouraged to remain in their special worlds, with the result that even if the economic and social organization of caste have suppressed individualism at one level, Hindus have remained loyal to individualism of another kind and never allowed themselves to be fused into one uniform mass.

Comparing Indian civilization with that of the West, Bose says that the Indian social or economic condition is predominantly an organization of peace. It encourages the co-existence of many cultures, many separatenesses; but it does not make a large community strong enough to wage war. It is natural that an organization designed for peace will fail in the event of war. But, on the other hand, it may also be true that an organization of war may fail men when they have to live in peace with one another. And here, let us try to observe and understand the shape which European civilization has taken during the last century or two. Even in Europe, there have been protests all through the past two centuries against the present state of affairs. Some have sought spiritual refuge in poetry or science, human service or mysticism. As the control over nature's material resources has gone on increasing, as large sections of the population have been saturated in plenty, men's minds have wandered away from this in search of something which would give them solace and anchor in a world which is engrossed in a perpetually unsatisfied search for satiety.

When we see India in course of its long history of three thousand years or so, we notice certain broad points of strength and weakness. Ever since the Afghan, Tatar and Moghul invaders professing Islam came to the land, it had been proved that the political structure of India was very weak in self-defense. The defence of the state became the exclusive business of several castes and not of all its inhabitants. Many cultures and religions existed side by side with one another; but the feeling of distinctness which was thus encouraged failed when there was a need of combining people into one 'nation' for purpose of defence. Further, Bose writes, perhaps this was indeed a source of weakness. All educated Indians are today conscious of this element of weakness in their social system; and those who wish to see in India the rise of a mighty nation which can match its strength against that of any other nation, are impatient with every element in Indian civilization which tends to weaken it from the military point of view. Caste has been held largely responsible for the absence of a sense of national unity. But what is overlooked is that caste was designed for one purpose, nationalism in Europe for another. The multiplicity of faiths in India, her variegated ways of life, with different kinds of food and dress, her many languages, have also been equally blamed for the lack of national unity. The fact that the spiritual quest for a transcendental view of truth has, again and again, proved attractive to the highest individuals in the land, has proved distressing to those who want to 'secularize' and 'modernize' India.

As said earlier, Bose said that tribals were a part and parcel of Indian civilization. The colonial anthropologist's approach for the tribals was of isolation. A tribe was isolated or a relatively isolated community–an anthropological whole. Bose said that this could be the situation for African tribes, Australian aborigines, tribes in North America and Melanesia. But the Indian situation was different where the tribes interacted with the wider society. He took the case of Juangs. The Juang were shifting cultivators. The British had put a ban on shifting cultivation. Then the Juang looked for an alternative mode of occupation. They moved to nearby multi-caste villages and took up some occupation. They got involved in the Jajmani system, became a part of pure and impure hierarchy. They started performing Lakshmi Puja, and the Hindu concepts of merit (*punya*) and demerit (*pap*) were used, but fowl sacrifice simultaneously went on. Undoubtedly, the scale of interaction differed—probably in middle and central India it was more compared to the south Indian tribes. The impact of the outside world was found more on the Oraon, the Munda and the Santhal. The land-tenure system among the Munda was more elaborate than the others. The technology of the Santhal was more advanced than others.

Here I would speak of the Kondh of Orissa. They are a good producer of tamarind, turmeric and tendu leaves. Today, the above three trades have reached the multinationals. Thus, indirectly the Kondh have gone global without getting its fruits (Chaudhury *in press*). The British administrator, Captain Macpherson, wrote that the Kondhs used to send cart loads of turmeric through middle-men, who used to be from neighbouring Oriya caste community. Even today, despite the government's best efforts through cooperatives and other marketing societies, middlemen are quite powerful (Chaudhury 2004). Thus, the point here is to focus on how tribals are interacting with the wider communities.

On the other hand, Sinha said that there could not be one common approach to the study of primitive society of different countries, because each community is a bounded unit having its own culture, notwithstanding the fact that cultural osmosis takes place between different communities. The British construction of Indian society has been based on caste system. Indian society consists of many self-regulating villages where various endogamous *jati* groups live, pursuing their hereditary occupations. They are arranged in a rigid system of birth-ascribed status hierarchy. The early British administrators also spoke of certain human groups who lived in hills and forests, or in the planes near the forests. They lived in relative isolation from the caste based peasant villages as unstratified endogamous groups. They were engaged in multiple occupations, including settled and shifting cultivation, hunting and gathering. They were pre-literate groups, placed outside the Brahmanic hierarchic civilization. They were called tribes on the analogy of similar groups in aboriginal America, Africa and Oceania. Then tribes were categorized as a special category for the purpose of census and administration. After independence, the government of India accepted the category of Scheduled Tribes for them (Sinha 1980).

Further, Sinha said that in ancient and medieval texts, there was no distinct term found for the category tribe. In rural India, the endogenous term for the so called tribes as well as castes was *jati*. In ancient texts, terms like *jana* indicated an ethnic group and *janpad* an ethnic territory. Some outlying *janpadas* were called *Atabika Rajyas (*forest kingdoms*)* and *Pratyanta Deshas* (frontier Regions); they included Kirat, Savara, Bhila, Nishada. Abhira, etc. Broadly speaking Sinha worked with the notion of tribe-caste continuum. He wrote in 1980:

> While reviewing the position of tribes in the context of their articulation with caste-peasant-based Indian civilization today we come across two contradictory sets of observation. On the one hand

> tribes continue to be drawn within the orbit of Varna-Jati civilization as a part of the broad spectrum of Indian peasant society; on the other hand, many tribal groups tenaciously hold on to their distinct ethnic identity as they seemed to have done in the past.

He tried to analyze the mutually interacting adopting strategies of Indian civilization vis-à-vis the tribes. He tried to understand how the tribes of India were absorbed into the civilization and continued their own identity.

For the definition of civilization he followed Redifield (1962), both culturally and structurally. The concept of civilization assumes the existence of critically systematized thoughts formulated by specialists (literati) above the level of the unsystematized local oral traditions. A civilization is characterized by the existence of hierarchies of urban centres for the cultivation of material and ideational excellence. These centres are connected with country-wide network of cultural communication with other centres, as well as village communities. In the context of a civilization as defined above, 'peasant societies' are stable agriculture-based village communities whose members, though largely guided by local oral traditions, have also channels of communication with specialists and centres of civilization. Sinha further says that in contrast to the peasant society, the tribe is ideally defined in terms of its isolation from the networks of social relations and cultural communications of a civilization. In their isolation, the tribal societies are sustained by relatively primitive subsistence technology such as shifting cultivation and hunting and gathering and maintain an egalitarian segmentary social system guided entirely by non-literate ethnic tradition.

Earlier, Sinha (1957) tried to distinguish between the tribes and Hindu peasantry on the basis of: (a) *habitat*—tribes live in hilly and forest areas whereas peasant live in deforested plateaus and plains; (b) *economy*—tribes have subsistence economy based on hunting, gathering and fishing, shifting cultivation and settled cultivation, crafts specialization like iron smelting, smithy, basket and bark rope matting and weaving; tribal village community is nearly self-sufficient where circulation of goods is based on barter; they have little incentive towards the accumulation of capital, whereas Hindu peasantry is based on intensive agriculture, intricate full time crafts specialization, beyond a limited degree of local self-sufficiency for the village communities and are tied to country-wide networks of markets ultimately related to commercial towns; they have strong incentive towards accumulation of capital in terms of land, storage of grains, cash, valuable metals and jewellery; (c) *social structure*—tribe is segmented in exogamous totemic clans with territorial cohesion and strong corporate identity, has a strong kinship system, village is their most important territorial unit, they have very little rigid stratification and have both secular and religious leadership combined in one person, whereas among Hindu peasantry, the larger group is the caste group which is hierarchically arranged and endogamous in nature and is segmented into exogamous clans which are often non-totemic; they have patrilineal descent; intensive crafts specialization and are full time traders; (d) *ideological system*: tribes have their own supernatural belief and pantheon, supernatural rites are explicitly directed towards happiness and security in this world; abundance in crops and children, and avoidance of sickness and death being the supreme considerations; they have no concepts of heaven or hell or of rewards and punishment for moral or immoral acts; there is a belief in re-incarnation and transmigration of souls into various forms of life, namely, trees, birds, animals, etc.; animal sacrifice is an essential part of rituals, magic and witchcraft predominate, whereas among Hindu peasantry there is a combination of monotheism, pantheism and polytheism; sun worship is an important element of Brahminical tradition; although the sun god is not regarded as the Supreme Being; the pantheon is much more elaborate in peasant Hinduism, which has some limited access to written sacred literature; it contains some of the gods of the Great Indian tradition; the concept of heaven and hell is very important; both temple and idolatry are very important; animal sacrifice forms an essential part of the rituals of many sects and there is a predominance of magic and witchcraft; and (e) *aspirational level*—the tribals have comparatively lower level of aspiration than the Hindu peasantry.

Broadly speaking, Sinha emphasized upon the fact that the tribal cultures of India are unique and are not necessarily universally shared by primitive tribes in other parts of the world. Besides, they shared many things with Hindu peasantry (Sinha 1957). He also studied the state formation among tribes (Sinha 1962). He analysed in detail the state formation among the Bhumij, and how they have created a myth of Rajput ancestry. There are several tribes in India which have become castes in their own manner, but they only adopted a few cultural traits like worshiping Hindu pantheon and following a few rituals. In this manner, Sinha (1965) mainly focused on tribe-caste continuum and tribe-peasantry continuum. He clearly mentioned that tribes in India are not living in isolation, rather they are always in some kind of contact with the wider caste and peasant communities.

REFERENCES

Béteille, André

1975 'Introduction'. In N. K. Bose, *The Structure of Hindu Society*, New Delhi: Orient Longman.

Bose, N. K.

1929 *Cultural Anthropology*. Calcutta: Arya Sahitya Bhawan.

1934 *Selections from Gandhi*. Ahmedabad: Navjivan Trust.

1940 *Studies in Gandhism*. Calcutta: D.M. Libarary.

1941 'The Hindu method of tribal absorption', *Science and Culture*, VII (4).

1952 *My Days with Gandhi*. Calcutta: Merit Publications.

1966 *Mahatma Gandhi and One World*. New Delhi: Ministry of External Affairs, Government of India.

1967 *Culture and Society in India*. Calcutta: Asia Publishing House.

1971 'Some aspects of Indian civilization', *Man in India* 51 (1).

1972a 'An anthropological view of Indian civilization', Man in India 52 (2).

1972b *Anthropology and Some Indian Problems*. Calcutta: Institute of Applied Anthropology.

Chaudhury, S. K.

2004 *Tribal Identity*. Jaipur: Rawat Publications.

in press 'Anthropology of tribal development: The Kondh case'. In S.K. Chaudhury and S.M.Patnaik (eds.), *Indian*

Tribes and the Mainstream. Jaipur: Rawat Publications.

Mahapatra, L. K.

2006 *Sixth Nirmal Kumar Bose Memorial Lecture 2006*. New Delhi: Indira Gandhi National Centre for the Arts.

Redfield, Robert

1962 *Human Nature and the Study of Society*. Chicago.

Sinha, Surajit Chandra

1957 'Tribal cultures of peninsular India as a dimension of little tradition in the study of Indian civilization: A preliminary statement', *Man in India* 37 (2).

1962 'State formation and Rajput myth in tribal Central India', *Man in India* 42 (1).

1965 'Tribe-caste and tribe-peasant continua in Central India', *Man in India* 45 (1).

1980 'Tribes and Indian civilization: A perspective', *Man in India* 60 (1 and 2).

16

Iravati Karve and the Production of an Indian Anthropology

SUBHADRA MITRA CHANNA

Iravati Karve's works cover a holistic conceptualization of Indian society, but in her methodology she moves beyond the static, homogenous version of society popular in her times to understand the multifaceted dimensions of social reality foreshadowing later theories in anthropology that take a critical stand on the earlier versions of culture and society as stable, timeless concepts. In her works, she definitely shows a greater influence of the cultural historical approach of Boas and the Culture-Area hypothesis of his student, Alfred Kroeber. The influence of the American cultural tradition is strong in her works as she dwells on evidences of cultural diffusion and a methodology that takes strong support from folklore and oral traditions. Her treatment of literary traditions as a major source to understand society and its evolution goes beyond the American cultural tradition and is better understood in a post-modern framework that gives authenticity to the written word and presents a contested version of truth where the subjectivity of the scholar is foregrounded. The feminist critique that follows upon this theoretical stance is very much reflected in Karve's works where in her interpretation of the written texts she dwells at length on the inner psychological states of women and she also does not fail to mention the patriarchal bias in the writings of the ancient texts. In fact, her literary and semi-anthropological work *Yuganta*, attempts to rectify this bias by presenting a feminist interpretation of some of the mythological characters of popular Hindu texts.

Even in her works on *Kinship Organization in India* and *Hindu Society–An Interpretation*, she emphasizes the complexity of Indian society and the possibility of alternate interpretations as well as the fact that gender plays a key role in interpretation and understanding. Coming at a time when both feminism and gender played insignificant role in anthropological theory, Karve was a true visionary possessing a keen sociological imagination that allowed her to understand society as a complex as well as an interpretative phenomenon rather than taking a static positivistic view.

A major understanding she brought to anthropological theory in India was an aversion to a blind faith in concepts and typologies generated by western scholars. She had insisted on definitions and understandings of concepts as they exist in Indian society, that included such kinship and sociological terms as *gotra, vansh* and *jati,* for which she claimed no meaningful western term existed. In this way she was able to reveal the true nature of culture as part of a local meaning system and the methodology of adhering to native terms for institutions rather that distorting them to fit in with a terminology generated by western anthropologists. In this she anticipated the colonial critique and the works of such cultural historians who gave a gendered historiography as Susan Bayley, Rosalind Hamilton, Bernard Cohn, and others. Hers was an effort to build up a true Indian anthropology, using native terminology and a meaning system not derived from the west but from the history of the South Asian society. In this she was a true believer in historical-particularism and a cultural historical interpretation of contemporary institutions. She firmly believed that the character of Indian society was that of absorption and not of division, a point of view reflected in her theory of caste.

In this paper, I will do a re-reading of her three major anthropological works in light of the critical approach developed in post-modern, post-colonial anthropology. My efforts would be to show how Karve anticipated both feminism and a post-colonial critique in her work while adhering to a methodology whose limits were defined by the existing American cultural tradition. But most of all her efforts to situate her work in the context of the Indian sub-continent and its special ethnographic content is what marks her out as a contributor to the production of a truly Indian anthropology. If she fails in that attempt, it is only because of her own reflexivity, her subject positioning as a Brahmin woman who in spite of all efforts failed to transcend to a level of encompassing the true diversity of India, confining herself to a largely Hindu and Brahmanical view of Indian society.

Iravati Karve was a leader from the front in more ways than one. In a Preface to the second edition of her work on kinship (1965) Hutton does not fail to mention her 'sex'.

> It is probably symptomatic of a new India, unknown to my generation, that this contribution has been made by one of her sex: at any rate it is one which anyone of either sex might feel proud to have accomplished (Hutton 1965: viii).

This quote makes it clear that even in world anthropology, at the middle of the twentieth century, there were not too many women scholars. To be a woman invited such comments as to the 'sex' of the writer especially if she belonged to a group that had earlier formed the "other" for colonial anthropologists such as Hutton. As understood in later theoretical developments, the identity of the anthropologist till the last part of the twentieth century was 'male, white' and not 'woman and non-white'. As Moore (1996: 1) has put it:

> A whole series of new questions has been posed by the sustained challenge third world, black and feminist scholars have provided to the established agenda of the social sciences and humanities in the recent years.

It would thus be theoretically rewarding to investigate whether Karve who fits the bill of being non-white and 'black' (implying non-western) also fits the description of being a feminist and whether and to what extent her work is a deconstruction of dominant concepts of her time, of paradigms developed within a specific cultural and social set-up situated historically in the colonial era; also to the extent to which she follows the theories popular in her age and the orientation of her contemporaries.

The influence of the American cultural tradition on her work is evident in the manner in which she has divided the Indian sub-continent into linguistic areas that she rightly refers to as cultural areas too. In the beginning of her book, *Kinship Organization in India*, Karve makes a rather profound statement,

> Three things are absolutely necessary for the understanding of any cultural phenomenon in India. These are the configuration of the linguistic regions, the institution of caste and the family organization.

She further develops the idea that to understand any of these elements one must conceptualize the regional diversity of India and translate it into methodology; in other words, situate one's analysis within a regional and linguistic framework. Thereby she states a fact made clear by later works on India that culturally and anthropologically, India is not a unified entity. This in fact would lead us to another rather relevant question, "Is there an Indian anthropology?"

Karve herself has already given the answer in the preliminary lines of her book as quoted above, anything in India can only be understood in the context of caste, family and linguistic regionalism. But as a criticism to her approach I would like to point to the distinct bias of her construction of a general picture of Indian society, especially kinship, one that upholds Brahmanical Hinduism and a distinct upper caste culture as 'typical' Indian culture. If we agree with Karve that caste should be a key factor to understanding Indian society, then what are we to do with the entire North- eastern part of the country and with all such groups that do not have a caste organization? In her classification of Indian languages, she mentions only three groups, namely Indo-European, Dravidian and Austro-Asiatic; then where is Tibeto-Burman? She herself admits to not analyzing data from Kashmir probably because it was not available at her times. But she should have made an honorable mention of all the areas and regions that she did not cover, instead of ignoring them totally as if they did not exist. Her book is also conspicuous by the absence of any data on the Muslims. In fact, she should have named her book, 'Hindu Kinship' rather than 'Indian Kinship', unless to her Hindu and India were the same!

Not only does her work reflect a definite cultural and political bias but it also reflects on the teaching of anthropology in India that till today sustains a largely Hindu and upper caste interpretation of society as 'The Indian Society'. Karve's book on kinship served as a text for at least two generations of scholars who kept learning by rote statements such as

> The behaviour pattern of the kin-group in the northern families is like that of the patri-family in ancient India. The man lives with his patri-kin among whom he is born and reared. He comes in contact with his wife's relations but rarely. The woman on the other hand spends her life, except for the few childhood years, with her affinal kin with whom she is not acquainted up to the moment of her marriage.

Further she writes:

> The northern joint family is a status group where husband, wife, parents-in-law, daughters-in-law, sons, daughters, sisters-in-law and brothers-in-law have each a definite place assigned to him or her vis-à-vis all others.

Though Karve has mentioned the existence of tribes and various other groups in her enumeration of the central and southern parts of India, her description of the northern joint family has captured the imagination of many. The fact that many lower castes and tribes and landless populations never had any concept of a joint family, and in India we also have matrilineal societies are realities that are not incorporated within the main descriptive framework of her book. Following the lead, many anthropologists in India try to explain away the fact that actual joint families are difficult to come by when they go to the field by attributing it to "change", so that an oft-repeated question in many question papers is, "Identify the factors that led to the dissolution of the joint family in India" or something similar. The assumption being that the normal state of the Indian family should be joint, and secondly, if it no longer exists, one assumes that it *changed* rather than it *never* existed.

Such assumptions also were rooted in the structural-functional methodology that concentrated on the present and ignored history. Thus when an anthropologist found that the majority of families in the field area was nuclear it was attributed to 'external' factors. But fieldworkers have subsequently critically questioned this ideal model especially when they began to use the historical method. A.M. Shah, a well known sociologist, highly regarded for his work on family, found in his social and historical study of a village in Gujarat that the kind of family assigned to tradition was not present even in the pre-colonial era. Let us see what he has to write about Radhvanaj, a village consisting primarily of upper caste Rajputs and Brahmins (Shah 1998).

> According to the Census of 1825 Radhvanaj had a population of 716 persons divided into 159 households and there were 25 castes, 73% of the total number of households were very small or small in 1825. The ideal of the so-called joint family household was not very strong in the village and this was even before the beginning of industrialization and urbanization.

But even though there were no joint families, the Rajputs, namely the Rathods of this region, formed exogamous lineage groups. But in the very same village such lineage groups were not found among the other caste groups. By and large, strong and elaborate lineage groups were associated with control over land. As Shah has further elaborated, land ownership provided stability of residence and facilitated growth of lineages. Land ownership also provided power and therefore, lineages with the help of the unity provided by the kinship bond, tended to be repositories of power.

In my own work on the Dhobi (washermen) in northern India, in Delhi (Channa 1985), I found no trace of any joint living. As rightly pointed out by Shah, landownership often provides the economic basis for joint living. For households which have to live off their daily earnings it is a difficult proposition to pool in the earnings at the end of the day and go for joint living. What the earlier authors had relied upon was an ideal basis for the family based on values and scriptural norms. But in reality the economic and political considerations determine at the actual level what shape is going to be taken by the household.

Thus, stereotypical definitions as given by Karve, do not reflect the truth, but only the author's vision of the truth, filtered through the lens of an upper caste Brahmin woman of an aristocratic class. Moreover, as was the climate of her times, her typology is static, it assumes a timeless classification rather than recognizing the dynamism of actual societies. At the same time, she was well aware of both history and archaeology and her theory on caste formation is both historical and takes into account the process of evolution of caste. Thus there is a tension in her work, where at some points she appears as a conservative scholar, depending upon the normative structures of society and ready to represent it in terms of her own subjective situatedness and at other points she breaks free of conservatism and goes into an analysis that is both reflexive and dynamic. She comes into her true mettle when she is discussing women.

Thus Karve's contribution becomes much more creative when she breaks out of the methodological bondage of a 'scientific ' approach and gives expression to her inner voice about women and their role in Hindu society. Though she is better known as a social anthropologist who interpreted the basic institutions of Indian society, I think her contribution as a feminist is much more laudable. But, at all points, her analysis must be viewed strictly as an interpretation of only a section of Indian society, largely Hindu sanskritic and upper class.

While describing the scriptural texts in her book on kinship (1965: 61), she gives us a sympathetic account of the lives of Sita, Draupadi, Kunti and Madri, contextualizing these lives to the cultural practices prevalent and the patriarchal social structure. She makes a sensitive description of the carefree and happy childhood of an Indian woman in her father's house and the privy and tribulations in her husband's house where her identity is submerged into that of her husband. Making a critical analysis of the concept of *pativrata* as it was interpreted in ancient times and as it is understood in contemporary Indian society, she works against the patriarchal interpretations of her own times and of her own culture. In ancient times, as the example of Kunti and Draupadi shows, virtue in a woman had quite a different meaning. These women would fail the test of being virtuous wives by contemporary definitions by not being virgins and exclusive sexual property of their husbands. But they were exemplary women of virtue in their own times; not because of their sexual purity or the fact that they belonged to only one man but by the fact that they bowed down to every wish of their husbands and the needs of his patriline. Thus, these women had to suppress their own desires and feelings to do what was required of them by the dictates of patriarchy. This norm is illustrated by the practice of a woman being passed on to her *devr* (or classificatory brothers of her husband) in order to procreate heirs for his patriline, a practice well illustrated in the Mahabharata.

Karve is able to understand the pain and suffering of these women, who are queens and princesses, but who have no control of their own bodies. She writes:

> To the honour of the poets may it be said that the husband of each of these women was blamed, *but we fail to get a glimpse of the woman's thought in all these circumstances* (1965: 73; italics mine).

Thus, Karve in her inter-subjectivity and reflexivity as a woman is able to understand and describe the suffering of women whose emotions had bypassed even the poets who created them. Her own reading of the ancient texts clearly indicates that she is guided by her feminine understanding as she picks up and emphasizes precisely those areas that throw a clear light on the plight of women and she makes it a point to comment that her interpretation has a feminine bias not present in the texts. In this case, her consciousness of her subjectivity is subsumed under her projection of an objective scientific methodology. Her disdain for 'conjectural' deductive reasoning led her to carefully document and substantiate her arguments, even if her perspective can be understood as interpretative from an analytic distance. That she set rigid standards of objectivity for herself is demonstrated throughout her works.

To clarify on the position of women, she looks into some of the laws and dictates of those times. The importance of a son in patriarchal Hindu society is demonstrated in two ways, one by the concept of *asramas* where as a householder a man is expected to discharge his dharma by paying off two debts : (1) debt to ancestors; and (2) debt to gods. Both the debt to ancestors and the debt to gods requires a man to marry and beget sons for not only must the ancestral sacrifices and offerings be made by the man himself but he must ensure their continuity by having a son; the third debt that to the sages is made by living the life of a pupil in the *brhamacharya asrama*.

In contemporary times, most scholars writing on this subject are happy to dismiss the preference for sons to practices of dowry or to economic considerations only. But, as Karve has rightly analyzed, such preferences may be far more deeply ingrained into the value systems that originated thousands of years back. More interesting is the definition of who is to be called a son? Here, Karve quotes from the Mahabharata where

> Pandu is supposed to be giving the authority of the law books (*dharmashastras*) for the following type of sons. The first six are kin (*bandhu*) and inheritors, while the next six are neither kin, nor have they the right to inherit (Karve 1965: 74).

What Karve notes is that the first six are all kinds of sons born to the wife, whether or not they were born of the father, whose name they are supposed to carry. The last six categories are of adopted and foster sons who are not born of the wife's womb. The only biological sons of wife debarred from inheritance is a son who was fully grown when a woman marries a man who was not his progenitor and the case of a son born to a woman of low caste. Both these types of sons are present in the Mahabharata as Vyasa, the son of Satyavati, before her marriage to the king Shantanu and Vidur who was born of a *dasi*. It is interesting to note that when there is a search for a suitable *devr* for the widows of queen Satyavati's two sons, *in lieu* of a prince of the Kuru lineage it is this son of Satyavati who has to stand in as a brother. This indicates that the woman was completely integrated into the husband's patrilineage in the *bija ksetra* analogy where her body is likened to a field on which the seed of the patriline is to be sowed. While on one hand this analogy raises the position of the mother in giving identity to her sons, it degrades the position of the wife who must provide her womb willingly or unwillingly so that it can be used to sow the seeds of her husband's patriline.

The present day cultural practices in most of India no longer conform to such values. In the absence of a son, it is considered appropriate to adopt one rather than use the wife's womb as a field to sow the seeds of the patriline. Modern day Indian families conform much more to the western ideals of virginity and monogamy considering the husband as the sole sexual claimant to his wife's body. More than sons, the purity of women is linked to the honour of a patrilineage. However it is also true that such values are more prevalent among the elite and middle classes and upper castes of Indian society, and marginal groups may be still or were till quite recent times having values nearer to those depicted in the ancient texts. Post-colonial scholars have often attributed colonial rule and the western values imposed by the foreign rulers to have brought about substantive transformations in Indian society, especially beginning from the top and permeating downwards. Thus, sexual purity of women, a rigid caste structure and enhanced patriarchy are now deemed to be more an influence of westernization than as part of ancient Indian traditions. Thus, the works of scholars such as O'Hanlon (1997), Dirks (1997, 2001), Cohen (1996) and Chatterjee (1993), to name only a few, have shown how the brahmanical model followed in a colonial production of knowledge about Indian society as well as the specific interventions based upon the western systems of morality and the artificial projection of Indian society as homogenous and static fulfilled the requirements not only of the colonial rulers but of a large section of Indian elites as well. One observation made by almost all these scholars was that the interpretations of Indian society were made largely by upper caste men, the only ones the British considered as trustworthy or respectable, as a reflection of their values derived from their own society. The glorification of the ancient 'Hindu' culture by those termed Indophiles by Trautmann also went into the emerging Hindu nationalism of the post-colonial era.

Karve's work upturns many of such myths that came to dominate upper strata of Indian society and was being passed off as 'Indian tradition' by the elite. In this way, she gives a true post-colonial critique and her work predates most of those who are now recognized as providing such a critique. Her commentaries would also make the advocates of glorious Hindu traditions of the past uncomfortable in the honest appraisal unclouded by any sentiments that she makes of the epics. Her brilliant commentary on the Mahabahrata, *Yuganta*, takes away from the commonly held norms of a Hindu family and an ideal woman or man. At this point, it becomes imperative to highlight the importance of her deep involvement with history and the ancient textual material. As Rosalind O'Hanlon has pointed out, one of the greatest fallacies of historical practice with reference to the South Asian data has been the assumptions of a static society.

> The strongest of these assumptions, enshrined in an intellectual tradition of considerable age and authority, has been of the essentially static character of Indian society (O'Hanlon 1997: 148).

Karve, by her methodology, had been attempting to refute exactly this kind of assumption. She shows quite clearly that Indian society has evolved and transformed over the ages and also in the character of a true feminist she is able to identify the cause of the assumption, the self-interest of the guardians of patriarchal authority.

To be objective, Karve by herself has not foregrounded the aspect of colonial influence in her work. But she is very clear about the prioritizing of male voice, a fact that she mentions several times. She was also deeply committed to the understanding of society as changing and dynamic. Refuting the assumption of the rigidity of caste structures that had been emphasized by colonial and patriarchal scholars, she is quick to point to both the elastic and loose structure of the caste system.

> By its very nature the caste society presented a loose structure which could take on new units and is so doing re-arrange old units (1961:109).

In this way, she fulfills aptly the requirements of a feminist methodology that has been expressed by Valle (1993: 7) as:

> More than any other field within the discipline, feminist anthropology is deeply connected to changes in society and the demand for change emanating from diverse interest groups. Concurrently, the degree of this connection gives a special element to the study of gender, namely questions about the many situations in which women live, and the many variations in what it takes to be a woman or a man.

Thus Karve by showing the transformative nature of Indian society and its dynamic nature refutes the assumptions of stagnation. She delineates the difference between *Shrutis* and *Smritis* and the fact that most of the laws governing family and marriage as contained in the *Smritis* are to be viewed as both dynamic and contextual, suitable for certain ages and interpreted situationally. The implication for the lives of women is tremendous as morality and family values are shown to be changing and changeable and not rigid and inviolable. Thus, Hinduism contains within itself the germs of development and is not by any means an immobile tradition. While she nowhere refutes the greatness of Indian civilization her approach is truly academic and non-political.

Many scholars as well as political interest groups use many of the stories and practices depicted in classical texts to project an image of women in ancient India as having a higher position than contemporary Indian women by saying that she had greater authority and freedom and could have more than one sexual partner. While it may be partly true that she had a better position vis-à-vis her progeny it was also a matter of interpretation. Karve has rightly indicated that such practices were causes of greater suffering for women as they subjugated her sense of self and personhood. She was always an instrument for the goals that were to be achieved by her husband. Thus while he paid his debt, she was only a partner whom he had to use to achieve his ends. The woman neither had personhood nor had she agency to act positively for her own good. Whatever she did was for her husband and his salvation. While she exposes the sufferings of women she also exposes the weaknesses and cowardice of men. In her analysis, women, though suffering, still emerge stronger.

Now I come to the question as to whether we can consider Karve to be a feminist. Here again one has to examine how one defines a feminist? As Valle (1998: 15) puts it:

> Acceptance of gender as a new analytical category implies the acceptance of knowledge that has already been considered marginal and on the periphery; it has been constructed, developed and expanded by those who are not placed at the center where recognized knowledge develops and expands.

Karve was definitely as a woman and as a South Asian placed at the periphery of anthropological knowledge of her times dominated by white, western males. Her analysis is sensitive to the facts of her womanhood, even though the concept of feminism had not found an expression in the theoretical discourses of her times. Thus while analyzing the more conventional institutions of caste and kinship, she remains confined to more conventional approaches of her times, in her interpretation of women and their position, she breaks free and is able to transcend the limitations of methodology imposed on her. Moore (1994: 4) has raised a question:

> Can people actively recognize and choose the subject positions they take up, and to what degree are they able to resist the term of dominant discourses?

When we analyze the works of Karve, it is clear that she was unaware of the concept of reflexivity at a conscious level, yet her observations and her theoretical orientations clearly indicate that she was deeply influenced by her own subjectivity and was inspired by her own individuality to take up an independent stand even when she was not required to do so by the norms of the times. It is her inner strength as a person and a deep conviction about her identity that makes her stand out, as a scholar who would not be cowed down by the 'dominant discourses'. Thus, it is irrelevant to raise the issue of Karve being a feminist unknown to her self. She was both aware of her identity and her responsibility to express the voices that were suppressed in the textual narratives she refers to. Such a point has been made explicitly by her in *Kinship* and she has in addition written a book *Yuganta* (originally in Marathi) in which she courageously reinterprets most of the characters well known in Hindu mythology and who have been stereotyped in common everyday life in Indian homes. For example, the act of Gandhari, bandaging her eyes, interpreted commonly as an act of sacrifice for the sake of a blind husband is revealed for what it was, an act of anger and hurt, to punish her husband and her own family for betraying her. The poignant conversation between Gandhari and Dhritarashtra, in the forest at the fag end of their lives reveals the bitter relationship of an angry woman and a husband who felt the resentment of his wife and the punishment inflicted on him by her, all his life. The interpretation is a truly feminist one in which Iravati is able to say out loud, what had been suppressed all along, the voice of a wronged woman. Thus, the male interpretations commonly given out by male scholars and priests had by their very misinterpretation, suppressed a voice of protest, converting it into one of passive suffering. Karve is able to show Gandhari for what she was, a strong woman, keen to inflict revenge on her kin and husband and not a passive suffering wife, a *pativrata*.

Moreover, Karve was fairly contemptuous of the 'greatness' of the Puranic characters such as the Pandavas or even of Krishna of whose identity as a historical character she has many questions. For example Karve brings to dust a much revered figure in Hindu mythology, Bhisma, the grandfather, the man usually upheld as one of the noblest figures of heroes of the

Mahabharata. Karve has nothing but contempt for a man she thinks spent all his life wronging women and bringing them to misery for his own glorification and ego. Throwing all conventions to the wind, she is able to write:

> How all these women must have suffered! How they must have cursed Bhishma! He alone was responsible for their humiliation. Bhishma was the active leader of the Kuru clan, the one who had wielded authority. In his zeal to perpetuate the house, he had humiliated and disgraced these royal women (1991: 14).

Thus Karve's voice has been a true feminist voice in deconstructing male voices and situating herself in the position of a marginalized section of Indian society, namely its women.

Not only women, but Karve is quick to catch on to all the injustices perpetrated by those in power and that has been conveniently overlooked in order to glorify some. For example, she has a sympathetic voice for the poor tribal woman and her five sons who are burnt in the *jatu griha* incidence. In *Yuganta*, Karve spares no one, not even Arjun, and Krishna whom she castigates for burning down the Khandava forest only to gain the land of the Nagas. Thus instead of glorification as divinity of the characters that emerges on the pages of the great epic, she is able to write of the high born prince and princesses like Dhritarashtra, Pandu, Gandhari, Kunti and the rest:

> ....all these Kshatriyas lived restless, intense lives. Their lives had heights and depths, loves and hates. Whatever real peace they had, came only after death. In old age, beaten by life, they finally achieved with great effort a resignation which was not so much peace as a desperate attempt to impose calm. ...What was true of the Kshatriyas was true of the Sutas. ...Even the Brahmins, Drona, and Ashvatthama, were not spared from the tormenting activity of the mind and body (1991: 70).

Thus, at the same time, as she takes a subjective stand with regard to women and men and their emotions and sufferings she also has a clear cut scientific and objective view of the texts that are in no way clouded by her sentiments as a Hindu upper caste woman. She nowhere treats the characters as divinity but regards them as flesh and blood historical people or as in the case of the *Ramayana* she is more inclined to treat it as a pure *kavya*, a run of the poet's imagination. While *Mahabharata* is for her a document of social conditions and cultural practices of a specific historical era and most of the characters appear to have a substantive reality, the *Ramayana*, appears as romantic poetry describing the ideal types rather than flesh and blood persons who may have lived on this earth. Therefore, her analysis concentrates more on the people who live in the verses of the *Mahabharata* than the *Ramayana*. The former she treats like a historical document that can be subjected to an anthropological analysis provided one dispels the clouds of religious sentiments. Thus she is able to make bold hypothesis as to the father and son relationship between Vidura and Yudhishtira, although in the text Yudhishitira is mentioned as the son of the god Yama or Dharma. To the social anthropologist that she was, the role of the *devr*, in impregnating his elder brother's wife was an appropriate cultural practice. Also the suppression of this fact could be related to the caste of Vidura who unlike his brothers was born of a *dasi* and hence of the *suta* and not the *kshatriya* caste. Although she makes many observations, some of them like the above, being quite startling yet her conclusions are drawn within the strict dictates of positivist methodology as she supports each of her statements with substantive data. Thus, we find that although her construction of Indian society is the construction of a Hindu society, yet she is a true critic of that society. While she cannot transcend her Hindu identity, her self-appraisal is highly critical.

Methodologically, she seems inspired by the Golden Age of American anthropology than by the static analysis of British structure-functionalism that seemed to have deeply influenced most Indian anthropologists almost up to the recent times. The reason could have been her deep-rooted interest in archaeology and history and the conviction that Indian society and culture could not be understood without referring to their roots. In this, she is guided by the theoretical commitment to understanding culture as a dynamic and historical process and not an entity in timeless equilibrium.

Her approach also leads her to studying Indian society as a holistic concept rather than fragmenting it into smaller 'community studies' that became popular as ethnographies at around the time she was writing. So that much before her we have ethnographies of tribes from scholars such as S.C. Roy.

Yet Karve chose an approach that was civilizational, confining herself to studying largely what may be termed as the Great Tradition. Yet it does not mean that she ignored the existence of a substratum of Indian society that was composed of rural and tribal people. But she was convinced that there was no significant difference in India between the higher and the lower groups as far as culture and traditions were concerned. She is critical of the term 'primitive' as used by Western anthropologists of her times as suitable for use in the Indian subcontinent. To her, what could be termed as Indian civilization had an over all identity that justified the use of titles such as *Kinship Organization in India* and *Hindu Society*. To her, what can be termed as Indian society was largely Hindu but again what she means by Hindu is not to be interpreted in the narrow sense that it is defined today but as 'inhabitants of this sub-continent' and an amalgamation of the various traditions and of people who live here, have migrated here and mingled with each other right here on this land. The association of culture with area comes again quite likely from the influence of the culture-area hypothesis popular in American cultural tradition. The rich diversity of Indian society is well recognized by her even though she uses terms such as Hindu society, in her analysis she breaks up this analytical category into its ground level manifestations of local and regional communities. She is keenly aware of the internal diversity of groups that profess the same *jati* name such as *kumbhar* (or potter), to give an example. She explains the internal diversity through the hypothesis of amalgamation rather than fission. She successfully explains the diversity as well as dynamism of Indian society by a single theory of addition rather than splitting.

She had done her anthropology, partly from Germany. The influence of German scholars, the diffusionists who had later influenced Boas, the founder of American cultural tradition, is clear in her orientation. But her individuality and her keenness to develop an Indian anthropology is exhibited in her rejection of terms coined by western anthropologists. She clearly finds it impossible to describe the Hindu social organization by making use of terms such as clans and lineages and instead builds up a vocabulary of kinship terms such as *sapinda*, *gotra*, *kul* and *vamsa* that are derived from Indian data.

A dimension of her scholarship was to take anthropology as a unified discipline of physical, social and prehistory, an amalgamation now long rejected that we find in her book *Hindu Society* and in her seminal paper on caste published in *Current Anthropology*. While discussing the material on Indian society in terms of geographical and cultural divisions, something that to her is concurrent, she also makes use of scattered references to physical anthropological variables. A typical example is the sentence in which she is describing the Saraswat Brahmins:

> epigraphic record shows that they have been occupying the coastal strip and the neighbouring places on the mountains at least since the Kadamba dynasty, i.e. since the 12th century. Anthropomorphic measurements show them to be one among the three broad-headed communities of Maharashtra (1961: 23).

Similarly with reference to the Chitpavnas, she writes:

> The Chitpavans distinguish themselves in having a larger percentage of hazel or cat's eyes than the other coastal communities (*ibid:* 24).

This mixture of physical and social anthropology was found only among the early colonial administrators like Hutton and Risely, but not followed by any reputed social anthropologists of the British or American school. Her opting for such a combined approach may be reflecting upon the trend existing at that time among her contemporaries like Ghurye who too had taken help of anthropometry to prove his theory of caste.

To her credit, she has tried to use physical anthropology not to prove a racial theory of caste as done by Risely that was supported to some extent by Ghurye but to dispel the myth of a concurrence of caste and race. She is clear in her condemnation of the colonial hypothesis linking caste and race and the British telling of the Aryan myth. She writes:

> It is wrong to suppose that the varna system arose out of a consciousness of racial distinctions as indicated by skin colour (1961: 53).

And she clearly dismisses the theory of the Aryan theory of caste propagated by British scholars as conjectural.

> Be this as it may looking at the Sanskrit record itself we have no evidence that caste was 'created' by race conscious Brahmins. It

> appears that the Aryans came upon the phenomenon of caste and fitted it into a scheme known to them (*ibid*: 58).

In her paper in *Current Anthropology*, co-authored by K.C Malhotra (1968), she provides enough statistical and biological evidence to support her hypothesis that the various castes are a result of amalgamation and the system as such shows no racial difference between one caste and another, least of all between the Brahmins and others.

> Thus there is no justification for assuming that the distance between the Brahmin 'castes' under investigation is less than the distance between a Brahmin 'caste' and a non-brahmin 'caste', for some Brahmins are closer to members of other 'castes' than to each other (1968: 115).

Thus, summing up on the contribution of Karve, one is overwhelmed by her single-minded pursuit of truth. True to her times, she considered that such a truth did exist and could be deciphered by objective, rigorous and painstaking academic endeavours. Her own academic methodology was based upon certain premises that she had derived from a theoretical orientation based upon the conviction of history and society being intrinsically connected. To her, no sociological analysis could be static and based upon observation only of the current situation as advocated by the British school of structural-functionalists but had to be understood by investigating as far as possible the development and transformations through the historical time. Her major theoretical premise is the futility of attempting to understand culture without its history; to understand society without its traditions. Her attempt to establish a true Indian anthropology and her conviction that such was possible led her to establish some extremely valid truths about caste, kinship and social organization in India; many of her observations are supported by later scholars. Take, for example, her observation on the changing and non-racial nature of caste. In her chapter on a historical survey of caste (1961: 50-77), she not only indicates how the castes were formed by historical processes spread over time but also makes the observation: "The process of caste-making has not stopped. New castes are coming into being even in the present age" (*ibid*: 65). Thus the complexity of the nature of caste, its fragmented nature, its situational nature, its historicity and the fact that it was not an institution devolving upon the existence of the brahman, were all ideas, glimpses of which we get in her works although she did not put it in the political framework as it was done by scholars in the latter half of the twentieth century.

She has certain convictions that are hers and not derived from any other scholars and most significant among them is her methodology in which she has treated the ancient Indian texts as a significant data base but first reinterpreting them in anthropological manner. She herself comes across as a person rooted in her traditions but innovative enough to project herself into the future as a post-modernist and feminist scholar. For a woman who was educated in India and abroad, who had reached the heights of professional achievements to write addressing her husband, "I place my head on your feet and ask for your blessing" is an achievement that can be equaled by few scholars, feminist or not. That Iravati Karve could not be cast in any stereotypical image is truly demonstrated by this one sentence.

REFERENCES

Channa, Subhadra Mitra

1985 *Tradition and Rationality in Economic Behaviour*. New Delhi: Cosmo.

Chatterjee, Partha

1993 *The Nation and its Fragments : Colonial and Post Colonial Histories.* Princeton: Princeton University Press.

Cohen, Bernard S.

1996 *Colonialism and its Forms of Knowledge: The British in India*. Princeton: Princeton University Press.

Dirks, Nicholas B.

1997 'The invention of caste: Civil society in colonial India'. In H.L. Seneviratne (ed) *Identity, Consciousness and the Past: Forging of Caste and Community in India and Sri Lanka.* Delhi: Oxford University Press.

2001 *Castes of Mind: Colonialism and the Making of Modern India*. Princeton and Oxford: Princeton University Press.

Hutton, J. H.

1965 'Foreword'. *Kinship Organization in India*. Bombay: Asia Publishing House: vii-viii

Karve, Iravati

1961 *Hindu Society –An Interpretation*. Poona: Deccan College.

1965 *Kinship Organization in India*. Bombay: Asia Publishing House.

(1953)

1991 *Yuganta : The End of an Epoch*. Hyderabad: Disha Books.

(1969)

Karve, Iravati and K.C. Malhotra

1968 'A biological comparison of eight endogamous groups of the same rank', *Current Anthropology* 9: 2-3: 109-124.

Moore, Henrietta

1994 *A Passion for Difference: Essays in Anthropology and Gender*. Cambridge: Cambridge University Press.

1996 'The changing nature of anthropological knowledge: An introduction'. In Henrietta Moore (ed.), *The Future of Anthropological Knowledge*. New York: Routledge (pp. 1-15).

O'Hanlon, Rosalind

1997 'Cultures of rule, communities of resistance: Gender, discourse and tradition in recent South Asian historiographies'. In H.L. Seneviratne (ed.), *Identity, Consciousness and the Past*. Delhi: Oxford University Press (pp. 147-176).

Shah. A. M.

1998 *Family in India: Critical Essays*. New Delhi: Orient Longman.

Valle, Teresa Del

1993 'Introduction'. In Teresa Del Valle (ed.), *Gendered Anthropology*. New York: Routledge.

M. N. Srinivas at the Crossroads of Sociology and Social Anthropology: The Issue of Common Identity and the Way Forward

S. GREGORY

Social anthropology and sociology are perceived to have much common ground today, though both have distinct historic traditions. Traditionally, while anthropology had been concerned with socio-cultural lives of simple and preliterate societies, with an emphasis on qualitative approach and field research, sociology was more concerned with complex and literate societies, with an emphasis on quantitative approach and survey research. While this distinction has been real, the pioneers of both the disciplines had left a mutual influence on each other in the formulation and development of theories and concepts about human society and culture. In course of time, the boundaries of these disciplines have been largely narrowed down with overlapping interests and approaches and with a greater realisation of the necessity for mutual interaction and exchange of their methods, concepts, and theories.

The relationship between sociology and social anthropology has been widely recognized. Kroeber considered the two sciences as twin sisters while in the view of Hoebel, these are, in the broader sense, one and the same. Evans Pritchard went to the extent of considering social anthropology as a branch of sociology itself, while Radcliffe-Brown treated it as nothing but comparative sociology. Redfield recognized the closeness of these two disciplines in the context of the United States, because of their similarity in the nature and subject of work.

In India, it is M.N. Srinivas (hereinafter referred as MNS) who is perceived to have been at the crossroads of these two disciplines, wearing the identities of both these disciplines. MNS had been widely considered as the founding father of modern sociology and social anthropology in India. Pauline Kolenda (2001: 374), in her biographical memoirs on MNS, calls him as India's leading social anthropologist who held that sociology and social anthropology should be a single discipline in India. While recognising his holding degrees in both sociology and social anthropology, she mentions that in the United States, he was known as an anthropologist. Parvathi Menon (1999), writing an obituary note on MNS, in *Frontline*, refers to him as India's most distinguished sociologist and social anthropologist. Coincidingly, if not ironically, of his two daughters Lakshmi and Tulsi, the former has a Ph.D. in sociology from the University of California while the latter has a Ph.D. in anthropology from Boston University.

With his most pioneering efforts, MNS had desired and worked for the integration of these two disciplines, as he used to insist time and again, as personally witnessed by the present author at close quarters, during his ISEC (Institute for Social and Economic Change) days between 1989 and 1994. In his Foreword to *M. N. Srinivas: Collected Essay*, Shah (2002: xi) emphatically brings out MNS' love for fieldwork. He also brings out MNS' conviction in finding it meaningless, in the present times, to insist on the association of social anthropology with the study of societies other than one's own, as well as on the distinction between the study of tribal and non-tribal societies, 'primitive' and modern societies, and between sociology and social anthropology. However, MNS himself realizes, to his own disappointment, that not only this had not materialised, but also he was even well aware of the fact that such a suggestion would not get a serious hearing. MNS further believed that even communication between the sociologists and social anthropologists was minimal.

André Béteille (2000), who has also been continuously preoccupied with the relationship between sociology and social anthropology in the footsteps of MNS, expresses himself to be disturbed on the question of his own professional identity as well as of all students of Indian society and culture. He finds the kind of division of labour between the two disciplines existing in the centres of learning in the United States and Europe as not conducive to his own 'personal project' of unifying sociology and social anthropology. Such a situation in these countries is, according to him, not only because of the marked separation between the two disciplines, but also the study of Indian society and culture is placed within the province of anthropology and outside that of sociology. He also feels that this not only harms the teaching of sociology in India but also has an unsettling effect on the identity of the Indian sociologists because of the tendency to label them as anthropologists abroad, though he asserts that he tries to present himself as a sociologist wherever he is.

In the context of the unification efforts of these two disciplines and the unsettling relationship between their adherents, the nature of concerns about identity is as much real in anthropology as is experienced in sociology, requiring serious examination about the whole issue. More than fifty years since the early efforts towards a common identity initiated by MNS, starting from his Baroda days, it would be worth looking at the affiliation of MNS to both sociology and social anthropology, the influence and impact of his integrating efforts, the ambiguity of their identities, and the future directions. The present paper examines these aspects in the context of MNS having been at the crossroads of these two disciplines, and in the light of his contributions and writings[2] as a sociologist and social anthropologist in his long and distinguished career, and addresses the issue of their common identity, especially from an anthropologist's perspective.

II

The titles of the two autobiographical essays of MNS, namely, 'Itineraries of an Indian Social Anthropologist' and 'Practicing

Social Anthropology in India' emphatically bring out his anthropological identity in no uncertain terms. However, in the first writing published in 1973, irrespective of the title of the paper, he mentions that he was concerned in that brief essay with narrating how he 'became a sociologist', while in the second writing, published in 1997, he says that his 'becoming a social anthropologist' was largely accidental. In the latter essay, however, in spite of the title and his proclamation, he perceives his career as in sociology, while he was analysing the reasons for the same. Thus, the dual identity in MNS had been very obvious in his perception as much as it has been in the perception of others. Such an identity, having its own impact on the professional identity of both the subjects, had been borne by his academic making, which gets reflected in his long professional career and writings.

MNS records many turning points in his life through his autobiographical essays, especially his all-inspiring paper 'All is not Lost if your Plans go Awry', published first in *Deccan Herald* in 1983. It is in 1936, when he is twenty, that he completes his B.A. Honours course in social philosophy, which included social anthropology and sociology. As per the direction by one of his teachers, Krishna, he moves to Bombay in 1936 to meet G. S. Ghurye, who, according to his teacher, is the best man in the country in sociology. He does M.A. Sociology under Ghurye, who himself had inherited the anthropological orientation from W.H.R. Rivers. As part of M.A. course, MNS is introduced to the empirical work, 'generally identified with anthropology', through his study of *Marriage and Family in Mysore*, which was published in 1942. Meanwhile he gets M.A. in 1940, and also passes L.L.B., and registers himself for Ph. D. under Ghurye. In 1943, his relationship with Ghurye goes soar. In 1944, he submits his Ph. D. thesis in sociology, based on his field-based study of Coorgs, using Rivers' approach.

In 1944, he proceeds to Oxford for doing D.Phil., under the leading anthropologist of that time, Radcliffe-Brown (RB), and later under Evans-Pritchard (EP), both of whom were themselves not particular about the boundaries of sociology and social anthropology. In fact, RB, who had been a student of Rivers as was G. S. Ghurye, believed that social anthropology itself is nothing but 'comparative sociology'.

MNS expresses an immense interest in the famous American anthropologist of the times, Ruth Benedict, and in her study of the *Patterns of Culture*. Even while he had been in Bombay, his reading of Benedict's work is said to have provided him an alternative to Rivers' approach with which he was fed up. Hence, in his application to Oxford for D. Phil., he proposes to work on the Benedictian approach with reference to three South Indian cultures without being aware of the fact that RB's approach was just contrary to this. Nevertheless, impressed by his Coorg material, RB asks MNS to write a paper on culture patterns which he does, using Kluckhohn, another famous American anthropologist, and a good deal of American literature. Though he was asked to proceed as per his original proposal, MNS himself, on second thoughts, decides to shift his attention to the Coorgs material, and proceeds to analyse it from a structural-functional perspective as suggested by RB and gets the D. Phil. degree in 1947.

Thus, Oxford provides a strong anthropological base for MNS and becomes a turning point in his academic orientation and foundation. One can notice a clear-cut influence of the perspectives of Rivers, Benedict, Kluckhohn, Radcliffe-Brown, and Evans-Pritchard in the moulding of MNS. In one place, MNS himself remarks that Evans-Pritchard influenced his outlook while Radcliffe-Brown, his approach. Moreover, the influence of his own anthropological colleagues like Mayer Fortes and Max Gluckman can never be undermined either (2002: 702).

In 1948, a university lectureship in Indian Sociology (and not anthropology) is created under the initiative of Evans-Pritchard at Oxford, and offered to MNS. Interestingly, this lectureship has now been converted into 'Social Anthropology of South Asia', though it is not clear why it was started as sociology in the first instance. Though MNS had a taste of fieldwork already during his Coorgs study, his profound experience of intensive fieldwork is realised only with his study of Rampura, a multi-caste village, undertaken for about ten months in 1948, as part of his university lectureship at Oxford. In his own view, he 'spent the best part of 1948 in making a field study of Rampura, a village 33 miles from Mysore' (*ibid.*: 658). However, his study of Rampura was published as

Remembered Village only in 1976, after a long twenty-five years. Thus, it is again Oxford that ultimately opens for him the door for sociology, when it comes to the question of pursuing a career, by offering him the lectureship in sociology.

III

The professional career of MNS, already started in Oxford as lecturer in Indian Sociology, has a continuation as a professor of sociology in the newly established chair at the M. S. University of Baroda in June 1951, as desired by Wadia, the then Pro-Vice-Chancellor of the University. With his new assignment, he begins to give a new direction to sociology, while he ignores 'making a distinction between Social Anthropology and Sociology', as he himself states, 'to the annoyance of some of my anthropological colleagues' (ibid.:.679). He does his most to encourage field studies using the method of participant observation.

From Baroda, at the invitation of V.K.R.V. Rao, the then Vice-Chancellor of Delhi University, MNS moves on to the Delhi School of Economics in 1959 to 'the newly established Chair in Sociology'. He develops the same as 'a Centre of modern sociology and social anthropology', and achieves the distinction of University Grants Commission's recognition as 'a Centre of Advanced Study in Sociology', in less than ten years. In his own assessment, he, along with his other colleagues, managed 'to combine sociology with social anthropological approaches', which he thinks is a positive thing about the department.

During his Delhi days, he goes to the Centre for Advanced Study in the Behavioural Sciences at Stanford University, California, once during 1964-5 and the other during 1970-1, mainly to reduce the feeling of 'academic illiteracy' from which he seemed to have suffered (2002:662). The second trip has been mainly meant to devote him to Rampura notes to bring out a monograph. However, with his notes having been burnt, it turns out to be a distress-turned-opportunity for the genesis of the *Remembered Village*. He leaves Delhi in May 1972, 'to start, along with the distinguished economist and educationist, V.K.R.V. Rao, the Institute for Social and Economic Change (ISEC) in Bangalore'. In 1979, he retires from ISEC, though he continues to associate with the Institute in different capacities.

He joins the National Institute of Advanced Studies (NIAS) at Bangalore as the R. D. Tata Visiting Professor in 1992 and starts a unit of sociology and social anthropology in 1997. He also establishes the women's policy, research and advocacy unit at the NIAS. He continues to be there till his end. In all, 'a great deal of his time and energies', as perceived by him, 'has been devoted to building up departments and institutions and promoting 'my kind of Sociology' (p.680), which places emphasis on intensive fieldwork (p.706). Thus, one could clearly notice in MNS, the identity of an anthropologist in his perspective, subject of research, methodology and approach, but a sociologist to the core in his allegiance to the subject.

IV

The interest of MNS in anthropology and his loyalty to sociology has been obvious in his early as well as later writings on the subjects. As early as in 1952, his paper on 'Social Anthropology and Sociology' (p.457-66) appeared in the first issue of the *Sociological Bulletin*, expressing his understanding and vision of both the subjects. He begins his paper, pointing to the unfortunate image of 'bearded and myopic ancients' that the term 'anthropology' suggests. This is especially so, as MNS believes, among the non-European countries, whose inhabitants tend to resent being studied by the anthropologists for fear of becoming branded as 'primitives', another unfortunate term under the glossary of anthropology. For MNS, the suspicion is much more so among the educated in these countries, against the anthropologist who is known to be digging into the unsavoury customs of the past. This seems to have left the social anthropologists to feel that their subject has been unlucky in the choice of its name (p.457).

Nevertheless, in his opinion, the social anthropologists (especially in Britain) had begun to study the 'non-primitive' societies for more than a decade or two, prior to 1952. He evidences this by referring to Seligman's preface to the sixth edition of *Notes and Queries*, an authoritative publication of the Royal Anthropological Institute, published in 1951, which talks about the marked advancement in social anthropology since its earlier edition in 1919. The same preface mentions that 'Part II-Social Anthropology' deals mainly with the

'Sociology of non-literate peoples', while admitting that the methods described are equally suitable in the study of advanced societies too. This implies not only the diversification of studies in social anthropology beyond the non-literate societies, but also the tendency in Britain then, to consider social anthropology as nothing but the 'sociology of non-literate peoples' (p.458).

According to MNS, it was Durkheim, more than any other individual, who determined the modern orientation of social anthropology, and exercised a dominating influence on Radcliffe-Brown and Malinowski. MNS also touches upon the differential anthropological emphasis on the twin concepts of 'culture' and 'society' as a matter of fact, and looks at it having a deeper implication of either historical/ethnological or sociological interests (p.459). On this count, he finds a hiatus between the two disciplines in the U.S., in spite of their contrasting reality (p. 459).

Emphasising the significance of fieldwork in anthropology, he says that 'no social anthropologist in England would regard anything less than 16 to 18 months with a strange people as at all adequate' (p.459-60). For him, what he would regard as the most important contribution of social anthropology to the social sciences is the insistence on the necessity of an anthropologist making an intensive study of all aspects of the selected society. In his opinion, it is here that the social anthropologist scores heavily over his sociologist colleague. For him, the experience of intensive fieldwork is an absolutely essential qualification for a social anthropologist. He even insists on the intensive study of a minimum of two societies preferably in two distinct areas, as a single piece of fieldwork might lead to certain lopsidedness in the anthropologist, though it may be overcome with his knowledge of other societies through a reading of ethnographic literature (p. 460-1).

In this context, it is worth noting the remarks of MNS that it is this dimension that has chiefly contributed to making social anthropology a respected and respectable discipline as evidenced in British universities, the seats of highest academic standards then, where social anthropology was an 'established and expanding' subject, whereas, barring London, no English university had a chair in sociology. As MNS further reports, even the few sociologists in Britain were all those who had conducted field investigations, which were social anthropological in nature (p. 461). Nevertheless, as MNS points out in another context (p. 705), even in Oxford, anthropology had been labeled as 'barbarolgy', prompting EP to be forced to move with the Orientalists who seem to have been enjoying an 'upper caste' status, a kind of academic sanskritisation at that.

MNS is appreciative of Ghurye for his insistence on fieldwork. While MNS dwells on the preoccupation of social anthropologists with the study of 'primitive' societies, he considers such studies not totally out of place, and in fact, perceives it as 'an essential preliminary to undertaking the study of one's own society' (p. 462-3). He also turns critical of the American sociologists for their subjectivism in spite of their claim of 'scientific objectivity'. His advice for them was to read anthropological monographs in order to learn objectivity. He also insists on the significance of an initial acquaintance with simple societies either directly or at least through reading, before undertaking a study of a complex and industrialized society (p. 463).

In the same essay, turning to sociology, he finds social philosophy and social work on either ends of sociology, but neither of these exercising any positive influence on the subject. In fact, he finds social work, which was then a more prosperous academic neighbour, as a great danger to sociology and considers it as a disaster for sociology if it does not assert its autonomy from both social philosophy and social work (p. 463-4). Does it imply a lesson for anthropology in the context of its acclaimed affinity to sociology today?

Realising the prospect of sociology becoming a 'popular subject in our universities,' MNS raises a deep concern about 'what type of sociology we want to be taught', even while he considers the uncritical acceptance of the existing kind of sociology to be 'a national intellectual disaster'. He declares an agenda for the kind of sociology to be evolved, which should include all aspects of society including the study of 'primitive' groups as well as to be of comparative in nature. It is very pertinent to note the kind of suggestion he makes, in this context, to make sociology most appropriate. He considers it good to insist that the students wishing to study 'sociology' should undergo 'a prior study of social anthropology for at least two years' for valid reasons, namely, to provide a cure from 'ethno-centrism' to develop a certain charity and tolerance towards ways of life other than one's own, to learn to consider small fragment of modern societies as integrated wholes, and to develop an empirical outlook, all of which are the basics of anthropology, which seem to become endangered today, even within anthropology.

Finally, MNS makes his suggestion 'to do away with the distinction between sociology and social anthropology and include them both under 'comparative sociology', which had remained as his pet topic throughout his life. However, the reason he puts forth for the union is strange, namely 'to separate social anthropology from physical anthropology and ethnology' and such a union, he believes, will be 'to the advantage of sociology'. His concern for sociology is further made clear, when he concludes that the evolved sociology should embrace 'all aspects of our society;' and 'include within itself the study of primitive groups, peasant communities, the various sects and cults and aspects of our urban life' (p. 465).

After forty years since then, he writes the paper 'Sociology in India and its Future' for his inaugural address to the 20th All India Sociological Conference held in 1993, the birth centenary year of G. S. Ghurye, and later published in *Sociological Bulletin* in 1994, in which he discusses the present status of sociology, being incongruent with the kind of sociology that he dreamt of in the fifties, and looks at its future. He himself remarks that 'there has been a sea-change in the position of sociology during the period. He considers Ghurye as 'an important figure in the history of sociology and social anthropology' and 'the most important proponent of the fieldwork tradition in Sociology', notwithstanding Ghurye's own status as 'an armchair scholar' (p. 467).

According to MNS, sociology in the 1930s was barely tolerated as a social science, and it was taught in only four universities, namely, Bombay, Lucknow, Mysore and Hyderabad, with only Bombay having a full-fledged department, while Calcutta University had an anthropology department (p. 468). He considers the increasing cultural and intellectual influence of United States in India and elsewhere, as one of the main reasons for the popularity of sociology in the post-independence years. Apart from the external influences, he also notes the new opportunities opened up in the post-independent era influencing the change in the position of sociology. In his opinion, the need to make sense of the rapid cultural and social changes in India in the post-1940 has also significantly contributed to the 'popularity of sociology and social anthropology'. Thus, though his intention has been to talk of 'the place of sociology in the social sciences', he does include social anthropology along with sociology, now and then, to drive home the idea of sameness, though his tone subsumes social anthropology under sociology. As Shah (2000) remarks, both Ghurye and Srinivas subsumed anthropology under sociology. He also points out that social biology is Ghurye's way of co-opting physical anthropology into sociology.

While MNS identifies the uniqueness of sociology as different from other social sciences in not having a clearly demarcated field, in being far more of an approach and a perspective, and also holistic and integrated in nature, one could not but wonder the extent to which MNS equates sociology with anthropology, and also the extent of his conviction about the transformation of sociology to take on the traditional features of anthropology. He goes on to remark that 'sociology is an empirical discipline, and fieldwork, either through survey method or by participant observation, is integral to it', though he does admit field work with participant observation to be 'usually identified with social anthropologists' (p. 472). Identifying the unique opportunities, the post-independent India provided in the growth of sociolgy, he explores new dimensions and emerging social realities, which could provide potential areas and fresh challenges for research in sociology in the near future. In this context, he appeals to the power-holders to 'support sociology and social anthropology', as these disciplines are indispensable to smoothen the transitional phase, the country has been undergoing.

He identifies a number of areas that had been or that should be subjected to sociological enquiries, as part of its indispensable role in the understanding of the increasingly complex world. He insists on making sociology admissions tough in its pursuit of excellence. He also insists on those in power, desiring science and technology to improve the living conditions of the people, to support 'sociology and social anthropology' as these are indispensable, in his opinion, in smoothening the transition. This would ensure, he argues, the attraction of able students with an aptitude for sociology, and concludes that only then will sociology become an integral part of the intellectual discourse of this country. Meanwhile, he also emphasises the point that 'only when sociologists undertake to seriously study problems bearing on the rapid improvement of the living conditions of the poor and the oppressed will the discipline's relevance be appreciated by those in power'. He also stresses on the importance of pursuing excellence to be the goal, in which case, 'all and sundry cannot and should not be admitted to sociology courses' on the one hand, while the employability of sociology should attract able students who have an aptitude for sociology, on the other (p. 478-9). Thus, while the core of the discussion in this paper has centred purely on sociology, his occasional inclusion of social anthropology along with sociology does indicate his inclusive approach to the dual identity of these subjects.

V

'The Development of Sociology and Social Anthropology in India' was an article MNS had jointly written with M. N. Panini (MNP), and was published in 1973 in *Sociological Bulletin*, approximately during the middle of the forty years span between the two papers discussed above. In this article, the authors proclaim to attempt 'to trace the development of two closely-linked and overlapping social sciences, viz., sociology and social anthropology' and relating the same with the corresponding cultural milieu (p. 480). Giving as a background discussion to the development of sociology and social anthropology in India, which itself, in their opinion, was intimately influenced by nationalism (p. 482), they suggest that the intellectual climate in Western Europe, which was closely linked with the political, economic and other forces of the day, favoured the development of the two disciplines (p. 481). As they rightly state, 'anthropology was the product of European expansion over the world during the last three to four centuries' (*ibid*). In the process, they also identify the emergence of different anthropological thoughts starting from evolution to diffusion, functionalism, and to structuralism and 'of the method of intensive field work' in native language as "the anthropologists' principal technique of data collection." They attribute the popularity of sociology in the USA during the corresponding period to the many problems like urbanisation, immigration, ethnicity, crime, juvenile delinquency, and prostitution (p. 482). They identify the growth of the two disciplines in India into three identical phases, namely, the period between 1773-1900, as foundational, from 1901 to 1950, as professional, and the post-independent years, as the period of research.

They consider the origins of sociology, as going back to the second half of the 18th century when the British officials realized that the knowledge of Indian culture and social life as indispensable to the smooth functioning of the government. Francis Buchanan's ethnographic study of West Bengal in 1807 is cited to be one such instance. Also important are the works of the missionaries, such as Abbe Duboi's *Hindu Manners, Customs and Ceremonies* in 1816, and the gazetteers. All these were considered as the forerunners of the more systematic attempts in the later part of the 19th century. The ethnographic surveys as part of the all-India Census started in 1871 by the British government have been one such attempt in this regard. The initiation of Indological studies with the starting of the Royal Asiatic Society of Bengal in 1787 and of a journal devoted to antiquarian and anthropological interests is also considered to have added impetus to the understanding of life and culture of Indian people. The works of Maine, Marx and Weber using the data on India are also considered to have 'an impact on the development of social anthropology and sociology in India'. Thus, they conclude that the soil was being made for the 'planting of sociology' (p. 485).

With the beginning of the 20th century, they touch upon the development of both the subjects being mutually inclusive, even while each having its own independent development as both entering into the early phase of professionalisation. Apart from the continuing efforts of the ethnographic works by British officials, the soil also attracts, according to them, professional sociologists and social anthropologists in Europe, starting from W.H.R. Rivers. Two of Rivers' students, G. S. Ghurye and K. P.

Chattopadhyaya, come to play an important role in the development of sociology and social anthropology. L. K. Ananthakrishna Iyer and S. C. Roy, even without formal training, make their mark in anthropology. The establishment of the Ethnographic Survey of India in 1905 becomes a milestone in the development of anthropology in India.

In their opinion, it is during the first two decades of the 20th century that these two disciplines are introduced as academic disciplines in Indian universities. Under Ghurye's leadership, Bombay becomes the leading centre for sociology. Lucknow becomes a centre for sociology and social anthropology, initially under the Department of Economics and Sociology, with the trimvurate, Radhakamal Mukharjee (RM), D. P. Mukharjee (DP) and D. N. Majumdar (DN) in the department. According to MNS and MNP, the foundations for the growth of Lucknow as an influential centre for sociological studies are laid by RM. Sociology is introduced at B.A. level at Osmania in 1928, under Fürer- Haimendorf and S. C. Dube and their work put Osmania on the map of Indian and international anthropology and sociology. A combined department of sociology and social anthropology is started in Poona in the late 1930s under the leadership of Irawati Karve, a student of Ghurye.

DN (a student of S. C. Roy and Ananthakrishna Iyer and later of T. C. Hodson at Cambridge) was instrumental in establishing the Ethnographic and Folk Culture Society in U.P. in 1945 and its quarterly journal *The Eastern Anthropologist* in 1947. The Anthropological Survey of India with its first director B. S. Guha and with his successor N. K. Bose, was another notable development for anthropology in the 1940s. Among the notable contributions of the missionaries, mention is made of Verrier Elwin, especially for his contribution to tribal ethnography. Among the learned societies, the Royal Asiatic Society of Bengal, later coming to be known as the Asiatic Society of Bengal, is conceived to be the foremost in promoting anthropology and sociology.

They also recognise that sociology and social anthropology suffered from many disabilities as well. 'If sociology was not respectable, anthropology was suspect of its association with the colonial policy'. The latter seems to have also been disliked especially by the nationalists, during the pre-independence period, for the fear of its stigma of 'primitivism'. During the first half of the 20th century, the study of these disciplines became professionalised, though only slowly, as these were taught in not more than half a dozen universities until 1950 while there seems to have been a sharp increase in their popularity after that. They find the increasing popularity of these two disciplines coinciding with their professionalisation, facilitated by different initiatives. For instance, they find the Indian Sociological Society, founded by G. S. Ghurye in 1951 who was also the first editor of its journal *Sociological Bulletin*, providing a forum, and the regular organization of All-India Sociological Conferences providing another national forum for the Indian sociologists and social anthropologists in their way to professionalisation. However, these just mentioned efforts, being as they are in their names, the impact had been real for sociology but not for anthropology, as such intensive and parallel mobilisation had not been much discernible in the arena of anthropology except for some individual initiatives.

The distinct theoretical line in sociology in the post-independent India is another factor acknowledged in favour of the popularity and professionalisation of sociology. They do recognise, within sociology itself, the existence of those who are hostile to the new line of sociology (using the 'structural-functionalist method'), and the group dubbing those adhering the new line, as social anthropologists, a species as distinct from sociologists (p. 500). In this context, they emphatically observe that the new research of studying social institutions using the structural-functional method based on field work rendered the distinction between the two disciplines, especially in the Indian context, untenable. For them, any attempt to erect an impassable barrier between the study of tribes and others is absurd, nor is the attempt to define a discipline by its dominant method of study any more successful. In their observation, while there are increasing attempts on the part of the anthropologists to incorporate quantitative and network analysis to tackle extensive data, sociologists refuse to regard the intensive study of communities, villages, and towns as the sacred preserve of anthropologists (p. 501).

They talk of the classical micro-level studies of 1950s, including that of Kathleen Gough's (1955, 1960) Tanjore village,

F. G. Bailey's (1957) monograph on caste and social mobility, S. C. Dube's study of U.P. villages, and Scarlet Epstein's (1962) study of two Mysore villages. They also touch upon the emergence of sociological analysis of caste and politics and educational sociology and the study of social change. The contribution of the foreign scholars both from the Europeon and American streams to the various facets and problems of Indian society had been significantly noted. The influence of American scholars either through Indian students trained in U.S. universities or through the writings of the scholars themselves on Indian sociology and social anthropology is found to be vast and varied. Having given an overall review of the development of the two disciplines in India, they summarise that sociology in India has been hospitable to divergent streams of thought, while they express hope for the development of an Indian approach to sociology, which was yet to emerge (p. 506).

Stating to look at the prospects for sociology and social anthropology, and the tasks ahead of them, they in fact resort to specify what sociology needs to do to grow properly. One such condition, they put forth is for sociology to go native if it has to be creative. They also underline the need for the Indian sociologists, for a commitment to comparative approach, which, according to them, has so far been conspicuous by its absence. Emphasising the overriding concerns with the issues of poverty and illiteracy, they recognise the operation of such impulse among the Indian anthropologists that led to the discussions on urgent anthropology with a new meaning. They also touch upon the trend of seeking the help of social sciences including sociology and social anthropology in the implementation of the plans but not of their formulations, and also on how modern India is a wonderful laboratory for social scientists. Underlining how sociology can play a useful if not an important role in both the formulation and implementation of policies, they conclude that a new dawn in Indian sociology may not be long in coming.

VI

MNS was convinced that the future of sociology and social anthropology in India lay in the use of the method of field work or participant observation and forcefully conveyed the implications and importance of fieldwork (Shah, 2002: xi) whenever an opportunity came in his way. The collection of his essays on Method (Part VII), which he had started writing early in his career, particularly after his fieldwork in Rampura and assumption of teaching and research responsibility in Baroda, profoundly reflects his approach. In his paper titled 'Village Studies, Participant Observation and Social Science Research in India' published in *Economic and Political Weekly* (EPW) in 1975, he credits the anthropologists with field work and participant observation method and dwells on its wider applicability while insisting on the social scientists in general to adopt a field based-empirical approach in order to be closer to reality. The lack of fieldwork tradition in the social sciences (excluding social anthropology and sociology), according to him, has had adverse results on their growth and development and most importantly, it has alienated them from grassroots reality. In his paper on 'The Fieldworker and the Field: A Village in Karnataka,' published in 1979, he dwells on the problems of fieldwork based on personal experience and identifies himself totally as an anthropologist.

In his paper on 'The Observer and the Observed in the Study of Cultures', published in 1983, MNS dwells on participant observation method of the social anthropologists in the study of culture. Only once he makes a mention of the sociologists and that too within bracket, when he refers to the anthropologists, taking on the role of a fieldworker, the need to feel inferior not only in the study of an alien community but even when it is in one's own country (p.544), as was the trend then. In another paper, 'The Insider versus the Outsider in the Study of Cultures', published in 1984, MNS, through and through, focuses on anthropology in discussing about the concept of insider and the outsider, in the study of cultures. In the article, while talking about the popularity of the two disciplines in the third world countries during the post-war period, MNS finds sociology to be able to spread more easily, mainly because of its non-association with the 'primitives', while there seems to be a strong feeling among the educated that to be studied by anthropologists would be sufficient enough to label a community 'primitive'.

The paper on 'Participant Observation' discusses the method, totally within an anthropological framework. Similarly, his paper 'Studying One's Own Culture: Some Thoughts' is totally confined to the anthropological framework, without trespassing to sociology except while discussing the following. Here, after touching upon the western bias in anthropology, MNS talks of how the colonial image of anthropology had affected its identity, and it was unpopular among the educated natives of the colonial countries, especially under the growing nationalism, mainly for two reasons. Firstly, anthropology was suspected to be a device in the hands of the colonisers, and secondly, the subject matter of its study traditionally being the apes and the 'primitives', there had been a fear of a stigma of primitivism, if subjected to study by the anthropologists. In this context, he finds 'sociology' being a more acceptable discipline than 'anthropology' for many and even a few anthropologists conveniently assuming the label as sociologists to escape from the counter-stigma (p.572). This could be contrasted to the situation in which some sociologists, with anthropological orientation, prefer to identify themselves to be sociologists within the country, while they come to be known as social anthropologists abroad. Then, he moves on to discuss how the focus of study in anthropology has transcended from its tribal fixity to the study of complex societies, and in the process, from its 'other culturedness' to 'the study of one's own culture'. He does recognise the importance of studying the other and experiencing the culture-shocks, which, in the Indian context, could be encountered not only in one's backyard but even next door, as his own experience vouches for. In retrospect, he is not surprised that he has become an anthropologist, all of whose fieldwork is in his own country. He studied societies that could be strictly considered as the 'other', while in a wider sense, they were his own, whether it was the study of the Coorg society, or of the Rampura village (Gregory and Gregory 2007: 255).

In his article 'Indian Anthropologists and the Study of Indian Culture', first published in the *EPW* in March 1996, MNS declares at the outset itself that he uses the term sociologists and social anthropologists interchangeably. Nevertheless, subsequently in the article, he uses the term 'sociologist' not more than once, and that too with reference to America, distinguishing them from the anthropologists of the same land, while he uses the later term as many as 13 times. In his article,

'Social Anthropology and Literary Sensibility', published in *EPW* in 1998, MNS states at the outset that he considers social anthropology and sociology as fundamentally the same, as both disciplines concern with the study and understanding of human societies in space and time (p. 596). Referring to fieldwork, he finds for good that in both sociology and social anthropology, as practiced in India, this tradition has come to be accepted as part of the disciplines. He also considers the post-war years to have been a creative period for sociology and social anthropology in India, for carrying field work studies of tribes, villages, castes, urban slums and factories. For the rest, he confines himself to the anthropological frame.

The identity question is also reflected in some of his papers included under the section 'Cultural and Social Change in India'. In his paper on 'Science, Technology and Rural Development', delivered and published in 1977, while dwelling on the importance of sociological knowledge, MNS expresses his surprise over the ignorance of scientists and technologists who have written on integrated rural development, about the concept of functionalism that has been so influential in social anthropological and sociological research during previous six decades or so (p. 421). According to him, the scientist and technologist must be able, like the social anthropologists, to get into the shoes of those they want to help (p. 427). Citing the example of caste factor as giving a common cultural idiom to the rural people, MNS notes, in his paper on the 'Dual Cultures of Independent India', written in 1977, that the anthropologists refuse to recognize the existence of such 'unpleasant' facts for fear of being labelled as reactionaries (p. 430). In the same article, he also makes a note of the cautious approach by the anthropologists, while probing the sensitive areas such as assets, liabilities, loans, household relations, sex life, factionalism, etc., during a fieldwork (p. 437). In the discussion on fieldwork and participant observation, MNS clearly spots the anthropologist at the core throughout. However, in his paper on the 'Changing Institutions and Values', first published in 1962 in *EPW*, he talks of sociologists as spending long periods in a single village, enabling to notice those changes that are invisible for an urbanite (p. 451).

VII

The contribution of MNS to social anthropology in India, especially in popularising its methodological orientation and in bringing out the importance of cultural studies in the development of the people, in freeing the subject from its obsession with the study of tribal societies and widening its scope, and in insisting on the value of field work in the study of human societies, is undisputable and highly valuable. He has brought laurels to the subject with his unique contribution to the study of various dimensions of Indian society, upholding his identity as a social anthropologist. Nevertheless, his loyalty to sociology and his unwavering interest in changing the direction of the subject by incorporating the methodological strengths of social anthropology are again undisputable facts that are clearly reflected in his works.

The redundancy in the existence of these two subjects and the necessity of their merger, as argued by MNS, is quite understandable. However, it becomes difficult to understand for an anthropologist, when he declares that such a proposition is only 'to the advantage of sociology'. This is also clear when Shah (2002: x) infers from his essay on 'Sociology and Social Anthropology' that MNS worked throughout his life to integrate social anthropology into sociology–clearly implying, in effect, a kind of assimilation rather than integration per se.

As reported by Shah (2000), subsuming anthropology under sociology was followed in every sphere of activity as a continuation of Ghurye's policy, visible all over western India where his students (including MNS) occupied leadership positions, with the sole exception of Poona. In Poona, according to Shah, anthropology has been given a separate status at the Deccan College Postgraduate and Research Institute, with a full-fledged department under the headship of Irawati Karve who subsumed sociology under it, although sociology eventually became a separate department. Otherwise, as accounted by Shah, none of the many universities that were established in Gujarat and Maharashtra after Independence set up a separate department of anthropology.

Srivastava (2000; 2004) observes that the main interaction of social anthropologists has been with sociologists, and not with physical anthropologists. According to him, the fear that this would lead to the merging of social anthropology with sociology is unfounded, as both social anthropology and sociology have retained their respective identities and their combined departments are in decline. For him this is an indication that each discipline asserts its identity and does not want it to be abrogated, regardless of the common interests and perspectives it may share with the other discipline. However, when there are strong attempts of co-habitation between two disciplines or if they are in a constant process of adoption of strong features from the other, there is possibility of one being subsumed under the other, depending on the circumstances, opportunities and the strength of advocacies, as noted earlier. Today, sociology has grown multi-fold while anthropology is mostly confined to a few colleges and a limited number of universities. In the process, sociology, with its anthropological orientation has become a more popular subject than its counterpart, leading to an uneasy co-existence between these disciplines with mutual suspicion and one-upmanship, creating a serious crisis, especially for anthropology of its identity and existence, as sociology has a vast network, acceptability and spatial spread as compared to anthropology (Gregory 2002: 287). The scenario is not much different in Europe, as is clear from Pat Caplan's (2001) address as part of her Sterling Memorial Lectures. According to Caplan, sociology is now a very large discipline while anthropology remains relatively a small one, in spite of her conviction that the latter is well capable of addressing crucial issues of our time in a globalising world. The question then is what should be the best option that would resolve the present crisis.

VIII

As for anthropology, it could justify its independent existence, relevance and significance, as long as it maintains its integrated identity. Extremity of its specialisations seeks for greater affiliation to their respective collateral subjects outside anthropology, while giving up its roots and basics. These have even led to suggestions for placing physical anthropology with zoology, archaeology with ancient history, as is the case of social anthropology with sociology, and doing away with the 'Departments of Anthropology' as reported by Srivastava (1999:

553, endnote 14). No specialisation, in itself, could claim to be anthropological if it loses the core and the central theme of the subject. Only in complementarity and connectivity among its specialisations, could there be a real anthropological identity.

Anthropology has come a long way to earn a coveted place among all disciplines, especially on the strength of its humanistic approach with a rich heritage to its credit. It has dynamically responded to the challenges of the growing world, effectively and appropriately. Its strength is its past and it has an immense potentiality to contribute to any situation of human development. It is only with concerted efforts in professionalising the subject, could it survive with its own exclusive identity especially in the changing times of globalisation and the consequent humanistic challenges (Gregory 2002). This does not close its door of establishing a healthy, constructive, and productive relationship with its collateral disciplines as should be the case between socio-cultural anthropology and sociology. As for the anthropological version of sociology, the kind of which had been advocated by MNS, and the subsequent claim for the socio-anthropological identity by a class of sociologists, it should be appreciated so long as they maintain a closer affinity to the anthropological perspective and an intensive collaboration with the anthropologists.

In this context, it is important to take a view of the current status of anthropology and its identity in our universities and the way forward. At the university level, anthropology had always struggled to establish its identity as different universities include the subject under different schools or faculties of disciplines (Gregory 2000:292). According to Srivastava (2000), because the so-called 'integrated' anthropology bridges biological and social sciences, it occupies a dual, sometimes uncertain, status of science as well as arts.

> Some universities list anthropology as a science subject, to be administered by the faculty of science; for others, it is a social science, or even a discipline of the arts and humanities, notwithstanding its biological content (Srivastava 2000).

However, there should be efforts to assert the unique identity of anthropology in demanding for a separate school or faculty, though its mere existence need not guarantee a unifying approach and an integrated identity unless strived. This is especially so, with the experience of the British universities, as reported by Srivastava (1999: 547; 2000), where separate departments of anthropological branches functioned under the faculty of anthropology with negligible interactions between them.

In the Indian context, there should be a school of anthropological sciences at the university level, which could co-ordinate the different specialised studies of anthropology, and offer a Master's degree in Anthropological Sciences (MAS), with the inclusion of specialised courses. The School could include specialisations such as rural anthropology, medical anthropology, human genetics, human ecology, folklore, gender studies, forensic anthropology, tribal studies, etc., depending on the specialised areas and strength of the faculty under the respective schools. This could help the students to acquire not only the anthropological value orientation but also command a demand, and suitable placement for anthropologists in different concerns, related to their respective areas of specialisation. However, such an approach presumes the intake of students with an anthropological background already at the intermediary or degree level, requiring only a general orientation and exposure to different specializations before they opt for one. This is also possible under a five-year integrated course, following the intermediary course. The school could also offer a one year post-graduate diploma in anthropology (PGDA) with a field work component, for degree holders who do not have any exposure to anthropology at the degree or intermediary level, so that to facilitate those who would like to take up a post-graduate degree under the school of anthropology. The diploma course could also benefit those who intend to gain a basic anthropological knowledge.

To channelise the schemes, orient the programmes and monitor the functioning of the departments of anthropology with a professional touch, there should be an apex body established under the name, Indian Council for Excellence in Anthropological Sciences (ICEAS). The Council could carry out a regular monitoring and assessment of the old and new departments and issue certificate of approval and accreditation. The Council can also take the work of identifying anthropological issues on an all-India basis and compiling the anthropological studies periodically. Such a Council can also bring out periodical updates on the nature of anthropological studies as well as facilitate greater co-ordination and integration among different anthropological studies and identifying the areas of dialoguing with the collateral disciplines for greater exchange of knowledge and information at the interdisciplinary level (Gregory 2002: 293). The researches in anthropology should have an inter-disciplinary approach while it does exhibit deeper orientation in the subject with strong motive for intensive fieldwork, the deterioration of which had been a constant concern of MNS. This would ultimately mould the subject into a status of professional identity, in order to meet the challenges of the new era of globalisation. Any specialised area of anthropology should be clear about what is anthropology in it, while every specialised study of anthropology should have a clear link with the principal concerns and perspective of anthropology.

With all these, however, anthropology has a long way to go to assert its existence, establish and popularise its own exclusive identity, and prove its mantle in the service of humanity without just resorting to its past glory. It would be appropriate to point out, in this context that in a review article, while presenting the view of one of the contributors as bemoaning the absence of their voice in public affairs and sayng that the anthropologists are doomed if they do not seek a voice, the reviewer adds that the iteration of this voice needs to be on a 'professional' level (Ratnagar 2006). Thus, howsoever and whatsoever assertion is made about the need for a voice in the contemporary society, it would carry weight only when it involves a committed professionalism with the real anthropological values and approach. Such a striving to anthropological professionalism and professionalising anthropology would be the right tribute to MNS, who had deep appreciation for the anthropological perspective and for its field-work tradition, and who initiated efforts to revitalise the subject, particularly its socio-cultural dimension, towards responding to the challenges of the times.

ACKNOWLEDGEMENT

[This is a revised version of the paper presented at the National Conference on Professor M. N. Srinivas: The man and his works, organised by Anthropological Association, Mysore, November, 16-18, 2004.]

NOTES

1. The reference to the writings of MNS in this paper is mainly confined to his autobiographical essays, as well as to the collection of his papers on 'cultural and social change in India', on 'sociology and social anthropology in India', and on 'method', all included in the volume *M. N. Srinivas: Collected Essays* (2002).
2. It is to be pointed out here that, in Kannur University, Kerala, a submission to this effect, placed before the Board of Studies in Anthropology has been accepted and a resolution passed, which has been later approved by the Faculty of Social Sciences, though still waiting for its implementation, probably for want of a nod by the Academic Council. In fact, the submission insists on the conversion of the newly formed 'School of Tribal and Folkloristic studies' into a 'Department of Tribal and Folkloristic studies' and on the elevation of the 'Department of Anthropology' into a School of Anthropological Sciences, under which the former could function as a specialist department, with a possibility for more such specialist studies in future.

REFERENCES

Béteille, André
2000 'Teaching and research', *India-Seminar.com*. November. 495.

Gregory, S.
2002 'Diffusionalising and professionalising anthropology: Towards a response to value-degradation and globalisation', *Man in India* 82 (3&4): 279-94.

Gregory, S. and Jancy F. Gregory
2007 'MNS the insider versus MNS the outsider: The researcher identity in the study of society'. In P. K. Mishra, K.K. Basa, and H. K. Bhat (eds.), *M. N. Srinivas: The Man and His Works*. Jaipur: Rawat

Kolenda, Pauline
2001 'Mysore Narasimhachar Srinivas', *Proceedings of the American Philosophical Society*, 145 (3), September 2001.

Menon, Parvathi
1999 'A scholar remembered: M. N. Srinivas, 1916-1999', *Frontline* 16 (26), December 11-24, 1999.

Ratnagar, Shereen
2006 'The canvas of anthropology', Book Review of *Issues and Themes in Anthropology*, edited by Vinay Kumar Srivastava and Manoj Kumar Singh. *Education Plus, The Hindu,* 17 January 2006.

Shah, A M.

2000 'Sociology in a regional context', *India-Seminar.com*. November. 495.

2002 'Foreword'. In M. N. Srinivas, *Collected Essays: M. N. Srinivas*. New Delhi: Oxford.

Srinivas, M. N.

2002 *Collected Essays: M.N. Srinivas*. New Delhi: Oxford.

Srivastava, V. K.

1999 'The future of anthropology', *EPW*, February 27, 1999: 545-553.

2000 'Teaching anthropology', *India-Seminar.com*. November. 495.

2004 'Anthropology in India: A comment', *The Eastern Anthropologist* 57 (2). April-June 2004.

18

S. C. Dube and Indian Anthropology

YOGESH ATAL

Twenty-fifth of July is the day of the birth of a man who never celebrated his birthday. On this day, in 1922, he was born in a small township of Seoni, in the then Central Provinces. His parents named him Shyama Charan. Born of a Brahmin caste, Dube was suffixed to his name. Shortened as S.C. Dube, his name was known the world over as one of India's most distinguished social scientists.

This great character in the history of Indian social sciences passed away on 4 February 1996 due to severe cardiac arrest. He died a preferred death: "I should die with a pen in my hand and with an incomplete sentence on the paper." That is what has happened. His three books were in press, and he had to contribute a paragraph or two on the phenomenon of post-modernity when suddenly he collapsed. But he was conscious enough to insist on calling his publisher to his bed for final instructions. He promised to dictate those paragraphs to his wife as soon as he recovered. That time unfortunately never came. His plans to do a book with me upon my return to India now remain like an incomplete sentence. In his last correspondence to me when I was stationed in Paris at UNESCO, he expressed the desire that I should come back to India. "Now you should return"; this was the briefest letter I had received from his pen. Hidden in the handwritten text was perhaps the message that his end was near. I decided to prepone my home leave to meet him in January 1996. When I informed him of my decision, he asked me in his characteristic style to bring a good pipe and some fine tobacco. Soon upon receiving the gift, he enthusiastically filled the pipe and enjoyed the puff. I knew that it was injurious for him, but I had no courage to ignore his wish. I was out of Delhi when he fell ill and had to be hospitalised. I rushed to Delhi, but by then he was back home. We spent full two hours together, with my doctor brother in company; for the first time, Professor Dube rose from his bed to see me off and came right up to the lift. He let me go to my home town and suggested that he would arrange a dinner upon my return when he would also invite some literary personalities commonly known to us. But that was not to be. The day I was preparing to return to Delhi from Udaipur, my brother phoned to tell me that he was no more. I regret my absence when he last breathed, but feel fortunate that I was there at the cremation.

II

Over the years our relationship, which began in 1957 as that of a teacher-pupil, developed into fictive kinship of filial ties. While he treated me as his son, my children always addressed him as "uncle". When *Jan Satta*– the Hindi newspaper, then edited by Prabhash Joshi, devoted one full page to Professor Dube, I was also invited to contribute an article on him that I faxed from Bangkok. The page carried a photograph of his nuclear family. When I met him during my sojourn in India soon after, he showed me the clipping and quibbled: "This photograph is incomplete. You are not there." Some time later we spent a week together in Paris for a UNESCO meeting. There I fell ill and he took my full care. Oddly enough, there he once remarked: "I very much hope you would be there to give me *mukhagni*." That rendered me speechless. I feel lucky that I was at his cremation to pay my tearful obeisance; but the electronic crematorium did not allow performing the ritual of *mukhagni*. On his death, I felt orphaned once more.

III

Professor Dube had an enormous circle of friends, colleagues, and admirers in fields as diverse as academics, politics, the civil service, and the media. He was a great host who welcomed every visitor irrespective of his age or status, and he excelled in conversations on diverse topics that matched the interests of the visitors. Other than English and Hindi, in which he was proficient both as a writer and speaker, Dube conversed with ease in Marathi, Urdu, Bundelkhandi, Chhattisgarhi, and the dialects of Western Uttar Pradesh. Even to his juniors and to those who were his subordinates – the clerks and chaprasis, he spoke in a polished and courteous language. While riding a taxi driven by a Sikh chauffer he would never forget to seek his permission to smoke. Dube was a perfect gentleman; a thoroughly cultured persona. He was an example of a queer mix of modernity with tradition; he displayed objectivity of a social scientist alongside the sensitivity of a litterateur; he occupied positions of power and yet he encouraged disagreement and dissent. Not the founder of any school, nor a narrow specialist, but rather a wanderer in search of new pastures, Dube was an investigator of the contemporary against the backdrop of history and against a vision of the future. He was a frontiersman, an itinerant explorer of new territories for research and reflection. To call him an anthropologist or a sociologist is to force him in a narrow cage. He transgressed disciplinary boundaries and encouraged others to do the same. It would be most appropriate to call him a social scientist.

Delivering the First D. N. Majumdar Memorial Lecture in 1972, he foresaw the contours of a newly developing paradigm for social sciences. Let me quote the prophesy he had made:

> By and large, academic anthropology in India continues to maintain a semblance of the classical "grand design" and keeps within its fold cultural and social anthropology, physical anthropology, and prehistory. It is becoming increasingly evident, however, that this federal character will not last. Ethno-linguistics could never become as effective a part of anthropology in India as it did in the United States. Now prehistory is discovering its natural affinity with archaeology and is slowly being absorbed into that discipline. Physical anthropology remains attached to cultural anthropology and is not making a determined bid to find a place for itself among the life sciences. This has contributed to its retardation. Anthropology and sociology have come closer in spite of the presence, in both these disciplines, of purists who make a deliberate attempt to avoid the pollution of their "own" subject by the other. Evidently, these purists are fighting a losing battle. With anthropologists seeking a new and

> larger unit of study the fusion of social anthropology and sociology is imminent. If we have to move from micro to macro studies this is both necessary and desirable. Nostalgia for the academic tradition and false pride in disciplinary labels are bound to be counter-productive. Those who care for understanding are increasingly rejecting the artificial disciplinary boundaries. Vested interests, rather than reason, appear to account for the continuing clash.[1]

At 74, he was alert, with a photographic memory, and an untiring urge to communicate his thoughts through his pen. In his later years, he switched over to Hindi in which he wrote numerous articles and made several speeches on topics ranging from hard core social sciences to contemporary concerns. He also served on the jury for the award of prizes in Hindi literature. He himself received the Moortidevi Award of the Bharatiya Jnanpeeth for 1993. Earlier he was awarded the S.C. Roy Gold Medal of the Asiatic Society of West Bengal in 1976, and the Doctor of Letters by the Kashi Vidyapeeth in 1987. Even as a student of B.A. (Honors) he won the World Politics Essay Gold Medal in 1943.

Orphaned by his mother's death when he was barely seven, Dube was socialized by his father who was Manager of the Court of Wards in Chhattisgarh. His schooling started in poorly equipped village schools, and later in residential schools. From the Model School in Jabalpur he did his matriculation and then went to Nagpur for his further studies. Even while at school, Dube developed the habit of reading and writing. As a child, he began producing a hand-written magazine for his family audience. His first published articles were on films, and then on other social issues. These were published in prominent magazines of the time such as *Hans* and *Vishal Bharat*. After doing his B.A. Honours in Political Science, with a first class first, from Nagpur University, Dube began his career as a Lecturer in Political Science at Hislop College, Nagpur. By this time, he had also published a collection of folk songs of Chhattisgarh in Hindi.

At Nagpur, he met Professor D.N. Majumdar of the Lucknow University–already a big name then in Anthropology—who had come to deliver some lectures based on his field research amongst the tribals. Majumdar was impressed to see Dube's monograph on the folklore of Chhattisgarh and offered to publish its English version through the Ethnographic and Folk Culture Society. Dube was introduced to Professor D.P. Mukerji, a pioneering sociologist teaching at Lucknow, by his sister-in-law (WiSi)–Mrs Sumati Mutatkar[2]— herself a great musician. She knew Mukerji because of his immense expertise in classical music. Meanwhile, Dube was appointed at the Lucknow University in the Department of Political Science. This further brought him closer to Majumdar and Mukerji. In addition to teaching classes in his own department, Dube was invited by Majumdar to teach anthropology classes, and to assist him in editing *The Eastern Anthropologist*.

His popularity as a teacher and his work on the Kamar drew the attention of Professor Christoph von Fürer-Haimendorf who was then teaching at Osmania University in Hyderabad and was planning to return to England. At his suggestion, the University appointed Dube to head the Department of Sociology. Later, the School of African and Oriental Studies (SOAS) of the London University invited him, in 1952, as a Visiting Lecturer. Upon return from there, he joined the Cornell-India Research Team and did field work in the Rankhandi-Jhaberan area of Uttar Pradesh. This assignment earned him also the visiting Professorship at Cornell. Returning from there, he joined the Anthropological Survey of India, but only a few months later, in the summers of 1957, he was appointed to the newly created Chair of Anthropology at the University of Saugar when he was still under thirty-five–the youngest person to be appointed to professorship in India then. Dube joined, in 1960, the Central Institute for Training and Research in Community Development at Mussoorie as a Director while maintaining the lien at Saugar. When the Institute was renamed as the National Institute of Community Development (NICD), and relocated at Hyderabad, Dube was made its first Principal.[3] As academic administrator, Dube also functioned as Director of the Indian Institute of Advanced Study, Shimla, Vice Chancellor of Jammu University, and Chairman of the Madhya Pradesh Higher Education Grants Commission. Apart from his assignments at London School of Oriental and African Studies and at Cornell, he did an 18-month consultancy at the United Nations Asia-Pacific Development Centre in Kuala Lumpur, Malaysia. He was also associated in various capacities with UNESCO, United Nations University, and the East-West Center, Hawaii.

Dube is mainly known for his books on *Indian Village* and *India's Changing Villages*—both published by Routledge and Kegan Paul in 1955 and 1958 respectively. Earlier he published *Folk Songs of Chhattisgarh* (1948) and *The Kamar* (1951)[4]. His other books include *Explanation and Management of Change, Contemporary India and its Modernization, On Crisis and Commitment in Social Sciences* (edited by Yogesh Atal), *Modernization and Development: The Search for Alternatives, Indian Society, Tradition and Development, Development Perspectives for the 1980s,* and *Understanding Change: Anthropological and Sociological Perspectives.* Besides this, he has authored six books in Hindi. His book on *Indian Village* has been translated in several Indian languages, beginning with Hindi that I did in 1974.

Quite individual and distinctive in style, Professor Dube was very versatile; he was a prolific writer and an eloquent speaker both in English and in Hindi. As a teacher, he enthralled his students and inspired them to work and explore unchartered territories. As a frontiersman, he did not create a "school" of his own. His doors were open to all[5]; even those who were not his formal students felt at home with him. He showed his genuine enthusiasm over the achievements not only of his colleagues and students but even of those who may have been his opponents. Wherever he went, he spotted the sparks, and encouraged them to become torches. Ultra modern in his life style, dubbed as a "deluxe professor", Dube was a teacher in the true Indian tradition. A great intellectual, an inspiring teacher, a generous human being, and a secular Indian, Dube was distinctly different.

Dube's intellectual journey coincides with the journey of Indian sociology and anthropology. He played an influential role in shaping these twin disciplines. Having a degree in Political Science, and having taught the subject at Hislop College, Nagpur and at Lucknow, he was increasingly drawn to Anthropology. As a researcher, he chose to be an ethnographer, studying for his Ph.D. the Kamar of Chhattisgarh, and then moved on to produce the first full-length monograph on an Indian village that became a classic, and made a publishing history with several editions and translations in various vernaculars of this country[6]. This book did not only mark a departure from tribal studies by an anthropologist, it also ushered in an era of team research. His next publication related to the study of India's Community Development Programme that was launched by the government of independent India to bring about planned change in rural India. This book again made a radical departure. As the title itself suggests, it focussed on *India's Changing Villages* and analysed the "human factor" in Community Development. It is interesting that in the first book on Kamar there was very little reference to change; the second book concluded with a chapter on change; and the third book was fully devoted to the changing scene. While preparing the second book, Professor Dube involved a multidisciplinary team from his own university; the third book resulted as part of an international team, called the Cornell-India Project. And from there on, Dube chose to write on broader issues related to development, bureaucracy, communication, leadership, modernization and tradition. I must, however, put on record that he undertook two research projects for the Planning Commission on Rural Health and Hygiene, and on Leadership and Communication while in Sagar[7]. While both the projects were completed and their reports submitted to the sponsors, they never saw the light of the day. I had seen the manuscripts ready for the press. But it is not known why he did not publish them.

Dube set the trend way back in the 1950s for village studies and for the study of change. His was the first full-length monograph on an Indian village that was of world standard. Again, on India's Community Development, he came out with the very first monograph in 1958. Both these publications made him a pioneer in village studies in India.[8] He was concerned about the gaps in the ethnographic map of India, and the need for monographs on tribes and villages. He also wanted sociologists to document the changes that were occurring. He encouraged his students to work on topics such as the changing frontiers of caste, unity and extensions of an Indian village, cross-cultural comparative studies, multi-village studies on health and hygiene, and on leadership and communication, and minority groups such as the Anglo-Indians. His own field work took him to tribal Chhattisgarh, Andhra Pradesh, Uttar Pradesh, and Madhya Pradesh. He was, in the real sense, a frontiersman. Rather than harping on the same theme and concentrating on a narrow specialty, he chose the challenging task of exploring new territories and extending the frontiers of knowledge to make Indian sociology more relevant to the cause of national development. He was an ardent advocate of interdisciplinary orientation and a promoter of research interests on a wide range of topics of contemporary significance. He did not believe in creating a "school" of his own and building a cadre of faithful followers. He encouraged his students to participate in the adventure of ideas, and to try fresh initiatives rather than walk on trodden paths. He did not allow his class of students to become an insulated endogamous group; he encouraged his colleagues and students to have wide ranging affairs with different intellectual traditions. That is the reason that he is regarded as pioneer in several branches of sociology and social anthropology in India: political sociology, sociology of mass communication, economic development, and rural development, sociology of education, modernization and development. In each of these fields, he made seminal contributions by raising issues of theoretical and national relevance. His writings led many scholars to focus on different issues and carry out field investigations.

Dube wrote in simple language without unduly burdening the text with abstract concepts. That does not mean that he wrote as a journalist. While reviewing his *Indian Village,* James Silverberg asked the reader to read in between the lines for theory. The descriptive accounts were couched in structural-functional terms, and the analysis of change invariably focused on the repercussions of an event of change in all aspects of the system—both cultural and social.

IV

We may briefly summarise below Dube's conceptual contributions to the understanding of Indian society.

The concept of an *Indian Village*

In his paper on "Social Structure and Change in Indian Peasant Communities", presented at the Third World Congress of

Sociology, held in France in 1956, Dube elaborated the framework that he had suggested in his *Indian Village*. Dube (1955: 3) wrote in his book,

> While it is true that many problems are common to the entire countryside, this practice tends to give one an impression that the village as a social and cultural unit possesses a basically uniform organization and structure of values all over the Indian subcontinent...For a proper understanding of their social structure as well as their problems, it is necessary to classify them into clearly distinguishable types. For such classification several criteria could be employed, including, among others, the following :
>
> (i) Size, population and land area.
>
> (ii) Ethnic composition and caste-constitution.
>
> (iii) Pattern of land ownership.
>
> (iv) Structure of authority and power hierarchy.
>
> (v) Degree of isolation.
>
> (vi) Local traditions.

Dube cautioned his readers that in

> ... view of the operation of factors delineated above, it is difficult to regard any one village as typical or representative of rural India as a whole. In fact, I would go a step further to say that such a village could hardly be regarded as representative even of its culture-area, except in a very general way" (*Ibid*: 6).

In view of this, he recommended a "series of studies of village communities from different parts of the country covering the many divergent patterns of organization and ethos. Until this is done our picture of social systems in rural India will remain vague and inadequate" (*ibid*: 6-7). While hinting at the need for village studies in different parts of the country, Dube did provide elements of the definition of an Indian village. He mentioned three features that seem to be common (Dube, 1955: 7-8):

1. "As a territorial, as well as social, economic and ritual unit, the village is a separate and distinct entity."
2. "These settlements have a composite population comprising a number of groups belonging to different Hindu castes, and in some cases to tribes as well as to other religious groups. As far as the Hindu section of the population goes, these diverse groups are inter-dependent and integrated in the social, economic, ritual and administrative organization of the community. No caste alone is self-sufficient, for it requires the services of several other occupational castes which hold the monopoly of certain crafts and

professions. This system of co-operative labour, based on a pattern of inter-caste relations approved by tradition, is not confined only to economic activities but also extends to ceremonial and ritual life. The hierarchical organization of castes within the community is so fixed that the structural patterns of rural India that the tribal as well as the non-Hindu ...segments of the population come to be regarded as other castes in the village."

3. "The members of this local group are bound together by ties of mutual and reciprocal obligations."

Advancing further his conception of the village in India, Dube said

> we have to view the village both as a distinct isolable entity and as a link in the chain of a wider inter-village organization. An individual village derives some of the characteristic features of its organization from the great national tradition of India, while the traditions of the region or the culture area in which it is located also contribute substantially toward shaping its value-orientation, ethos, and general pattern of life (1956: 259).

He felt that the Indian village is "sufficiently isolable, but it is not an isolate, and has therefore to be viewed as a community within a larger community" (*ibid*).

Establishing links of the village community with the wider society, Dube suggested that the village community is to be seen as organised both in terms of kin and caste and also in terms of territorial affinities. Thus, an individual is linked to the wider community, on the one hand, through his family, group of near kin, lineage, affinal kin, sub-caste, caste, and *varna*; and on the other, through family, village, inter-village organization, region and nation. These two sets of groupings constitute the social structure of a village as a subsystem of the national society. This is shown in the following diagram:[9]

> The village as a unit of social structure cuts across the boundaries of kin and caste and unites a number of unrelated families within an integrated multicaste community.

Dube classified Indian village communities in terms of their structure into three main groups: (i) single settlement village; (ii) nucleated village; and (iii) dispersed village. According to him, the

> first two have a number of common features. They are stable populations generally, with a common past and a number of shared values. They recognize and emphasize their individual identity, and

> in certain situations act as a unit. Their economy is built largely around agriculture; economically and socially the agricultural castes are the most important, while the non-agricultural occupations are subsidiary to agriculture. Land is greatly loved and valued, and the community as a whole shares some common problems and acculturative influences. Being largely caste-structured, the community finds itself integrated in terms of traditional patterns that define the interactions between the different segments of the community in the fields of economy, socio-religious life, and village administration (1990: 112).

He offers the general outline of the social structure of Indian peasant communities as a "structural model". In suggesting this, Dube said:

> while few village communities will present exactly the same picture, a large number of them will be found to possess the major characteristics and features delineated above.

Paradigm for analysing change in India

Dube suggested that changes should be located in the various units of the social structure. In doing so, various forces and

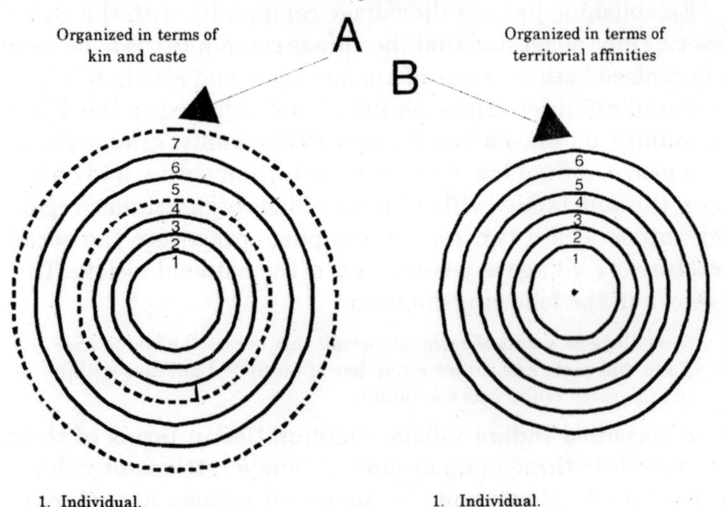

factors operating in the society must be identified and the outcome of the interplay of these should be studied to gauge the trends of change. Indian social structure is exposed to a number of influences. Here are some of the prominent ones:

(i) Western impact resulted in the introduction of the new administrative pattern resulting in the evolution of a set of executive, judicial and legislative institutions;
(ii) Modern systems of transport and communication, and industrialization have given greater national cohesion to the land;
(iii) Western-type education also has been influential in bringing about change;
(iv) Nationalist revival set in motion a series of important changes; and
(v) Nation-building activities of the government in the British days and community development activities after independence served as powerful influences.

As a consequence of these forces and factors, many changes were noticeable in the structure and organization of Indian village communities. Some of these listed by him are:

(i) Shift from an ascribed status system to an achieved status system. "The society being largely caste-structured, the ascribed or caste status of a person still contributes materially toward determining his status, but there are unmistakable signs that a rival system is growing, which takes sufficient account of an individual's distinctive qualities and attainments in ranking him."
(ii) "While there is a general loosening of caste structure at one end, there are signs that it is consolidating at the other end in some rather unexpected directions."
(iii) There is the "general weakening, and even breakdown of the formal authority structure of individual castes".
(iv) "In recent years, there has undoubtedly been a change from a kin-oriented outlook to an interest-oriented outlook, and a gradual breaking up of large effective kin groups has been in evidence".
(v) "While higher levels of the community take to modernization, the lower levels take to Sanskritization".

Writing in the 1950s, Dube did not subscribe to the view that the village community is disintegrating. While recognising the trends of change that are affecting the traditional social structure, Dube was of the view that because "the primary groups of kin and caste have continued to be effective units of social control even in semi-urbanized areas, there is no immediate threat to their position in the village communities, and consequently the latter are likely to continue to be organized on their basis. Even with the growth of rural towns, these structural features are not likely to change beyond recognition" (*Ibid*: 114-115).

Phenomenon of directed cultural change

Dube's involvement in the study of the Community Development project in a district in Uttar Pradesh led him to focus on the "human factor" in a programme of planned culture change. While his formulations about social and cultural change in India as a whole took note of the general trends initiated by the processes of Westernization and Modernization that became prominent during the British rule, his intensive study of a project area helped him understand the actual dynamics of change that resulted in either acceptance or rejection of innovations introduced by external change agents. His book, *India's Changing Villages*, offers insights through carefully prepared case studies into the dynamics of change. The personality factor (both of the change agent and the recipient), social status of the recipient, administrative rigmarole, and cultural-traditional factors including faction-politics and group-dynamics within the village were identified as key variables affecting the prospects of any innovation.

In his later writings, Dube built upon his field experiences and readings of sociological and anthropological theory to reflect upon India's development. All his essays and books, published after *India's Changing Villages* are devoted to theoretical explications of the concepts of "tradition" and "development". They provide good guides to new researchers and policy makers as they clarify the concepts and suggest directions for interpreting change and developing blueprints for development. They can well be called paradigmatic essays.

Perspective on tradition

Dube drew attention to the fact that early thinking on development not only neglected culture, but regarded tradition as an obstruction to modernity.

> The basic flaw in a great deal of thinking related to development and modernization was that it made some erroneous assumptions

> regarding tradition and traditional societies. It attributed to these societies a static quality, denying them an inner dynamic, adaptability and variability (1990: 18).
>
> A second fallacious assumption concerned the homogeneity of their culture and social structure (1990: 19).

Elaborating this point, Dube wrote in another essay:

> When we speak of Indian culture, we often envision in it a degree of unity and integration that is really not there...There is such a thing as *Indian Culture*, but its intricate and complex weave must be understood in terms of stabilized cultural pluralism. It essentially represents a heterogeneous growth, i.e., in different periods of history and in different regions a multiplicity of sources have contributed to the texture and designs of its fabric. It would be inappropriate to compare Indian culture with a tree; it is not as if it has grown from one seed, has common roots and trunk, and is linked organically with branches growing in later periods of its development. It would be more appropriate to think of it in terms of a river–many streams, rivulets, and minor rivers mingling at different points to create a powerful mainstream, one in which the reality of mighty river does not obscure the identities of the different currents whose waters go into its making. The contemporary culture of India is richer for the diversities that are built into its mosaic. It represents hundreds of folk forms as well as several sub-cultural and religious traditions that are blended into a functional and reasonably balanced and harmonious pattern (1990: 55-56).

Dube was critical of the cavalier treatment meted out to tradition. He asked:

> Is it the real villain–a roadblock to progress? Can it be dispensed with?"

He was of the view that traditions "cannot be treated as vestigial remains of an ancient past. They survive because they have definite functions. They contribute to a community's special sense of being, they provide bases of social integration, and offer guidelines to action during periods of uncertainty. Without replacement by adequate functional analogues, one cannot contemplate dismantling traditional structures. They cannot be wished away just to facilitate economic growth and development (*ibid*: 21). It must, however, be said that while Dube acknowledged the critical significance of culture, he was aware of the flaws in the culturist position and warned against an overargument of the case. In this regard, his following observations are very pertinent:

(i) "Cultural identities are important but their overmystification can result in contorted rewriting of history, doing grave violence to facts."

(ii) "There is a global aspect to human cultural development."

(iii) "In cultural processes, centripetal tendencies are as important as centrifugal ones. The demand of cultural autonomy necessitates decentralization, but there are several problems common to all humanity that call for a massive collective effort and global solutions and strategies."

(iv) "The politicisation of culture has its own inherent dangers. It can lead to vulgarisation (including erosion of core values and creativity) and to promotion of discord, conflict, and violence."

(v) "Some of the bizarre manifestations of ethnicity and fundamentalism demonstrate the convolutions and distortions resulting from the inept handling of culture. It is a double-edged weapon. It has great reserves of energy and creativity, but it can all too easily be manipulated towards counter-productive ends" (1990: 22-23).

On social science situation in India

Apart from reflecting on problems of contemporary India and suggesting doable paradigms for investigating social and cultural change, Dube wrote extensively on the prevailing social science situation in India. I had put all his essays on this theme in a book titled *On Crisis and Commitment in Social Sciences* (1983). While he was happy to notice quantitative expansion of the social sciences, and an explosion of publications, he found in them very little of national relevance or of theoretical significance. He was worried that both teaching and research in social sciences in India continued to be cast in the colonial mould, characterizing Indian sociology as "largely a sociology of borrowed concepts and methods". He lamented that the:

> colonial virus...has greatly debilitated Indian sociology by sapping its creativity. It is time we stop chasing the mirage of high prestige models and avoid the quicksands of pseudo-intellection.

Dube was, however, not an advocate of an insulated social science for India. In fact, he took issues with those adumbrationists who assigned all virtue to sacred texts and derived explanations for the existing reality from the prescriptive commentaries of ancient sages. He was equally concerned about the emergence of radical criticism of the structure of Indian society and of those scholars who had rediscovered Marx. He was of the view that such critics function only as a demolition squad and rarely produce dependable Marxist analyses.

Dube was disturbed about the lack of relevance in social science research, and was concerned about the blind pursuit of the trivia.

> Why the response of Indian sociology to the travail and trauma of independence was so feeble and why its efforts to deal with the ferment and convulsions characterizing the post-independence decade were so half-hearted? Why have we not produced a relevant and meaningful sociology–a science imbued with social concerns, a discipline with a human meaning and purpose?

Commenting on the kind of research that was carried out and reported, he wrote:

> Through a series of logical acrobatics, tortuous statistical procedures, and mystifying model building we appear to arrive at convoluted generalizations that often turn out to be statements of the obvious, their pseudo-profound terminology notwithstanding.

In his address to a Plenary session at the time of the 10th International Congress of Anthropological and Ethnological Sciences, held in December 1978 in New Delhi, he said that the Third World anthropologists have not played "a more decisive role" to

> enrich the discipline with the articulation of a grass roots consciousness...Some of the self-proclaimed leaders of the profession in these countries have not been able to decolonise their minds either in respect of theory and method, or in the choice of themes for research and analytical treatment....Their intellectual styles continue to be imitative.

Without hiding his anger at such development, he boldly remarked:

> A curious aspect of international social science is that some operators of little academic worth, who are subject of endless private jokes and a favourite theme of discussion at cocktail parties, can get catapulted to dizzy heights. This recognition of chicanery and willingness to serve any patron confuses the honest social scientists.[10]

Advocacy for commitment

Dube was of the view that Indian sociology is suffering from a certain crisis of commitment. The book of his essays that I had the privilege to edit was titled *S.C.Dube on Crisis and*

Commitment in Social Sciences. Although he did not specifically define his concept of commitment, one can decipher some of its indicators from his writings. He expected a committed social scientist to carry out 'relevant' research, focussing on national needs and key problems of vital concern to society. He also preferred the role of a social critic for the social scientist. Regarding the distinction between 'pure' and 'applied' research as artificial and futile, he wanted a committed social scientist to carry out "purposive research on vital and live issues of the day". Dube made a fine distinction between *objectivity* and *ethical neutrality*.

> *Objectivity* involves also questioning and evaluating the assumptions implicit in theoretical formulations and research programmes. *Ethical neutrality* can induce one into playing it safe and even turning away from controversial issues; objectivity makes more exacting demands. Balanced appraisals are a better help to thought than prescriptive arguments. Objectivity does not rule out deep human concerns; it should not.

In my Introduction to the book of his essays, I took a somewhat different stand. While he disagreed with what I had to say, he did not protest and let it remain. Let me quote what I had to say:

> To me, this appears to be too fine a distinction, and one on which many may not agree. The question of commitment is not easy to resolve. Commitment to what? To whom? Who shall decide whether one is committed or not? Can there be consensus on commitment–even on relevance, national needs and priorities, or on solutions to problems? A social critic opposed to the establishment may be viewed as non-committed. Similarly, someone taking sides of the establishment–and thus regarded as committed–may be decried as a sycophant or, worse, an opportunist. Furthermore, where does one draw a line between journalism and social science? ...I feel that ethical neutrality is one of the elements of objectivity. While I agree that in the selection of a topic for research, or fixing priorities, there is no need to be ethically neutral –to that extent commitment to national goals in whatever they are defined is possible–but the treatment of the problem will have to follow the principles and procedures of science. The danger that a "committed" scholar would manipulate facts cannot be ruled out. Professor Dube himself makes reference to Project Camelot and Project Agile. As long as the two roles–that of a social scientist and of a committed citizen–are separately defined and performed distinctly, there is no problem, but if the two are allowed to be merged, they create a crisis of identity.

> We must accept that everything a social scientist writes is not social science. His being a social scientist is his public status–his description in terms of his major preoccupation, but like any other individual, he occupies various other statuses and changes many caps. When an economist or a sociologist becomes a minister, he may have occasions to use his economics or sociology in that role, but he is certainly not doing economics or sociology most of the time that he plays the role of a minister."[11]

But he was firm on his position. In his reflective essay, published in the *Festschrift* that I edited in his honour, he said : "I will continue to plead for commitment even if some of my own students, including very dear ones,[12] misunderstand." Elaborating his view, he further said:

> At no stage have I had a commitment to a person, a party, or an ideology, but at all times I did think of our commitment to the people we most often study. Do they have a voice in the decisions concerning their lives? Do they have choices and options in respect of what are known as development aims? In the name of 'national' development must they suffer the erosion of their cultural autonomy and the loss of their self-esteem? Must they accept goals formulated and foisted upon them by the elite? Is it their inexorable fate to gradually lose control over their resources, accept servitude, and submit to frequent uprooting for a kind of development that benefits them only minimally? The ambit of individual commitment, in my view, included such questions of public policy. Anthropology and sociology, in addition to their scholarly function, should also seek to give voice to the voiceless. I detest populist rhetoric. Anthropology and sociology should resist the temptation to coin catchy slogans. But their analytical insights and cultural criticism should certainly bring to light the degenerative and destructive aspects of well-intentioned policies.[13]

Concern for proper growth of the social sciences in India

As was said earlier, Dube was worried about the deterioration in standards in Indian social science. He expressed this worry in several of his essays. His book *On Crisis and Commitment in Social Sciences* represents this concern. To quote him:

> The major weaknesses of Indian social science are all too well known. Both in teaching as well as research we place excessive reliance on foreign models. The so-called international styles of scholarship, rather than contemporary national relevance, determine the content of our university curricula as well as the themes and models of our research. In general we fail to ask the right questions, and all too willingly accept the tyranny of established concepts. Our efforts

> reflect the absence of conceptual innovativeness and methodological rigour. In order to equal or excel our counterparts abroad in technical virtuosity we willingly undergo the torture of techniques and often end up murdering by methodology, both research problems and their insightful analyses. ..Our theoretical constructs are largely vacuous and we are timid in responding to the challenges of the day.[14]

He drew our attention to the following weaknesses in Indian sociology and anthropology:

1. "The discipline appears to have become prisoner of a pattern. There is need for a different perspective: "In the world of today the *problems* to be investigated matter much more than the disciplinary labels under which research is conducted. These problems are best investigated through interdisciplinary perspectives and research procedures....but this needs most careful thought and adequate intellectual preparation. Runaway enthusiasm for a newly discovered interest can be self-defeating." (51)
2. "Our attachment to foreign conceptual models and research tools has been pathetic." (51)
3. "One of our basic weaknesses is that we are not asking the right questions." (52)
4. "We have been overly concerned with segmental perfection to the exclusion of valid macro generalizations."
5. "We appear to have emphasized the autonomy of academic pursuits so much that they have been largely divested of social concerns."
6. "There is a regrettable absence of *meaningful* social criticism." (53)
7. "While a proliferation of institutions of social science research has occurred, little attention appears to have been given to the problem of institution-building." (54)[15]

Dube was very cautious about theory. He admitted that

> we need sound theory. But how do we go about it? Shall we start running from nowhere in hot pursuit of theory? Such a blind race would yield perhaps only vacuous and spurious theory. The emphasis on theory building should not imply the undervaluation of data gathering...It is not being suggested that social sciences can rest with assembling a great mass of data.

However, he cautioned that "we should not fail to be cognizant of the tyranny of established concepts. Without wide-awake awareness they can set invisible limits to thinking and data gathering." In his own writings, he never displayed over-enthusiasm for theory with the result that his reviewers talked of his "lucid style",[16] implying thereby that there was absence of theory in his work. To such a comment his retort was: "To be readable is not necessarily to be un-scholarly; and a social science book may have functions beyond the mere cultivation of scholarship." He discouraged "narcissistic intellection and the feverish search for theory" for, he felt that, such "theory, often phoney, distracts attention from larger issues of public policy...Theory is important, but the search for theory at the cost of human concerns is very disconcerting... And why do we shy away from hard and sustained field work? I am all too aware of the limitations of empiricism, but I am more distrustful of theorizing without a solid data base".[17] Prefacing this statement, Dube said that his "concerns are more serious...Why the loss of interest in tribal studies, especially at a juncture when the emergence of new forces is creating unprecedented turbulence in several tribal areas."[18]

Utilization of social sciences

In making critical remarks about the growth of Indian sociology and anthropology, nay the entire gamut of social sciences, Dube showed his concern for the utilization of social sciences for public policy. In his paper presented at the National Seminar on *Social Sciences and Social Realities*, held at the Indian Institute of Advanced Study, Simla, in 1973, Dube listed six major possibilities of the utilization of social science research towards national development. I reproduce them below:

1. Social science research throws up valuable background data from which the planner can make his own assessment of the prevailing situation, especially of the magnitude, complexity, and ramifications of the problems he has to handle.
2. Carefully designed analytical studies can illuminate critical areas of policy. The overt and covert dimensions of a given problem emerging in such studies provide the planner with a measure of foresight to deal with them effectively and efficiently.
3. These studies open up the possibility of testing the validity of the assumptions that must, of necessity, be made by the planner in setting his proximate and ultimate objectives.
4. They enable the planner to estimate the possible consequences and costs of the different choices available to him in determining the path for the attainment of his goals.
5. Diagnostic studies suggest *where* and *why* particular projects go wrong. Their unintended consequences are also brought to light.
6. Wide dissemination of social science research findings increases general awareness in respect of the situation to be met as well as

> the policy designed for this purpose. This may enhance credibility of particular policies and prepare the people for them. It may also help towards building up popular pressures for the reformulation of certain policies or for weeding them out altogether.[19]

The message that we get from Professor Dube is significant. As social scientists, we must not shut our eyes from issues of public policy, and we must not give up our strength that lies in empirical fieldwork. We must resist the temptation to be theoretical without firm grip over the data, and we must not offer unsolicited prescriptions for the problems that we hardly understand.

While he frankly admitted that "Social science research, let there be no illusion, is not a substitute for national development", he emphasised the explanatory power of the social sciences. As he grew in stature, Professor Dube was increasingly drawn towards policy making and planning. He continued to encourage young scholars to do rigorous field work, but he devoted his energies to engage in dialogue with policy makers and in popularising social sciences through his writings and lectures. His books were essential readings for the new initiates in administration. He also used popular weeklies, such as *Dharmayug* and *Saptahik Hindustan*–the most widely read Hindi magazines–to popularise social science orientation. Both within administration and in the reading public, S.C. Dube gained popularity, and succeeded in popularising social sciences. He was one of the few who could write and speak with the same ease and facility in both Hindi and in English. He also encouraged me to do the same.

V

In his contribution to the *Festschrift* that I edited in his honour in 1993, he looked back at the path he had travelled in an essay that was aptly titled "The journey so far". He remarked:

> Indian sociology and social anthropology represent a significant intellectual quest. Now their edifice is solid; ideas-wise they matter...The younger generation has taken over with élan and vigour new themes and made some significant innovations...These developments are taking place in an environment of free dialogue and discussion–a fact that augurs well for the health and future of the disciplines.[20]

He began his end piece with the words:

> I am coming to the end of my story, but it is not quite the end...A working retirement can be a glorious experience. Free from the constraints and pressures of office one can do just what one likes. I am in this happy position.[21]

He knew, however, that he was going. But he did not accept the defeat. In his letter of 8 August 1995, he wrote to me: "...my health is deteriorating and work seems to be the best remedy."

Like a sage, Professor Dube died in harness.

But did he die? Could he?

NOTES

1. S.C. Dube, *Social Sciences in Changing Society: D.N. Majumdar Memorial Lectures,* 1972 Ethnographic and Folk Culture Society, Lucknow, 1973: 49.
2. She retired as Professor of Music from Delhi University. She gave several performances at the All India Radio. She died recently in 2007.
3. Now it is called National Institute of Rural Development (NIRD) and the Principal is renamed as Director-General.
4. The Kamar has been republished by Oxford University Press in 2003.
5. Concluding his piece titled "The journey so far" in the *Festschrift* that I edited for him, he wrote: "our house is open to young colleagues who seek to discuss their ideas and projects, and many of them receive our warm welcome". See *Understanding Indian Society* (ed. Yogesh Atal), p. 42.
6. It may be noted that in 1955 four books on Indian villages came out, but Dube's was the only full-length monograph; others were collections of essays, reporting the progress of field work.
7. I worked as a research investigator in one of them.
8. Both S.C. Dube and M.N. Srinivas are known for their pioneering work on village India, and both inspired several young researchers to undertake village studies. But Srinivas gained popularity because of his concepts of Sanskritization (published in *The Far Eastern Quarterly*, Vol. XV, No. 4, August 1956), and of Dominant Caste (published in *American Anthropologist*, Vol.6, No. 1, 1959). His book on Rampura that threw up these concepts was published much later in 1976 as *The Remembered Village* (Oxford University Press), based on his memory as his field notes were destroyed by an arson at Stanford where he had gone to do the book after so many years of his field work. Fame came to Srinivas earlier than his first full-length monograph on Rampura; Dube earned a name and fame through his *Indian Village* way back in 1955 when no other village ethnography was published; and it remains the most quoted reference.
9. Taken from his essay presented at the Third World Congress of Sociology

in 1956, and reproduced in his book, *Tradition and Development*, Vikas Publishing House, New Delhi, 1990, p. 108.

10. See Atal (ed.) *S.C. Dube on Crisis and Commitment in Social Sciences*, 1983, p. 61.
11. See Yogesh Atal, *S.C. Dube on Crisis and Commitment in Social Sciences*, 1983. "Introduction", page 11.
12. This was a reference to me on my above comment.
13. See Yogesh Atal (ed.) *Understanding Indian Society: Festschrift in Honour of Professor S.C. Dube*, New Delhi, Har Anand Publications, 1993, page 23.
14. From his essay on The social sciences: Crisis and commitment, *On Crisis and Commitment in Social Sciences* (Atal Ed.), 1983: p. 15.
15. From his *Social Sciences in Changing Society: DN Majumdar Memorial Lectures 1972* (1973), pages 51-54.
16. In his reflective essay in the Festschrift issued in his honour, he responded to this criticism in the following manner: "I suspect that at least a few of these observations are intended as left-hand compliments. This raises two important and interconnected issues–of the audience of the social scientist and of style. Are we always and necessarily addressing our professional peers alone? Or do we also have to carry our findings to the general reader? If an interventionist role is envisioned for the social sciences, should we not make our research results intelligible to the policy maker? I believe that social sciences have a conscientization function and a policy dimension. Recognizing them we have to adopt an appropriate idiom and style. Tortuous, abstruse, and convoluted writing may give the illusion of profundity, at least to the uninitiated." "The Journey So Far" in *Understanding Indian Society* (ed. Yogesh Atal), p. 34.
17. *Ibid*: 40.
18. *Ibid*.
19. *On Crisis and Commitment in Social Sciences*, p. 29-30.
20. From "The Journey So Far", p. 40-41.
21. *Ibid*.

REFERENCES

Atal, Yogesh (ed.)

1993 *Understanding Indian Society: Festschrift in Honour of Professor S.C.Dube*. New Delhi: Har Anand Publications.

Dube, Leela and Sudheesh Pachauri (ed.)

1997 *Seemanto Ke Anveshak* (Hindi). Delhi: Vaani Prakashan.

BOOKS [IN ENGLISH] AUTHORED BY S.C. DUBE

Folk Songs of Chhattisgarh, Lucknow: Universal Publishers, 1948

The Kamar, Lucknow: Universal Publishers, 1951. (Second Edition in 2003 by Oxford University Press, New Delhi)

Indian Village, London : Routledge & Kegan Paul, 1955.

India's Changing Villages, London : Routledge & Kegan Paul, 1958

Explanation and Management of Change, Bombay : Tata-McGraw Hill, 1971

India Since Independence : A Social Report 1947-72 (ed.), Delhi : Vikas Publishing House, 1972

Social Science in Changing Society, Lucknow : Ethnographic and Folk Culture Society, 1973

Contemporary India and Its Modernization, Delhi : Vikas Publishing House, 1974

Man, Society and Education : Some questions concerning a Preferred Future, New Delhi, NIE Series, NCERT, 1977.

Tribal Heritage of India: Ethnicity, Identity and Interaction Vol.I, (ed.) . New Delhi, Vikas Publishing House, 1977.

Public Services and Social Responsibility (ed.). New Delhi, Vikas Publishing House, 1979.

On Crisis and Commitment in Social Sciences (ed. By Yogesh Atal). New Delhi, Abhinav Publications, 1983.

Development Perspectives for the 1980s. New Delhi, Abhinav Publications, 1983.

Secularization in Multi-religious Societies: Indo-Soviet Perspective (edited with V.N. Basilov). New Delhi, Concept Publishing, 1983.

Modernization and Development: The Search for Alternative Paradigm. Published for the United Nations University by Zed Books, London. 1988.

Tradition and Development. New Delhi, Vikas Publishing House, 1990.

Indian Society. New Delhi, National Book Trust of India. 1990.

Understanding Change: Anthropological and Sociological Perspectives. New Delhi, Vikas Publishing House, 1992.

19

C. von Fürer-Haimendorf: Half a Century of his Imprint on Tribal Welfare in Andhra Pradesh

URMILA PINGLE

What was to be a brief reconnaissance in the Hyderabad State turned out for Fürer-Haimendorf and Betty, his newly wedded wife, a life long commitment to the welfare of the tribes. They arrived in Hyderabad in August 1939, at the invitation of Sir Theodore Tasker, the Revenue Member of the H.E.H. the Nizam's government. Tasker informed the young couple that the War had just been declared and that Fürer-Haimendorf was to be interned as an enemy alien (his Austrian nationality was converted into a German one) and had to cancel his plans to go to the Naga Hills as earlier planned. The bright side to this disaster was that instead of Fürer-Haimendorf languishing in the internment camp till the end of the War, the Nizam of Hyderabad was wise enough to offer him the opportunity to work among the tribal people of his dominions. Thus for the next nine years from 1940-49 Fürer-Haimendorf devoted himself to the meticulous study and evolution of development policies for the different tribal cultures he studied. This forced internment gave him a unique opportunity not only to do concentrated research on the tribes but to gain the confidence of the Nizam's government and become an official adviser on tribal matters and policies in 1945. After four years of directing tribal welfare work, Fürer-Haimendorf left Hyderabad to take up an academic position at the School of Oriental and African studies (SOAS), University of London. Thereafter, he returned to Hyderabad for short intervals to direct the handing over of the work he had initiated. Retirement from SOAS in 1976 would release him again to revisit the tribes of Andhra Pradesh and undertake a series of restudies on the changes occurring among these tribal communities (Fürer-Haimendorf 1982). From 1978 to 1988, he participated in active field work. The result of this work was published as a series of monographs.

Ethnographic studies of the tribes (1940-49)

Fürer-Haimendorf consulted with various officials familiar with the geography of the state and this helped him to choose in an evolutionary way to first study the Chenchus, food-gatherers (1943), then the Hill Reddi who were shifting cultivators (1945) and finally completing his ethnographic work among the more complex Raj Gonds who were settled agriculturists (1948). In all these three monographs he used a multidisciplinary approach to the holistic understanding of the tribes. The detailed observations of the geography and ecology of the areas the tribes inhabited coupled with their agricultural and forest activities enriched the studies and made them useful for administrators to make important decisions for the welfare of these communities. The meticulous study of the traditional customs of land ownership and usage in these tribes as varied as food-gatherers to shifting cultivators to settled cultivators helped administrators in prioritizing the important economic issues to be tackled in each one of these tribes. Most important, his sensitive perception of the early signs of the troubles to come in the tribal areas and the appropriate steps taken to stabilize the economy of the tribal societies helped strengthen tribal cohesion for more than a decade.

The Chenchus—jungle folk of the Deccan (1943)

The Chenchus lived along both banks of the Krishna, the river forming the border between Hyderabad State and the British administered Madras Presidency. The Chenchu that Fürer-Haimendorf studied lived on the high plateau atop the Nallamallai Hills. Fürer-Haimendorf and Betty settled down in an abandoned forest bungalow in the village of Farahabad as their main camp for the next nine months of their anthropological stay. As Fürer-Haimendorf noted in his autobiography (1990):

> Compared with the splendid Nagas with their colourful ornaments these Chenchus were a poor lot, and I felt sorry for Betty who had expected to live among Nagas in the magnificent scenery of the Assam hills.

So their honeymoon was spent in the most difficult of terrain, under war time conditions of rationing of food and medicines and the summer heat with very little shade that the deciduous forest had to offer. Their resilience helped them adapt to seasonal vagaries and they began to forge a close relationship with the local Chenchu. They started bartering with the Chenchu, obtaining forest fruits, honey and tubers and giving in exchange rats which they caught with their mouse-traps. The Chenchu were delighted with this valuable food as they themselves had noted the skill to trap small animals. In retrospect, Fürer-Haimendorf notes in his autobiography that they realized they made a mistake by not having eaten the rats themselves and depriving themselves of the only available source of protein. For, by the beginning of the monsoon in the Chenchu area, there was acute food shortage and they were reduced to a Chenchu diet, living on edible roots and tubers and wild berries. By the end of the nine months spent among these people, Fürer-Haimendorf had a deep understanding of this unknown tribe and the problems they were facing. He had made many friends among them and with whom he remained in touch in his subsequent visits. Both Fürer-Haimendorf and Betty walked the extensive forest areas and followed the Chenchu groups in their annual summer migration down to the river banks. They traveled as lightly as the Chenchu themselves carrying a blanket, mosquito net, tea and a few handfuls of rice and their notebooks and cameras. The constant mobility of this bandgroup in searching for forest food would often hamper Fürer-Haimendorf in seeking lengthy discussions with the Chenchu who would get very restive. So the Haimendorfs hit upon the idea of doling millets to their informants who would then be no longer under pressure of time to leave for their collecting grounds. They would then talk at length about their gods and their myths. In between interviewing the Chenchu he carried out a detailed census on all the families (426) on the upper plateau. The outcome of this work was published in 1943, with an appendix on the Notification of the Nizam's Government in establishing the greater part of the upper Amrabad Plateau as a "Chenchu reserve" covering one lakh acres. This important step to protect the welfare of this vulnerable group was the outcome of Fürer-Haimendorf's work among the Chenchu. The rules governing the Chenchu reserve ensured the Chenchu living within this reserve to follow their way of life without restrictions and to extract all minor forest produce without payment for their domestic use. The forest department was made responsible to organize a purchasing and sale center to purchase all minor forest produce brought by Chenchu and supply them with their requirements. No tradesmen were allowed to deal with the Chenchu from the reserve. The forest department was to help the Chenchu within the reserve to take up forest industries such as bamboo weaving, etc. A specially selected Chenchu forest guard and forest watchmen sympathetic to the ideas underlying the creation of the Chenchu reserve were to be employed.

The Reddi of the Bison Hills (1945)

The next stage of Fürer-Haimendorf's journey took him to the relatively isolated Papi Konda or Bison Hills in the South-Eastern part of the State. Access to the Hill Reddi was only by boat, for there were no roads or cart tracks along the banks of the Godavari. The Konda Reddi lived on the river bank settlements and the hills on both sides of the river and were traditionally shifting cultivators growing small millets, maize and pulses. They were independent farmers, but at the time Fürer-Haimendorf started his research it had come to an end with the forest department of the Samasthan of Paloncha auctioning bamboo growing on the hill slopes. Timber merchants of the nearby town had acquired the right of bamboo extraction and they employed the Hill Reddi in this operation. However, the relationship between the merchants and the tribals turned into one of exploitation, the tribals being led into debt by the merchants who advanced them grain and other provisions. The illiterate Reddi had no means of calculating the sums of money the merchants owed them as wages and the value of foodgrains they received. The Reddi were warned by the merchants not to divulge any information to the Haimendorfs, so the naturally friendly tribals became sullen and uncommunicative. In spite of these initial problems, the Haimendorfs continued on their tour of the Reddi villages observing and gathering information on the varied activities of these hill people. They spent a year in these areas, both suffering from bouts of malaria and greatly weakened. They shifted camp to the hill top village of Gogulapudi where the Reddi were more traditional and remote from the influence of merchants. It was in those months that many of the tribals in that region came to the Haimendorfs to seek help and advice in their struggle against the oppressiveness of forest contractors, merchants and minor officials. Fürer-Haimendorf used this information in drafting his powerful reports to the Nizam's government entitled, "Tribal Hyderabad—Four reports" (1945) which enabled the administration to take the appropriate steps to improve the condition of these tribal communities.

The Raj Gond of Adilabad (1948)

The Haimendorfs after their return from Bison Hills and a brief stay in Hyderabad left for their tour of Adilabad in December, 1941, which was the Northern most district of the Nizam's State. Through the use of Survey of India maps they made their way up these highlands with extensive stretches of forest scattered with tribal villages and cultivated areas. There were no motorable roads, so they hired two bullock carts from Asifabad, the headquarters of the subdivisional officer. After having paid their respects to the Gond Raja living at Pangri village, they accepted the invitation of Lachu Patel of Marlavai to establish their permanent camp at his village. Fürer-Haimendorf was greatly impressed by this articulate Gond who had an excellent understanding of the rituals connected with their clan-god worship. Besides, the highland area was scarce in drinking water and Lachu Patel assured them that Marlavai had a good well. So it was that the Haimendorfs settled down in Marlavai in a house built for them by Gonds. They lived in a community which was occupied throughout the year with agricultural activities, seasonal festival, participating in rituals connected with birth, marriage and death and visiting neighbouring villages. A valuable task that Fürer-Haimendorf set for himself was the detailed recording of Gond myths from the Pardhan bards who had an outstanding knowledge of these myths, a cultural heritage which was being lost in areas where Gond were living with other populations. This had never been put down in writing but was orally recited over generations by the Pardhans. Fürer-Haimendorf also studied in great detail the organization and functioning of the tribal panchayats presided over by the Utnur Gond Raja, the most influential among the Gond local chiefs. The Raja settled disputes and was the custodian of Gond customs. After some length of time in Gond country, Fürer-Haimendorf realized that though at first the Gond seemed prosperous farmers without harassment of moneylenders and outsiders, they were, in reality, facing many difficulties. Marlavai soon became the gathering point, for Gonds from other villages to come to the Haimendorfs with tales of woe. At that time, though Fürer-Haimendorf had no official position as Adviser he was prepared to listen and note down their grievances but he made it clear to the Gond that he had no authority to solve their problems. However, he assured them that he would convey their petitions to the concerned officials and explain personally the circumstances of each case. The Gond too were happy to get a sympathetic hearing and thus Fürer-Haimendorf came to build up a picture of the socio-economic and political situation that these people were facing. The picture that emerged was that already in the 1940s the Gond were ousted from the lands cultivated by their forefathers in the lower regions of the riverine tracts drained by the Penganga and Godavari. They had lost much land to Hindu and Muslim settlers. The highlands around Marlavai were still protected from encroachment with compact areas of forest and exclusively tribal villages. The alienation of land had already spread to the highlands of Utnur and Fürer-Haimendorf noted the beginning of the influx of Maratas, Kunbis and Banjaras from neighbouring district of Maharastra. Most of the village accountants (Patwaris) were Maratha Brahmans and had little empathy for the Gonds and were easily bribed to abet the non-tribals in occupying Gond clan land. Later with the help of W.V.

Grigson, a former administrator of the state of Bastar who joined the Nizam's government in the position of Revenue Member, Fürer-Haimendorf was able to place proposals for tribal rehabilitation which were promptly sanctioned by the Nizam's government.

Anthropologist-activist

During his stay at Marlavai, Fürer-Haimendorf had no official position to tackle the land problems of the Gonds, so he thought of other means to strengthen the Gonds in their struggle against exploitation by non-tribals. Since much of their inability was due to illiteracy and ignorance of government laws and rules, he wanted them to be prepared for this eventuality. With this objective in mind, Fürer-Haimendorf began to formulate the Gond education scheme and in May 1943 the training school was formally established in Marlavai under the guidance of Fürer-Haimendorf and with the support of the Revenue Member. It had a modest budget and this enabled the young Gond students to receive stipends for the period of their training. In this school a new set of tribal leaders-teachers and Patwaris were taught to maintain village records. It worked well as the new leaders worked harmoniously with old leaders as they were sons of the soil.

In order to open up primary schools in Gond villages, the medium of instruction had to be Gondi as that was the only language spoken by the Gond. Hence, the second function of this education scheme was to identify and train young and intelligent Gondi-speakers to become primary school teachers. Fürer-Haimendorf spent most of his time recruiting the first teacher candidates and working out the basic principles of their teaching. He appointed a teacher to head this centre and with his help began composing primers and readers in Gondi written in Devanagiri script, which is the script used for Hindi, Marathi and other Indian languages. It lent itself to the transcription of Gondi phonetics and familiarized the Gond students with an all-India script. Urdu, the language of Hyderabad state, was to be introduced only in the higher classes (Fürer-Haimendorf 1990). By 1946, thirty primary Gond schools were functioning. By 1949, at the time of Fürer-Haimendorf's departure, the number of schools had trebled. By 1951, this centre which in

1943 had begun with the training of five semi-literate Gonds had produced ninety-five teachers, five village officers, one revenue inspector, five clerks and seven forest guards. One of the trainees of this school went on to become the president of the Panchayat Samithi of Utnur Tribal Development Block. The success of this centre helped establish a second centre at Ginnedari village in Asifabad taluk. Teacher training centres were also established among the Koya of the Godavari valley.

Anthropologist-administrator

Between 1945-49 Fürer-Haimendorf functioned as the Adviser to the Nizam's government for tribes and backward classes. Besides giving advice, he had the heavy responsibility of dealing directly with the problems of the tribal population of the State. This was an enviable position for him as few anthropologists ever get the authority to bring about change and improvements among tribes. Fürer-Haimendorf had immediate access to the Revenue Secretary and the Director-General of Revenue, being allotted an office in the Revenue Secretariat. He could thus obtain information on the current developments of tribal policy. During this period Fürer-Haimendorf undertook tours to different tribal areas of the state, co-ordinating the various schemes concerned with tribal problems throughout the State. Several of his reports were published by the Revenue Department entitled *Tribal Hyderabad*.

Fürer-Haimendorf was also appointed a Warden to the Civil Service House which was an institution to instruct freshly recruited young men in subjects that they would be required subsequently to know as district officers. His close proximity to these officers and interaction with them helped sensitise these people on tribal matter.

Besides these two positions he was appointed as a part-time Professor in Anthropology in the Department of Sociology at the Osmania University. This was the first time that anthropology was to be introduced in this university. This gave Fürer-Haimendorf an opportunity to turn out a cadre of officers trained in anthropology who would later join the Social Service, a department specifically concerned with tribal welfare.

Systems of land tenure in tribal areas

In homogeneous tribal populations, there are hardly any problems of enchroachment. Their ancestral or clan lands are owned by the village community, and therefore, the concept of having permanent rights to individual plots was foreign to the tribes. The cultivation based on clan ownership was not recognized by the Nizam's government. The majority of the Gonds in Adilabad highlands then cultivated according to a system of land tenure known as *siwa-i-jamabandi.* The land they tilled remained government land, although they had permission to cultivate and annually pay the land revenue. They were not registered as owners (*pattedars*) in the village register. The allotment of land on this tenure system was within the powers of the *tahsildar* who endorsed the actions of the *patwari* and revenue inspector without inspecting the rights and wrongs of individual cases. This meant that the *patwari* had the final say in the matter. This allowed the lower revenue staff with opportunities to enrich themselves by shuffling land from one cultivator to another, and every year many tribals were evicted from lands which they were cultivating on *siwa-i-jamabandi* tenure. The Gond practice of frequently shifting their fields and being the inhabitants of large expanses of cultivable land and forests became an attraction for new settlers who then obtained title deeds for the occupied land. At the turn of the century it was the government's policy to open up the district and encourage the influx of new settlers and to grant them title deeds free of charge for as much land as they could make arable. Moreover, the reservation of forests had begun to encroach on the traditional habitat of these tribes.

Tribal rebellion

Until the British rule, the tribal people were left relatively undisturbed. The extention of a centralized administration under the British over areas which had previously been outside the effective control of princely rulers reduced the autonomy of the tribal rights and customs, and the establishment of "law and order" in these areas exposed the tribes to the pressure of more advanced populations. Traders and moneylenders were able to establish themselves under the protection of the British administration. Often they were followed by settlers who succeeded in acquiring large tracts of tribal land. By imposing an alien system of land tenure and revenue collection developed in advanced areas on the tribals, the government unintentionally facilitated the transfer of tribal land to members of other ethnic groups. This set about a deterioration of tribals' position in Peninsular India as early as the middle of the nineteenth century and continued into the twentieth century. This gave rise to a series of rebellions of tribals against the authority of the government, and resulted in defeat and loss of lives among the ruled who had to struggle against the organized power and sophisticated system established by the ruler. One such rebellion was the Rampa Rebellion in 1879, which involved the Hill Reddi of the East Godavari Agency of Madras Presidency, now part of Andhra Pradesh. This Rampa country was in possession of a feudal lord who was not Reddi. He had managed to control the lives of these tribals. He had leased out his villages to subordinate chiefs for an annual income of Rs. 8,750. The last straw of this oppressive rule was leasing the toddy revenue to contractors entitled to collect taxes at their own discretion. Simultaneously, the feudal chief brought an excise regulation forbidding the Hill Reddi from drawing toddy for their own use. Compounded with this the civil law operating there was an additional grievance of the tribals whose trustfulness and ignorance of court proceedings enabled the traders to play mischief by making unfair contracts with them. When the tribal people could not fulfill their contracts, the traders would file suits against them, obtain ex-parte decrees and acquire as much land as they could lay hands on. The hill people blamed the government for all these injustices and therefore, carried out attacks on police stations and this movement spread to neighbouring hill areas covering an area of 5000 square miles. Government forces countered this guerilla war and did not quite succeed in entirely suppressing this rebellion until 1880.

The aftermath of this movement instituted special methods of administering tribal areas in Madras Presidency to protect the tribals from exploitation and enchroachment by outsiders. The various orders that were passed from time to time were consolidated in a legislation known as The Agency Tracts Interest and Land Transfer Act, 1917. This served as a blueprint for future legislations in other tribal areas. The four important regulations of this Act were:

(1) The interest on any debt or liability shall not as against a member of a hill tribe be allowed or decreed at a higher rate than 24% per annum nor shall any compound interest or any collateral advantage be allowed against him.

(2) The total interest allowed or decreed on any debt or liability against a member of a hill tribe shall not exceed the principal amount.

(3) Notwithstanding any rule of law or enactment to the contrary any transfer of immovable property situated within the Agency tract by a member of a hill-tribe shall be absolutely null and void unless made in favour of another member of a hill tribe or with previous consent in writing of the Agent or any other prescribed officer. (Agent was the revenue officer comparable to the Collector of a district).

(4) Where a transfer of property is made in contravention of sub-section (1) the Agent may on application by anyone interested decree ejectment against any person in possession of the property claiming under the transfer and may restore it to the transferor or his heirs.

This act remained in force till the promulgation of the Andhra Pradesh Scheduled Areas Land Transfer Regulation, 1959.

Protective tribal land legislation in Hyderabad State

Large scale evacuations occurred in the 1920s in Adilabad district as a policy of forest conservancy and continued until 1940. This policy of clearing large tracts of forest of human habitation, including old, established villages, led to the only case of armed resistance by Gonds in this district. It was a small rebellion called Babijheri named after the locality in which it occurred and has found a place in Gond folklore. The leader of the Gonds was one Kumra Bhimu who tried repeatedly to get some land as most of the land in his village had fallen into the hands of non-tribals. He finally settled in the village of Babijheri which was subsequently established as an enclave in the state forest. Since Bhimu and the other Gonds had no *patta* rights they were asked to vacate the place. As they had not vacated the place by the specified date, all their houses were burnt by the forest guards. They then moved to Jhoreghat, east of Babijheri and with the permission of the *patwari* and revenue inspector cleared some land. The forest guard then came and told them that they could clear as much forest as they liked provided they paid him Rs. 500. They borrowed the money and paid the forest guard but he continued to harass them to pay more.

Bhimu and four other Gonds went to Hyderabad and obtained printed permission to cultivate 57 acres. In spite of showing this permission, the forest guard threatened to burn their houses if they did not pay the money he demanded. However, the forest ranger without the knowledge of his superior officer sent a party of his forest staff with a gun to enforce the evacuation of these Gonds. They resisted this party and overpowered them and finally the forest staff ran away after they got a good beating. The negotiations between the district forest officers and Bhimu and his supporters were mismanaged and Bhimu refused to give himself up. The police party then advanced into the hills where Bhimu and his supporters had gathered and Bhimu fired the first shot without wounding anyone. Thereupon, the police opened fire, killing Bhimu and ten other Gonds and wounding many others. This left the Gonds deeply resentful of the government and it was not until four years later that the measures for their rehabilitation were implemented.

Fürer-Haimendorf knew that a fundamental change in tribal economy would be achieved only by securing the rights of the tribals to the land which their forefathers were cultivating. This could be done only by new legislation modeled on the 1917 Act and creating an agency concerned with the protection of tribal rights. Hence Fürer-Haimendorf identified a zone covering tribal villages in Adilabad district and notified it to bring protective legislation to the tribes living within this area. With the support of the Revenue Member, W.V. Grigson, he helped formulate and execute the farsighted and radical Tribal Areas Regulation 1356 Fasli (1946 A.D.). This swung into action in 1949 during the interim period when Hyderabad State came under military government. This law assured the tribes of permanent rights in the land they cultivated and empowered their traditional panchayats to run their affairs and decide any cases without outside interference. This regulation empowered the government to make the rules which vested the administration of the Notified Tribal Area in the first *talukdar* (Collector) as agent, in the special social service officer as assistant agent and in a panchayat to be established by the agent. Instead of having to deal with numerous officials and distant courts whose proceedings were unfamiliar, the tribals were now under the care of officers of the Social Service department who were sympathetic to their cause and vested with sufficient powers to prevent land alienation among the tribals as well as exploitation of tribals by non-tribals. Fürer-Haimendorf helped correct the injustice done to the tribals of Adilabad when large areas of tribal clan land was taken away from the tribals by the Nizam's government and held as reserved forest. He persuaded the government to dereserve 160,000 acres of fertile land for allocation to 12,000 tribal families (15 acres/family) along with title deeds, popularly known as "Haimendorf *pattas*". This had a positive impact on improving the economy of the tribals, 85% of whom now had adequate land for cultivation.

Implementation of land legislation

To implement these protective measures, Fürer-Haimendorf created a special agency attached to the revenue department and known as Social Service. This agency which he directed until he left in 1949 provided the field staff for carrying out the tribal welfare work. These officers were trained in anthropology in the Osmania University and even learnt several of the tribal languages (such as Gondi). They were posted in tribal areas and their activities helped forge friendly relations between tribals and government officers. The tribals had easy access to the officials sympathetic to their problems and able to provide quick remedial measures. Also, the presence of officers of the Social Service department acted as a check even on the high-handedness of forest-guards and *patwaris*. The organization of co-operative societies to inculcate the habit of thrift and self-reliance provided social security to the tribals. There was also provision for the supply of plough bullocks to needy tribals on long-term credit. The establishment of village grainbanks helped provide food security to the tribals in any eventuality of crop failures.

When Fürer-Haimendorf returned in 1977 to do intensive research on the Gond of Utnur he found that the whole demographic scene had changed with numerous settlers from

Maharashtra. This non-tribal movement into the tribal area of Utnur had reached a climax between 1965-1975. They occupied cultivable land at the expense of the Gond in the span of a few years. The laws prohibiting the acquisition of tribal land by non-tribals were obviously ignored. The methods used to achieve this were similar to those used fifty years ago to dispossess the tribal of the lowlands. Apart from outright trickery and bribing of *patwari* and revenue staff to change entries in the land register, the immigrants deliberately led Gonds into debt, then induced them to lease their lands and finally refused to return this land to the owners.

The occupant's name was entered in the village records as owner in place of the original owner with the connivance of the patwari and revenue officials. The demographic figures for Marlavai Circle in 1941 show that it was purely tribal in composition, the percentage of tribals in 1961 was 90%, but by 1971 it had dropped to 65%. To compound this invasion into the tribal areas, in 1970s the Banjara (an immigrant community from the district of Berar) succeeded in dislodging many Gonds from their holdings. At that time, Banjaras were not notified as tribes, but in 1977, with their inclusion in the list of scheduled tribes, there remained no legal bar to the transfer of land from Gonds to Banjara. Such transactions between tribals were permitted by law. Hence, with these two important events, the position of the Gond which had stabilized, turned a full circle to return to the precarious position Fürer-Haimendorf found them during the 1930s. There was one important difference though, there was no more vacant land available in the forested highlands for the Gond to take refuge and they were thus reduced to becoming landless laborers.

Breakdown of tribal cohesion

The author's own independent studies among the Gonds of Adilabad district from 1970s and the unique opportunity she had in accompanying the Haimendorfs on their annual revisits from 1977-88 resulted in two publications co-authored with Fürer-Haimendorf entitled, *Gonds and their Neighbours (1982)* and *Tribal Cohesion in the Godavari Valley (1998)*. The picture that emerged was that in spite of protective legislation, the wholesale immigration of non-tribal settlers and the introduction of commercial cash crops, mainly cotton among subsistant tribal groups, was too great an onslaught on the Gonds' way of life. The entire cropping pattern of Utnur taluk underwent a transformation that was detrimental to Gond economy. The high prices for the cotton transformed a food producing area into a region concentrating on growing cotton. The increasing number of commercial centres in the area and exploitation of the tribals by traders led them into debts and ultimate loss of ownership of their lands to non-tribals.

Added to this, Gonds had to face the change in governments twice in the span of a decade: the partition of Hyderabad state in 1956 and the merging of the Telengana districts with Andhra districts into Andhra Pradesh. This change of administration also brought about the repeal of the Hyderabad Tribal Areas Regulation in 1963, replacing it by the Andhra Pradesh Scheduled Areas Land Transfer Regulation, 1959. While the latter regulation also protected the land of the tribals, prohibiting any transfer to non-tribals, it did not contain any provision for the maintenance of the tribal panchayat. Most importantly, it stripped the social service officers of the authority and judicial powers with which the Hyderabad Tribal Areas Regulation had provided in all cases involving tribal land. Moreover, any non-tribal whose occupation of tribal land was challenged by a revenue official could now, and still can, lodge an appeal in a civil court. The termination of the functioning of tribal panchayats ended an institution which had regularly brought together the headmen of groups of villages in settlement of disputes according to the rules of tribal customary law. The commercialization of the local economy further resulted in the breakup of tribal solidarity, as it inevitably tended to encourage individualistic tendencies as opposed to the welfare of the community.

The imposition of a grassroot democratic system, the panchayati raj in tribal areas was designed more for the needs of more advanced regions of rural India and undermined the traditional authority of tribal panchayats. Previously, the village was the basic unit and now the smallest unit was a cluster of villages or the gram panchayat. Hence, the splitting up of villages and the reconstitution of blocks from parts of different villages was done more for beauracratic convenience, but it definitely undermined tribal village cohesion and created division within tribal society. Since tribal areas are no more homogenous due to the demographic transformation, the constitution of villages dispersed over large distances and consisting of other ethnic groups, the elected members could seldom meet and had little sense of solidarity and purpose to accomplish anything.

In 1977, Utnur Taluk had 40 gram panchayats, and in 29 of these the sarpanch was a Gond or Pardhan, while in seven gram panchayats an immigrant Banjara held that position. Even in gram panchayats with a tribal sarpanch, non-tribal members exerted a far greater influence, especially if they were economically more powerful.

In view of all these problems highlighted by Fürer-Haimendorf, the Bhuria Commission was appointed to re-examine the provisions of the 73rd Constitution Amendment Act, 1992, and recommended a system of *panchayat raj* in harmony with existing traditional tribal institutions. The Panchayat Raj (Extension to Scheduled Areas) Act, 1996 was passed by the parliament and in 1997 the Andhra Pradesh state too enacted a law in pursuance thereof. However, the Act is still to be implemented since the panchayat raj elections have not been held in the state. The gram sabha is empowered to safeguard its customary law and settle disputes. They have the control over the management of community resources and have power to decide on land alienation cases and restoration of the land back to the original owner. They have the powers to grant mining leases and licenses. This is the ghost of Hyderabad Tribal Areas Regulation, 1949 rising from the grave after half a century.

Future role

The younger generation of anthropologists cannot afford to sit in ivory towers any more but move into the difficult yet challenging role of focusing their attention on the future welfare of tribal societies whose very survival is being threatened by the process of modernization. The trend today, even among the educated class as well as administrators is a growing unwillingless to accept that more than eighty million tribal people continue to need special protection. The ecologists are fighting to save the forests, but very little attention is being paid to the displacement of tribals living for millennia in these forests which have now been reserved or established as wild life sanctuaries. For example, the Rajiv Gandhi Tiger Sanctuary in Andhra Pradesh, which was earlier a "Chenchu Reserve", protecting the rights of this small group totally dependent on the collection of minor forest produce, is now a reserve to protect tigers. The forest department has been trying to resettle some of the Chenchu outside this reserve. This programme has failed, with Chenchu returning to their forest homes. It is ironic that so much hue and cry is made for the protection of tigers by the environmentalists but so little attention is given to the plight of this threatened tribal group. It is for such issues that both anthropologists and ecologists need to come together to help put this matter in a proper perspective. They should approach the government to work out the modalities of implementing programmes in a scientific and humanistic manner.

The author has been taking part in these programmes and debates with the government which involve tribals and other rural poor in participatory management of forests in Andhra Pradesh. She has evaluated the JFM programme as an independent consultant teaming up with senior foresters in suggesting strategies to make this programme sustainable, by tying up the economic improvement of the poor with the scientific management of the forests. She has been involved in analyzing the process of empowerment of grassroot institutions in decision making and implementation of forest management and protection (1993, 1998). She has also stressed the importance of strengthening women's thrift groups to take a more active role in their own development process. The JFM programme in A.P. has clearly shown that when tribal communities are handed over the responsibilities of protecting and sharing the usufructs from forests, the impact on forest regeneration is good. Besides, the attitude of the tribals to the foresters has undergone a sea change in a short span. The tribals who used to disappear on seeing a forest jeep, on the contrary, now see them more in the light of development agents who come to their doorstep to help attend to their basic problems. The Andhra Pradesh government is now designing rural programmes based on the participation of the community, such as water users committees, watershed committees, forest protection committees, thrift groups, education committees, etc. The earlier top down developmental approach which the government had been following has failed to trickle down to the grassroot level. However, for the participatory approach to work, the mindset of the beauracracy has to be re-oriented to take up these new challenges where the answers are not known. They have to be determined through a scientific approach and involvement of the village communities which have a repository of empirical knowledge on the soil profiles, the flora and fauna, which they are so closely in touch with. It is here that anthropologists and ecologists should work together to help gather the information for effective implementation of these programmes.

The political empowerment of tribals at the grassroot level through active participation in panchayat raj elections will give them a capacity to influence decision-making process, planning and implementation of their welfare programmes. The one-third reservation for tribals and their women guarantees their representation. In the states of Madhya Pradesh and Karnataka, poor rural and tribal women have already won representation in Panchayat Samathis, often more than the minimum of one third seats reserved for them. The women who were previously shy to appear in public are now confidently bringing basic amenities to the villages they represent. They are active in improving education, health and sanitation in their villages giving more priority to these programmes than their men. In this sphere of activity too, the anthropologists have an important role in creating awareness and capacity building of tribal women and men to participate in both the political and development process. These efforts cannot be done by the government alone and NGOs, anthropologists and sociologists should pitch in to give a helping hand.

The educational backwardness of tribals in Peninsular India co-relates with continuing high levels of poverty among them. The government in Andhra Pradesh has made very little impact on imparting quality education to tribal people. The latest overall tribal literacy in A.P. is 17% as compared to 44% in the general population. The dropout rate of tribals in the primary and middle school level is 82% in boys and 89% in girls. All this indicates an apathy of the government to impart good education to the tribals and make it their top priority.

The work that Fürer-Haimendorf did for the welfare of tribal people half a century ago is still so relevant and radical for providing deep insights in tackling the complex problems facing the tribals in India. Those of us (anthropologists, administrators and NGOs) who have had the opportunity to interact with him have come away a little bit wiser than before. Marlavai was the home of the Haimendorfs and they returned so often to watch anxiously over their beloved Gonds, often somewhat helplessely in their struggle for survival. Not having the authority anymore to bring about change, Fürer-Haimendorf resorted to persuading and gently prodding many a young civil service officers working for the welfare of the tribals to take appropriate steps in the right direction. Hence, the annual visits of the Haimendorfs helped rally and inspire a group of people seeking ways and means to help the tribal cause.

The Haimendorfs had endeared themselves to the Gond who have immortalized them in their myths. The Gond of Marlavai have built mausoleums for their beloved ancestors, Christoph and Betty Haimendorf.

REFERENCES

Fürer-Haimendorf, C. von

1943 *The Chenchus-Jungle Folk of the Deccan. Vol. 1. The Aboriginal Tribes of Hyderabad.* London.

1945 *The Reddis of the Bison Hills-A Study of Acculturation. Vol. 2. The Aboriginal Tribes of Hyderabad.* London.

1945 *Tribal Hyderabad—Four Reports.* Hyderabad.

1948 *The Raj Gonds of Adilabad.* Vol. 3. *The Aboriginal Tribes of Hyderabad.* London.

1982 *Tribes of India: The Struggle for Survival.* Delhi: Oxford University Press.

1990 *Life among Indian Tribes.* Delhi: Oxford University Press.

Pingle, U. and Fürer-Haimendorf, C. von

1987 *Gonds and Their Neihbours: A Study of Genetic Diversity.* Lucknow: Ethnographic and Folk Culture Society.

1998 *Tribal Cohesion in the Godavari Valley.* Hyderabad: Book Links Corporation.

Pingle, U.

1993 *Tribals and Forest Development.* Report submitted to the World Bank, Andhra Pradesh Forestry Programme.

1993 *Role of Tribal Women in Joint Forest Management in Andhra Pradesh.* Report submitted to the World Bank.

1998 *Evaluation of JFM and Eco-Development Programmes in Andhra Pradesh.* Bangalore: Om Consultants.

Part V

20

Experiencing Anthropology in the Nicobar Archipelago

VIJOY S. SAHAY

The title of this paper is also the title of my forthcoming book on the Nicobar Islands. At the very outset, I would like to quote a few lines from the book of a Nobel laureate, Gunnar Myrdal. In the Preface of his book *Asian Drama* (Volume I), Myrdal (1968) writes,

> ...books have their own destiny, even while they are being written and before they are published. Often the simplest way of explaining what a book is about and what it aims to achieve is to tell why and how it came to be written.

While agreeing with Myrdal's observation, I would very humbly appeal to the readers of this article, not to consider my unconventional way of presenting it as self-reflective.

The paper is an outcome of the intensive data collected by me during the two courses of fieldwork conducted over a period of twenty-seven years: first, during 1974-75, and second, during May-June 2002. During the first phase of fieldwork, I was a young researcher, and during the second phase, a matured and a professional anthropologist. The changes witnessed by me in the Nicobar Islands were unprecedented. Most of my informants, more importantly the key informants in different islands, were lying in their graves. The island of Chowra, which was then known as the *land of wizards and the witchdoctors* had turned into a *land of medical doctors*. Three Chowrians, I was told, were studying in different medical colleges of the country. Gone were the days when canoes ceremonially plied between different islands for inter-island trade relationships, somewhat like the *kula* of the Trobriand Islanders. Women in Chowra no more made earthen pots, which were earlier used by all the Nicobarese due to magico-religious beliefs, supposedly, associated with Chowra pots. Nor could they be found, expectantly, awaiting their husbands along the beach near the *elpenam* (community houses), who brought coconuts, yams, banana, cloths, pigs, tobacco, and various other domestic items from far off islands. Wearing a loincloth by men had become history. On the one hand, the standard and quality of life of the islanders had developed; on the other, many of their traditional rituals, beliefs and practices were either on the verge of extinction, or had already become extinct. For me, to witness the changes over twenty-seven years was a great anthropological experience. This paper has been written in a somewhat post-modernistic fashion. Therefore, instead of using the third person, as an objective and passive spectator of the phenomena like a natural scientist, I have taken liberty to explain my anthropological experiences in the first person.

II

My association with the Nicobar Islands

My association with the Nicobar Islands is quite old. Altogether I have been six times to the Bay Islands. From time to time, I also contributed articles on different aspects of the Nicobarese life and culture in different journals (Sahay 1976, 1979, 1981, 2007). My Ph.D. thesis entitled *The Nicobarese: A Study in Nature-Man-Spirit Complex* was twice accepted for publication abroad in a book form; however, this particular title, *Experiencing Anthropology in the Nicobar Archipelago*, emerged in my mind during my fourth visit to the Nicobar Islands in the summer of 2002. Twenty-seven summers had passed since I had last set my foot on the shores of Nicobars; and had bid good-bye to Abednigo in Car Nicobar and Gabriel Kulilong in Nancowrie. Both of them (now dead) were my interpreters and key informants in my two consecutive visits in 1974 and 1975, respectively. I had collected all the relevant data during these two visits for my doctoral thesis. After my return from the archipelago, I considered myself the champion of the Nicobar Islands. I often claimed that I knew about the Nicobarese more than the Nicobarese knew about themselves. And, such a claim of mine was not very unfounded.

Off the deep southeast, of the long stretched eastern coast of the Indian peninsula, between Sumatra and the Andaman Islands in the Bay of Bengal, lies a chain of twelve inhabited and seven uninhabited islands, known as the Nicobar Archipelago. The situation of the Nicobar Islands is 8.00 N and 94.00 E. The inhabited islands are Car Nicobar, Chowra, Teressa, Bompoka, Nancowrie, Kamorta, Trinket, Katchall, Great Nicobar, Little Nicobar, Pulomilo, and Kondul; and the uninhabited islands are Tillanchong, Battimalve, Menchal, Taraik, Tries, Miroe and Kabra.

Geographically, we can divide the Nicobar Archipelago into three zones, viz., the Northern, the Central, and the Southern. The Northern Zone consists of Car Nicobar only; the Central Zone consists of Teressa, Bompoka, Chowra, Katchall, Kamorta, Nancowrie and Trinket; and the Southern Zone comprises the islands of Little Nicobar, Great Nicobar, Pulomilo, and Kondul.

Linguistically, Nicobarese dialects are from Mon Khmer speech family, and five different dialects are spoken here. Car Nicobarese have a separate dialect, people of Teressa and Bompoka speak one dialect, Chowrians speak a separate dialect, the people of Kamorta, Katchall, Nancowrie and Trinket speak one dialect, and people of Great and Little Nicobar, Kondul, and Pulomilo speak a separate dialect. In addition, there is a dialect for an 'uninhabited island.' It appears paradoxical that how could there be any dialect of an 'uninhabited island?' However, it does exist. I will present a brief account of it in the later part of this paper. Inhabitants of one island hardly understand the dialect of other islanders.

Culturally, we can divide the Nicobarese into four groups. Car Nicobar has a distinct culture; Teressa and Bompoka have common cultural traditions; Chowra has a very distinct culture; people of Kamorta, Katchall, Nancowrie, and Trinket share common cultural traditions; and similarly, people of Great and

Little Nicobar, Kondul and Pulomilo have common cultural traditions.

Although during the course of my fieldwork in 1974-75, the inter-island trade and exchange existed among them, some of the islanders exchanged their goods indirectly with the third party (see trade route map). Thus, all the islanders did not get frequent opportunities to communicate and interact directly with each other; therefore, a Car Nicobarese little knew about the affairs of Great Nicobarese, or for that matter any of the islanders of the Southern Zone, and vice versa.

On the contrary, I had lived in nine of the twelve islands during the course of data collection; therefore, I claimed that I knew about the Nicobarese more than anyone did. However, all my claims shattered when I revisited the islands after twenty-seven years. When I witnessed the changes that had taken place during the last twenty-seven years, at first, I thought that all I knew about the Nicobars had now become history. For a moment, I was as perplexed as Rip Van Winkle. I began worrying that how should I arrange and integrate my data collected after a gap of over two and a half decades. Nevertheless, as I started again to interact and mingle with the people there, I also began to realize gradually that 'the more and more an anthropologist knows about a people, the less and less he thinks he knows about them.'

I received my doctoral degree in 1979. Thereafter, Anna Hohenwart, my Ph.D. examiner from Austria, wrote more than three letters to my guide, late Professor L .P. Vidyarthi. She wanted my thesis to be published from Austria. In her report as an examiner, she had adjudged my thesis as excellent. Vidyarthi referred all her letters to me with instructions to prepare the manuscript in a book form, and send it to Anna. It was both my carelessness and misfortune that I could not set my mind to rework on the manuscript, and thus, years after years passed by. Vidyarthi died in 1985; and I had no personal acquaintance or contact with Anna. Thus, the very idea of publication of my thesis from Austria was finally dumped.

In 1998, I was attending the XIV International Congress of Anthropological and Ethnological Sciences (ICAES) at Williamsburg in U.S.A. I met the Edwin Mellen publishers there. They also offered to publish my thesis. I told them that over two decades had passed; and I needed to update the data. They agreed and I signed a contract with them that within six months I would send the updated manuscript. Unfortunately, despite all my efforts to revisit the islands, I failed to do so. And thus, my contract with the Edwin Mellen also ended in grief.

In spite of such disappointments, I never lost hope. I knew it well that my work in the Nicobar Islands during 1974-75 was very thorough and intensive. It carried immense anthropological potential. In my two consecutive visits for data collection, I had spent altogether 13 months with the Nicobarese in different islands. The most important being the Island of Chowra, which was then referred to as the land of wizards. During the entire course of my fieldwork, I lived in Nicobarese huts, often with my interpreter. Neither I knew then to cook meals, nor had I even a stove with me to prepare tea for myself. Thus, even for my food and drink I was absolutely dependent upon the Nicobarese. Very often we took meals in the houses of our informants. The meals were invariably preceded by a toddy session. Thereafter, typical Nicobarese meals that consisted of yams, banana, pandanus, baked fish, half roasted pork, and sometimes rice and chicken were served.

I had spent three and a half months in Chowra in 1974, completely cut off from the outside world. I didn't have even a transistor with me to know the news of the world outside. Before leaving for Chowra, I had posted two letters, one to Professor Vidyarthi, and one to my mother at home. I had explained to both of them that as no ship or boat ever went to Chowra, no communication could be possible with me, until I returned from this relatively 'inaccessible island'. During my stay there I had witnessed the extent of incredible superstition that prevailed in Chowra life. Many a times I had journeyed with them to the island of Teressa in their primitive type of canoes. I had witnessed their open burial system. I had witnessed their inter-island trade. Fear of Iwi, i.e. spirit, both malevolent and benevolent, was so profound in Chowra life that one day as I woke up in the morning, I found pin drop silence prevailing in the entire island. Except for the roaring sound of the sea waves dashing against the shores, and the rustling sound of the leaves of the trees in the blowing wind, one could hear nothing. People silently walked along the village paths with hands folded at the back. On enquiring, my interpreter Abednigo, a Christian, told me with a frown that it was the festival of *bunglav*. The Chowrians, who were then all non-Christian, believed that if they produced any sound that day, the devil in the island would become angry; and its wrath would cause death and disease in Chowra. At that moment I had the first experience of the contradictions involved in the life of an anthropologist during the course of his fieldwork.

While Abednigo was shouting at his peak, and condemning the pagan beliefs and rituals of the islanders, at that moment an old woman approached him, and whispered something into his ears. After listening to her Abed became even more furious. He frowned the woman into silence, and told one of his confidants to ring the bell of the makeshift chapel as loud as he could in order to denounce the superstitious beliefs and practices of the islanders. Out of scare, the woman disappeared from the scene. For the islanders, Abed was far superior and powerful, as he could interact with the world outside in different dialects. The Chowrians, on the contrary, knew little about outside world, except the neighboring islanders with whom they traditionally interacted. No one had the courage to oppose and stop Abednigo from making loud sounds. I was in a fix. As an anthropologist, I was examining the phenomena with great interest, and with a Chowrian's perspective. I had deep regard for their indigenous beliefs and rituals. I empathized with the old woman. I wanted to stop Abed from hurting the sentiments of the old woman and the islanders. However, at the same time, as a humanist, it also occurred to my mind that should we allow such people, in this case the Chowrians, to remain forever, at whatever stage of development they were. Honestly speaking, till this date I have not received a convincing and satisfying answer to the problem. Nevertheless, the life in Chowra was then a rich anthropological experience. Today, all the Chowrians have been proselytized to Christianity.

III

The threat of Chowra

In the last week of December 1973, while I was in my early twenties, as a Junior Research Fellow of the University Grants

Commission, I set out for the Bay Islands to study the Nicobarese. Earlier, in December 1971, as a postgraduate student of the Department of Anthropology, Ranchi University, I had already visited Andaman and Nicobar Islands with Professor Vidyarthi. Then I had set my foot only in Car Nicobar, Nancowrie and Kamorta, though I had read and heard a lot about the 'inaccessibility' and 'inhospitality' of Chowra and its people. As I said earlier, the Chowrians were then regarded as wizards. It was commonly believed that a Chowrian could change the direction of the wind and the waves during a voyage. No one would offend a Chowrian for the fear of misfortune befalling upon him. In a way, they were respected as 'Brahmins' in the Nicobar archipelago. In Car Nicobar, we had met Bishop John Richardson, the architect of modern Nicobar, and in Nancowrie, Rani Laxmi, the influential political leader of the Central Islands. Thus, having received theoretical and fieldwork training under Vidyarthi, I was already fascinated by the island studies. Malinowski, Margaret Mead and Franz Boas were my ideals.

I received the first warning about the island of Chowra in the library of the Anthropological Survey of India (ASI) at Calcutta. Some colleagues in the ASI, who had been earlier posted in Andamans, when came to know of my resolve to go to Chowra, asked me whether I wanted to die or commit suicide? How would I go there as no ship ever went there? How shall I protect myself from filarial infection, as most people suffered there with this disease? What shall I drink there, as only the dirty ditch water was available in the island? How shall I communicate with the people there? Would the witch doctors ever tolerate the presence of an outsider in their island? These and many other queries were fired upon me, one after another, of which I certainly had no immediate answer. I could only say that I had learnt from the available sources that the Chowra people came to Teressa in their canoes during summer to fetch drinking water. I would contact them and like to go with them. Chowra was then considered so formidable to reach.

Landing on Chowra

The office of the Anthropological Survey of India was then at the Aberdeen in Port Blair. I spent most of my time in its library as long as I stayed in Port Blair. Then, R. S. Mann was the Station Director. Hari Ram, the office assistant, one day called me and asked whether I was really determined to go to Chowra. When I told him in the affirmative, he gave me the first clue. He said that he knew a person, named Abednigo, in Car Nicobar who knew the Chowra language. I procured a letter from him for Abed, as he was popularly known in Car Nicobar. I landed in Car Nicobar in the first week of February 1974. I knew it well that without the blessing, or better said, the permission of the Bishop, who was then considered as the uncrowned king of the Nicobar Islands, it would be futile to roam about the Nicobar villages. In want of it, hardly anybody would bother to talk to me. Therefore, with the help of the then Additional Deputy Commissioner (ADC) of the Nicobar Islands, Janak Juneja, I sought an appointment with the Bishop. And, the Bishop obliged me by giving an appointment.

One morning (I do not remember the date), at 11.00 a.m., at his residence at Mus village, I met him. I first congratulated him, as the Government of India had awarded him Padmashree, only a couple of days earlier on the Republic Day. During our meeting, the conversation ran as follows:

> "What can I do for you, young man", asked the Bishop.
>
> "I want to go to Chowra", I said.
>
> "No ship ever goes to Chowra. How will you go there?" said the Bishop.
>
> "The Chowrians come to Teressa on their canoes to fetch drinking water. Can't I go with them?" I asked.
>
> "Do you know swimming?" enquired the Bishop.
>
> "Yes, I can swim for ten hours at a stretch," I replied.
>
> "But how will you talk to them? You don't know the Chowra language," He said.
>
> "That's why I have come to you for your help. Can you tell Abednigo, your cousin, to accompany me to Chowra? I have learnt that he alone knows the Chowra language," I said.

The Bishop thought for a moment and thereafter told someone to call Abed. After a few minutes, Abednigo appeared there in *khaki* half pants and white half shirt. The Bishop had some conversation with Abednigo in Nicobarese, and then announced that Abed had agreed to accompany me to Chowra. I thanked him and left his premises with Abed. I told Abed that by the very next ship to the Southern Islands we should leave for Teressa. We decided that we would contact the

Chowrians at Teressa and request them to take us to Chowra in their canoes.

Nevertheless, luck had something else in store for us. Two days later, the ADC Miss Juneja, in her office in Car Nicobar, introduced me to one gentleman, Captain Beals, an Anglo-Burmese, who owned a small cargo ship named *Katherina*. Miss Juneja told him that I was determined to go to Chowra. Captain Beals also asked me the same questions about Chowra; and, I too, gave the same answers that I had replied earlier to many others. Thereafter, the Captain told us about his expedition to the South Sentinel Island with the German scientists, who were after the *robber crabs*–the species supposed to have become extinct. He also told us that the Germans paid him Rs. 7500 per day for chartering his ship. I had little interest in his narration, as I could not imagine paying any amount to charter a ship to Chowra. However, to my great surprise and astonishment, before his departure from the ADC's room, Captain Beals put one of his hands on my shoulder and suddenly announced, "O.K. young man, when I next go to the South, I will drop you at Chowra." Miss Juneja congratulated me after Captain Beals left her office; however, I could not believe. I told her that I could not give any money to the Captain, as I was merely a Junior Research Fellow of the U.G.C. receiving a meager sum of Rs. 300 per month. Nevertheless, Miss Juneja assured me that she knew Captain Beals very well; he was the champion of these waters, and a man of principles and integrity. And, so was Captain Beals.

Just after a week one afternoon, Miss Juneja's driver came to where I had been put up. He had brought a message from the Headquarters sent through the Police Radio. It read, "Chowra party, be ready to move on Wednesday- Captain Beals." I was as delighted as surprised. I immediately went to Miss Juneja to confirm the message. She smiled and reminded me of what she had told me earlier about the Captain. I only nodded my head; however, I was still skeptical and worrisome, and thought that if Captain Beals demanded money then what should I do? At last, I resolved that if the Captain so demanded, then I would tell him the truth; at most, he would drop me in any Island. Thus, I resigned worrying, and spiritedly went to Abednigo to tell him the good news. To add to my delight, I found Abed more enthusiastic than even me.

The next two days, I was busy with Abednigo in purchasing a lot of food items and medicines. I learnt from the ADC's office that *Katherina* had arrived and anchored at Sawai Bay; and that after unloading the cargo, would sail sometime in the night hours. At about 4.00 p.m. we reached Sawai Bay; first, boarded a canoe, bag and baggage, which took us to a raft about one hundred meters away from the shore. There we waited for the ferryboat that finally took us to *Katherina*, which had anchored about a mile away from the shore. I boarded *Katherina*, and went to Captain Beals; who, resting his hands on the railing of the upper deck, watched us board the vessel. He greeted me with a smile and offered me a cigarette. I shook hands with him and thanked him. He called one of the members of his crew; instructed him to arrange a cabin for me; told Abednigo to go downstairs in the bunk; and ordered for two cups of tea and biscuits. Thereafter, I was treated as a VIP by the crewmembers on board the *Katherina*—a very special guest of the Captain. Sometime around 10.00 p.m., anchor was lifted, and *Katherina* slowly began to sail towards the south. However, after supper at 7.30 p.m., I had already retired to bed in my cabin.

It was midnight that a crew member knocked the doors of my cabin. When I opened the doors, he informed that the captain immediately wanted to see me in pilot's room. I went there and found the captain was a little worried. I asked him what the matter was. Instead, he asked me whether I had earlier visited the Southern Islands. I told him that I had been up to Nancowrie earlier. Then he explained that *Katherina* though was passing through the waters of Chowra, it was difficult to anchor near it because of darkness and abundant coral reefs around the island. It was risky to approach the island until the day broke. The captain finally offered me to accompany him up to Campbell Bay (Great Nicobar); and assured that on return journey he would drop me at Chowra during the day hour. I had neither any option nor any objection; so, I accepted his offer happily, and retired to bed.

Next morning I woke up early. The sun was bright. We passed through Teressa and Bompoka. Flying fishes were abundant in these waters. Thereafter, we entered the open sea. The ship rolled because of high waves. In the afternoon, we passed through Katchall on our right, and Kamorta and

Nancowrie on our left, then again the open sea. Far in the south, the Little Nicobar came to sight. I felt exhausted because of moist wind and ship-roll. Therefore, I retired to bed early only to wake up in the morning. I never knew when we reached Campbell Bay.

Though exhausted, I was a little excited to land on the Island of Great Nicobar at Campbell Bay. After unloading the cargo, the ship was to leave for Katchall. We had a few hours at our disposal; so with a hope of meeting the Shompen, I climbed down the ladders of the ship with Abednigo. Shompens lived in the interior of the Great Nicobar. Their estimated population is around 200 souls. There was a small settlement of ex-army men belonging to Sikh community at Campbell Bay; some shops and some government quarters were there. We were told to go to the Block Office to find any Shompen. An office assistant there told us that a few of the Shompen often visited the Block Office in order to receive some gifts supplied by the government. By the time any Shompen came to the Block Office, the siren of the ship blew; and we hurriedly returned to the ship.

We reached Katchall a little before sunset. There was no jetty then at Katchall; therefore, *Katherina* anchored three to four hundred meters away from the shore. People came on canoes to unload the cargo. As the cargo was not much, so it took little time in unloading. However, by the time the unloading completed, fast wind began to blow; and within no time, it turned into a storm with heavy rain. The weather in these islands is always very unpredictable. We could not lift anchor before the storm stopped. Around 8.00 p.m., the weather began clearing. Captain announced that after dinner at 10.00 p.m. *Katherina* would sail. I was again a little anxious; as I guessed that we would again pass through the Chowra waters in the midnight. Anyway, as I could help little in this regard and already had vomited twice due to sea sickness, I went to bed in my cabin.

At midnight, again I woke up at the knock of the doors of my cabin. A crew informed me that captain wanted to see me. It was around 1.30 a.m. I went upstairs to pilot's room. With a binocular set on his eyes, Captain Beals was watching the long stretched sea before him. A quarter size of moon was visible along the western horizon. There was absolute lull after the storm. *Katherina* was moving as smoothly and leisurely as if sailing on a calm lake. I entered the pilot's cabin and said, "Hello Captain, you wanted to see me?" Without removing binocular from his eyes, he asked, "Would you like to see Chowra?" It startled me at once, as if, I had suddenly received a jerk. However, in no time, I understood the situation; and then I felt animated. Within seconds, all my exhaustion and fatigue was gone. I could only say, "Really, could I?"

Captain Beals handed over the binocular to me and pointed towards the north-west direction to look at. I set the binocular on my eyes, and tried to locate the island. Under the faint light of a quarter size moon, I located a tiny speck over the calm surface of sea. It was the cliff at the southern end of the island, locally known as *tahop*, meaning the *Devil's Abode*. My excitement knew no bounds. I was having the first glimpse of Chowra, for which everyone who had come to know of my desire and resolve to go there, had scared me, and warned me of dire consequences, even to the extent of my life and death. However, no one knew that my resolve to go to Chowra was not because of any desire for adventure, but because of my topic of research—"Nature-Man-Spirit Complex." I was convinced from the literature of Nicobars that without the study of Chowra, my study on the nature-man-spirit complex of the Nicobarese would remain incomplete.

I was very thrilled as I realized that I was nearing the destination. I went downstairs to Abednigo, woke him up and informed him. I again climbed upstairs and went to the upper deck. Captain was very busy; every now and then, he gave instructions to the crewmembers. Slowly, *Katherina* was nearing the island; and gradually, her speed slowed down. Finally, she moved at snail's pace. Captain was very serious. Navigation chart was spread before him in pilot's cabin. In fact, he was trying to locate a suitable place for anchoring; neither too near nor too far from the island. Now we were quite close to the island, less than a quarter mile I believed. To our left down the western horizon moon was about to set, though still dimly visible; and to our immediate right was the Island of Chowra, almost engulfed in darkness.

Suddenly with a roar, *Katherina* anchored, and the siren began to blow. All the lights of the ship, including the spotlights, were put on; and for the first time I saw thousands of fish at a time jumping over the water surface, especially following the spotlights. Whichever direction the spotlight moved, hundreds of fish jumped over the water. It was a spectacular sight for me. Continuously the siren of the ship blew, and the spotlight was thrown towards the shore with the hope that some one from the shore would come by canoe, as it usually happened during the day hours in other islands. But, there was no response, no sign of life along the shore. Only the white surfs could be seen under the spotlight, as the waves dashed against the shore. Captain was getting puzzled. "Why not anyone is coming?" he asked Abednigo. Abednigo too looked puzzled. He shouted in Chowra language at the top of his voice, so that some one would hear him and come on his canoe near the ship, but of no avail.

Finally, Captain brought a small mike attached with a portable loudspeaker from pilot's cabin, which could be carried on one's shoulder, and gave it to Abednigo. Then he told his crew to lift down a boat from the ship to take Abednigo near the shore, and told me to stay on board the ship. A boat was lifted down the ship, and under the spotlight, Abednigo and a few members of the crew climbed down the ladder for the boat. The boat started and followed the spotlight towards the shore. We all watched them go from the upper deck. With the small loud speaker on his shoulder and mike in his hand, Abednigo was continuously shouting and calling in Chowra language. Though they reached very near the shore, and Abednigo shouted at his full voice, no one responded. At last, Abed lost his patience; he lifted down the mike and loudspeaker from his shoulder; removed his shirt, jumped into the water, and swam across to the shore.

From the deck of the ship, we saw in spotlight, Abednigo emerging out of water along the shore; thereafter, the site was even more spectacular. At least a few hundred torches, made of dried leaves of coconut were lit, which the islanders carried in their hands. In fact, all the islanders were hiding behind the *elpenum*, and throughout watching our activities, without showing any sign of their presence. They all encircled Abednigo. We were too far from the shore to hear their conversation. However, the inhabitants recognized Abednigo, who had earlier lived in Chowra for quite some time to proselytize the natives.

After Abednigo jumped down the boat, the crewmembers returned near the ship. With fingers crossed, we were watching the next move of the islanders. Intermittently, the spotlights were thrown towards the shore.

At last, we saw some people launching a canoe along the shore. Within no time a canoe with three men on it came near the ship. A crewmember threw a rope from the deck, which they caught hold of. While I was talking to the Captain, they saw me; I shouted in Hindi and English both, and asked them where Abednigo was? They perhaps did not understand what I had asked. Then the Captain told me not to board the canoe unless Abednigo came. Later, I learnt that Abednigo had in fact sent them to fetch me. A state of confusion had emerged there. Meanwhile they left the rope and started to return. The crewmembers shouted at them to stop, but they did not. Abednigo later told me that they had refused to take me on their canoe, as they found me talking in a foreign language.

After some time the same canoe returned near the ship. Now Abednigo was with them. He caught hold of the rope that was still hanging from the ship. I saw Captain smiling and waving his hands at Abednigo. He told the crewmembers to lift down my baggage. I told them to carry the small bag of Abednigo also, which he had given me before climbing down the boat. When all the baggage was lifted down to the canoe, I turned towards Captain Beals. He looked relaxed; lit a cigarette, and offered me one. I was emotionally a little perplexed. I did not know what to say to him, and how to thank him. I shook hands with him and said, "Captain, I wouldn't thank you because it will be a mere formality; however, I will never forget what you have done for me; I will always remember you Captain." He pressed his hands against mine, as if with concern, and said, "Don't worry young man; if I came to the South again, I would pick you up from here." But he never came. Nor could I ever see Captain Beals again.

I don't know whether he ever came to the South again or not. After four months, I returned to Port Blair. I enquired about Captain Beals and *Katherina*. I learnt that *Katherina* was at dry dock at Madras (now Chennai). Thus, without meeting Captain Beals, I returned to the main land. In 1975, I again went to Andaman and Nicobar Islands with a batch of postgraduate students of Ranchi University. This time we camped at Enunga village in Nancowrie Island for one and a half months. Thereafter, the team returned to Ranchi, and I stayed there for the next three months. However, *Katherina* never came to Nancowrie harbour; and I never got a chance to meet Captain Beals again; though he remained always fresh in my memory, as he remains even today. After twenty-seven years, I again visited the archipelago in the summer of 2002. I wanted to enquire about all the people whom I had earlier met. When I went to Marine to buy my ticket for Car Nicobar, in the Marine Office, I enquired about Captain Beals and *Katherina*. To my shock and dismay, I learnt that Captain Beals was dead long ago, and soon thereafter, *Katherina* also went out of sea.

After bidding goodbye to all the crewmembers, and finally to the Captain, I climbed down the ladders of *Katherina*, and boarded the canoe. The high waves had started again, so the canoe rolled turbulently from one side to another. I sat down at the centre of the canoe, with both the hands holding the pole on which the sail was fastened. The spotlights fell on the canoe. As the canoe moved and began distancing from the ship, I saw Captain Beals waving his hands. I too wanted to wave my hands; but involuntarily, I stood up with my right hand raised, and I saluted him. In response, I only saw him raising his hands. That was the last glimpse I had of Captain Beals.

Soon we reached ashore. The spotlights still followed us. As we climbed down the canoe and stood on the shore, the lights went off and the siren of the ship blew again. We saw *Katherina* turning and slowly moving towards the north. By then we were surrounded by hundreds of half or semi-clad men and women; many of them still had torches of dried leaves of coconut in their hands. While I was trying to locate my baggage, Abednigo appeared from the crowd and said to me, "You are welcome at Chowra, Mr. Sahay." I said, "Thanks Abed."

IV

Life in Chowra

Thus, I landed on Chowra. Abednigo talked to the chief of the island named Laklalul. Some men carried our luggage at the instance of Laklalul, who led us through the village to a separate hut. It was around 3.00 a.m. We climbed up the ladders of the rectangular hut. After everyone left, I applied mosquito-repellant cream (Odomos) all over my body, set my mosquito net, and tried to sleep; however, despite being tired I could not sleep. Cocks had begun to crow. Since we were very near the shore, we could incessantly hear the dashing sound of the waves. As the day broke, Abednigo told me that the witchdoctors had organized a meeting, where they would decide whether I should be allowed to stay in the island or not. Abed left for the meeting and instructed me not to move outside the hut. He returned after four hours.

I learnt from him that in the marathon meeting, initially, the witchdoctors, particularly Kamitonp (the chief of the witchdoctors) opposed my presence in the island. However, when Abednigo told them that I was from India, the innocent islanders became scared of me. Later, I learnt as to why they were so scared of India. Earlier, quite often, they practiced 'devil murder.' If ever a person in Chowra was considered as a 'black magician', the islanders unanimously decided to kill him, as it normally happens in cases of 'witchcraft accusation'. Thus, he was killed; his body was cut into pieces and on a raft, his mutilated body was thrown into the sea. Whenever such a mutilated body was found on a floating raft, the administration immediately made out that the victim must have been a Chowrian. As a result, the policemen raided the island, and indiscriminately arrested people from Chowra, and put them in Port Blair jail. On interrogation, however, all such accused persons replied that they had killed the 'devil' in the deceased, not the man. Therefore, this practice was known as 'devil murder.' But because the policemen were necessarily Indian, the islanders were scared of India. I admonished Abednigo for it (i.e. for false presentation of my identity), and told him that anthropologists seldom hide their identities.

Anyway, I was allowed to stay in the Island. Gradually, I began to move with Abednigo and mingle with the people. With the help of Abednigo, I learnt some words and sentences of their dialect, which helped me in establishing initial rapport with them. For the next two and a half months, I was absolutely cut off from the outside world. I did not even know when the festival of Holi was celebrated in the country. Only after my return to the mainland I learnt that during those months, when I was in Nicobar Islands in general and Chowra in particular, a lot of political upheavals had taken place in the country under the movement launched by late Jai Prakash Narayan.

In a small island of barely 2.8 square kilometers, the roaring sound of waves dashing against the shore could be heard from anywhere and anytime. I never knew when and how I would leave the island. People were extremely superstitious. Any misfortune was caused because of the wrath of the *iwi*, i.e. spirit. They worshipped and offered sacrifice to anything that scared them. There was a broken canoe along the beach near the *elpenum*, locally known as *hanvooha*. It had perhaps been left by some unknown pirates of the medieval period. The witchdoctors periodically offered sacrifices of a chicken or a pig there. They hold it sacred even today. Inside the forest, there were birth houses, where a pregnant woman was taken just before delivery. Instead of a midwife, the witchdoctor helped her deliver the child. Very near to our hut, there was burial ground. People of Chowra then practised open burial. They split a mini canoe into two halves; put the corpse in one of them that served as coffin, and on a 'V' shaped stick erected on the ground, placed the canoe with the corpse and thereafter put the other half of the canoe over it. The stinking smell spread all around as the corpse decayed. However, after the complete decay of the corpse, when only the bones were left, upper lid of the coffin was removed and the bones were reburied nearby. Surprisingly, only women did all this.

During the entire period of my stay in Chowra, I was very scared of malaria and filarial infection. I saw hundreds of people in the island suffer from elephantiasis caused by filarial infection. It was frightening to see their enormously large and swollen legs and scrotum. Every now and then, I applied Odomos on my hands, and legs, and all over my body to protect myself from the bite of mosquitoes. Earlier, I did not move alone. Abednigo always accompanied me. Later, however, I could move alone anywhere in the island. Men in the island wore loincloth only; women moved bare breast with a Burmese type of *lungi* that covered their lower part of body; only unmarried girls wore blouse and *lungi*. All the five villages in Chowra are situated at a stretch along the western coast. There is hardly any line of demarcation between two villages. The rest of the island is forested. Inside the forest, they made their gardens where they produced yams, banana, tapioca, pandanus. They kept their pigs and chicken in the forest. In spite of living in scarcity and adversities, I observed that Chowra men and women knew the worth of laughter, which I always found very natural and spontaneous.

Our daily routine in Chowra was to get up early morning; go to the seashore for call of nature; brush our teeth, and then take some biscuits and drink coconut water. We also consumed the kernel inside the coconut. Then we moved to the village; sat in the house of any informant, very often in the house of a witchdoctor. People soon started flocking around us, and with the help of my interpreter, I started collecting information on different aspects of Chowra life and culture. On all such occasions, toddy was served as essentially as any ritual. Often we went to the forest in the gardens of our informants. Mostly we took our lunch and dinner in the houses of our informants. Seldom did Abednigo prepare meals for us. He would supply raw items of food that we had purchased in Car Nicobar to any of the informants to prepare meals for us. We had carried a lantern with us. In the night, I wrote the details of all the information collected in the day hour.

After two months and a half, one morning we saw a ship anchored about half a mile away from the shore near the *elpenum*. Along with my interpreter and an informant, I went near it on a canoe. It was *Tarmugli,* a ship owned by the Andaman Administration. On board the ship were a unit of the Films Division of India, and some colleagues from the Anthropological Survey of India. Prem Vaidya, the Director of the film unit was making a film titled *Man in Search of Man*. Someone had told them in Car Nicobar that an anthropologist was working in Chowra. Thus, they came there and requested me to help them shoot in Chowra. And, so I did. Later, the film received the President's Award for the best documentary of the year. After the shooting was over, the unit members requested me to avail the good opportunity and wind up my work in Chowra, and leave the island with them. After having lived for two and a half months completely cut off from the outside world, I could not check the temptation; and though half-heartedly, told Abednigo to pack our luggage. The next morning we were in Car Nicobar by *Tarmugli*.

Return to Chowra: A great anthropological lesson

I must confess I had done a great blunder in leaving the Island in a huff with the film unit. Sheerly because of comfort of a ship journey, and in order to avoid the risk of a canoe journey, I had left Chowra by *Tarmugli*, despite my unwillingness. In Car Nicobar, I developed a feeling of guilt. I tried to recapitulate and arrange my Chowra data meaningfully, but I always failed to do so. Whenever I attempted to write something, there appeared emptiness in my mind. In spite of all my notes, I failed to recall anything of Chowra systematically. I cursed the moment when I had taken the decision to leave Chowra unceremoniously, and so abruptly. Then I realized that an anthropologist must not leave his field unless he is fully satisfied and convinced with his data.

After a couple of days, I went to Abednigo's house in village Mus, and expressed my feelings. I told him that unless I went to Chowra again, and verified my data, I would not feel satisfied; rather I would not be able to write my thesis. I again requested him to accompany me to Chowra. And Abed did oblige me, for which I shall ever remain thankful to him. In 2002 when I revisited Car Nicobar after twenty-seven years, I went to village Mus; and there I learnt that he too had died long before. Anyway, by the first available ship, Abednigo and I left Car Nicobar for Teressa. We landed there and within two hours, we learnt that several Chowrians had come to Teressa to fetch drinking water. We already had good rapport with them so they did not hesitate to take us in their canoes. Thus, I was again in Chowra within a fortnight. I felt immensely satisfied then. In my second round, I stayed in Chowra for one month and thirteen days. This time we were put up in a beehive type of hut in the *elpenum*. Once I fell ill and was surprised to find that all the witchdoctors including Kamitonp, the chief witchdoctor, looked after me. They applied all sorts of folk medicines on my body. Such medicines were invariably mixed with the blood of a pig or chicken.

This time in Chowra, I applied a novel method of data collection. Abednigo always remained with me as interpreter whenever I interviewed an informant. During the course of interview, I noted down all the information in my notebook right on the spot. In the night hours, not only did I elaborate the contents of information collected during the interview, I also persuaded Abednigo to write down in detail, as he had acted as interpreter. His English was tolerably well, and, he had a better knowledge of Chowra and the Chowrians, for he had earlier lived in Chowra for over three years in order to spread Christianity. Though he had been unsuccessful in proselytizing the islanders then, in his effort to do so, he had gained complete mastery over their dialect. This helped him understand better the intricacies of Chowra life and culture. However, in order to obtain as much of objectivity as possible, during every leisure hour, and especially during the evenings, I taught Abednigo anthropology, specifically, the methods of data collection, importance of objectivity in doing so, and the meaning and significance of cultural relativism. Thus, I was able to instil sufficient anthropological interest in Abednigo. The result was very positive. First, I spent a very good time in Chowra in healthy and creative anthropological discussions with Abednigo; and secondly, I could cross-examine my data from Abednigo's report, even after my return from the field. I remember Abednigo had given me a report on Chowra religion in sixty pages.

My rapport with the Chowra people had developed so well that when I was finally leaving the island, a little before the monsoon (I do not recollect the exact date), almost the entire population of the island assembled along the beach near the *elpenum* to bid me good bye. I had received enormous items as gift, including nine live chickens, which we consumed during our nine days stay for the return ship at Teressa. Today, whenever I remember of my ceremonious farewell at Chowra, it instills confidence in me and assures me that my anthropological sojourn to Chowra was a great methodological success. Cohen (1978) has very aptly observed:

> Ultimately, the ethnographer's success does not depend upon intellectual mastery (alone), but upon the competence with which he/she can interact socially with the members of the field studied, and on the help provided by informants.

He further observes:

> The latter (i.e. help provided by informants) is of crucial importance, for the anthropologist is a nuisance. We (i.e. the anthropologists) need help not only to negotiate the tortuous social paths of the field, but often also for our very physical well-being. We intrude upon people and require them to bear the burdens of our presence. Our intellectual task is, (therefore), to represent them fairly. Our moral responsibility is to approach them with humility and integrity (*ibid*).

V

Making of Chowra pot

I have discussed, in detail, the entire process of pot and canoe making in Chowra in several of my earlier articles (Sahay 1976, 1979, 1981, 2007). However, I would like to present a brief account of both of them here also.

Chowra pot had two significant purposes in the life of the Nicobarese. First, it was considered the harbinger of fortune and prosperity; therefore, meals were cooked in it on special occasions. Secondly, it was thought that if children were bathed in water boiled in a Chowra pot, they would be immunized against black magic. Therefore, it was held sacred and universally employed for use by all the Nicobarese. People made ceremonial voyages to the island of Chowra to fetch such pots. Chowrians had monopoly on this item of trade. The pots prepared by other islanders were not acceptable to anyone, as such pots were supposed to be devoid of magical powers. The Chowrians also went to different islands to exchange their pots with pigs, coconuts, clothes, tobacco, etc. Those who had no direct contact with Chowra might not go there. However, they exchanged it indirectly with the third parties, who were in direct trade with Chowra, as was the case with the inhabitants of the Southern Zone (see map trade route).

The making of Chowra pot was very fascinating. Chowra people were ignorant of wheel pottery. They made these pots with their hands only. Chowra is one of the smallest islands with thickest density of population; its size being merely 2.8 square kilometers, and the population while I worked there was over 2600 souls. As the pot clay was not available in Chowra, the Chowrians made ceremonial voyages to the islands of Teressa to fetch it. Teressa is about fourteen nautical miles from Chowra. The clay was collected from a particular place, which is held sacred even today. An eye-witness account of fetching clay from Teressa and the making of earthen pots in Chowra is as follows:

> During a calm season, Chowrians unanimously decided to fetch clay from Teressa. A meeting was held in the presence of the chief of the Island, all the fourteen witch doctors, and several heads of the families. A date was fixed for the expedition. On their voyage, they carried everything in odd numbers, i.e. the number of persons, coconuts, fishing hooks, lines, etc. Thus, materially and mentally equipped, they set out for their ceremonial expedition in ecstasy. During such a voyage, the Chowrians joyfully sang songs in praise of their canoes. The rhythm of the songs was maintained in tune with the rise and fall of the sea waves.

When people reached Teressa, they went to a particular spot where the clay was available. And, as soon as their canoes entered the calm and still waters of the shore, everyone stopped singing, as well as talking. This place is held sacred even today. It is believed that if any sound were made there, vegetables would cease to grow in Chowra. Therefore, a perfect silence was maintained there. No one spoke in his local dialect. When necessity arose, they communicated either by signals or by driving their canoes away from the shore. They landed ashore and started collecting clay by their hands. Several heaps of clay were made and a small plant, which was easily available in the vicinity, was plucked and placed on top of each clay-lump. Then the clay was brought aboard the canoe. On completion of the job, they left the place in silence. This was all done in perfect harmony. As soon as they left the place, they again started singing as before and joyfully returned home. When they arrived at Chowra, female members of their families welcomed them on the shore and they jointly carried the clay lumps to their houses. The task of the male members ended here.

A few days later the married women went to *hiva* (a sacred place in Chowra) to collect sand. It is said that the earliest ancestors of this island first landed at *hiva*. They had brought with them coconuts and had planted there. *Hiva* was the earliest village in Chowra. Later this place was abandoned and they moved to *Rahion* (another village). It is said that the oldest coconut tress are found at *hiva*. The women also went in odd numbers with bare breasts. Only a piece of black cloth covered the lower part of the body. They also silently collected sand and returned home. The sand was mixed with clay very carefully so as to preserve its elasticity. Then the rolls of clay were made, and on a wooden platform, the skillful maneuverings of the clay in shaping the pots by the Chowra women could be seen. Since the Chowrians were ignorant of the use of the wheel in pottery, it was a time consuming job. It required an expert hand to make such pots. Every girl in Chowra, from her childhood, started learning the skill of pot making which was considered an essential qualification for her. She learnt it from her mother and other senior members. Thus, when the pots of different sizes were ready, they were first baked in the sun. The pots were then painted by employing the juice of the fibrous mesocarp of tender coconuts. Fibers of unripe coconuts were removed and with its help, beautiful vertical stripes were made on the pots. Thereafter, such pots were baked in fire. They prepared as many fire receptacles as the number of pots. Thus, each pot was baked separately.

Canoe making

The traditional system of inter-island trade, which was earlier carried out by organizing ceremonial voyages, has now completely stopped in Nicobar Islands; however, canoes still occupy an important place in Nicobarese life and culture. It is still an important item of trade there. The canoes differ in their shapes and sizes depending upon the locality. They could be named as the Chowra type, the Nancowrie type and the Kondul type. The Kondul and the Nancowrie types of canoe are more or less similar in shape, but they differ in their sizes. The Nancowrian canoes are relatively smaller.

Broadly speaking, the canoes in the Nicobar Islands are of three sizes viz., the mini, the midi, and the maxi. A mini canoe could accommodate two persons only, one at the front end and other at the rear. It is used only for fishing purpose. No long journey is undertaken on it. Two persons, however, can go miles away from the shore on such a canoe during calm weather for fishing. This size of canoe is found almost with all the Nicobarese families. A midi canoe has two useful purposes. It could accommodate eight to twelve persons, and is used for fishing as well as journey purposes. It generally has two sails. A maxi canoe is mostly for ceremonial voyages and racing competition. It could accommodate 25 to 40 persons and could go a long distance. All the ceremonial as well as trade voyages were earlier made on such canoes. Now they are used for racing purpose only. Canoe race is an important feature of entertainment in the Nicobars. Canoe race is prevalent in all the islands. Only rich persons afford such canoes. It is generally held in Chowra and Car Nicobar that bigger the size and more the number of such canoes, the higher the social status of a person. The hulls of the canoes are carved out of the trunks of big trees. The Chowra type of canoe is very largely used in the islands of Teressa, Bompoka, Car Nicobar, and Chowra of course. The people of Teressa, Bompoka and Car Nicobar do not make their own canoes. They get them from Chowrians in exchange for their articles. In the rest of the islands, canoes are of Nancowrie or of Kondul type.

In fact, canoes are not made in Chowra owing to the deficiency of suitable flora for this purpose. Therefore, Chowrians go to Teressa or any other island of Nancowrie group to make their canoes. Whenever a Chowrian wants to make a canoe, he goes to any of the above-mentioned islands, though never to the islands of the Southern Zone, because of his deep-rooted traditional belief that even a particle of sand from there would lead to the destruction of Chowra. However, it was necessary for the people of the Southern Zone also to keep Chowra pots in their houses, which they received from their family-friends in Nancowrie, Kamorta, Katchall or Trinket. Thus, when a Chowrian goes to other islands, he asks his friend to allot him some work. It is notable that whereas the Chowra people are recognized, on the one hand, as the spiritual leaders of the Nicobarese; on the other hand, they are also recognized for their manual labour and skills in house construction, horticulture, roof thatching and copra making. They do such works for the other islanders, and in return ask for a suitable tree for making canoe. So long as a Chowrian stays in the house of his family-friend, he is treated as guest. His host does not offend or displease his Chowra counterpart for fear of misfortune in consequence.

After the work allotted to him is over, the Chowra man is asked to choose a tree. The selection of the tree depends upon its proximity to the sea. After selection of the tree, he returns home. He then persuades his near relatives and friends to help him make the canoe. His friends and relatives voluntarily help him in this endeavour. First, they clear the jungle and make a path from the seashore to the tree-site. Then the tree is cut down and the branches are removed. A place for temporary settlement is made and many persons are employed on the job. No wage is given to anyone, and together they manage their food as long as they stay in the forest for this purpose. Such is the extent of reciprocity and cooperation among the Chowrians. Thus, when the canoe is half-ready, both of its ends are horizontally stretched in mild fire; an outrigger is made and the canoe is brought near the seashore. Then it is towed to Chowra with the help of another canoe.

The finishing work to make the canoe sharp and beautiful is done in Chowra. When the canoe is completely ready, a date is fixed in consultation with the witchdoctor for its inaugural launching. On the inaugural day, the canoe worship is done with sacrifice of a pig; and this is followed by a canoe-race in the evening. Earlier, Chowra people made canoes for their own use as well as for trade. Car Nicobar was the main market for Chowra canoes. The people of Teressa and Bompoka asked their Chowra counterparts to make canoes for them, as and when these were required.

Inter-island trade and exchange and ceremonial voyages

The importance of trade to subsistence level economies is seldom realized. Exchange of goods and services among them is certainly limited in extent. Nevertheless, trade (i.e. a regular series of acts of exchange) is a distinct feature in all such economies, even among the poorest, who live by hunting and collecting forest products. The principles of reciprocal transfer of goods and services, and their tradition of give and take, in fact, seem to be deep rooted in human nature.

In my articles (of 1976, 1979, 1981, 2007), I have also discussed the traditional system of inter-island trade in Nicobar archipelago. Trade in Nicobar Islands had two aspects, first, inter-island trade, i.e. with the people of other islands, and secondly, intra-island trade, i.e. between the members of the same island. The former is of significant interest to anthropologists. The traditional system of inter-island trade in the Nicobar Islands has unfortunately disappeared from the waters of the archipelago today; however, it was a well-established institution of trade till the mid-1970s, when I worked there. Now it has assumed altogether a new form. Earlier, it noticeably resembled the *kula* of the Trobrianders, sans the use of *soulava* and *mawali*. With reference to the ceremonial voyage and traditional system of inter-island trade and exchange in the Nicobar archipelago, in a recent book, entitled, *In the Sea of Influence: A World System Perspective on the Nicobar Islands*, Simron Jit Singh (2003:144) writes,

> The first lucid, field based account comes from the Indian anthropologist, Vijoy S Sahay (1976, 1979), apparently the last witness to the system of inter-island trade as it existed then.

Unlike the system of weekly markets in rural and tribal India, from the beginning, there has been a complete absence of open-market-system in Nicobars. However, every island had either an indigenous industry, or possessed an indigenous item of trade. The people of Car Nicobar made baskets and mats, the Chowrians made pots and canoes, the Nancowrians also made mats and baskets, and the people of Kondul made canoes and collected honey from the forests in Great Nicobar. We find that the people of Teressa, Bompoka, Great Nicobar, Little Nicobar and Pulomilo did not have any indigenous industry. It is obviously because these islands are sparsely populated in comparison to their size and the natural abundance of food there; this perhaps rendered the inhabitants of such islands inactive, indolent and averse to hard work. One of my observations about these islands has been that smaller the island the more industrious its people, and bigger the island the lazier its people.

In fact, in small islands the pressure on land is very high, as is the case with Chowra. Density of population in Chowra is about 600 persons per square kilometer. Naturally, the foodstuff is not sufficient; therefore, the adult male members of the island have to go necessarily to their family-friends in other islands. They work in the gardens of their friends, thatch the roofs of their houses; and in return, receive gifts of coconut, yams, banana, pandanus, cloth, and other items of use. If a Chowrian does not do so, he and his family might have to starve. Therefore, even during a rough weather and turbulent sea, he ventures to make a voyage in his canoe. This has made them more industrious than the other islanders; and gradually this has also given rise to the notion that the Chowrians are wizards; and they can change the direction of the wind and the waves during their voyage.

We have earlier mentioned that there is no open-market system in Nicobar Islands. In such a situation, one could not just go to another island to exchange his goods arbitrarily. It took long hours and quite an effort to reach other islands. Therefore, people developed family-friendship bonds with other islanders. Such family-friendship bonds were maintained through generations. It has been said about the Trobrianders, "Once in Kula always in Kula" (Malinowski 1922:83). In the same tune, it could be said about the Nicobarese, "Once in family-friendship-bond, always in such bond." When a Chowrian made a voyage to another island, he went to the house of his family-friend only. He stayed with him for a couple of days and exchanged his articles with the articles of his need. Both treated each other as guests and hosts, and not as buyers and sellers. This generated a strong 'we-feeling' among them. The other islanders made reciprocal visits to Chowra, according to necessity. Thus, the inter-island trade relationship had developed among the Nicobarese since times immemorial. A man who did not have any family-friend in a certain island or a village would not go there, nor would he be able to exchange goods with any one else; he might have to starve there. Therefore, people of these islands wished to develop and strengthen such family-friendship bonds with each other to flourish their trade and maintain solidarity of the Nicobarese society.

Let us now examine the trade route (see map). If we start from the southern end, we find that people of these islands were in direct trade with Nancowrians. The people of Kondul are the most industrious in this zone. It is to be noted that the island of Kondul is even smaller in size than the island of Chowra. They made maxi canoes and collected honey from the jungles of Great and Little Nicobar, which they exchanged with other islanders for pigs, cloth, tobacco and sometimes money.

They were the sole manufacturers and distributors of maxi canoes in this region. They brought their canoes, honey, etc., to their family-friends in the Nancowrie group of islands. From the Nancowrians they received Chowra pots, mats, baskets, etc. Thus, the Nancowrians acted as mediators between the people of Southern Zone, and those living north of Nancowrie group of islands, viz. the islands of Chowra, Teressa and Bompoka, except the island of Car Nicobar. Neither the Nancowrians nor the Car Nicobarese directly traded with each other, though the Nancowrians made ceremonial voyages to the islands of Southern Zone, and carried Chowra pots and other articles of trade for exchange with the people of the south.

The Chowrians came to Nancowrie group of islands to work as labourers, as also for trade and exchange. They carried pots with them. In return they received mats, baskets, cloth, pigs, coconuts, tobacco, sometimes a tree for making a canoe, and money. Thus, both the Nancowrians and the Chowrians had developed family-friendship bonds from very early times; and they maintained, strengthened, and developed such bonds necessarily with each other through reciprocal visits. Some rich Nancowrians had coconut plantations in Teressa. Therefore, they made frequent visits to Teressa and Bompoka; and carried gifts for their friends and relations there. In return they received tobacco as gift from their counterparts in these islands.

The Chowrians had most varied and extended trade-relationships with others. On the one hand, they directly traded with the Nancowrians, and on the other, they also traded with the people of Teressa, Bompoka and Car Nicobar. They supplied Chowra pots to all these islanders and in return, they received pigs, coconuts, cloth, money, etc. The Chowrians made most elaborate and ceremonial expeditions for the purpose of trade to the island of Car Nicobar, situated 40 nautical miles north. The Chowrians before going to Car Nicobar made a considerable number of pots. A date was fixed by the chief of the island in consultation with the witch doctors. The date and time of departure depended on the favourable hours of tide and current in the sea. The departure was preceded by canoe-worship. Canoe-worship was imperative on such expeditions. A chicken or a pig was sacrificed on such occasions and the canoe was tastefully decorated with tender leaves of coconut. Several tender coconuts were hung on the canoe and the inner soft edible part of the coconut was squeezed and mixed with pig's or chicken's blood for pasting on different parts of the canoe.

The Chowrians had a maximum number of family-friends in different villages of Car Nicobar. During their voyage to Car Nicobar, every Chowrian carried three pots, because the canoe could accommodate 12 to 15 persons only with all the items of trade and exchange at a time. Thus, a Chowrian on each visit handed over all the three pots to only one of his family-friends in Car Nicobar. He also carried with him *talua*—a sort of cake prepared from pandamus, banana and coconut—carefully wrapped in areca nut leaves. He distributed these cakes not only to the one receiving his pots, but also to all his family-friends there. In return he received a number of articles such as cloth, tobacco and other utensils from each one of them; but the one who received his pots, gave him three pigs, one pig for each pot. When a Chowrian supplied a canoe to his family-friend in Car Nicobar, his demand was sometimes very high, which often included heavy amount in cash. This practice of cash was not in vogue before. In early times, coconuts were the recognized currency of exchange in the Nicobars. The Chowrians made canoes on order only. Sometimes it took a year or so for a Chowrian to supply a canoe to his family-friend in Car Nicobar, depending upon the availability of the raw material.

When the Car Nicobarese ceremonially visited Chowra to meet their counterparts, the latter were under obligation to supply pots to all their visitors. The Car Nicobarese brought for their family-friends in Chowra, pigs, cloths, and different types of utensils for exchange. In Chowra, the visitors were put up in the *elpenam* (public houses), and treated as honourable guests. For a young Car Nicobarese boy, the first visit to Chowra on a canoe was treated as an initiation ceremony. The tradition had it that a man in Car Nicobar attained manhood only after he had successfully made, at least, one such expedition to Chowra. Another interesting feature of the voyage between Car Nicobar and Chowra was that they made stopover for a few hours in the small island of Battimalve, located midway between the two islands. Battimalve is an uninhabited island abounding in luxuriant growth of coconuts. The voyagers necessarily stopped over there and waited for the favourable wind and current.

Dialect of an uninhabited island

The above sub-title appears to be enigmatic and paradoxical. How could there be any dialect of an island, where no one lives? Nor any one has ever lived there. However, in case of Nicobars it is true. There are altogether seven uninhabited islands in the Nicobar group. It is surprising that the island of Tillanchong, though uninhabited, has its own dialect, which is different from the dialects of the neighbouring islands. Tillanchong comprises an area of 15 square kilometers; and is situated along the eastern flank of the archipelago. The island abounds in coconut, pandanus, tapioca, yams, and many other edible roots and fruits. It is also famous for python and a variety of birds, including an endangered species, the megapode.

Six families of the central group of Nicobar Islands, consisting of Nancowrie, Kamorta, Trinket and Katchall considered the fauna and the flora of Tillanchong as their property, since times immemorial. Each year, one family is entitled to make a voyage to Tillanchong and that too once only. Thus, the turn of any family to visit the island comes once in six years. During one's turn the family members, relatives, and friends ceremonially organize a voyage. They carry everything in odd numbers, such as the number of persons, canoes, implements, etc. Wearing a black loincloth is necessary. Once they approach the island, for fear of superstition, they maintain absolute silence, as long as they stay there. To speak in one's own dialect is strictly tabooed, lest the spirits/devils in Tillanchong become angry and cause death and disease in their native island. When necessity arises, either they communicate in signals, or a dialect specially invented for use in Tillanchong. Their general belief is that any one, even if accidentally, landing in Tillanchong, would forget his native dialect, and spontaneously speak in Tillanchong dialect.

During my second visit in 1975, I spent over three months in Nancowrie group of islands, with base camp at Enunga village in Nancowrie. Gabriel Kulilong was one of my key informants. With Kuli, as he was popularly called there, I had collected a number of ancient songs that were sung during *kinrauk*, the reburial festival. Due to spread of Christianity such songs were fast disappearing, rather getting extinct. During the course of recording such songs, I first came to know of the Tillanchong dialect. There were a number of songs relating to Tillanchong. Then I could not collect the vocabulary of Tillanchong dialect. However, during my visit in 2002, I spent over a week's time in Nancowrie. Gabriel Kulilong had already died in 1977. I went to his grave and observed two-minutes' silence there. After paying homage to the departed soul, I began to search for someone who could tell me about this unknown and secret dialect. At last, I came across Mark Paul and Isigal Joel. They recognized me. Though Mark Paul helped me a lot in drawing several genealogies and collecting other information, he was not very conversant in Tillangchong dialect; and Isigal Joel remained sick and bedridden as long as I stayed in Nancowrie. Thus, I could collect only limited vocabulary of this strange dialect. This is one area of anthropological research in the Nicobar archipelago that requires immediate attention, as it is a question of now or never. If it is not done today, it might be too late to do it tomorrow. The posterity will remain incognizant and unenlightened of this unknown dialect, which is the product of the creative mental faculty of an indigenous population.

VI

Epistemological issues

I am aware that I have presented the account of Chowra life and culture in the above paragraphs in an unconventional way. To many, it may appear as 'subjective' and 'self-reflective'.

> Ethnography has traditionally been written in a way as if the anthropologist was a neutral, omniscient observer (McGee and Warms 1996: 481).
>
> Throughout the history of our discipline, anthropologists have claimed to be authorities on other cultures. They have fortified this claim by emphasizing upon the mystique of fieldwork... (*Ibid*: 480).

However, very little account of the process of fieldwork in earlier ethnographic accounts was to be found.

> One of the more insidious writing conventions is that of the omniscient narrator, the authoritative third-person observer who replaces the fallible first-person (*ibid*: 481).

As a result, instead of writing "I saw in Nicobar my informants doing such and such thing", which is the result of direct observation, many ethnographies would contain statements like "the Nicobarese do such and such things", as if, the use of omniscient narrator heightens the sense of scientific objectivity. But today it is questioned whether an anthropologist could really be 'objective'? Post-modernists claim that because the collection of data is 'subjective', it is not possible to analyze the data 'objectively' (Taylor 1979).

> The conduct of fieldwork is also a crucial issue because traditionally most ethnographies have contained very little information on the actual process of research (McGee and Warms 1996: 480).

However, today, this process is considered very crucial in the creation of ethnographic texts. In India, Srinivas was perhaps the first to describe the actual process of fieldwork and research in *The Remembered Village* (1978). I wrote my thesis in a true modernistic and conventional style of anthropology. Modernism, applied to anthropology, broadly refers to the years between the 1920s and the mid-1970s (Manganaro 1990). And, I conducted fieldwork in the mid-1970s. In my thesis, I remained completely detached, assuming the position of scientific neutrality and rationalism. I considered my first approach to the land and the people, my interaction with them, my stay in Chowra, my participation with them on their ceremonial voyages, on their fishing expeditions, as acts of my personal adventure. Therefore, I did not mention a single line about how I reached Chowra. How the witchdoctors were opposed to my presence? How did I tackle them? How I once fell ill, and was looked after by the same witchdoctors, who were earlier opposed to my presence in the island? How did I travel with them on their primitive type of canoes several times from Chowra to Teressa and back? How I participated with them in their fishing expeditions, and once entered even the shark-infested area.

Two factors significantly changed the very concept of ethnography that I earlier held. First, in *The Remembered Village* (1978) I discovered that Srinivas had exquisitely described his approach to the field and his interaction with the people in general and his informants in particular. Then, I began to think about the anthropological significance of my approach to the field, and my interaction with the people there. Had I read *The Remembered Village* prior to the completion of my thesis, probably the presentation of my data in my thesis would have been different.

Secondly, in 2002, when I revisited the islands after a gap of twenty-seven years, I was quite bewildered to witness the changes that had occurred there. Hardly one or two of my earlier informants were alive; and those alive, were in their seventies or eighties. For a moment, it appeared to me that I knew nothing about the Nicobars. I began to question myself. What was the use of writing ethnography? Was it only to leave the records of the life and culture of a people for the posterity? Even if it was so, was it a final record? Was not an ethnographic report merely an instant history? Would any one believe what I had witnessed in Chowra over two and a half decades earlier? If I wrote the account of life and culture there, would they not consider it a reconstruction? Whereas I was a living witness to the changes that had taken place during this gap, it appeared to me that writing ethnography was a really difficult task, if not impossible. In addition, could an anthropologist ever claim that he had been able to write a complete ethnography?

I was so disgusted and frustrated then that I began to curse myself that why on earth did I come here at all, leaving a peaceful and scheduled academic life in Allahabad. However, as I began to re-interact with people, new informants came forward to help me. I met some of my old informants too. And, I gradually began to realize that writing ethnography was a process of learning. The ability to learn differed from one individual to another; likewise, ability to write ethnography also differed from one anthropologist to another. Writing ethnography is a long process, rather a life long process. The examples were that of Trobriand Islanders by Malinowski, and Kwakiutls by Franz Boas.

My 2002 visit to the Nicobar Islands made me realize more than ever before that the success of an anthropologist did not merely depend upon the amount of data that he brought from the field, but it also depended upon the amount of help and cooperation that he received from his informants and the people whom he studied. After all, as long as an anthropologist stays in the field for data collection, despite being an undeniable intruder, the people whom he studies must accept him as a 'social person' at least, as long as he stays there. Moreover, here lies the skill of an ethnographer. This realization completely changed my conception about ethnography; and thus, I resolved to include my personal account in the account of the Nicobarese. I was convinced that anthropologically, it was of course significant to describe what I knew of the Nicobarese; nevertheless, it was equally significant to explain how I came to know of them.

I do not consider myself to be a protagonist of postmodernism in anthropology. The postmodernists claim that anthropology is not a science. I do not agree with this claim of the postmodernists; however, as stated in the beginning of this paper, their challenge has led anthropologists to examine the very basis of their discipline. Some of the issues that they have raised deserve discussion here, such as:

(i) Should an anthropologist include his personal experiences in the account of 'other's culture'?

(ii) Can an anthropologist/ethnographer ever claim to be authentic?

(iii) Whether the *reconstruction* of a culture is justified?

Let us discuss the above issues, one by one.

With regard to the first issue, I believe an anthropologist *must* include his personal account in the account of other's culture. If he does not include it, then for a century the misconception about a culture may continue in anthropology. His version will be transmitted to the next generation as a prophecy, and he will be remembered as a prophet. This has precisely happened with the Birhors, as described by Roy (1925). The Birhors are still understood and described by most anthropologists as gatherers and hunters. In fact, they are so in the annals of anthropological literature. Today, the carrying capacity of the forests in Jharkhand and the adjoining states has so unsparingly depleted that hardly a band of Birhor could subsist and survive on gathering and hunting economy. The personal account of an anthropologist may also throw light on the cultural dynamics of a people. It can very well explain the extent and process of cultural change among the group. Today, unprecedented changes have taken place in the Nicobars. The motorboats are plying in the whole of the archipelago so frequently that those ceremonial voyages for inter-island trade and exchange have completely stopped. People now dare not make such voyages on primitive types of canoe for fear of their lives. Articles of daily use, including all the domestic utensils, are available even in the most remote islands; as a result, Chowra pot has lost all its importance, and has become obsolete. Personal account of my journey and stay in Chowra would only demonstrate the momentum and the factors of culture change that have taken place in the archipelago during the last three decades.

With regard to the second issue that whether an anthropologist/ethnographer can claim to be authentic, I think he must not do so. After all, I believe that anthropologists can never be unbiased observers of all that goes on in a culture. As a field worker, he necessarily collects data at a specific place and at a specific time. As a result, he sees some things and not others. Besides the above, the particular circumstances in the field, the political context in which the events occur, the investigator's preferences and predilections, and the people/informants whom an anthropologist meets by chance or by design, all these very critically condition the very understanding of the society and culture one studies. Although, in order to defend anthropology as an empirical science many scholars accept that some aspects of ethnographic data collection are 'subjective', they also consider that it is not impossible to do 'objective' anthropology. My opinion is that as far as possible, an anthropologist must remain objective while collecting data in the field, as also while interpreting it. And, this can be very safely done by remaining faithful to 'cultural relativism' while collecting and interpreting data. However, he should leave the authenticity to be decided by the readers themselves.

Lastly, whether the reconstruction of a culture is justified? Today, Chowra is a changed island from what it was three decades earlier. However, the way I have attempted to describe Chowra life and culture in this brief article, may appear to some, as if, I have attempted to reconstruct it. However, it is not like that. After all, what does an anthropologist do? According to Linton (1936), every anthropologist *constructs* a culture. There is ideal culture, real culture, and the culture construct. Every anthropologist constructs a culture the way he perceives and conceives it in his mind. That is a good reason that anthropologists differ in their interpretations of the same culture.

However, a deliberate attempt to reconstruct a culture must not be encouraged in anthropology, as was perhaps done by Franz Boas in the 1930s. The American government had banned the Potlatch of the Kwakiutls in the 1920s, because of extravaganza, and the random destruction of property involved in it. In order to leave the accounts of Potlatch for the posterity, Boas persuaded some Kwakiutl chiefs to organize and stage the drama of a Potlatch, and recorded it in a film. Such construction, or for that matter reconstruction of cultural events, cannot be regarded as natural, and therefore, an anthropologist must refrain from doing so.

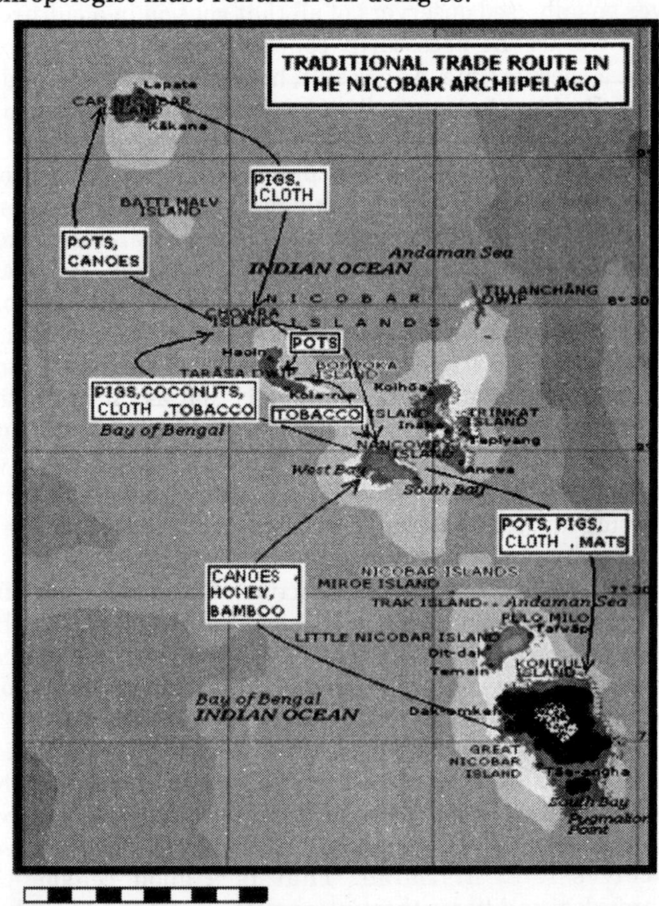

REFERENCES

Cohen, A. P.

1978 'Ethnographic method in the real community', *Socilogica Ruralis*, 18 (1), 1-22. Also in R. F. Ellen (ed.) (1984), *Ethnographic Researches: A Guide to General Conduct*. London: Academic Press.

Linton, Ralph

1936 *The Study of Man*. New York: Appleton.

Malinowski, B.

1983 *Argonauts of the Western Pacific*. New York: Routledge & Kegan Paul.

(1922)

Mangararo, Marc (ed.)

1990 *Modernist Anthropology: From Fieldwork to Text*. Princeton, N J: Princeton University Press.

McGee, R. Jon and Richard L. Warms

1996 *Anthropological Theory*. California: Mayfield Publishing Company.

Myrdal, Gunnar

1968 *Asian Drama: An Inquiry into the Poverty of Nations*. Volume I. New York: Pantheon.

Roy, S. C.

1925 *The Birhor: A Little Known Jungle Tribe of Chotanagpur*. Ranchi: Man in India Office.

Sahay, Vijoy S.

1976 'Traditional system of inter-island trade in the Nicobar Archipelago', *Journal of Social Research* XIX: 2.

1979 'A note on the system of exchange in the Nicobar Archipelago', *The Eastern Anthropologist* XXXII: II.

1981 'The Nicobarese: A study of nature-man-spirit complex'. In L.P. Vidyarthi, R. S. Mann, and Vijoy S. Sahay (eds.), *Nature-Man-Spirit-Complex of Tribal India*. Delhi: Concept Publishing Company.

2007 'Loss of traditional knowledge in the Nicobar Archipelago'. In K. K. Mishra and K. K. Basa (eds.), *Traditional Knowledge in Contemporary Societies*. Delhi: Pratibha Prakashan.

Singh, Simran Jit

2003 *In the Sea of Influence: A World System Perspective on Nicobar Islands*. Lund: University of Lund.

Srinivas, M. N.

1978 (1976) *The Remembered Village*. New Delhi: Oxford University Press.

Taylor, Charles

1979 'Interpretation and the sciences of man'. In Paul Rabinow and W. M. Sullivan (eds.), *Interpretative Social Science: A Reader*. Berkeley: University of California.

21

What is not Anthropology?

BINOD C. AGRAWAL

In over a century of field based anthropological researches and later teaching have five high growth points. These dates are independent of European and American anthropological traditions though often influenced by intellectual fervour of both continents. There could be other milestones in Indian anthropology that I might have missed. These are:

(a) Inclusion of "Caste and Tribes" ethnographic description in 1881 Census of India leading to publication of *People of India* by *Herbert Risley* (1915).

(b) Starting of anthropology teaching at Calcutta University (1920), publications of anthropological journal – *Man in India* (1921) and world's first *Cultural Anthropology* text book (1929).

(c) Setting up of Department of Anthropology by Government of India (1945), later renamed as the Anthropological Survey of India.

(d) Setting up of Ethnographic and Folk Culture Society and starting of publication of *The Eastern Anthropologist* (1947).

(e) Holding of Tenth International Congress of Anthropological and Ethnological Sciences at New Delhi and in a dozen other cities (1978).

These five high points have had profound influence on the perception and performance of the emerging "colonial discipline" of anthropology until 1947 followed by independent India's anthropology that some of us have witnessed after 1947. The first three dates are reminder of "colonial anthropology" whereas the last two are symbols of strength and eclectic progress of Indian anthropology. The event of International Anthropological and Ethnological Congress in India highlighted the growing recognition of Indian anthropology.

Passage of Social to Social-Cultural Anthropology

The second significant point relates to shift in the use of "Social Anthropology" on the pattern of British social anthropology to social-cultural anthropology under the influence of American anthropology without qualitative changes in the content and approach in teaching and research of anthropology.

For the first time, Sarana and Sinha (1976), while reviewing Indian social anthropology, coined hyphenated term "Social-Cultural" as prefix to anthropology. Both had American Ph.D. after having M.A. degree in Social Anthropology from Lucknow University. Since social-cultural anthropology has been accepted by anthropologists, the Indian Council of Social Sciences Research continued to review "Sociology and Social Anthropology" without serious efforts to recognize the new developments in anthropology. I have indicated this point to emphasize continual lack of understanding and integration of British social anthropology and American cultural anthropology in spite of several serious intellectual discourses by a number of Indian anthropologists, the latest being in the 2007 issue of *The Eastern Anthropologist.*

In retrospection, whether Indian anthropologists have benefited from social and cultural anthropology in improving the understanding of the Indian civilization or society is yet to be realized. I fumble in answering the question, as I do have fragmented and partial understanding of multilingual, multi-religious, cases and tribes of the Indian civilization.

Little convergence

Teaching of anthropology remained largely devoid of Indian ethnographies carried out by Indian anthropologists. I read T. N. Madan (1965) and K. S. Mathur (1964), excellent studies in the United States during 1964-66, while in India I read Evans-Pritchard (1940) and Mayer (1960) during 1961-63. Incidentally, Mathur and Mayer both had conducted their village studies in

Central India as a part of their Ph.D. thesis (Mathur from Australia and Mayer from U. K.).

A bitter truth is that social or cultural or social-cultural anthropologists remained under the hegemony of British or American anthropology in spite of over hundred years of first hand field work, knowledge and experience of the village, caste, tribe, religion and topics they had chosen to study. In this context, it would be important to point out that intensive extended field work often has been absent in the research studies of the Indian anthropologists as compared to non-Indian anthropologists who carried out field work in India. Most of the field work was carried out by the Indian anthropologists as if the anthropologists were "non-Indian" or "outsiders". Very few could carry out field work as one being "native" who was studying his/her own caste, religion or region.

In spite of this these glaring theoretical and some time methodological problems, anthropological field research flourished and expanded in the country though uneven and highly "personality focused" or "individual centred" programmes under the leadership of a few eminent anthropologists. Depending upon the individual interest, opportunity and research fundings, a range of studies were carried out spanning rural, urban, industrial, tribal, women, children and weaker sections in a number of geographical regions covering national spectrum. What was anthropology then could not be deciphered.

Anthropological research

Today, in India, multiple research agencies like Anthropological Survey of India, State Tribal Research Institutes, Ministry of Tribal Affairs, university departments, privately and government funded social science research institutes, development departments to mention a few are all involved in anthropological researches, training and teaching. These institutions have diluted both theoretical framework and methodological rigour of fieldwork. The fashion of "in-depth studies", focus group discussions" and "qualitative research" all have replaced the serious intensive field work.

I have often fumbled and felt sad in front of the so-called qualitative researchers, who would like to have quick-fix answers to their problems whether in "market research" or "media research" or problem solving studies. I must confess, I do not know, what kind of anthropological research, I am asked to carry out? I often feel everything that relates to human beings, if studied, is anthropology. At the same time, I question myself: What is not anthropology?

Social and Cultural Anthropology: The Indian brand

Anthropologists due to lack of opportunities within anthropology continue to migrate into a variety of applied fields like health, family planning, media, communication, design, architecture, planning, rural development, management, information technology to mention a few. Each of these anthropologists has tried to expand the scope of anthropology.

For example, a dozen anthropologists participated in anthropological field work spanning eighteen months period in seven linguistic regions of India during 1974-1976. Since these studies involved evaluation of satellite television effects on rural cultures in 1976, Agrawal coined the term "Communication Anthropology" taking clues from Majumdar's anthropological study of caste and communication (1958 and 1958a). In order to support my view, I took shelter from the writings of Sapir (1936). Now, I find that a number of anthropology departments are teaching courses like "anthropology of communication" and "communication and anthropology". I now wonder "what is not anthropology", based on my personal experiences.

Similarly, a dozen anthropologists carried out anthropological field study of one year CLASS (Computer Literacy in School Studies) project in 1984-85. The computers were installed in urban school to understand adoptive behaviour and impact of computer literacy on the students in the school. Since then anthropologists have been carrying out a number of studies in the country during the last few years. The findings of these studies have influenced the educational policy and helped policy formulations of computer education.

I have been asking myself: What is not anthropology after spending over two decades in carrying out a series of research studies related to India's space programme. I have been able to use four major anthropological premises (namely, "holistic view", "process analysis", "emic approach" and "participant observation") in these evaluative studies of the impact of satellite television, computer and other technologies on the rural viewers, students and urban population of India (Agrawal 1978, 1981 and 1986).

Teaching of Social and Cultural Anthropology–then and now

Over forty years ago, in 1966, I got an opportunity to teach an introductory anthropology course to undergraduate students in an American university. I prescribed the then available text book (Sol Tax 1964) and supplemented it with a few other reading materials. After forty three years, in 2002, I again taught a course on introductory cultural anthropology which I have been teaching for three years since then as "summer course" in an American college. This time I have been using a text book by Kottak (2008).

During these forty three years, the anthropology that I studied and taught during my formative years, seemed to have changed so much that often I feel I am studying and teaching a new discipline. At the same time, when I think of some of the fundamental premises of anthropology I feel comfortable and at peace since these continue to be unchanged in social and cultural anthropology.

At this juncture, it would suffice to say that both social and cultural anthropology share common fundamentals to a large extent about the scope and methods of the subject matter. I have do doubt that social and cultural anthropology evolved two distinct approaches to understand humankind to fulfil different historical, administrative and intellectual needs in their respective countries. Since Indian anthropologists came in contact with these two countries, leaving a large body of anthropological knowledge of other European and Asian countries and followed these two traditions, exception being Karve (1961 and 1953) who had her education in Germany.

Since I left the American university department of anthropology about four decades ago, I have been involved in teaching anthropology in various institutions of professional and technical education. I have been deeply involved in the teaching and research schools of agriculture, architecture, planning, design and interior design. In all these schools, I have been offering courses of cultural anthropology and have guided diploma and degree theses.

The need to offer such courses emerged from the realization that art, design and architecture are material manifestations of cultures shaped by production technology and available raw material in a given environment. Architects and designers have been using anthropological theories and methods in their research over several decades.

My first course outlined for architecture students was titled "Architectural Anthropology". Similar courses are being independently offered in Europe and the United States of America. These courses are seriously taken by the students of architecture and design schools. Rappaport (1969) provided a cultural explanation for explaining the variation in house types. Urban designers followed anthropological route to design growing needs of urban spaces in Asia and Africa. The closest explanation found in the anthropological literature is objectification of culture in artefacts and architecture which was thought to be the result of human behaviour and material. "That is, material artefacts were the material residue of culture, but not culture itself' (Taylor 1948: 100).

Since Majumdar's publication of *A Tribe in Transition* (1937) having several editions with a new tile (Majumdar 1950), no text book of Social Anthropology until Majumdar and Madan (1961) and collection of essays in the memory of D. N. Majumdar entitled *Indian Anthropology* were published in 1962 (See Madan and Sarana 1962).

Madan and Sarana (1962) made a pioneering attempt to bring together "Prehistoric Archaeology", "Physical Anthropology" and "Social-cultural Anthropology". In this book, the editors for the first time used the term "social-cultural" anthropology which Sarana has been using in his writings since then (Sarana and Sinha 1976).

A number of text books in anthropology specially social and cultural anthropology have been published in Indian languages which are literally translations of some of the American text books. Recently, I reviewed a Gujarati text book in cultural anthropology which was trans-literation of *Man and His Works* by Herskovits (1952). Similarly, a whole lot of anthropology books specially prepared for competitive examination are available. These books are collections of papers or chapters from various books. These books are prepared by Indian anthropologists and several unknown ghost authors with or without the acknowledgement of original authors. Several Indian anthropologists have been quite energetic and enthusiastic in preparing such books along with other social scientists. Without doubt these books are highly focused, examination oriented and edited as per the prescribed syllabi of national and provincial civil service examinations.

The content analysis of anthropology syllabi of selected universities support my observations vividly. However, these syllabi continue to reflect the unresolved issue of social or cultural or social-cultural anthropology. For example, Lucknow and Hyderabad Universities continue to teach social anthropology and not cultural anthropology though in outline of the course cultural anthropology is mentioned. Other universities call it social anthropology and continue to follow what was designed half a century ago at Lucknow University, Department of Anthropology. Since many professors were trained at Lucknow, they have continued to teach Social Anthropology and carried out field work with the help of *Notes and Queries*.

Since Majumdar's students went to several continents for higher studies in anthropology, they brought back with them both social and cultural anthropology. Social and cultural anthropology today as it stands is a unique combination of British and American academic thought processes. A critical examination of these unique combinations has been discussed in an article, "Culture" in *Wikipedia,* the free encyclopaedia (*http://en.wikipedia.org/wiki/Culture*).

On the other hand the text book, *Cultural Anthropology* (Kottak 2008), which I used reflected the Cultural Anthropology tradition of United States of America. This book takes the American perspective of anthropology and illustrates American cultural experiences and demonstrates cultural diversity both from biological and social perspectives. The topics discussed in the book based on the historical experiences of the Americans like "ethnicity and race", "language and communication" and "gender", "modern world system", "colonialism and development" and "cultural exchange and survival" have also been described and elaborated.

Cultural Anthropology in America since the very beginning included anthropological linguistics as a part of cultural anthropology. A full length chapter is devoted to "language and communication" which is generally ignored in India (Misra 2007). Cultural anthropology in American universities is context specific and is ingrained in the American way of life, whether it is marriage, family or religion.

On the other hand social and cultural anthropology in India is largely devoid of context specificity and Indian perspective. The Indian anthropology can be contextualized by prescribing *The Nuer* (Evans-Pritchard, 1940) along with *The Dhurwa of Bastar* (Thusu 1968).

This discussion clearly indicates anthropology continues to evolve and redefine its scope. Hence, it is difficult to indicate "What is not Anthropology". But certainly being an experiential and reflective knowledge, it has to respond to the contemporary needs in context specific situations. One example of "What is not Anthropology" was recently discussed by Dunleavy who in consultation with an anthropologist Anne Chambers felt that photo-journalism is not anthropology as it is not reflective and photo-journalists do not take time "to understand what the act of producing pictures would mean for them as well as for their subjects prior to the act of making images" (Dunleavy 2007).

I continue to wonder 'What is not Anthropology?'

REFERENCES

Agrawal, Binod C

1974 *SITE – Madhya Pradesh (Chattisgarh) Audience Profile*. Ahmedabad: Space Applications Centre – ISRO.

1978 *Television Comes to Village: An Evalaution of SITE*. Bangalore: Indian Space Research Organization.

2004 *Ethnography of Communication*. Shillong: North-Eastern Hill University.

2008 'Culture, communication and development: An Indian perspective'. In M. S. Gore (ed.), *Third Survey in Sociology and Social Anthropology*. New Delhi: Indian Council of Social Science Research and MANAK Publications Ltd.

Bose, N. K.

1929 *Cultural Anthropology*. Calcutta: Arya Sahitya Bhawan.

Dunleavy, Dennis

2007 'Photojournalism in not Anthropology'. *http://ddunleavy.typepad.com/the_big_picture/2007/10/photojournalism.html.*

Evans-Pritchard, E. E.

1940 *The Nuer: A Description of the Modes of Livehood and Political Institutions of Nilotic People.* Oxford: Clarendon Press.

Herskvoits, Mclvile J.

1952 *Man His Works – The Science of Cultural Anthropology.* New York: Alfred A Knoff.

Karve, Irawati

1953 *Kinship Organization in India.* Bombay: Asia Publishing House. (Second edition 1965)

1961 *Hindu Society–An Interpretation.* Poona: Deccan College.

Kottak, Conrad Phillip

2008 *Cultural Anthropology.* Boston: McGraw Hill (12th edition).

Madan, T. N.

1965 *Kinship and Family: A Study of the Pandits of Rural Kashmir.* Bombay: Asia Publishing House.

Madan, T. N. and Gopala Sarana (eds.)

1962 *Indian Anthropology. Essays in the Memory of D. N. Majumdar.* Bombay: Asia Publishing House.

Majumdar, D. N.

1937 *A Tribe in Transition: A Study in Culture Pattern.* Calcutta and London; Longmans, Green & Co.

1950 *The Affairs of a Tribe: A Study of Tribal Dynamics.* Lucknow: Universal Publication Ltd.

1958 *Caste and Communication in an Indian Village.* Bombay: Asia Publishing House.

1958a Rural Life and communication', *The Eastern Anthropologist.* 11: 175-188.

1960 *Social Contours of an Industrial City.* Bombay: Asia Publishing House (assisted by N. Subba Reddy and S. Bahadur).

Majumdar, D. N. and T. N. Madan

1961 *An Introduction to Social Anthropology.* Bombay: Asia Publishing House (4th Edition).

Mathur, K. S.

1964 *Caste and Ritual in a Malwa Village*. Bombay: Asia Publishing House.

Mayer, Adrian C.

1960 *Caste and Kinship in Central India*. London: Rotledge & Kegan Paul.

Misra, Kamal K.

2007 'The passions and perils of anthropological linguistics in India: Some personal observations', *The Eastern Anthropologist*. 60 (3-4): 431-453.

Rapoport, Amos

1969 *House Form and Culture*. Milwauku: University of Wisconsin.

Risley, Herbert H

1915 *The People of India*. London: W Thackerco. (Second edition).

Sarana, Gopala

2007 'Indian social-cultural anthropology: A brief review'. *The Eastern Anthropologist*. 60 (3-4): 307-325.

Sarana, Gopala and Dharni P. Sinha

1976 'Status of social-cultural anthropology in India'. *Annual Review of Anthropology*. 5: 209-225.

Taylor, Walter

1948 *A Study of Archeology*. Memoir 69 American Anthropological Association, reprinted, Carbondale IC: Southern Illinois University Press.

Thusu, K. N.

1968 *The Dhurwa of Bastar*. Calcutta: Anthropological Survey of India.

Wikipedia.

2009 'Culture'. *http: / / en.wikipedia.org / wiki / Culture.*

22

The Impact of Anthropology[1]

VINAY KUMAR SRIVASTAVA

One of the oft-repeated statements about the impact of education on people is that it enlarges their vision and changes their view of life. If this hypothesis has some merit, then each subject the student studies in his school or college should exercise its impact on his thinking, often contesting the information he has inherited from his family and community. That the different systems of knowledge co-exist in a society is a fact known full well. Also known is the conflict, and dialectics, of different knowledge-pools, with each competing to gain ascendancy over the other. That each system and practice of knowledge is intimately connected with politics and power is equally well known. Among many of these issues, what has interested me is the probable impact that the subject a person studies for some years exercises on his outlook, meaning of life, and rationality.

Considering that there may be a grain of truth in this hypothesis, from 1995 onwards, each year, I have advised the students of post-graduate degree (final year) in anthropology, in the month of March, a couple of weeks before they appear for their final examination, to write up a short piece on what they think and believe has been the impact, if any, of anthropology on them.[2] Neither do I prescribe its word-limit nor language; they are free to write in English or Hindi. Further, realizing the advantages of the incognito research, I also advise them to refrain from writing their names (or any mark of personal identification) on their respective notes.[3] However, I request them to mention their gender and the fact of whether they have studied anthropology at the undergraduate level. The aim beneath this is to discover if there are any gender differences with respect to the impact of anthropology, and what kinds of differences can be discerned between those who study anthropology for five years vis-à-vis those who study it for two years. In addition, I have also conducted several structured and unstructured interviews with the students, research scholars, and faculty members of anthropology and those who read anthropology for the Civil and Provincial Services Examinations.[4] It is an ongoing project on the subjective perception of the impact, in the typical mould of before-and-after research, and some day I wish to publish its detailed findings.[5]

Many of these write ups are detailed, beautifully crafted, bubbling with ideas, enthusiastic, creative, and personal (almost like the 'daily diary' that some of us write). Some of them blame their teachers for not exciting them enough to explore the dimensions of anthropology. Some think that mass media have not done enough to popularize anthropology, or have just talked about one of its specializations (such as forensic science or molecular anthropology), as a consequence of which not many know of the existence of the discipline, or confuse it with one of the super specializations of the medical science. As expected, some are more concerned about the job prospects after reading anthropology, and the economic value of anthropological knowledge.[6] Will the expanding global market ever seek this knowledge, and, if so, for what purpose? Besides those who have identified a definite impact of anthropology on their selves, there are some who are not sure if the changes they view in them, of which they are certain, can be attributed in any way to their study of anthropology. A couple of them thought that if at all these changes were there, they could be a part of growing up in a secular, democratic, plural and multicultural, and global society. And, of course, a handful of them have stated categorically that they felt no change in their perceptions. In their opinion, a subject one studies at college does not necessarily alter one's value framework or the collage of thoughts. Notwithstanding these varied responses, an overwhelming majority each year has been of those who have delightfully written about the impact they think that the subject of anthropology has exercised on them, and further, they think that this impact is indelible, hopefully life-long.[7]

II

The social categories in which the impact of anthropology has been classified run into more than fifty, and each year, a couple of new ones are added.[8] But each year, certain values the students claim to have acquired as an outcome of reading anthropology are repeated. Let me list some of these. That anthropology made them realize the essential equality of all human beings was one of the common values.[9] The lengthy ethnographic fieldwork inculcated in students the virtues of patience and persistence. The students thought they had become more tolerant after knowing about cultural differences that would never be transcended. Many students admitted that earlier they were biased and nurtured prejudices, but anthropology helped them overcome these values.[10] That the other cultures should be studied sympathetically and respectfully was an oft-repeated theme. All human beings are geniuses and creative, but culture plays a cardinal role in flowering or constraining these traits was another aspect that figured in the replies of many. It was obvious therefore that culture should be the focus of study, for the answer to why human beings differed from one another could be found in how they were socialized in different cultures. Anthropology sensitized, the students thought, to different facets of the social world. Then, they could understand it better, criticize it in a balanced manner, with an open mind, and think positively in terms of bringing about changes, thus ameliorating the human lot. Interestingly, a large number of students thought that the differences in their attitudes owed to their gradual internalization of social and cultural anthropology, since physical (or biological) anthropology was not much different from what they had expected and learnt in biology courses earlier.[11]

Let me make two submissions at this juncture. First, I am not suggesting that the other social sciences and humanities do not inculcate certain values among its students or practitioners. In fact, a study of students and practitioners of other disciplines will help us in understanding comparatively the findings from anthropology presented here. Second, for a long time, I did not come across any research work that dealt with the impact of anthropology on its learners, with which I could have compared my findings, but during the course of writing up a paper on the future of anthropology I read an article by Raymond Firth (1963) wherein he had referred to a similar study he had conducted at two points of time on his students. Although he used this material to show a wide variation in the interests of the students in anthropology (p. 131), he definitely came across a significant proportion of graduate students who

> thought that the training in social anthropology had tended to increase their tolerance and understanding of social differences of hitherto unfamiliar ways of behaving and to lessen ethnocentric beliefs....About half the members of the seminar said positively that a knowledge of social anthropology had given them a wider range of ideas about social life and an improved ability to ask themselves relevant questions when making value judgments (p. 130).

Among Firth's sample were those students who thought that they already had a template of 'partly formed ideas' about tolerance and anti-ethnocentrism, and the role of social anthropology figured in supporting and systematizing them. In other words, it did not 'create new ideas or values' (p. 130). It led Firth to ask whether it was social anthropology which was responsible for broadening of their minds, or those whose minds were already broadened sought to study social anthropology (p. 131).[12]

This query directs us to the questions about the social background of the students and why they join anthropology for a degree programme? Do people have many of these values (such as of tolerance, equality, relativism), acquired during socialization and schooling, which drive them – consciously or unconsciously – to look for social anthropology for their further nurturance and systematization? My information on the students' background and the reasons for joining anthropology does not lend any support to this hypothesis. Do parents want their school-leaving or graduate children to opt for a degree in anthropology as the first option? To this question, the answer my data can give is that of course parents have pushed their children, particularly daughters, to anthropology when they were unable to get admission to some other career-oriented course.[13] A significantly large number of students have maintained that they had no option but to seek admission in anthropology because of low scoring in the earlier examination, which disqualified them from admission to other high-prestige and market-driven subjects.[14] Many had absolutely no idea of what the subject was before they joined.[15] Some looked into the dictionary for its meaning, and were unclear as the definitions given therein were all-encompassing: 'Anthropology is the study of man in the widest sense.' After graduation, quite a few (especially from the states of Bihar, Jharkhand, and Orissa) joined a post-graduation in anthropology, for they thought it was an attractive, marks-fetching option for Civil and Provincial Services Examinations.[16] In other words, barring isolated and exceptional cases, the intake of students in anthropology departments in Indian universities and colleges is generally of those who have not been able to get admission in other preferred courses.

III

But, once he is an anthropology student, albeit the subjects he studied in school or at the level of graduation, he starts feeling the change in his thinking and orientation to life. He might have watched television programmes on tribes with interest and profit, but what he lacked was an explanation in comparative terms of why these customs and practices prevail among certain communities.[17] Once he is in anthropology, not only does he become familiar with an enormous diversity of human living, with a variety of societies and their lifestyles, but also with the basic values to which anthropology adheres and has always championed. As his study of anthropology progresses, he begins having introspective looks into his family, neighbourhood, and community to find out why they are what they are. Like the popular aphorism 'charity begins at home', the student initiates his career in fieldwork with a study of his domestic group, although he may or may not write about it, or, write about it pseudonymously. Gradually, he also becomes aware of the methodological problems in the study of one's own society, the problems that emerge from 'homeblindness', that is, certain phenomena being taken-for-granted because of the investigator's assumption that he knows the local facts full well because of his socialization in that culture. Over time, he also learns that it is better to have two field studies to one's credit, of which one should be in a society different from his own society, as they would make him comparative.[18] Anthropology is a way of thinking comparatively.

Anthropologists learn to treat their 'self' as the 'other', and the 'other' as their 'self'.[19] The first is the methodological vantage point, a requirement. In fact, otherness should not be viewed as stating physical distance, or remoteness. Rather, it is a frame of mind, a methodological principle, stating that our approach should be of, what is called, the 'clean slate' mind, the *tabula rasa* mind, or what is stated as: 'I do not know a social fact unless I study it'.[20] The second aspect, when the other is treated as the self, is of empathy, stepping into the shoes of the other and then, experiencing the reality as it is natively experienced. This duality is central to anthropological work as well as the experience accumulated thereof. Living and viewing the self as the other and the other as the self surely induces a paradox – a sort of 'schizophrenia' – but then, gradually all anthropology students acquire the skill to resolve it. Through this doubleness, anthropologists learn about the others and themselves.[21] In other words, the self is revealed in an intellectual engagement with the other. The anthropological work begins with treating every phenomenon, every social fact, whether of a different or one's own society, as the 'other', and then getting immersed in it, feeling and experiencing it as much as possible, to know it as much as the insiders, the bearers of culture, do.[22] Anthropologists describe the social phenomenon, which they have understood subjectively, in objective terms. It is herein lies the distinctiveness of anthropology.

Anthropology students learn the several explanations, espoused from different angles, of why a particular custom or practice prevails in a community. For knowing why and how a social fact has come into existence, what are the various stages through which it has passed, and what have been its earlier forms, it is essential that we firstly know what it is and why and how does it exist. A contextual explanation has to be found first before we move into any other realm of understanding. The method of cultural relativism helps us at this level. That things are meaningful in their respective cultural contexts and should be understood in these terms is the first lesson of an anthropology student. But it does not imply that anthropologists justify the practice just because it exists in a society. Finding an explanation does not imply its justification. Cultural relativism is not ethical relativism.

If, on one hand, anthropology students learn that specific values are relatively understood, in the context of the society in which they exist, on the other, they also learn of the universal values, which must be reinforced; and if they are non-existent, attempts should be made to bring them in. That all human beings are equal; there should not be any discrimination between people; no one should be subjected to torture and dehumanization; no one should starve; are some examples of universal values. If a local value or practice comes in conflict with the universal value, it must be criticized. Anthropological practice does not teach one that whatever is local is good, valid, just, and needs to be promoted. If it is contrapuntal to the universal values, to which anthropology adheres, the people must be communicated why their practices demand change.

In fact, the distinction between 'theoretical' and 'applied anthropology', or 'value-neutrality' and 'activism', or 'understanding the things as they are' and 'initiating changes in social consciousness', is of heuristic nature. In reality, they all fall on a continuum, concatenated, one leading to the other. When I find that people are seeking their treatment for snake-bite from their traditional religious practitioners, instead of approaching the nearby hospital, and in the process, many of the victims die, it is my duty to apprise people of the advantages of an allopathic treatment in these cases. I would not ask people to give up their traditional curative lore, but to combine it with other practices which are scientific and offer a more certain cure. From this would result medical pluralism, and it is left to the people to weigh the advantages of the respective systems under operation.

What I do is that I start a dialogue with people – listen to their viewpoint, gently place before them for their scrutiny a rejoinder of their opinions, put forth my own view, wait for the reactions of people, reply to their counterpoints. Through this, I am able to initiate a process – a democratic one – whereby people look at their cultural practices critically, and commence endogenous changes, which, as is well known, last. I am able to start this process, which requires a one to one, friendly relationship with people because of a lengthy participant observation I carry out with them. Because of this role of the anthropologist – to start a dialogue in the community – it is imperative that the set of the development specialists includes him, whom we may call the 'resident anthropologist'. He knows the people well. They also trust him. He can explain the nuances of a project to people, and also communicate their apprehensions, doubts, and problems to the planners, thus seeking an amicable solution. This role of an 'intermediary' – between the people and the development specialists – can be skillfully and suitably filled by an anthropologist.

Although I do not want, desiring to remain a dispassionate observer of social reality, the inevitable humanistic dimension of the social situation pushes me, almost involuntarily, to take up the role of an interventionist. In course of time, I may become an activist, an advocate of a certain ideology or a programme of change and development. When this happens, we realize how artificial the distinction between the 'pure' and the 'applied' dimension is. All fieldworkers know that this distinction, although maintained at the theoretical level, is collapsible in reality. Needless to say, when human beings study others of their species, they cannot remain robotic, howsoever hard they may try. Whilst some of us become grotesquely emotional on seeing people suffer, the others think of certain objective and operational ways of ameliorating human condition. And, of course, some completely avoid any direct practical involvement with people, restricting them to pure academic concerns, but even they cannot remain totally detached from the problems and sufferings of people they encounter during the course of their fieldwork. That they do not talk about it does not imply they are iron-clad. No human being can remain totally disengaged from the sufferings of others. This has great implications for the concepts of objectivity, value-freedom, and ethical-neutrality.

IV

In class rooms and fieldwork, anthropology students gradually imbibe the values of human equality, tolerance, anti-ethnocentrism, plurality, and non-exploitation and anti-suppression. They hail the virtues of diversity and argue for a system that fulfils the basic needs of all. I am not arguing that anthropology has necessarily created these values, for they have also resulted historically from a myriad of social and political ideologies and movements. But, what I am submitting is that all these values also precipitate from a comparative study of different kinds of society, simple and complex, and the intellectual discourse on them. In this, anthropology emerges as a 'first-hand way of experiencing society in its enormous diversity'. Anthropologists are always 'field-working', always observing the phenomenon, whichever comes in their way, consciously; and if they are habituated to writing their 'daily accounts', they analyze the everyday life, the quotidian facts, anthropologically. Anthropology, thus, becomes their 'way of life', their 'second nature'. So, when the student speaks of the changes, which in his opinion have surfaced in his orientation and thinking after studying anthropology, we should not only take it seriously, but treat it as a social fact, which would guide us to studying why such an impact occurs.

One of the criticisms of this study could be that what the students have said about the change anthropology brought about in them was because of the lead that the investigator provided, by specifically asking them to think about the change; in other words, by telling them that anthropology brings about a change, and then asking them to describe the changes that have occurred in them. It is quite likely that what the students have written are the values for which anthropology stands rather than the changes that have really occurred in them. With respect to the first charge, it can be said that unless questioned people do not systematize their thoughts, presenting them in an arrayed form. Asking questions does not imply giving them a lead. However, there is some substance in the second, for it is likely that the changes the students of anthropology describe in their thinking are the 'imagined' rather than the 'real'.

The society in which anthropologists (like the others) live has all sorts of inequality, domination, exploitation, suppression, intolerance, ethno- and ego-centrism, and untiring attempts towards homogenization, although, at the normative and theoretical level, it may claim to subscribe to those values for which contemporary anthropology stands. The gulf between the ideational and the existential levels, what societies say and what the reality is, is an important sociological question for investigation. But, considering the values anthropology propagates and the impact it exercises on its students, who are expected to practice and pass it on, it should have really changed the world.

Furthermore, the change should come since to the credit of anthropology are those tasks which no other discipline does. First, it offers a biological-cum-cultural (or behavioural) perspective on human populations and their society. Second, it regards a lengthy, direct observation of social phenomena occurring at a micro-level as the prime method of information collection. Third, although it studies all types of societies comparatively, notwithstanding their respective levels of complexity, its chief commitment is to the so-called 'simple societies'. And, finally, it offers several, contesting theoretical perspectives on society, but what unites them is that they try to explain the contemporary reality – what it is – on the basis of which some anthropologists envisage the kind of society they would try to build in future. Today, fieldwork as well as the study of tribal societies has been de-centered, as a number of other disciplines of social science and humanities have entered into what at one time were called the 'territories of anthropologists'. But this certainly has not conquered the hold that anthropologists have on fieldwork and tribal studies. In fact, when other disciplines embark on these areas, their point of commencement and comparison is the anthropological work.

The future of a subject depends upon, first, its contribution to the world of knowledge, in terms of what it does, its specialized task, which is not done by any other discipline. This aspect is linked to the question of how other disciplines with which it is grouped, because of closeness, look at it. For instance, if anthropology is classified as a science under the faculty of science, as it is in the University of Delhi, a pertinent question to ask is how botany, zoology, physics, chemistry, and geology, the other sciences, view anthropology, and what they think about the relationship (of research or interdisciplinary teaching) they can have with it.[23] Similarly, if it is classified as a social science, as it is in the University of Hyderabad, then we have to ask is how economics, political science, linguistics, and sociology view it.

Second, the distinctive contribution a discipline makes to the wider society also conditions its future. Take, for example, disciplines like physics, biology, economics, and history. Each of them is theoretical, contributing to a particular dimension of knowledge. By comparison, disciplines such as law, medicine, and engineering, are chiefly applied, though a relationship definitely exists between certain theoretical and applied disciplines, for example, between physics and engineering, or biology and medicine. To each category of disciplines – predominantly theoretical or predominantly applied – one may add several more examples. We know in recent years a wide variety of new disciplines (such as public administration, actuarial science, forensic science) have emerged, which serve one or the other vocational need.

Against this 'ecology' of disciplines, and the ever-dynamic relationship between different specializations, the question pertains to the place of anthropology in the world of academics, for this would condition its future. Anthropology is neither a specialized study of an institution nor is just a social or a biological science. One of the branches of anthropology, namely social anthropology, studies each segment of the institutionalized human behaviour, but in relationship with the other. Therefore, a good way to define social anthropology would be that it is a study of the theoretical and operational interrelationships between different institutions. Second, as has been submitted previously, although anthropology has specializations, some super-specializations as well, which apparently seem to be unconnected, its strength lies in providing a forum where the human being (or whom we earlier called 'man') is seen not as atomized and segmented, but in the round, as made up of biological and socio-cultural entities, on which there is an unremitting effect of the habitat.

V

Elsewhere, I had submitted that there are definite similarities between social anthropology and sociology, or biological anthropology and zoology, or archaeological anthropology and prehistory, or linguistic anthropology and linguistics, and there has also been an argument in favour of distributing the distinct specializations of anthropological knowledge to other cognate disciplines, with which each one of them bears familial resemblance (Srivastava, 1999). In this way, the subject of anthropology could be easily dismantled. Some of us think that this is required, for there exists scant unity between different branches of anthropology and the super-specializations that have occurred have struck at the root of whatever unity was envisaged by our founders. This will also put to rest the internal badmouthings between representatives of different branches, surfacing because of meager resources (funds, positions) for which they are constrained to fight. Against this background, the solution suggested is in favour of dismembering anthropology, and attaching its respective parts to those disciplines with which they have intellectual proximity. Whenever there is an argument regarding the distribution of resources to the different branches of anthropology, one may hear aloud the opinion for amputation of anthropology in line with the specializations. Social anthropologists have often been angrily told to 'go away to sociology' and join hands with it. However, I have not heard of physical anthropologists being 'sent to zoology or medicine'![24]

Arguments for fragmentation of anthropology, which often come up, have been rebutted. When Barkatullah University at Bhopal (Madhya Pradesh) advertised for a post-graduate degree programme in *social anthropology*, rather than *anthropology*, many thought that it was a wrong move, detrimental to the interests of the subject and the students. The correct move is to start a department of anthropology, rather than of any of its specializations; however, depending upon the faculty and resources available at that time, the department may temporarily offer specialized training in a particular branch. With the passage of time, attempts should be made to include all specializations, but even when the department is in its formative stage, introductory training in all branches of anthropology should be imparted. In fact, to the best of my knowledge, segmented departments of anthropology, which have emerged from time to time, have found it extremely difficult to survive, and have collapsed sooner or later.

Surely, not many studies in anthropology draw upon its different branches. Collaborative projects involving different specializations of anthropology are few. That anthropology is a 'group of subjects', each having its own set of specialists interacting more with the outside world, has been noted frequently.[25] But, in spite of these differentiations in anthropology and differences between its professionals, the infallible and unconquerable argument for a 'united anthropology' is that it is the only discipline that gives an opportunity to approach the human being as 'total', in terms of its bio-cultural aspects, yet also suggesting its practitioners to follow the systemic approach, break each part of human existence in its building blocks, examine the relationship between them, and continue further with this procedure till one reached the boundary of one's specialization. As an outcome of following this approach, one may indulge in a fruitless exercise of preparing taxonomy of different branches of anthropology, but they are basically an application of anthropological theory and practice to specific realms of human life. Because of this character of anthropology, it cannot be classified in a rather simplistic manner, as is the case with several other disciplines.

Against this backdrop, my submission is that anthropology is neither a 'science' (to be classified with other natural and biological sciences), nor it is a 'social science' (to be classified with economics, sociology, linguistics, political science), nor it is a branch of 'arts' and 'humanities' (to be classified with history, philosophy, psychology, literature). Yes, indubitably, a segment of anthropology may bear affinity with any of these other subjects. But, when our concern is with the 'whole' of anthropology, that is, anthropology providing a forum to undertake the study of human beings in the round, we shall have to transcend the existing nomenclatures (of science, arts, humanities) in which anthropology is classified and look for it a separate and distinct place. Elsewhere, I have suggested that the state of anthropology is similar to that of mathematics. For keeping its distinction, as is the case with mathematics, and also to take care of its specializations, which, although having tenuous relationship among them, give unparalleled opportunity to explore the 'roundness' of human beings, we should establish for the purpose of its training and research, and administration, the 'faculty of anthropology', which would govern the three separate departments, respectively for physical anthropology, social anthropology, and archaeological anthropology, with certain compulsory courses to be taught notwithstanding the specialization the student opts for (Srivastava, 2005).

VI

When an insider looks at anthropology, he finds that his co-disciplinarians are engaged in a wide range of important and crucial issues, approached in an original, authoritative, and comparative manner. They may include the rights of communities inhabiting international borders, or the question of bio-ethics and the original genetic material, or the rise of insurgency in tribal areas, or the ecological crises. They may also discuss certain micro-level issues, such as dwindling sex ratio in Punjab villages, or reasons behind the shortage in the supply of onions. Anthropologists have also examined critically the drafts of various policies the government has released from time to time in recent years. The insider knows that anthropology with its holistic perspective and comparative knowledge is greatly equipped to provide an analytical view on each issue of human importance. Then, why it is that anthropology has not been able to create the impact it should have made?

Our dismay surfaces when we finds that anthropologists are absent from those institutions that shape public opinion. Generally speaking, anthropologists also do not seem to participate in general intellectual discourses. They hardly write for common public and refrain from speaking across disciplinary boundaries. Undoubtedly, the word 'anthropology' is not absent from the media. When Rupkund Mystery (of Uttarakhand) is discussed on a television channel, anthropologists are invited to participate in the discussion. Often, when national issues pertaining to caste or tribe come up, or when a bizarre incident occurs (say, Hindu idols drinking milk, sea water near a Sufi shrine in Mumbai turning sweet, tears flowing from eyes of

Virgin Mary, monkey-man holding a neighbourhood to ransom, etc.), anthropologists are often interviewed and quoted in newspapers. The media may also note that Prince Charles was a student of social anthropology, or the Miss World of 2005 had also studied it.

But when it comes to a discussion of national and international issues, on the terms and conditions of anthropology, with the initiative of its professionals, a common observation is that the anthropologists lag behind. Anthropologists can communicate the experiences and representations of the 'others', the people whom they study, to those who just share their own experiences. In this way, they can certainly increase the knowledge-pool of societies, making people far more comparative than what they are. They can also explain to people why they differ in their lifestyles and that each way of living is an historical adaptation to a given habitat. That there is no ranking of cultures and the value of universal humanism is supreme can be one of the principal lessons of anthropology.

There has been a tendency on the part of many to regard anthropology as a sort of journalism (or, 'ethno-journalism'), which is not really correct. Anthropology may deal with current issues, but it certainly is different from the media. The messages of anthropology do not flow from the media since its priorities and stories are different. And, they have to be, because as a business proposition, the media generally cater to the interests of a particular section of society, the middle and upper classes. The class bias of media is well known. The stories of human suffering are not absent from media, but sensationalism may often mar their objectivity. Being too insignificant, small communities of tribal foragers may not enter the media discourse. It may be speculated here that being too much confined with their own interests and preoccupations, the middle and upper classes do not wish to have close encounters with the naked facts of how states and markets ceaselessly suppress lower classes and poor people to uphold the interests of the privileged.

Moreover, journalists are constrained (and trained) to write quickly about the events and fast occurring changes, as a result of which they may churn out impressions, simplistic explanations, incorrect facts, and wrong quotations. By contrast, anthropologists write slowly, after having undertaken a time-consuming, detailed survey of facts and figures. It may be several months (sometimes years) after the event has taken place that anthropologists start its study. By the time they emerge with its intellectual explanation, the public has already lost interest in it. Notwithstanding the ingenuity of their findings, anthropologists (as 'late-comers') are unable to seize public attention. What anthropologists have to learn is to write as fast as possible in the midst of the events, drawing upon their vast field experiences and the knowledge of diverse societies. And surely, they can do that, for during their fieldwork years, they write each day, analyzing all sorts of daily events of varying significances, and committing these analyses to their field notebooks and diaries. However, I have observed that when they are formally out of the field, they usually renounce their practice of writing and commenting on each day's happening. Its panacea may be located in the idea I submitted previously that anthropologists should realize that they are 'always fieldworking'. An outcome of their long term fieldwork is that they don't *see*, they *observe*; they aren't eager to *answer*, but *listen* to people patiently; they not only absorb the empirical facts as a blotting paper, but keep on analyzing its every bit theoretically. If anthropologists follow this frame of mind, they can significantly contribute to the understanding of the contemporary world, handsomely supplementing the understanding that the other disciplines have achieved, and enlightening the public on various issues.

During the formative years, anthropologists energetically engaged themselves in the debates of their time. Other intellectuals and social thinkers read their works with interest and profit. Who does not know that Karl Marx and Fredrick Engels read Lewis Henry Morgan, and Charles Darwin, Edward Tylor? Sir James Frazer inspired a poet, T.S. Eliot, and a philosopher, Ludwig Wittgenstein. Bronislaw Malinowski was well known for his writings (particularly on war) in popular magazines and popular lectures on topics of general interest. Franz Boas was a publicly acclaimed intellectual for his anti-racist views. Both Ruth Benedict and Margaret Mead were extremely popular public figures; in fact, Benedict's *The*

Patterns of Culture, written poetically, was read as a remarkable piece of literature. Edward Evans-Pritchard and Edmund Leach, famous for their B.B.C. lectures, actively participated in the discussion of the issues of their days.

Back home, we have examples of several anthropologists who gained public attention because of the contribution they made to the understanding of their times. S.C. Roy, D.N. Majumdar, N.K. Bose, M.N. Srinivas, Irawati Karve, L.P. Vidyarthi, and S.C. Dube applied anthropological knowledge to understand the problems of the then Indian society (Rao, 1999). They also wrote extensively for newspapers, thus entering the public domain. The term 'vote bank' appeared for the first time in a newspaper article that Srinivas had written. Bose and Srinivas wrote a great deal on the issues of national integration. These (and some other anthropologists) were also members of several committees that formulated national policies. In other words, anthropologists were at the centre of the debates that mattered the nation.

In other words, the cocooning of anthropology we note now was certainly not the order of the day in the past. The vibrancy anthropologists showed in understanding the complex society of their time and participating in public debates was remarkable. Then, why has anthropology become inward gazing and non-engaging with audiences outside the academy? This surely does not imply that academic anthropology and its application areas have become stagnant. The theoretical developments in anthropology would make any one proud. And, there is no doubt that anthropology has emerged as one of the strongest critics of development.

VII

One of the works by Eriksen (2006) has seriously analyzed the aloofness of anthropology and its self-imposed ghettoization. He thinks that the withdrawal of anthropology from the public sphere and the general intellectual discourse can be traced to the latter half of the twentieth century. Of course, there have been some exceptions. For instance, in India, among anthropologists, André Béteille and T.N.Madan, and sociologists, Dipankar Gupta, Shiv Visvanathan, and Nandini Sundar have from time to time participated in public debates and contributed extensively to newspapers and magazines. Béteille has already published two collections of his articles published in newspapers. Some of the authors have expanded their newspaper articles into full-length academic papers.

One of the reasons for this state of inwardness has been sought in the anthropologist's lack of confidence in dealing with a changed scenario. Not only have vast changes occurred in society, but also a large number of perspectives have come which have challenged the foundation of anthropology. The idea of scientific anthropology based on participant observation in a bounded social unit, which came with Malinowski, and guided us for a long time, is no more the guiding principle. One submission is that anthropology's cocooning is an outcome of the kind of societies (closed, preliterate, simple, and small) they have been studying for a long time, and when these societies changed, merging gradually with the outside world, anthropologists found them difficult to study with fieldwork techniques and methods that had evolved earlier. As anthropologists studied societies which were devoid of any historical documents on them, they certainly acquired expertise on the art of observation but lacked acquaintance with the historical method and the art of handling the historical material. When they shifted to the study of modern societies, their incompetence with respect to fieldwork in a vast agglomerate and dealing with survey and historical facts was greatly exposed. The result was that although anthropologists produced excellent, worth-emulating ethnographies on 'primitive societies', they were unable to reproduce the same skillfully crafted works on urban and industrial societies, with perhaps the sole exception of Lloyd Warner's study of the Yankee City.[26] Against this background, some think that the survival of social anthropology in modern times is imperiled because of the gradual disappearance and dwindling of simple societies, what is popularly termed the 'loss of the native'.

In addition, the confidence of anthropology was considerably shaken by its post-colonial critique. For all these years, the task of anthropology was to identify and tell the world what it meant to be the 'other' (the preliterate, small community). Now, with a myriad of changes that have transformed the world, linking different communities together, the 'other' thinks it can perfectly identify and represent itself. In many cases, it has challenged the knowledge and the analysis that the 'outsiders' have attempted of its lifestyles. In my study of why students have joined anthropology, some students from the tribal communities of the north-eastern part of India said that they had read colonial officers' writings on their respective communities before joining anthropology. These accounts infuriated them, for they were erroneous at places and presented their people in derogatory and unacceptable terms. These students thought that they would write a 'correct' and 'sympathetic' account of their community after having done a degree in anthropology, thereby equipping themselves with the necessary skills to correctly represent the other. This augurs the beginning of 'auto-anthropology', challenging the representations of native communities by the outsiders. If 'natives' are capable of representing themselves, the anthropologists are at the verge of losing their vocation.

Lévi-Strauss (1987) notes this in his lecture of 1959-60 where he says that the future of anthropology is doubly threatened. First, the 'primitive societies' have greatly dwindled as a consequence of acculturation, the asymmetrical changes. Threatened by famine and demoralization, almost at the brink of the state where their desire to live has ceased, they have lost their distinctive characteristics. Not only does the concept of *indigène* become blurred, it is also giving place to a whole class of *indigent*, the necessitous, needy, and poor people. Second, Lévi-Strauss says, there are areas in the world (such as Central America, Africa, South-east Asia) where the population of 'primitive' people is multiplying, but they are hostile to any type of ethnographic enquiry. In both cases, anthropologists would be left with the study of the 'native theories about culture' (what do the native scholars say about their culture) rather than the 'native culture' *per se*. If these societies are not amenable to study, because of one or the other factor (local hostility, insurgency, government restrictions, etc), anthropologists will have to shift to the study of modern societies, where they should be prepared to compete with other social sciences that have a long tradition of studying urban-industrial, complex societies.

Little we realize the damage that the post-colonial critique has done to the morale and confidence of anthropologists. For a long time, during the second half of the twentieth century, we were told about a painting in the ante-room of Kwame Nkrumah, which showed the anthropologist as a 'tiny, pallid figure', running away with his copy of the *African Political Systems*, and the popular conclusion from Katheen Gough, according to which anthropology was the 'bastard' child of European imperialism and colonialism. In the years that followed, anything that fell in the lineage of the colonial science was despised, looked down upon, and rejected, because of its association with the knowledge that was used for exploiting people, siphoning off their local wealth, and subjugating them, perhaps forever. Anthropologists were told time and again, by their own tribespersons, that their work served the colonial masters, helped their rule. Anthropologists were almost equated with 'spies', who accumulated local knowledge for the administration, which used it, to say the least, for its own interests. In this line of thinking, participant observation became a metaphor for "uncovering people's secrets and weaknesses". All this, which happened with anthropology, did not happen with sociology, since it was defined not with reference to the study of the 'other culture' but "one's own society". In sociology, so to say, the 'natives were representing themselves'. Therefore, the question of the prejudiced, exaggerated, incorrect, and romantic representation did not arise. In other words, sociology was free from the 'crisis of representation'. This would explain that the 'identity crisis' we have in anthropology is non-existent in sociology, except that portion of sociology which happens to be anthropological.

To say that anthropology as a whole or all anthropologists served the colonial interests is wrong. To generalize from the activities of some anthropologists who served (or were constrained to serve) the establishment about the entire community of anthropologists is a synecdochic fallacy, i.e. generalizing from the activity of a part about the whole (Eriksen, 2006).[27] In fact, some well-known anthropologists, who greatly influenced the public opinion, worked for the interests of the communities they had studied much against the chagrin of the state. J.H. Hutton, for instance, who was the Political Agent to the Naga Hills, argued in favour of giving people autonomy to manage their affairs. Verrier Elwin is well known for the idea of establishing a 'national park' for the Baiga, where they could live, as they would like to without being exploited by the outsiders (e.g., moneylenders, liquor vendors, landlords, supervisors, etc.). The notion was that the so-called primitive people were quite like 'us' (the advanced and modern) in many respects, and if they were not able to become our replica, it was because of the historical context in which they were entangled. Once the barriers that thwarted their growth and progress were weakened, they were able to change like any one of us.

Anthropologists held colonial governments responsible for the conditions of poverty, alienation, demoralization and dehumanization, and malnutrition in which small communities found themselves. In other words, anthropologists fought – at least with pen and paper – for the rights of tribal communities rather than serving the colonial interests at all times and places. But, as we noted previously, the image of anthropologists as 'stooges of the colonial regime' has continued, which has irreparably damaged their reputation. Some anthropologists in their unrestricted enthusiasm to prove that anthropology has served the colonial regime have gone to the extent of saying that its concepts (such as great and little tradition, folk-urban continuum, elite-emulation like Sanskritization and Westernization) conceal the facts of exploitation. They want to liberate anthropology from the enduring colonial and neo-colonial yoke by making it Marxist (or leftist) or a component of the practice of Marxism. The issue is not of their success or failure. It is of the damage that the subject has suffered, which has made its practitioners more and more cocooned.

VIII

Well known to anthropologists is the ambiguity concerning the status of social and cultural anthropology, which has also contributed to inward gazing among anthropologists.

For positivists, anthropology was one of the natural sciences and methods from physics were considered to be eminently applicable for the study of social and cultural systems. The positivists searched for the laws of human society – applicable for all times and places – quite like the laws that the natural and biological scientists yielded for the systems of action they respectively studied.

That human behaviour is amorphous and unpredictable and not conditioned by a battery of laws was a salient criticism of the positivist view. Instead of looking for laws of social behaviour, which did not exist, the critics documented the meaning that people assigned to their thoughts and actions. Search for laws was futile, for what was regarded as an 'invariant proposition' about human behaviour turned out not to be so. Positivists (and the later variants known by different appellations) were utterly frustrated when they found that although social and cultural anthropology could be regarded as a 'science', it was not a 'science' in the sense natural and biological sciences were.

Doubts came to be raised about the scientific status of social and cultural anthropology. Evans-Pritchard considered social anthropology as a kind of historiography. For Geertz, it was a literary exercise. Similarities were drawn between fiction writing and ethnographic work. Those for whom social and cultural anthropology was anything but 'science' ('a branch of natural science') did not see any problem in its classification as a branch of humanities or social sciences. An outcome of this problem regarding its classification is that different universities place anthropology in different faculties: in some universities, anthropology is within the faculty of science; in some, the faculty of arts; while in some, the faculty of social sciences. Perhaps, with the sole exception of psychology, no other discipline has this ambiguity about its classification.

Not only this, internal bickering also exists: physical anthropology call social and cultural anthropologists 'soft scholars', 'storytellers', 'narrators', 'non-scientists among scientists'. Social and cultural anthropologists think that physical anthropologists feign as 'clinicians' in the field. The laboratory is seen as essential to physical anthropology, which gives it a scientific status. When funds granted to anthropology departments have to be divided, the physical anthropologists demand a lion's share, for they have to spend on equipments, chemicals, and maintenance of the laboratory.[28] Not to be left behind, social and cultural anthropologists also want to establish their 'laboratories' (such as of psychological anthropology, medical anthropology, communication anthropology). They also call their classroom exercises of data collection and analysis 'practical', knowing full well that for them the entire society is their field and their data come from it rather than a bounded laboratory. For claiming that they are also 'scientists', social anthropologists turn more towards generalizations – some even resorting to mathematical anthropology and model building – rather than spending a lot of their attention to a vivid description of social life. The art of writing up the detailed accounts of quotidian facts – the imponderabilia of social life – suffers a lot when we want to be like econometricians or physicists. Needless to say, one of the central tasks of anthropology is to render what Geertz has called the 'thick description'. Not only are these descriptions valuable to anthropology, they are also being read with profit in other disciplines. Analysis is inbuilt in these descriptions.

IX

At this juncture, when the clan of anthropologists is becoming more and more marginalized and anthropologists, more and more inward gazers, there is a need to have a critical look at our practice.

A general feeling among us is that we are not heard. None reads us. Our subject is old fashioned: Who is interested in reading about marginal societies?[29] Only we understand what we say, what the others in our academic community do. There may be a grain of truth in what we think. Not many people are keen to know about tribes. Anthropology, as we saw earlier, is not a preferred subject in universities. But the truth is that researchers from other disciplines read a lot of anthropology and they have been greatly benefited by it. Our concepts and theoretical perspectives have enriched other disciplines. We may cite the examples of the functional approach, organic analogy, structuralism, interpretive approach, and many others, which have influenced and enriched other subjects.

Our shortsightedness is that we do not want to know how the others – whether they are in pure academics or in policy and applied research – have used and developed our concepts and perspectives, the enriching they have made to them. For instance, the methodological cluster of RRA/PRA/PLA, which is extremely popular in NGO research and evaluation programme, has borrowed tremendously from the teachings of participant observation. At the same time, its espousers and practitioners have contributed quite a lot to the concept of participation. It becomes imperative for anthropologists to have a critical look at the contribution that the others have made to their concepts. We always learn in a feedback relationship. Nevertheless, anthropologists have generally refrained from making a comment – not to speak of an extended commentary – on the techniques and methods that the NGOs use. It may be interpreted as an example of arrogance on the part of anthropologists.

I have observed that generally anthropologists avoid working on multi-disciplinary projects, with specialists from different fields, for they think that they would be eclipsed; their expertise will make no dent on others. The consequence of this thinking is that we do not want to become leaders of these projects. When we have no option but to work along with the others in a multi-specialty project, we merely contribute our bit, what is asked for or expected from us; we are least interested in knowing what the others are contributing and also, how the entire programme (or study) is taking shape. What we do not realize is that we are in a multi-specialty project or study because of our worth. The others value it; but when they find us too inwardly to participate, then they themselves take up our role notwithstanding the effectiveness with which they perform. As was stated previously, India produces far fewer anthropologists than they can meet the demands of the multi-specialty world.[30] This provides an opportunity for people from other disciplines to take up anthropological work.

Anthropologists are the critics of modernity, globalization, racism, particular cultural perspectives, and inequality at differential levels. In fact, much of anthropology is read for its criticisms of the contemporary social systems. However, when it comes to suggesting alternatives to the present state of affairs, anthropologists are tight-lipped. They do not want to commit themselves to a particular type of social formation. We want to be 'critics' but not 'builders' – we object to being called 'social engineers' or 'social doctors'. Applied and action anthropology is viewed with suspicion. Although critical, our tacit subscription to value-freedom continues, resulting in our being unresponsive and uncommitted to social problems and issues. The net effect of this is that we are least public; we least contribute to how the system should shape itself in future.[31] We do not want to work for the others; suppose we work for an industrial house (or business family) or even the government, we are criticized as being 'sold out'. If we work for NGOs, we are said to dilute the rigours of anthropological methodology. Against this backdrop, we think the best way for us is to remain 'independent' and 'lonely' scholars, participating less in public debates and forums.

Since anthropology was never a study of a particular type of society (i.e., 'primitive' or what is now called 'tribal'), but of all types of society in comparative terms, it is important that it devotes itself to the study of different kinds of society, irrespective of the locales in which they are found. Unfortunately, as noted earlier, we have lagged behind in the study of urban and industrial societies. Institutions that characterize these societies – such as banks, corporations, universities, hospitals – have remained virtually unstudied using the typical anthropological methods of fieldwork. But, much to our dismay, we are witnessing a sharp decline in the tradition of fieldwork.[32] Unless it is invigorated and students advised to carry out their first fieldwork in a community different from their own, and thus, have a first-hand experience of working in the 'other culture', neither would good anthropology be produced nor would it create its impact in the academic world.

Our greatest commitment is to the study of those societies (i.e., tribes) that are not studied by any other social science discipline. Undoubtedly, in recent decades, some other social sciences (particularly history) have evinced an interest in the study of tribes, but the subject fully devoted to their study is anthropology, and therefore, we must continue with this work. It will not be wrong to say that we are the true subalternists and should be proud of it. We have to put forth the tribal perspective and share it with the contemporary world. The knowledge gained from the study of tribes should be publicly shared, not only through writings, but also through visuals, lecturing, and participative discussion.

To sum up, anthropology should not remain confined to a narrow group of academics. We need to attend to the issues of public importance. We should not lose confidence in the merits of our discipline in the wake of postmodernism that has made us less sure of ourselves, of our methods, conclusions, and even aims. Anthropology has made a tremendous contribution to the understanding of human behaviour; it has given impetus to other disciplines; it has rendered viable solutions to many social problems; and therefore, its inward gazing is detrimental to its potentiality.

NOTES

1. This is a revised version of the text of the Platinum Jubilee Lecture I delivered in the Section of the Anthropological and Behavioural Sciences (including Archaeology, Psychology, and Educational Sciences) of the Ninety-fourth Session of the Indian Science Congress Association (2007) on 4 January 2007 at Annamalainagar, Chidambaram, Tamilnadu. I am grateful to Professor Kishor K. Basa, who presided over the lecture. Certain ideas from this paper were presented in the Chancellor's Lecture I delivered at Vinoba Bhave University (Hazaribagh) on 4 May 2009. I am thankful to Professor Chaturbhuj Sahu, the head of the anthropology department at this university, for this honour. This paper also formed the base of the lecture I delivered on 27 August 2009 in the University of Delhi under the Popular Lecture Series. My thanks to Professor V. Suneja for presiding over the lecture.

2. The students are told in advance that this write up of theirs is not for evaluation. The students write a number of other essays (known as tutorials) which are evaluated for internal assessment marks added to the marks they obtain in the main examination conducted at the end of the third term (i.e., March) every year.

3. Since these write-ups are not discussed with students as are discussed their tutorial essays, they do not get a chance to know what each one of them has written. Most of the final year students do not return to the department for a research degree; therefore, they do not get to share their views with their junior students who would attempt to write on this a year later. In other words, one set of students does not lead the other.

4. I am not submitting here the opinion of the civil servants who had opted for anthropology as one of the subjects for the examination and who think that it has really profited them in terms of understanding human beings and their predicaments. See Srivastava (1999).

5. Besides this, since 1995, every year, in the month of July, I have been advising the newly admitted students to the first year of post-graduation in anthropology to write a note on why they have chosen to study anthropology, when they could have sought admission in any job-oriented

and vocational course. An interesting comparison can be made between what the student said when he joined anthropology and when he was passing out. For want of space, many of these issues will not be taken up here.

6. One of the reasons of why these write-ups are like that is that the students know that they are not for evaluation, and hence they can open themselves up. Moreover, their frankness could be because they do not identify themselves in these notes. The tutorials they write are usually conventional, less polemical, adhering to the expected standards.

7. Commenting on this aspect, Vijoy S. Sahay said (on 3 January 2006) that like 'Once in *kula*, always in *kula*', 'Once in anthropology, always in anthropology.' His point was that one's engagement with anthropology never ceases, even when one happens to be in a different profession. Incidentally, *kula* is the name the Trobriand Islanders use for the ceremonial exchange of necklaces and bracelets they have with people of other neighbouring islands. The statement 'Once in *kula*, always in *kula*' is from Malinowski's work of 1922 on this community.

8. A few examples of these social categories may be given here – 'Anthropology has helped me to understand each situation in contextual terms'; "Anthropology has taught me to understand the others' points of view"; 'After reading anthropology, I am impressed by simplicity and honesty of people'; 'Anthropology has made me less materialistic'; 'I never thought anthropology would exercise such an impact over me'.

9. A female student, who had studied anthropology for her B.Sc. (Hons.), wrote the following in March 1996:

> Anthropology has definitely, certainly changed my point of view towards life in certain respects. Some other subjects like zoology, mathematics, and geography, etc., could never have brought about radical change. Now I no more restrict my viewpoint to my own surroundings and environment. I think and feel concerned about the whole human society. Candidly speaking, I had a lot of superiority complex earlier. When thinking about my own society and the tribal society, I felt that tribes were indeed inferior and was the Black community of Africa. I simply could not stand the sight of Blacks for long. Now definitely, I have come to know that that was a big, stupid mistake on my part. I feel, on the whole, I am a better humanitarian now.

This excerpt and what follow below from the write-ups of students are unedited.

10. A male student of 2000-2 academic year, who joined anthropology after his B.Sc. (General, with Botany, Zoology, and Chemistry) with the sole aim to appear in the Civil Services Examination with anthropology as a subject, wrote the following:

> During the course of attending classes, I found the subject [anthropology] engulfing, profound, multifaceted,

> multidimensional, and consuming. Anthropology has given me a lot of insight, developed a broader perspective, and radically transformed my attitude, criteria, and way of thinking. Before taking this course, I was having a very prejudiced and biased view, but now that hypocritical behaviour has deserted me. I feel as if it [anthropology] has opened my eyes. My overall personality has altered significantly. My ideas have become flexible. A good sign, I am ready to accept new ideas, rather than cling on and hold to my own conceited or biased convictions. Thanks to anthropology!

11. A female student, who came to anthropology after her graduation in zoology, wrote the following in March 1998:

> ....Though the basic facts of physical anthropology were as expected, it is cultural anthropology which really makes a person think. Cultural anthropology does induce a lot of thoughts. Earlier, when I was not an anthropology student, I used to have disregard for other cultures and the way people behaved and talked which I didn't approve of. I could not see any logic of any sort in it. I used to look at things in a very careless and nonchalant way. Earlier, I used to be indifferent or condemned it.
>
> But, ever since, I've started reading social and cultural anthropology, I've realized that there is quite a logic involved and people are products of their respective socio-cultural environments, and in most cases, they really can't help being the way they are. This has made me more understanding and matured....

12. Gregory (2002: 282) writes the following: 'Anthropological knowledge has the potential to control the biases of sex, class, race, nation, religion, ethnic group, or culture. By adopting the broad view of the totality of the human eperience, anthropology could help the students tear off the blinders put on them by their local life styles and help them see themselves as they really are.' Prasad (2007: 353) writes: 'Anthropology is a science of democratic learning and sharing, and it is a humanizing science.' Edmund Leach, writes Stephen Hugh-Jones (1989: 14) believed that "the value of anthropology lay in its message of tolerance and in its ability to come to terms with human difference, not in the eradication of such differences".

13. A number of female students admitted that they joined anthropology not with an intention to look for a career in it, but to spend some years in the university before attaining marriageable age and their respective parents succeeding in arranging proper matches for them. The gender dimension in enrolment to different subjects is an important social fact for study. It appears that the parents hesitated greatly in sending their sons to study anthropology because of want of career in comparison to other subjects.

This however was not the case with their daughters. In the University of Delhi, girls outnumber boys in both B.Sc. (Hons.) and M.Sc. in anthropology. Seats for M.Sc. rarely remain vacant, whilst those for B.Sc. (Hons.) are rarely completely filled. Some students join M.Sc. to retain hostel seats, and prepare for competitive examinations.

14. One of the former teachers of the Department of Anthropology of the University of Delhi, Abhimanyu Sharma, was quoted in *The Hindustan Times* (26 June 1976) as saying that the male students who joined anthropology were 'rejected lot', whereas their female counterparts were 'first-rate students.' This was questioned by Srivastava (1976). However, it has also been observed in other parts of the world that those who have not been able to obtain admission to high profile courses come to anthropology.

15. An exception to this was a set of students from the north-eastern part of India, about whom we shall read a little later.

16. However, after the syllabus of anthropology for the Civil Services Examination was revised in 1997 (and later) and increased manifold, making it almost unmanageable, its popularity as an optional subject has sharply declined (Srivastava, 1996). We are told that now not more than a couple of hundred students appear in this examination with anthropology (Vaid, n.d.). Some protests have also been registered against the syllabus (Srivastava, 2004).

17. In their classes, the anthropology teachers have time and again said that they studied the so-called 'primitive' societies; and they studied that aspect of behaviour which appeared 'irrational' to the others (see Gell [1998] in this context). Notwithstanding the fact that anthropology is 'global' and 'comparative', to borrow words from Gregory (2002), in the teaching of anthropology, the dimension of 'social oddity' has received a lot of emphasis. See Descola (2005) on this point.

18. One remembers here Louis Dumont's famous statement for the anthropological work: 'comparison is the fulcrum' (quoted in Madan 1995: 136).

19. Madan (1995: 136) expresses this idea in the following words: 'One has to learn not only to *live intimately with strangers* but also to *live (behave) strangely with intimates*. One has to cultivate empathy for other cultures; contrariwise one has to create distance between oneself and one's culture and society in order to be able to see oneself in the round, as it were.'

20. This is basically an idea from Durkheim's treatise on the sociological method (1964[1895]).

21. In an aptly titled article 'On the Mutual Interpretation of Cultures', which anthropology is, Madan (1995: 133) writes that anthropology is a 'kind of knowledge', a 'form of consciousness', which results from the 'encounter of cultures', one's own and the other, in the 'mind of the anthropologist'. But when one studies one's own culture, the encounter is between one's subjective and objective understanding of the same phenomenon. Besides

this, during their phase of apprenticeship in anthropology, the students learn about the social organization of a large number of societies, and at each step of their study, they compare what they learn from a specific situation with what they know about other societies. Anthropology is essentially a comparative science.

22. One may recall here Lévi-Strauss's (1973: 15) words: 'It [Anthropology] is undoubtedly the only science to use the most intimate kind of subjectivity as a means of objective demonstration.'
23. If anthropology is classified as a social science or as a branch of humanities, it will obviously try to establish its relations with the other subjects of its faculty.
24. This shows the affinity that social anthropology has with sociology and the distinction that physical anthropology has from zoology and medicine.
25. See Srivastava (2005) on this point.
26. It may also be noted here that some specializations in anthropology – such as urban anthropology, industrial anthropology – have not become very popular. Most of the books read as part of the syllabus of urban anthropology were written by sociologists. Still we have books in urban anthropology that the anthropologists had written (such as by R.G. Fox, A. Southall), but none in industrial anthropology. In a recent meeting to prepare the syllabi of anthropology for a university, the committee thought of half a paper on industrial anthropology, but was constrained to drop it for want of proper anthropological readings for students.
27. Also see Goody (1995), Eriksen and Nielsen (2001).
28. These days, comparative studies of DNA profiles of different populations have become quite popular in some anthropology departments, with the consequence that physical anthropologists undertaking DNA studies have started thinking that 'molecular anthropology', the name used synonymously for DNA studies, is far more important than the other specializations within physical anthropology. In one of the seminars in my department, a young teacher of physical anthropology proposed that 'molecular anthropology' should be regarded as the fifth branch of anthropology.

    Regarding physical anthropologists in the field, Gupta (2004: 5), a social anthropologist from Patiala, wrote about his Master's fieldwork: "Students specializing in physical anthropology also came with us to Manali for fieldwork. But they were not given any instructions by their supervisors about the basics of fieldwork. Collecting finger prints and taking anthropometric measurements, these students posed as if they were medical doctors. The villagers got suspicious and somehow discovered that they were lying. They refused to cooperate with them."
29. An old colleague of mine once told me that the problem of anthropologists is that they work on tribes and not on estate agents, property dealers, and 'builders'. Barring a few, he said, who is interested in tribes? I have

heard an anthropologist say that as the communities anthropologists study are marginal to the mainstream, so is their subject. A former civil servant, reacting to my paper on the Draft National Policy – 2006, said that as tribes are marginal so is the Ministry of Tribal Affairs.

30. Anthropology is taught in not more than thirty-five universities in India, the latest additions are Bastar University in Jharkhand and Mahatma Gandhi International Hindi University, Wardha (Maharashtra). In post-graduate course, the number of students in a university department is not more than fifty.

31. See Peacock (1999). He has argued in favour of 'going public or perishing.'

32. Students wish to return to their native places for doctoral fieldwork, where they can live with all comforts and pursue the belief that they already know about the community they are investigating. Senior academics in anthropology rarely have more than one fieldwork to their credit.

REFERENCES

Descola, Philippe

2005 On Anthropological Knowledge. *Social Anthropology*, 13 (1): 65-73.

Durkheim, Émile

1964[1895] *The Rules of the Sociological Method*. New York: The Free Press, and London: Collier-Macmillan.

Eriksen, Thomas Hylland

2006 *Engaging Anthropology, The Case for a Public Presence*. Oxford: Berg.

Eriksen, Thomas Hylland and Finn Silvert Nielsen

2001 *A History of Anthropology*. London: Pluto Press.

Firth, Raymond

1963 Aims, Methods, and Concepts in the Teaching of Social Anthropology. In David G. Mandelbaum, Gabriel W. Lasker, and Ethel M. Albert (eds.), *The Teaching of Anthropology*. Memoir 94. American Anthropological Association (pp. 127-140).

Gell, Alfred

1998 *Art and Agency. An Anthropological Theory*. Oxford: Clarendon Press.

Goody, Jack

1995 *The Expansive Moment: The Rise of Social Anthropology in Britain and Africa*. Cambridge: Cambridge University Press.

Gregory, S.
2002 Diffusionalising and Professionalising Anthropology: A Response to Value-Degradation and Globalisation. *Man in India*, 82 (3 & 4): 279-294.

Gupta, Surendra K.
2004 Introduction. In Surendra K. Gupta (ed.), *Emerging Social Science Concerns, Festschrift in Honour of Professor Yogesh Atal*. New Delhi: Concept Publishing House (pp. 1-25).

Hugh-Jones, Stephen
1989 *Edmund Leach, 1910-1989*. Cambridge: King's College.

Lévi-Strauss, Claude
1973 *Structural Anthropology*. Volume II. London: Allen Lane.

Madan, T. N.
1995 *Pathways, Approaches to the Study of Society in India*. Delhi: Oxford University Press.

Peacock, James L.
1999 The Future of Anthropology. *American Anthropologist*, 99 (1): 9-17.

Prasad, R. Siva
2007 What Ails Indian Anthropology? *The Eastern Anthropologist*, 60 (3&4): 349-354.

Rao, P. Venkata
1999 Anthropology as Career: Towards Better Prospects. *Man in India*, 79 (1&2): 191-196.

Srivastava, Vinay Kumar
1976 Anthropology and Males. *The Hindustan Times* (2 July).
1996 Interview published in Hindi in *Pratiyogita Samrat*, 4 (12): 53-4 (January Issue).
1999 The Future of Anthropology. *Economic and Political Weekly*, XXXIV (9): 545-552.
2004 Letter to the UPSC, published under the column 'News', *South Asian Anthropologist*, 4 (2): 235-7.
2005 The State of Indian Anthropology. *Humankind*, 1: 31-52.

Vaid, N. K.
n.d. Sustainable Development of Anthropology in India – Is it Possible? Confessions of a Student of Anthropology for the Last Thirty Years. Unpublished Paper.

23

Problematique of Unification of Social Sciences

K. N. SHARMA

I am grateful to Indian Social Science Association in general and Professer Rajeshwar Prasad in particular for providing me with another opportunity to pay tributes to my guru, Late Professor D.N. Majumdar. The hard academic training which I received from him has come to my rescue. He faced many hurdles in his life. But he remained undaunted. He could cross all obstacles with fortitude, commitment and struggle. He had an abiding interest in almost all branches of anthropology. He was an emulous field-worker and an ideal teacher. His management skills were also praiseworthy. He also provided imperceptible soft training in *guru-shishya* (teacher-student) relationship. He was extremely helpful to his students. For a traditional guru like Professor Majumdar, the success of a student was like his own success. That is why he is still loved, respected and fondly remembered.

II

The focus of all social sciences, as is generally made out, is on society and all of them are wedded to scientific method. Therefore their unification is logical. The main purpose which the unification will hopefully serve is that comprehensive and holistic understanding of society will help in finding effective solutions to the myriad social problems which humanity is facing. John Gillin (1955: 5-7) has proposed esoteric benefits flowing from a unified social science. He says that we will find "reliable answers to the question of sheer continued human existence in a world of confusion" and "some guidance towards fuller realization of human potential". I do not know how these esoteric goals will be fulfilled through a unified social science. At the esoteric level, the only possible thing is self-satisfaction of social scientists in developing a unified social science.

When we look at the origin and roughly three and a half centuries old history of various social sciences and nearly a century old history of efforts for unification, it becomes obvious that there are in-built obstacles in this project of unification. However, I may hasten to add that all social sciences have been borrowing from each other both at the theoretical as well as practical micro-level.

Before we focus attention on the origin and history of social sciences, it is incumbent to sketch a brief history of modern science and technology. Basically, the aim of natural sciences is to explore the laws of nature. Technology (and sometimes even science) attempts to use this knowledge for the practical benefit of human beings.

In the first stage of development of science, we can put pre-Darwinian and pre-positivist thoughts. Mathematics and astronomy are the oldest sciences. They inspired and helped in the growth of several sciences. They were deductive rather than inductive. It may not be out of place here to mention that the contribution of India to both these sciences was immense. It may also be mentioned that Ayurveda, the Indian system of medicine, including surgery, is also equally old. At least the practice of surgery (as propounded in *Sushrut*) was based on the inductive knowledge of human body. In the second category can be placed discoveries and inventions attempted by common men. The development of agriculture and invention of the wheel, for example, come in this category. Many of these empirical developments preceded both mathematics and astronomy.

Now we can distinguish between the traditional and modern scientific methods. I agree with Whitehead (1926) that the traditional scientific method focused on classification, while the modern approach is towards measurement. The seventeenth century may be considered as the watershed for the development of modern science. In this century, the debate over faith vs. reason in Christianity in Europe was won by those philosophers who propagated faith in reason (which belongs to mind) and sensual perception (belonging to body). Hannah Arendt (1958) has detailed these developments. The final nail in the coffin of faith was provided by Tom Paine in his long article entitled "The Age of Reason" in 1793 (see Fast 1945).

This debate between faith and reason was associated with three developments. The first development was oriented to the source or means for knowing the truth. When divine revelation is rejected, can one depend on reasons for the senses for knowing the truth? The old persistent belief was that the capacity of the senses to recognize truth was inferior to rational truth. Arendt says,

> Democritus' (a Greek scholar of the 5th century B.C.) early prediction that a victory of the mind over the senses could end only in mind's defeat had come true (*ibid.*: 350).

For the invention of instruments, which enlarged and deepened the capacity of the senses, seemed to have won a victory over both the mind and the senses. And this was heralded by Galileo's use of the telescope in such a way that the secrets of the universe were delivered to human cognition "with the certainty of sense perception". Apffel-Marglin (1999) gives credit to Robert Boyle who invented the air pump in the seventeenth century. He instituted a practice of public viewing of the experiments. Thus, the value of instruments was further enhanced. Arendt (1958) informs that in the sixteenth century itself, Niccolo Tartagalia of Italy coined the term "New Science" when he discovered ballistics, by applying geometrical reasoning to the motion of projectiles.

The next important development was in the perspective on nature. If nature is sacred, man must not interfere in its operation. If it is profane, then man has freedom to manipulate nature. I think the Christian tradition laid the foundation for viewing it as profane. For example, Genesis 28 says,

> After the creation of earth, and all that is on it, are separated from divinity and made available for human mastery.

I may add that it was Durkheim who called nature profane. Contrastingly, Indian tradition does not regard nature as profane for divinity is present in every part of nature. Therefore, it is sacred. Francis Bacon advanced the perspective of Genesis 28, when he declared that

> Nature is a lady not to be left free and at large. Only when by the art and the hand of man she is forced out of her natural state and squeezed and moulded will she tell us what we want to know?

Such a perspective paved the way not only for unravelling of the law of Nature, but also her exploitation and degradation. Their pernicious consequences we have already started experiencing.

Arendt (1958) outlines the role of state and organized research in the development of science on this basis of the example of the functioning of the Royal Society of England. It was founded in 1662 A.D. Its members had to agree to take no part in political or religious strife. One may conclude that modern scientific ideal of objectivity was born here. The origin of science, according to her, was political and not scientific. Besides, even an organized activity of scientists is always a political institution. Of course its output was vastly more important than the work done outside the Royal Society. What Arendt misses is recapitulated by Apffel-Marglin (1999:80). She says,

> By 1765 science was becoming an indispensable tool of the state to collect revenue, carry out census, do cadastral mapping to know land ownership and many other things.

Today the state is playing a two-fold role in the development of science and technology. Almost all defence research is controlled by the state. It leads to the development of technology for production of armaments for mass destruction. The hegemony in this sphere, for example, in case of the U.S.A., has ushered in the economic domination of developing societies. This helps the private industry of consumption goods to procure raw materials and ensure expanding markets through W. T. O. for mass production and sale of consumer goods throughout the world.

Finally, let us look at the impact of these developments on the emergence of social sciences. Quoting Toulmin, Apffel-Marglin (1999) says,

> During the course of the seventeenth century scientific ideas about the order of nature were to be transposed to the ideas about the order of society... the order of Nature and the order of Society turn out to be governed by a similar set of laws.

Furthermore, Comte's positivistic perception of science led to the belief that science is universal knowledge. On the dangers of such a perspective of science, Pathak says (2004; 36):

> It is, therefore, important to understand what Feyerabend wanted us to remember: if science is allowed to become the only voice that matters, it would negate the foundation of a pluralistic society.

In the course of these developments modern science acquired several characteristics and a broad framework of scientific method. These characteristics are unicity, objectivity, certainty, utilitarianism, universality and hegemony.

Both Protestants and Catholics, despite wars, claimed unicity and exclusivity of their version of the divine truth. Modern science discarded the role of both Churches in claiming the exclusive monopoly over truth. However, amazingly and imperceptibly, it acquired the characteristics of exclusivity and unicity claimed by Christianity. Consequently, it insisted that only science holds the key to truth. I have already mentioned the birth of objectivity in science research. "The postulates of objectivity which place the mind outside of all contingency, all context, relates unicity to certainty" (Apffel-Margin 1990:79) Certainty of facts is established not only by the use of tools and instruments for observing facts but also by rationality, formal logic, and geometry.

> It is bound up with unicity by the fact that these procedures require a unitary mind positioned outside and beyond the shifting realities and ambiguous contingencies of the world (*ibid*: 79).

It may be underlined that Apffel-Marglin (1999) does not characterize the churches and their teachings with unicity. But it is obvious that all the sematic religions can be characterized by unicity, for they all require a unitary mind, undisturbed by either the teachings of other religions or shifting phenomenal realities, which remains focussed on Christian (as well as other sematic religions) "other-worldly absolutism". It is with this perspective that both unicity and certainty of the divine truth are associated. Modern science replaced it with its own absolutism.

The universality of scientific laws is based on decontextualising the conditions surrounding a particular fact. When a cause-effect relationship is established, it is a relationship between an independent and a dependent variable, which has been divorced and isolated from other surrounding conditions or variables. Therefore, scientific laws can be universally applied not only for knowing additional facts but also for developing universal technology. Thus, it emerges that in the pursuit of the analytical method science ignores a holistic perspective on nature, in which isolated variables are integral parts of the whole. By scientism, I mean a dogmatic faith in positivist empirical perspective for knowing the laws of nature as well as man and society in order to control and manipulate nature, including man.

III

In this presentation it is neither possible to cover the history of all social sciences, nor even a brief history of core social sciences, i.e. anthropology, sociology and psychology in order to bring out their distinctness as well as mutual exchange. I hope my purpose will be served by identifying major landmarks in their history.

Anthropology, sociology and psychology remained amorphous probings into *Homo sapiens* and his social and cultural context between the seventeenth and the last quarter of the nineteenth centuries. These intellectual exercises could be characterized as philosophical or historical, if one is keen to put academic labels on them. The main centre of these activities was France. The French Revolution, the enlightenment, the success of natural sciences in unravelling the laws of nature and Darwin's evolutionary theory prepared the congenial environment.

When scientific developments in France spread to the study of man, it manifested a strong interest in "natural man" and "natural reason". "Natural man" implies "biologically natural man" whose reasoning is not influenced by society or culture. By and large there was agreement among the French intellectuals on three things: (a) continuity of human nature; (b) the biological unity of mankind, and (c) the importance of accumulation of culture and the clash of cultures as the principal source of growth of knowledge and power.

The twin biological beliefs about man, i.e. biological unity of mankind and continuity of human nature, contributed to the development of all the three core sciences. In the beginning, psychology focussed attention on mental processes of 'natural man' by studying the individual, isolated from his social environment. Anthropology turned its attention to the study of physical form of man on the one hand, and study of second-hand reports on tribals living in the colonies of various European powers, on the other. The former activity was later named physical anthropology combined with archaeology, while the latter was called ethnography (simple description of culture and social life of peoples or tribes). Though France considered itself endowed with natural reason and superior culture, it was tolerant towards the study of primitives.

In France, anthropology meant physical anthropology. For descriptive accounts of tribes the French used the term ethnography and for analytical, comparative and explanatory studies, they used the term ethnology. Adolf Bastian (1826-1905) is considered the 'father of anthropology.' His field-work and rich ethnographic material on tribal life earned him the title. However, some work of anthropological nature had already been carried on. A considerable amount of ethnographic material on tribes of colonial societies was collected and reported by travellers, missionaries and administrators. In the nineteenth century, palaeolithic and neolithic sites were excavated in France. It led to the development of archeology as an early branch of anthropology. Folklorists were collecting folklore from the reported ethnographic material. All of these became part and parcel of the emerging science of anthropology. Thus, it can be said that anthropology was born of "a union between antiquarianism and natural history."

In the beginning, anthropologists were guided by Darwin's doctrine of organic evolution. It led to unilinear theories of social and cultural evolution. The primitive tribes were considered at the lowest end of evolution, while the Europeans were regarded as the highest end of the evolutionary scale. By the end of the nineteenth century, these theories of social and culture evolution were discarded under the influence of Herbert Spencer (1820-1903), Wiliam Graham Sumner (1940-1910) and Emile

Durkheim (1858-1917). It is noteworthy that today none of them is regarded as an anthropologist.

There are three noticeable contributions of Spencer: the concept of universal culture pattern, organization and classification of data on the people of the world, and advancement of cross-cultural research. Sumner's main contributions are the doctrine of cultural relativity and functionalism. Durkheim's contribution to both anthropology and sociology was much more fundamental than the above two sociologists. He also used the available ethnographic data, but his perspective was conditioned by the ameliorative perspective of Saint-Simon and positivism of Comte, on the one hand, and the societal conditions of France on the other. On the basis of the ethnographic data, he developed structure-functionalism. It buried the prevailing interest in evolutionism and historicism. About the other contributions emanating from his sensitivity to society, we shall have occasion to discuss in the section on sociology.

The developments in Germany were distinguishable from developments in France. Several German scholars contributed to the concept and the study of 'culture' between the seventeenth and the nineteenth centuries. The term 'culture' probably was originally derived from the equivalent Latin word. However, at least indirect influence of France cannot be ruled out. There are five major contributions of German scholars to the meaning of culture, and its association with the concept of society:

(i) Originally culture signified personal cultivation. Later its emphasis shifted to indicate a somewhat less personal and more objective aspect of the non-material achievements of mankind.

(ii) Alexander von Humboldt called attention to the fact that mankind has many cultures.

(iii) It led to the use of a German word which meant ethnography. It implied description of peoples.

(iv) Herder, a philosopher, made special reference to regularities in the succession of changes and the recurrent regularities in their interrelations. British anthropologists later called them synchronic and diachronic perspectives respectively.

(v) In the late eighteenth and nineteenth centuries German scholars developed the concepts of political-rational and irrational cultures. The concept of political-rational culture was equivalent to the French cultural absolutism, which was represented by French

> culture. Contrastingly the concept of irrational culture tended to regard "culture as a complex of qualities, achievements and behaviour patterns which were local/national in origin... They are non-transferable, and non-repetitive". In fact, the latter term refers to the culture of tribals.

Most of the contributions of French and German scholars were not based on their own field work. In many cases, they used secondary ethnographic data. The year 1900 is a watershed in many respects. Both anthropology and sociology discarded the apron-string of evolutionism and historicism and thus also parted company. Field-work became a *sine qua non* of anthropological research. The area of research was tribal societies in various colonies. The field-workers concentrated on patterned behaviour of people for which they collected data from judiciously selected informants, while living in the field for eighteen months or so. Their operational objective was to find out how these people could be controlled. In this sense anthropology became a handmaid of colonial administration, at least in England.

On the theoretical side, the British anthropologists borrowed structure-functionalism from Durkheim and developed many nuances of these terms. As the focus of British anthropology was on society, they were and are still called social anthropologists. In the U.S.A. anthropology became cultural but essentially American theoretical framework is comparable to social anthropology.

Here, I may point out that the claim of anthropology is that it is the study of mankind. Analogically, it is a bird surveying the human world by flying with the help of two wings—physical and cultural-social. In the twentieth century anthropology developed many specializations on both sides. Therefore, as Srivastava (2004) puts it,

> The unique character of anthropology is seen neither in natural, nor biological nor in social sciences, for it combines both the biological and social and cultural aspects.

The inspiration to call the study of society as sociology came from two sources: concern for social reform and positivism. As mentioned earlier, Saint-Simon and Auguste Comte were the philosophers behind these ideas.

The difference between Spencer and Sumner on the one hand and Durkheim on the other was that the latter was extremely sensitive to the socio-political condition of France and this helped him develop his socio-centred vision. He was not alone in France in viewing "the crumbling of the old order and the splintering of the new with a degree of alarm". There were many traditionalists who thought and believed that the reestablishment of social stability rested upon the disciplining of the individual and a restoration of the respect for authority. Secularization in the aftermath of defeat of faith by reason led to normlessness and disorganization. Durkheim combined sociocentric perspective with historical functionalism and the prevailing view that society was an organism. His main contributions are the concepts of organic and mechanical solidarity, collective consciousness, anomie and structure-functionalism. While the concept of collective consciousness led to the development of symbolic interactionism, his structure-functionalism was borrowed by most British and American anthropologists as well as sociologists.

Max Weber (1864-1920) of Germany was a contemporary of Durkheim. Karl Marx (1818-1883) preceded both of them. Weber's interests were very wide. He studied not only the German society and the role of Protestant ethic, but made a comparative study of Chinese, Indian and Palestinian civilizations and the role of religion in them. In addition, he contributed to the study of political sociology and of bureaucracy. Briefly speaking, his main ideas about society and individual are the following:

(1) Every society is divided into several competing social strata. Each has a style of life. Therefore social structures cannot be conceived as wholes.

(2) As members of a status group, individuals are products of a social organization.

(3) Status groups are fountainheads of moral ideas. Such ideas are not only responses to the material environment but also the products of human inspiration and spiritual challenges.

(4) Sociology is a study of the understandable behaviour of individual in society and the nexus of individuals to the stability of a society.

(5) The action of an individual actor has to be understood in terms of the meaning which the actor has in his mind.

Max Weber thus differed from Durkheim in two respects. One, he considered the study of individual action necessary. Two, he did not subscribe to the idea of solidarity of society. For Karl

Marx class structure and class conflict characterized all societies excepting primitive communism and modern communism. His views on class conflict preceded Max Weber's idea of conflict of interests between status groups. In any case, both of them, especially Marx, replaced socio-centredness of Durkheim by class-centredness.

Weber's recognition of the significance of the study of individual action for the study of society or civilization foreshadowed Talcott Parsons' grand theory in which socio-centredness was combined with ego-centredness. In fact, from the beginning of the twentieth century, when reliance on ethnographic material, collected by others, was discarded, four distinct trends emerged in sociology. First, some sociologists continued to be armchair philosophers like Sorokin. Second, some sociologists, following the footsteps of Durkheim have become system-builders and grand theory-builders, and have been fighting valiantly to develop a science of universal validity. Third, many sociologists have contributed to middle-range theories or small-range generalizations on the basis of the selection of a problem and collection of data with scientific method, followed by analysis and generalization. Fourth, a number of sociologists are engaged in the study of social problems of their own societies in order to find solutions without bothering about theory or scientific method. The best example of the last trend is England, where sociology is engaged in social work and public welfare administration.

During the last fifty years of the twentieth century, critiques of Euro-centred sociology have emerged, especially in Europe. Some of these trends are symbolic interactionism, post-modernism, Frankfurt School, critical theory and post-structuralism. They have questioned the claims of sociological theory of universal validity as well as the claims of scientific method to know objective truth in social life.

The focus of psychology is the individual. If we look at the relationship between society, culture and the individual triangularly, then society and culture should be conceived to form the baseline and the individual as the apex of the triangle. The commitment and triumph of natural science to understand and control nature led some philosophers of France to conceive man as a product of nature. Therefore, as has been pointed out, they believed that "natural man" can be studied as scientifically as any other natural product. The natural thing about man is his organism, including the mind. His behaviour, therefore, flows from his psychological make up. As all men have the same mechanism of organism, the study of the psychological processes of a single individual would lead to generalisable laws of human nature.

The application of the theory of organic evolution raised three questions. First, how far are human brain and psychological processes developed from other animal forms, especially from apes? Second, what is the process of development of child psychology into adult psychology? Can we not consider the psychology of primitive man as an earlier stage of evolution of the psychology of modern European man? Or, alternatively, is it comparable to the psychology of a European child?

The first line of enquiry led to the development of laboratories where experiments on apes, rats, etc., could be conducted. It helped psychology to acquire scientific status. In many cases even "natural men" were subjected to such experiments. For an answer to the second question, psychologists not only leaned on the rich ethnographic material, but also joined anthropologists in joint expeditions for first-hand field-work among primitive tribes.

The development of the third line of enquiry was preceded by the contributions of philosophers and Durkheim. The French philosophers later on rejected the concept of "natural man" on the plea that man lives in society. He is not an isolated being; he is a social being. Therefore, man cannot be studied without the context of society. Some called man as a "social man" while some called him "social natural man". The traditionalists of France, including Durkheim, underlined the significance of society. In their view, society is in essence something external to and constraining the individual. Social institutions and traditions cannot be given an individualistic explanation. The study of child psychology and the learning process, development of the study of culture and personality and social psychology are evidences of the realization by psychologists that the study of the individual has to be in the context of his society and culture.

In the background of these thoughts, let me mention briefly the major landmarks in the theory of psychology. The first is the theory of instincts developed by McDougall. Pursuing the biological perspective and accepting the rationality of man, he held that the behaviour of man is guided not only by rationality, but also by instincts and sentiments. The latter are rooted in the biological make up and lead to non-rational behaviour.

The second is the behaviourist movement and development of learning theory. The major outcome of this movement was the perspective that the external environment, including society, provides stimulus to which man responds. These theorists held that stimulus-response is the elementary unit for the study of any behaviour or social process. It undermined the genetically given instincts and sentiments and paved the way for learning theory which recognized the significance of social entities like language, family, school, etc.

The third landmark is the emergence of Gestalt Theory and its associated theories and thoughts. In a non-technical language, we may say that it emphasizes that the objects of perception of an individual are systematically integrated. When these objects are internalized they also get organized. Memory plays an important role in internalizing the external objects. Thus human behaviour is not a simple product of instincts and sentiments, nor it is an entirely passive conditioned response to external objects, whether social or non-social.

Psychoanalytical theories have provided the fourth major landmark. By and large, these theories emerged from the study of pathological cases. They attempted to explain the dynamics of the personality structure of man with the two-pronged perspective of (a) the role of unconscious, biologically rooted impulses; and (b) organized cultural mode of man's social existence. Freud, the founder of these theories, underlined the significance of early experience in the family for personality development of the child. With the concept of super-ego, he provided insight into the process of internalization of values of culture.

Psychology has nearly forty branches, mostly of applied nature. However, its three branches have a direct interface with sociology and anthropology. They are (a) culture and personality; (b) social psychology; and (c) learning society theory. Time does not permit me to detail the exchange of ideas which has been going on between psychology, anthropology and sociology since the beginning of the twentieth century. These exchanges have cross-fertilized all the three core social sciences. Before we take up the central question of probability of the development of a unitary or unified social science, it would be in order to reflect on their developments in India.

IV

Social sciences in India derive their sustenance from the umbilical cord which binds them with Euro-American social sciences. Dhanagare (2004:23), in his Presidential address delivered at the XXIX All India Sociological Conference in 2003, observed:

> In a country like India, the discipline of sociology would not be considered as a fundamental intellectual unit in the structure of academia if it failed to relate its research work to the body of theoretical systems developed by sociologists from the developed world. This is as much true of other social sciences as of sociology.

Anthropology has a large number of branches. However, the main branches are archaeology, physical anthropology and social-cultural anthropology. Thus it combines both the biological and socio-cultural aspects. On the socio-cultural side, Indian anthropology does not distinguish between cultural and social anthropology on the pattern of the difference between American and British Anthropology. Besides, in Britain social anthropology and sociology are indistinguishable in so far as theory and research are concerned. Similarly, in India, sociology and social anthropology are indistinguishable. So far as tribal studies are concerned, they were started by travellers, administrators, missionaries and the British and American anthropologists long before the teaching of anthropology was started in Indian universities. They were also commenting on Indian social institutions like caste and joint family. Therefore we shall discuss the growth of social anthropology with the growth of sociology, although some orthodox Indian sociologists may object to my perspective.

The development of sociology in India can be divided into two parts: pre-independence and post-independence. In the pre-independence period Calcutta University had started teaching anthropology earlier than Bombay and Lucknow Universities introduced sociology. Bombay and Lucknow universities were active, although sociology had been introduced in Bardoa as well as Pune. The Bombay School was responding to the writings of foreigners on India on the one hand and social problems on the other. Ghurye, Kapadia and Karve wrote on caste, tribe, joint family and kinship, while the founder of the Bombay school, Sir Patrick Geddes, who was a geographer and town planner, had started taking interest in civic and urban problems as well as in policy-making and planning for urban development. Institutionally there are two major contributions of the Bombay school. Soon after independence, i.e. in 1951, it founded the Indian Sociological Society, which started publishing the *Sociological Bulletin.* Both of these institutions have contributed immensely to the growth of sociology in India.

In order to illustrate how Ghurye and others were responding to British writers, let me draw your attention to Ghurye's views on tribes in India. Varrier Elwin favoured the policy of preserving tribals in India as "National Parks". Ghurye's reaction was that tribes were the constitutive elements of Indian society since time immemorial. Therefore they should be integrated with rest of the society. Of course, in his view, the problem of integration was an administrative problem in which he did not want to participate. In September, 2004, Mahashweta Devi published a short biography of Bisra Munda in *Manohar Kahanian* on the basis of her travel and personal experience in Chotanagpur. On this basis, it can be stated categorically that Elwin's idea of "National Park" was a cover up for the exclusive role of missionaries converting tribals and supporting the colonial set up for the exploitation of forest resources directly and tribals indirectly. Probably Ghurye could sense it very well.

In contrast to the Bombay school of sociology, the Lucknow school was started as a combined department of economics, sociology and anthropology. Later on social work was added. But these disciplines could not stay together for long. Each discipline was separated to form four departments. In the words of Rajeshwar Prasad, the hallmark of the Lucknow school of sociology was "Philosophical, Traditional and Theoretical Orientation". A.K. Saran was a scholar of traditional Indian philosophical thoughts, especially Adwait Vedanta. His pioneering work in developing logico-dialectical philosophical method was recognized by Tom Bottomore very early. D.P. Mukerji introduced Marxist thought in sociology. It must be mentioned that none of these three was an empiricist. Contrastingly, D.N. Majumdar was a pure empiricist anthropologist.

After the independence, anthropology was introduced in very few universities in contrast to sociology. Many departments of sociology teach social anthropology as one of the papers at the Master's level. However, the field-work tradition of social anthropology has been widely used, especially in sociological studies of villages and small communities. The credit or discredit for the introduction of field-work in rural studies must go to M.N. Srinivas. I have deliberately used the word "discredit', because some orthodox exclusivist Indian sociologists have been raising questions on hyphenated coexistence of sociology and social anthropology in India.

Community Development Programme encouraged rural studies in the early fifties. They dominated during the fifties and sixties. Gradually, other specializations have also emerged. Now there is such a large number of specializations that it is difficult to keep their count. Still I must mention a welcome trend of publication of insider's views on some social problems. The study of women's problems by women and Dalit problems by Dalit writers are noticeable. The sociological publications in general indicate several trends. It is difficult to study and portray Indian social system at the macro level only on the basis of empirical, primary or secondary studies. Therefore Indian sociologists have concentrated on micro level studies of various social problems, including political and economic.

In this scenario, M.S. Gore's book (2002), though a collection of papers, is a welcome contribution. Gore holds that Indian social reality is too complex to be amenable for a purely sociological analysis. It warrants an inter-disciplinary approach. Hence Gore has adopted an integrated social science approach combining historical and comparative perspectives with sociological analysis.

The study of social problems raises several issues. Are we analyzing social problems in terms of any theory? Have the studies of social problems contributed to theory-building nationally or universally? And whether this engagement has contributed to solving our social problems. It appears that most of the studies are not theory-oriented. I agree with Dhanagare (2004:3) that the record of Indian sociologists' contribution to theory is 'below expectations, if not dismal'.

Let me dwell upon solutions to social problems. Social problems cannot be solved by sociological analysis and publications. They require both public awareness and action, and state action in terms of policy-making on the basis of available knowledge and its honest and sincere implementation. On both these counts the record is poor for which sociologists alone need not be blamed. I agree with Dhanagare (2004: 25) when he says:

> In the ultimate analysis, the actual use of sociological research would hinge on the extent to which politicians and bureaucracy, responsible for people-oriented governance, are sensitized to social science research.

In fact they are part of the problem. So far as the contribution to theory is concerned, one of the explanations for dismal contribution is provided by Becker and Barnes (1952: 793). They say,

> For in contrast to natural sciences, in the social sciences, the central core of any theory one cares to name is almost inseparably connected with the language in which it is formulated... Not only this, the cultures of different countries in which social sciences have developed possess a number of aspects other than language which vitally affect the theories that develop within them.

On the theoretical side, there are three identifiable developments. First, a few middle or short range concepts have developed, e.g. sanskritisation and resources networks. However, they are out of currency in current research. But, recently a few social scientists have started questioning the Euro-American theoretical discourse and its relevance for India. In this connection, I may refer to the names of André Béteille, Ashish Nandy, Avijit Pathak and Sheej Hegde. Such critiques of Euro-American sociological tradition indicate the possibility of contribution to theory.

Another line of development is what is termed as "Indian Sociology". It is seeking to understand Indian social phenomena in particular and social phenomena in general within the framework of Indian traditional thought. The direction shown by Radhakamal Mukherjee, D.P. Mukerji and A.K. Saran is being pursued by a few sociologists, though it is a fact that the actual philosophical theoretical-methodological contribution of these path-setters has not been advanced. In this direction T.N. Madan has done pioneering work. The journal, *Contributions to Indian Sociology* has provided a focal point for exchanging and advancing the ideas on "Indian Sociology".

In closing this section on social sciences in India, I may point out that about thirty institutes of social sciences have been established during the last half century. The central government also established the Indian Council of Social Science Research. None of these institutions has taken any significant action to promote the process of unification of social sciences. It will be worth-while to study the objectives and programmes of these institutes and inclination or interest of social scientists working there. What prevented them in this attempt? V.K.R.V. Rao was an economist. He established the Institute of Economic Growth as a multi-disciplinary institute, for he was convinced that economics alone cannot contribute to the success of policies of economic development or growth. It has very eminent social scientists including persons like Ashish Bose, T.N. Madan, Ashish Nandy, P.C. Joshi, P.B. Desai, etc. But they did not proceed towards the task of unification of social sciences in India.

V

The problem of developing a unitary social science or unified social sciences has been bothering American and European social scientists for almost a century. However, the American social scientists have been most active during the later half of the twentieth century. The first step was the development of Human Relations Area File based on ethnographic studies of almost all societies of the world. This work started in the nineteenth century. Development of a unified social science out of cross-cultural studies is a recent unintended consequence. Besides, Social Science Research Council, Carnegie Corporation, the Rockefeller Foundation, the Wenner-Gren Foundation, Ford Foundation and UNESCO are all seriously engaged in this task.

Wenner-Gren Foundation for Anthropological Research funded the organizing of two conferences of eminent American anthropologists, sociologists and psychologists in the early fifties of the twentieth century. It is apparent that these scholars did not welcome the idea of a unitary social science. The aim was to strengthen the linkages between social sciences, and not making a case for an old fashioned and spurious unified science.

At this stage let us distinguish between a unitary social science and unification of social sciences. A unitary social science may borrow from the existing social sciences, but in the final analysis it must have its own theory and methodology so that it can handle studies of all kinds of people, irrespective of their traditional and cultural differences. The other possibility is that one of the existent social sciences rises to the occasion to encompass the specialized areas of existing disciplines. Linton's work entitled, *The Study of Man* (1936), had expressed such an agenda for anthropology, but such a holistic, totalizing social science may become hegemonic and authoritarian. So far, no evidence has emerged about the probability of a unitary social science. In case it emerges against all evidences it is very likely to become an instrument in the hands of the state, especially the United States of America, as the natural sciences have become instruments for domination, exploitation and annihilation.

The second choice is to develop a unified social science. This is what American social scientists are advocating. As I see, this may allow the existence of disciplinary regimes, while concentrating on the unified social science. In addition it will draw on the existing repository of various disciplines. In so far as unification of social sciences is concerned, the process is hindered by an abundance of theories, concepts and technical terms. While some theories emerge because of new insights, many theoretical perspectives are responses to the changing problems of human societies. Besides, it has to be borne in mind that cultures of societies vary. These problems explain the failure of the American social scientists in developing a unified social science theory, despite the path shown by the conference on the "Science of Social Man" half a century ago.

Let us now start from the other end, i.e. social problems. American scholars suggest that if 'area research' is undertaken by a team of scholars of various social sciences, then they will be exposed to each other's theories, concepts and perspectives operationally. In such a collaborative exercise they will be forced to provide a unified explanation which will also be effective in solving the problems of that area. However, the idea of area research is not workable in India for two reasons. The first is the problem of funding. The second one is rooted in conflicting political interests.

Between the above two, i.e. between theory and practice, comes scientific methodology. The ultimate test of social sciences being "science" lies in exploration and identification of causation of social phenomenon. Recently John Gerring, an American political scientist, had put his paper on the internet. Its title is 'Causation: A Unified Framework for the Social Sciences'. (Its references is–*wtp://www/.a.s.u.edu/das/polisci/eqm/APSA2003/ Gerring-APSA-2003. pdf.*). He identifies two approaches to causation–unitary positivist approach and plurality of causes approach. The first one is reflective of a narrow conception of cause, while the second one embraces the whole range of causes. But, even in this second perspective, there are difficulties which must be overcome. My argument is that only positivist unitary approach is 'scientific', in the sense that it can identify a single independent variable as cause. If it can be controlled, then the dependent variable of social phenomenon can be manipulated. Multiple causes cannot be controlled. At best they may provide post-facto explanations.

In view of the above difficulties and record of the failure of the American social scientists, it is obvious that unification of social sciences is also improbable. Indian social scientists need not join this American bandwagon which has serious political implications also. Indian social scientists, in my view, have three options. The first one is to take up one of the nationally important problems like poverty or unemployment and form a multi-disciplinary team and ask I.C.S.S.R. for funding. If they succeed in taking these three steps, they will acquire first-hand practical experience of obstacles in unification. The second option is to engage individually in the study of any social problem of one's choice within the parameters of one's discipline, without bothering about unification.

The third option is for those social scientists, who have grounding in philosophy and who are oriented to theory. My advice to them is to understand Indian traditional thought and if possible, study Sanskrit. They will be exposed to Indian cosmocentric perspectives. It is their duty to explain the dangers of scientism, including those of modern science and technology. They have caused irreparable exploitation and pollution of nature on the one hand, and the exploitation of developing societies on the other. They have contributed to the emergence of the U.S.A. as a super-power, with concentration of enormous economic and political power.

Finally, let me express my views and refer to my initial contributions to theory based on Samkhya philosophy. Science, whether natural or social, cannot provide a holistic vision for they are all instrumental. In the absence of or weakening of a holistic vision of cosmos in which everything is functioning interdependently, Euro-American homo-centric vision is spreading globally. This has created insolent hubris, unsustainable exploitation and pollution of nature. Nature is meant to provide for the needs of all, but not for the greed of even a few giants. Poverty is rising. Peaceful as well violent reactions of people are rising. Terrorism has become enigmatic trauma. How do we explain all these and other social phenomena?

I was a student of the Lucknow school and was exposed to the ideas and perspectives of Radhakamal Mukherjee, D.P. Mukerji and A.K. Saran and through them to the contributions of Anand Coomarswamy and others. However, I was not fully satisfied. Finally, I leaned on my father who was one of the greatest Sanskrit scholars of the twentieth century. After teaching me Indian philosophies he directed me to work on Samkhya *darshan.* Fortunately, the *triguna* theory satisfied me. It has both analytical as well as prescriptive potentiality. That is why it has been adapted in both religious and nonreligious (I do not want to call it secular) texts for more than two thousand five hundred years of Indian thought.

[This is the text of the Professor D. N. Majumdar Lecture that I delivered in 2004 in the meeting of the Indian Social Science Association, Agra.]

REFERENCES

Apffel-Marglin, Frédérique

1999 'Secularism, unicity and diversity: The case of Haracandi's grove'. In Veena Das, Dipankar Gupta and Patricia Uberoi (eds.) *Tradition, Plurality and Identity*. New Delhi: Sage.

Arendt, Hannah

1958 *Human Condition*. Chicago: University of Chicago Press.

Becker, H. and J. Barnes

1952 *Social Thought from Lore to Science*. Washington: Harren Press.

Dhanagare, D.N.

2004 'Social policy concerns in Indian sociology', *Sociological Bulletin* 53 (1).

Fast, Howard (ed.)

1945 *Encyclopaedia of Philosophy*. New York: Carlton House.

Gillin, John

1955 *Human Ways: Selected Essays in Anthropology*. Pittsburgh: University of Pittsburgh Press.

Gore, M.S.

2002 *Unity in Diversity*. Jaipur and Delhi: Rawat.

Pathak, Avijit

2004 'Teaching/learning sociology: A critical engagement with modernity'. *Sociology Bulletin* 53(1).

Srivastava, V.K.

2004 'Anthropology is India: A comment', *The Eastern Anthropologist* 57(2) : 127-152.

Whitehead, A.N.

1926 *Science and the Modern World*. Pelican.